T0244593

Praise for *Chasing We-ness*

"William Marsiglio thinks big in *Chasing We-ness*, an elegant and passionately written book that asks what you and I can do to reduce the surging social turmoil of the modern world."

Mark W. Moffett, author of *The Human Swarm: How Our Societies Arise, Thrive, and Fall*

"*Chasing We-ness* takes on an impossible task: to lay out a plan for unifying an America that has fragmented in a dramatic way since 2016. William Marsiglio comprehensively reminds us of the features that create a sense of caring community with detailed examples that make his points brilliantly clear. I know of no one who has brought all this data together with a blueprint for change so well!"

Jacqueline Olds, Associate Professor of Psychiatry, Harvard Medical School

"We have both too much we-ness and not enough. *Chasing We-ness* offers a brilliant diagnosis of today's polarizations. But even more importantly, it suggests productive ways forward. The strategies offered hint at ways to afford we-ness that embrace difference rather than reject it. These are precisely the interventions needed as we experiment with ways to keep our social networks, and social and civic institutions, from spinning further apart."

Michael S. Carolan, Professor of Sociology, Colorado State University, and author of *A Decent Meal: Building Empathy in a Divided America*

William Marsiglio

Chasing We-ness

Cultivating Empathy and Leadership in a Polarized World

Aevo UTP
An imprint of University of Toronto Press
Toronto Buffalo London
utorontopress.com

© William Marsiglio 2023

Library and Archives Canada Cataloguing in Publication

Title: Chasing we-ness : cultivating empathy and leadership in
    a polarized world / William Marsiglio.
Names: Marsiglio, William, author.
Description: Includes bibliographical references and index.
Identifiers: Canadiana (print) 20220396582 | Canadiana (ebook) 20220396620 |
    ISBN 9781487544775 (cloth) | ISBN 9781487545208 (EPUB) |
    ISBN 9781487545840 (PDF)
Subjects: LCSH: Empathy. | LCSH: Leadership. | LCSH: Belonging
    (Social psychology) | LCSH: Mindfulness (Psychology) |
    LCSH: Altruism.
Classification: LCC BF575.E55 M35 2023 | DDC 152.4/1 – dc23

ISBN 978-1-4875-4477-5 (cloth)
ISBN 978-1-4875-4520-8 (EPUB)
ISBN 978-1-4875-4584-0 (PDF)

We wish to acknowledge the land on which the University of Toronto Press operates. This land is the traditional territory of the Wendat, the Anishnaabeg, the Haudenosaunee, the Métis, and the Mississaugas of the Credit First Nation.

University of Toronto Press acknowledges the financial support of the Government of Canada, the Canada Council for the Arts, and the Ontario Arts Council, an agency of the Government of Ontario, for its publishing activities.

Canada Council   Conseil des Arts
for the Arts   du Canada

ONTARIO ARTS COUNCIL
CONSEIL DES ARTS DE L'ONTARIO

an Ontario government agency
un organisme du gouvernement de l'Ontario

Funded by the   Financé par le
Government   gouvernement
of Canada   du Canada

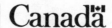

I'm honored to dedicate this work to all the generous professionals who celebrate the spirit of we-ness by collaborating with coworkers to help others in need, especially the dedicated teams of frontline health care workers who sacrificed so much during the COVID-19 pandemic.

Contents

Illustrations

Preface

As a professor, I've always enthusiastically lectured about "we-ness" – a sociological concept I define at length in the introduction. I've been curious about why, how, and with what effect people develop special bonds to others as well as to the ideas that bind them in common cause. Most people, including me, know the comfort that comes from belonging to something bigger than themselves. We-ness, or the sense of togetherness, is common and consequential. Although it is a typical part of human life, we each have our own stories about group belonging that uniquely define us. As a social force, we-ness generates strong feelings, both good and bad. At times it solidifies and polarizes simultaneously. It affects all of us directly and indirectly, as well as individually and collectively. Thus, we-ness is a personal and powerful concept that has implications for everyone.

Our social landscape is full of examples that illustrate the process of group belonging, ranging from intimate loved ones negotiating their private orbits to millions of people sharing a collective identity and similar convictions. I highlight the significance of the we-ness concept in all my courses. For example, I talk about gang members creating a sense of family, stepfamilies navigating their new familial arrangements, athletes establishing team chemistry, social activists bonding over a political cause, and much more.

In January of 2019, I began to ponder writing a book about this core concept that is pivotal to our everyday lives and the social arrangements that define our society. At the time, Trump's first impeachment trial was taking place, the #MeToo movement had gained traction in the American psyche a few years earlier, and the Black Lives Matter (BLM) movement had contributed much already to the public conversation about racial inequalities. Various environmental movements and the gun control movement, Never Again MSD, had recently captured the public's attention, revealing how collective expressions of we-ness can contribute to transformative historical moments. However, we were still a year away from the chaos of the COVID-19 era. We also had not yet witnessed how consequential BLM's massive demonstrations would become in the spring and summer of 2020. In short, I began my writing surrounded by the histrionics of Trumpism, but before the cataclysmic social events of 2020–2, including the tribalized and bitter presidential election. In 2019, unbeknownst to me and to others, we were on the cusp of cascading into a profound transitional period. It would be defined by a health calamity, an economic crisis, renewed demands for social justice, and unruly politics. These developments have influenced how many of us define and practice certain forms of we-ness. In various cases it amplified our need for this experience.

I initially set out to interrogate the social psychological processes that influence how we navigate the different phases of we-ness in diverse settings, including intimate relationships, leisure and sports, community groups, paid work, and the thought communities that guide our convictions. That initial story line was intended to be loosely informed by my political sensibilities. However, my political perspective grew more relevant over time when the compelling events of 2020–2 altered the social landscape in America and elsewhere. As a result, I both sharpened and broadened my vision of what was needed to promote healthy forms of we-ness in different areas of our lives. I saw more clearly and felt more deeply how politics and social justice issues inform our understanding of the complex forces that shape our experiences with we-ness and group belonging.

I was reminded too of the powerful message the acclaimed historian Jon Meacham conveys about fear and hope in *The Soul of America: The Battle for Our Better Angels*: "Fear points at others, assigning blame; hope points ahead, working for a common good. Fear pushes away; hope pulls others closer. Fear divides; hope unifies."[1] When we reflect on a people's broader collective soul, I agree. But, as Meacham astutely notes, consistent with the flow of history, the social forces of the twenty-first century that have generated more equality and opportunity for so many have also incited reactive forces. Thus, the same sentiments of fear that undermine an expansive form of we-ness that celebrates the common good also perpetuate a narrower, yet fiery expression of we-ness that polarizes.

As 2020 unfolded, my passion for writing *Chasing We-ness* intensified. I, like so many others, witnessed Americans become more and more divided. Raised in a working-class setting by parents and other adults who valued hard work, honesty, and humility, I was both startled and troubled to see so many working-class Americans aligning themselves with Trump and his brand of divisive politics. Seeing everyday people and self-serving politicians become part of a cult-like movement underscored how commitments to misguided forms of we-ness can be a destructive social force. I repeatedly asked myself the pointed question: How could those people – the ones who shared the rituals and rhythms of my blue-collar upbringing – fall under the spell of Trump's myriad lies and appalling words and deeds? My childhood memories, bolstered by my father being a "union man," impressed upon me that those who had walked in my shoes should demand that leaders demonstrate some semblance of integrity. Yet, as the months passed, I saw on Facebook how some of my former high school classmates were enthralled with being part of the Trump movement. I realized then that I had underestimated how ingrained and pervasive the roots of racism, sexism, and xenophobia had been in my youth. I came to see, too, how these roots were still very much alive and spreading. Trumpism extends well beyond Trump the public figure – the politician. Trump has also provided the fuel to ignite a new firestorm of hate, disrespect, and delusion that has marked his critical time in the political limelight. Trumpism reveals the cultural divisions in America. It showcases a tribal mentality steeped throughout history in white privilege and patri-archal masculinity that defies basic logic and common decency. But on the grassroots level, the movement is also reinforced by a deep, emotional story that captures why so many white people on the political right feel as though they have been maligned in their own country.[2] These folks feel forgotten and misunderstood.

In contrast, it was inspiring during this time frame to see people harness the power of we-ness to promote the common good. Thus, for many people, the despair during the Trump era was offset by watching the protests and marches that brought people of varied backgrounds together to support progressive issues related to, most notably, immigration, the environment, gun control, sexual harass-ment and assault, and racial justice. For me, the scope and intensity of this activity gave me renewed hope that we can do a better job of generating healthy forms of we-ness. I'm optimistic about the pros-pects of constructing well-intentioned, nurturing forms of we-ness.

Although I highlight numerous uplifting examples of we-ness, the countless health care workers who selflessly treated patients during the COVID-19 pandemic deserve special recognition. They stead-fastly honored both their caregiving ethic to help others and their shared commitment to work alongside colleagues. Unfortunately, many risked and ultimately sacrificed their lives as they embraced feelings of we-ness, both as caregivers to patients and their families and as members of a dedicated health care team. In addition, the mixed messaging in political and media outlets about the pandemic – including the loud and false declaration by some that COVID-19 was a hoax – denied health care workers the resources and respect they deserved. In short, politicians and media personalities offered alternative and incompatible visions of what we-ness meant in the COVID-19 era. Some visions, regrettably, were based on conspiracy theories, the rejection of science, and disinformation. These anti-science efforts diluted any chance of creating a prolonged, unified, and effective type of patriotic "American we-ness," one that could have resembled what older generations had demonstrated fighting a different kind of enemy in World War II.

The competing messages that have dominated American public life in recent years, culminating in the events surrounding the deadly insurrection at the Capitol and Trump's second impeachment trial, highlight the essential role leadership, or the lack thereof, can play in altering why, how, and with what effect different forms of we-ness matter for individuals and society. This period also accentuates the media's increasingly disruptive role in segmenting our society into recalcitrant factions. As entrenched and isolated groups generate and consume different sets of facts, they revamp the basic ground rules for civil public discourse.

On the world stage during the spring of 2022, as this book entered the final phases of the production process, we witnessed unspeakable atrocities that deepened our appreciation for the cultural and social forces that breathe life into the human pursuit of we-ness. Appallingly, innocent Ukrainians were being slaughtered, raped, tortured, and displaced because of Russia's unprovoked invasion. Homes, schools, hospitals, day-care centers, and the rest of the built environment that gave Ukraine its unique identity were being demolished. Yet, Ukrainians' hearts were filled with a spirit of we-ness rooted in their love for country, community, and each other. In addition to the Ukrainian military, millions of loyal, brave, and angry civilians from every imaginable station of life, irrespective of gender, age, or economic standing, collectively marshalled creative, sometimes lethal, strategies to resist. International observers who paid attention, me included, were impressed by President Volodymyr Zelenskyy's courageous style of leadership and Ukrainians' unflinching willingness to fight, and even die, for their land and way of life. In a resounding display of empathy and solidarity in the early months of the invasion, most of the Western world rallied to stand with the people of Ukraine. The inspirational power of we-ness and group belonging was palpable. Unfortunately, the forces that drive us to embrace a sense of we-ness and a national identity also compelled millions of Russians to support their ruthless leader, Vladimir Putin, as he and his military sought to obliterate Ukrainian cities and the Ukrainian identity. Putin messaged this despicable "special military operation" on the pretext that it was necessary for Russia's self-preservation. However, the destructive power of we-ness was also evident for anyone with a sober mind, and access to the truth, to see. This tragic international event revealed in dramatic fashion the complex social and ethical implications of our need to experience we-ness and group belonging.

On a personal note, my own feelings of we-ness with my youngest son, Phoenix, framed various aspects of my writing as well. As a seventh grader, Phoenix was taking an advanced civics course in 2018–19 that inspired me to reacquaint myself with our founding fathers' messages regarding the ideals of democracy. Notwithstanding their prejudicial views on racial and gender justice, their convictions about the virtues of democracy stoked my angst over the vigorous assault on our political system and institutional norms. I interpreted in a new light those early writings that gave us the phrase "we the people of the United States." The phrase projects a portrait of an empowered "us," one that defines who entrusts power to political leaders. It honors a collective, grassroots type of we-ness. The founding fathers also championed another theme relevant to my book: Americans are expected to establish healthy forms of we-ness while balancing the aspirations of individuality and a commitment to supporting the common good. A critical, yet difficult task. I build upon this notion to highlight how the struggle to resolve the tension between "me" and "we" is one that permeates our experiences with togetherness in all areas of our lives, not just our politicized social activity.

Framed by these historical and personal realities, I decided to envision a roadmap that would help us to build healthier forms of we-ness for ourselves and others. For starters, we must recognize that the need to feel a sense of belonging touches us in numerous and unique ways. We need to appreciate more fully how our experiences reflect a series of choices that are predicated on our desire to build, belong to, or to avoid certain groups and identities. Despite the political undercurrents that inform this book, I emphasize how our choices about the expression of we-ness are intertwined in areas of life often far removed from traditional politics.

Throughout our lives, we each consider opportunities and make choices that define how we see ourselves relative to others. These choices differ according to how inclusively we incorporate individuals into our trusted, inner circle of "we-ness." With some choices, we open our hearts to those who differ from us; other choices compel us to restrict who we invite into the fold. Our choices can empower us. They can also sabotage others' rights and opportunities.

The main message I convey is that we are likely to make healthier choices if we improve our approach to mindfulness, empathy, altruism, and leadership; use these skills more effectively in our daily lives; and express gratitude for our life opportunities. My insights draw on eclectic literature that speaks to our shared humanity and social instincts to form groups. Our shared humanity is based on our mutual awareness that we need each other on some level and that we ultimately face the same future: death.

Many of the ideas I introduce in this book emerged organically as I integrated new insights from multiple fields into my narrative. I'm indebted to a diverse set of creative thinkers whose work enabled me to reframe and deepen my approach to we-ness. I was informed by complementary ideas from anthropology, studies of artificial intelligence (AI), Buddhism, gender studies, history, medicine, neuroscience, philosophy, political science, psychology, sociology, urban studies, and more. That so many disciplines contribute to a deeper appreciation for we-ness should not be surprising. Our desire for a sense of belonging is a fundamental yet complex aspect of who we are as a species.

Throughout the writing process, I came to see displays of we-ness everywhere I looked. Images of we-ness emerged when I talked to friends, family, and students; studied the news; read books; went to faculty meetings; followed college and professional sports; participated along with other parents in Phoenix's sports training and competitions; and bonded with him watching numerous TV series (e.g., *Arrow*, *Blacklist*, *Dark Matter*, *Legends of Tomorrow*, *Lost in Space*, *The Mandalorian*, *Seinfeld*, *Supergirl*, and *Stranger Things*) that accentuate themes of group belonging and team dynamics. Consequently, I seek to display in the chapters to follow how ubiquitous the we-ness experience is in our everyday lives. I also show how our openings to experience it are forever changing and expanding as we adopt new technologies, such as social media, online gaming, social robots, and virtual reality. Unfortunately, we are simultaneously losing other opportunities to develop we-ness. For instance, by restructuring our communities to make them more car-oriented, increasing our online consumption patterns, and becoming more obsessed with our cell phones, we are in effect minimizing the personal rituals that once helped us build precious forms of we-ness. Thus, in some respects, the book serves as a wake-up call that documents how expressions of we-ness dominate the social landscape and our personal lives yet are precarious. It also offers constructive suggestions for how we might do better individually and collectively to promote healthy forms of we-ness in various aspects of our lives.

I'm thrilled that writing about we-ness created rewarding mentorship opportunities for me that were imbued with the we-ness spirit. I had the good fortune to work with nineteen bright and meticulous undergraduate students at various points throughout the writing process. I'm delighted to acknowledge the following former students who made invaluable contributions to this project: Emmaleigh Annas, Kiara Cazares, Nicole Cecil, Lauren Cook, Abigail Dumonceau, Carrie Hight, Ian King, Kathryn Kuchman, Tessa Melson, Annie Montalto, Heidi Neff, Gloria Ponce, Emily Primm, John-Robert Rodriguez, Nicola Strouse, Madison Todd, Jamie Venezia, Garrison Wells, and Sara Zarb. My students brainstormed with me; informed me about aspects of popular culture relevant to my work; edited my drafts meticulously for poor grammar, incoherent ideas, and substantive shortcomings; tracked down scholarly and popular press literature; and shared personal stories that illustrated and sometimes expanded my thinking. They revealed, for example, how important we-ness is in their lives and how they pursue it. I learned directly from them how the COVID-19 pandemic and social media negatively affected their sense of we-ness by fostering anxiety, fear, frustration, and loneliness. But they also enlightened me on how the health crisis and recent social movements enhanced their options to experience we-ness. Without exception, they brought an infectious energy to the project that confirmed that I was not alone in believing that thinking, talking, and writing about the pros and cons of how we experience we-ness is a worthwhile undertaking. Some of these students also collaborated with me when I developed a new sociology course, Empathy, Leadership, and Civic Engagement, which I taught for the first time in the spring of 2021, and again the following spring.

I'm also indebted to the thousands of students who have entrusted me with their personal analytic essays. These stories reveal in intimate detail how young people build and manage their sense of we-ness with family, friends, romantic partners, and mentors. Similarly, the hundreds of interviews I've conducted with men, but also with some women, about their experiences as parents and mentors highlight the power of intergenerational bonds formed in different settings.

Most recently, throughout the middle and later stages of this project, I was inspired by my supportive and astute acquisitions editor, Jodi Lewchuk. From our first exchanges, I felt her enthusiasm for the way my project explores how we-ness is built, expressed, and shapes the social landscape. She immediately "got" my idea in a way that mirrored my own understanding. I thank her for being an effective advocate for my message and my vision of how to structure the project. The process has left me with the sense that we've forged our own version of deep dyadic we-ness. I am also grateful for my conscientious and good-natured copy editor, Dr. Emily Reiner, who meticulously answered my queries and pushed me to sharpen my narrative. I assume responsibility for whatever shortcomings may remain in my writing, but far fewer will appear in print because of Dr. Reiner's impeccable editing skills.

Finally, I'm grateful for the sabbatical I received from the University of Florida, which I put to good use in the fall of 2020. The award gave me the freedom to engage in a style of academic quarantine that afforded me the focused time to weave together the numerous substantive threads of my project. Ironically, spending my sabbatical monitoring my son's digital schooling during the pandemic also gave me the chance to add new layers to how we express our we-ness as father and son.

Introduction

"My ultimate responsibility is to protect my *babies*," Charles firmly tells me while sharing his story early one Monday morning. He quickly adds, "I can't let anyone, or anything, hurt them." Charles, a director of a Boys & Girls Club in a low-income section of town, is talking about the neighborhood kids who hang out at his facility. Mentor to most, father figure to some, Charles is passionately committed to the kids and his job.

In my public talks and classroom lectures, I often recount Charles's words. I also share my firsthand stories about shadowing Charles at his club because they reinforce my perception of how strongly he feels about "his" kids. Despite having no children of his own, Charles presents himself as an attentive and caring father-like figure.

I'm struck by how this single, thirty-two-year-old African American man uses the word "babies" to define the neighborhood kids who visit his club. Charles's word choice conveys his unique conviction to look out for the neighborhood youth. He has clearly established an affinity with them. They are not merely club members; they are like family to him. As such, Charles believes they deserve his affection and protection. The kids in the club make it easy for Charles to identify as their father figure and mentor because they see him as a comforting and caring presence in their lives.

Charles's story illustrates a basic and universal feature of human existence – our quest to experience a feeling of "we-ness." He feels that he and the kids relate to one another because they have a shared identity and sense of belonging as active participants in the neighborhood club. In addition, Charles feels that he shares a broader type of we-ness with nearly all the kids that is rooted in their shared African American heritage and life experiences as persons of color.

Coincidentally, another Charles, the famous American sociologist of the early 1900s Charles Horton Cooley, is often credited with introducing the "we" label into the academic lexicon. He used it to refer to a feeling state that often emerges out of primary groups.[1] These groups are home to the intimate face-to-face interactions between people who share a special association with one another; these associations often include common traits, feelings, and experiences. For Cooley, primary groups are distinct largely because they are instrumental in "forming the social nature and ideals of the individual." With an emphasis on families, playground groups, and neighbors as sites for this "we-feeling," Cooley tries to capture the sentiment shared by those who experience this state of mind: "One lives in the feeling of the whole and finds the chief aims of his will in that feeling."[2] In other words, a person's experiences in everyday life are often emotionally linked to and motivated by their membership in a larger group.

A clever illustration of both Cooley's thesis and the symbolic power of we-ness when expressed as part of a close friendship can be found in Mitch Albom's best-selling novel, *Tuesdays with Morrie*. As a professor, I've used this book to encourage thousands of students to reflect on the meaning of life and how they prioritize their personal relationships. For those unfamiliar with it, Mitch recounts the life lessons Morrie Schwartz, his former sociology professor at Brandeis University, imparts to him. Mitch integrates into his narrative a series of intimate face-to-face conversations that take place over the course of many consecutive Tuesdays when Mitch visits Morrie at his home. Morrie, afflicted with the debilitating neurological disease amyotrophic lateral sclerosis, or ALS, shares his wisdom with Mitch and anyone willing to listen, while gracefully navigating his last several months of life.

On one occasion, Morrie retells an animated story about two waves having a conversation as they approach the shoreline. One is distraught over its impending fate when it sees the waves in front crashing against the shore. The other wave calmly assuages these fears by reframing their identities. It tells the frightened wave, "You don't understand. You're not a wave, you're part of the ocean."[3] Hope, for these waves, emerges from their expanded vision of life. For us humans, peace of mind can be achieved by embracing our connection to all of humanity.

Both Cooley's work on primary groups and Morrie's aphorism inform my observations in the pages to follow. However, I use the "we-ness" label more broadly than Cooley does to emphasize how people both intentionally and unwittingly pursue the feeling of affinity and group belonging with others – some intimately familiar to them, others not – in a much wider range of groups and scenarios of all types and sizes.

This interdisciplinary book explores why, how, and with what effect we build we-ness into our lives, and it examines strategies to promote healthy forms of we-ness within and between groups. The strategies strengthen our capacity to cultivate and integrate what I label *MEAL* life skills into various aspects of our lives: Mindfulness, Empathy, Altruism, and Leadership.

These issues demand our attention because of our current vulnerabilities as individuals, as a society, and as a global village. Confronted with transformative advances in communication platforms, artificial intelligence (AI), genetic engineering, pharmacology, and more, we grapple with new options for defining ourselves. These changes also affect how we relate to people as well as to smart machines in diverse social situations. In addition, the remarkable events of 2020–2, most notably the COVID-19 pandemic, the Black Lives Matter (BLM) social movement, and the contentious presidential election and impeachment trials that heightened anxieties over the precarious state of American democracy, have highlighted the long-standing divisions and inequities that permeate our fractured society. Despite the debilitating change and turmoil, our deep-seated desire as humans to experience a sense of we-ness, along with our uncanny ability to cooperate if motivated, signals that we still have the potential to create a promising future.

When we ponder our long-term collective future, like the moral philosopher Toby Ord does in *The Precipice: Existential Risk and the Future of Humanity*, we engage the notion of we-ness from an expansive, intergenerational perspective.[4] Speculating about the anthropogenic (e.g., nuclear war, pandemic, unaligned artificial intelligence) and natural scenarios (e.g., asteroid or comet impact, supervolcanic eruption) that could fundamentally alter or extinguish humanity highlights our moral standing as human beings and our cooperative potential. Scholars use phrases like "the principal of intergenerational equity," "intergenerational cooperation," "intergenerational global public good," and "longtermism" to signal a consciousness that respects our precious human legacy. The New Zealand philosopher Annette Baier captures this sentiment: "The crucial role we fill, as moral beings, is as members of a cross-generational community, a community of beings who look before and after, who interpret the past in light of the present, who see the future as growing out of the past, who see themselves as members of enduring families, nations, cultures, traditions."[5] In addition, Ord calls for a "more imaginative compassion" – which is essentially an "intergenerational public good" – that seizes on the "humanity of people in distant times as well as distant places" in order to protect humankind from an existential risk.[6]

Part I. Framing We-ness

Scholars from various disciplines have used numerous broad and sometimes overlapping concepts (e.g., we-ness, group belonging, social connections, bonds, ties, interdependencies, networks, communities, tribes, and more) to wrap their minds around the subjective perceptions and activities that define us as *social* creatures. A selective sampling of these approaches includes those that focus on the evolutionary and biological roots for social groupings; how we use others to develop our self-perceptions; how we physiologically and socially react to loneliness; how we are interconnected via a national identity or in social networks; and how social relations influence our prosocial tendencies, including our willingness to act altruistically, kindly, and mindfully for current and future generations.

The we-ness concept, as I use it here, is informed by how John Cacioppo and William Patrick describe three categories of "social connections" in their book, *Loneliness: Human Nature and the Need for Social Connection*. Consistent with other scholars, they distinguish intimate, relational, and collective forms of connection to people and groups.[7] As they note, "Humans have a need to be affirmed up close and personal, we have a need for a wider circle of friends and family, and we have a need to feel that we belong to certain collectives."[8]

Cacioppo and Patrick's three-category model of connectedness is a useful framework to capture the wide-ranging forms of connections that enable us to feel as though we matter in some way to others or share something in common with them. Many of the connections that fit within the relational category include acquaintances, superficial friends, distant associates, and domestic employees (e.g., babysitter, yard crew, handyperson) with whom we interact at home or in the context of stores, schools, work settings, neighborhoods, and other public venues. According to the model, these interactions differ from the up-close and intimate ties we have with individuals that presumably involve more consequential obligations and expectations. The more superficial connections can be of value, and even minimize our loneliness, but they are not central to this book. In addition, while this book addresses much of what is relevant to this three-category model, I concentrate on the distinction between the "me" and "we" that enables us to define who we are and how we fit in with others, or distance ourselves from members of specific groups. Seeing ourselves as being connected or wanting to be connected to something larger than ourselves shapes our self-perceptions and many of our life decisions.

I differentiate what I call *deep dyadic* we-ness (dyadic we-ness for short) from *ideational* we-ness. We can use these concepts to show how we connect in unique ways to other people and to ideas that represent thought communities that appeal to us. As I discuss below, processes related to mindfulness, empathy, altruism, and leadership are often critical elements of the we-ness expressed in these (and other types of) relations. I also comment on how trust affects our experiences with group belonging and the different forms of we-ness.

Dyadic we-ness overlaps with what Cacioppo and Patrick appear to mean when they use the phrase "intimate connection," but it differs as well. They do not provide a precise definition of intimate; instead, they mention that people need to be "affirmed up close and personal" and they refer to "marriage" and "close family connections" as two examples of this type of connection. Although the terms "close" and "intimate" generally convey a positive sentiment, they acknowledge that "close family connections can be a mixed blessing."[9]

In contrast, I explicitly use the "deep dyadic" label to capture various relationships. Some include family ties; many others transcend typical family relations, as I elaborate below. In addition, by using "deep dyadic," a relatively neutral phrase in terms of feelings, I signal the importance of capturing how we navigate a we-ness process that may produce either good, bad, or mixed results for our own and others' well-being. More specifically, deep dyadic we-ness captures how we perceive a coupled identity with others. It necessitates that we relate to them in a way that sustains the we-ness we've built together, for better or worse. Although some dyadic relationships stand independent of other ties, many dyads, and the we-ness they manage, are embedded in groups with additional members. The other group members are likely to influence to varying degrees how two people frame and sustain their distinct we-ness.[10]

Our perception of how we-ness matters to us is related to the meanings we assign to certain rights, obligations, and expectations that permeate our connection. Those meanings will be mutually shared with dyadic partners at times but contested on other occasions. Romantic partners, close friends, those in a mentorship relationship, parents/grandparents and their children/grandchildren, and business partners are some of the relationships that typically generate this type of we-ness and enable us to interact with others as part of a small group.

Ideational we-ness, similar in many respects to Cacioppo and Patrick's use of "collective connection," speaks to the ways in which we cultivate our ties to a collective ideology or group identity. I chose "ideational" to emphasize whatever idea is the driving force behind our decision to embrace a thought community, group, organization, association, or shared collective identity. We are likely to feel a sense of belonging or connectedness to at least some of the people who share a formal or informal commitment to this larger entity. However, the underlying sense of we-ness we experience is most likely tied to our shared beliefs that are represented by the collective. In other words, our core feeling of we-ness is anchored to a perspective or set of beliefs, even though this may be shared by the folks who are like-minded and have similar experiences or attributes. Still, when we have established dyadic we-ness alongside our ideational we-ness, our interpersonal exchanges and felt obligations to group members will reinforce our broader affinity.

Unlike dyadic we-ness, an ideational connection is not as intimately tied to the hands-on, interpersonal work we do with another person to develop and preserve a shared identity. Nonetheless, it can give us a strong sense of belonging and purpose in life. Those who experience this broader form of we-ness would include, for example, people who share a particular condition (cancer survivors, hearing loss), identify themselves as being a member of a historically marginalized category (LGBTQ+ community, persons of color), are affiliated with a religion (Christianity, Islam), follow a particular life philosophy (feminism, white nationalism), pursue a specific lifestyle (nudists, triathletes), or feel a part of a community or nation state. It can even capture the intergenerational sentiment of those who feel a spiritual bond to the unborn generations whom they feel deserve to inherit a healthy, peaceful planet that will allow humanity to flourish indefinitely.

Dyadic and ideational we-ness often flow from our activities in small group settings. In *Tiny Publics: A Theory of Group Action and Culture*, sociologist and ethnographer Gary Fine dissects how small groups operate and serve as the building blocks for social life. They are, according to Fine, "aggregations of persons who recognize that they constitute a meaningful social unit, interact on that basis, and are committed to that social unit."[11] He celebrates small groups as "tiny publics" that represent "not only a basis for affiliation, a source of social and cultural capital, and a guarantor of identity, but also a support point in which individuals and the group can have an impact on other groups or shape the broader social discourse."[12] My analysis of we-ness throughout the book is selectively informed by Fine's theory of group action and what he labels "idioculture." Idioculture represents the

> system of knowledge, beliefs, behaviors and customs shared by members of an interacting group to which members refer and that they employ as the basis of further interaction. Members recognize that they share experiences, and these experiences can be referred to with the expectation that they will be understood by other members and can be used to build a shared reality.[13]

Among other things, a group's idioculture frames how a member navigates their journey to bond with others in a group or rejects the sense of we-ness they once experienced.

Following Fine's lead, small groups can be viewed as "opportunity structures" that are shaped by participants' shared pasts and projected futures. These tiny publics are central to how civil society is organized and they are a powerful force in promoting civic engagement by providing the "platform for collective action."[14] Small groups are particularly relevant to the position presented in this book because these tiny publics are critical sites for teaching and demonstrating the skills of mindfulness, empathy, altruism, and leadership that can enhance our chances to experience healthy forms of we-ness that benefit individuals' well-being.

Both dyadic and ideational forms of we-ness are often associated with many types of social networks that are increasingly studied by social scientists. A social network basically refers to a collection of people. Many social networks "evolve organically" as people make decisions about developing friendships, having children, taking jobs in small or big organizations, living in isolated or densely populated neighborhoods, and more. To be clear, while both represent a collection of people, a network differs from a group because the former includes a

> specific set of connections between people in the group. These ties, and the particular pattern of these ties, are often more important than

the individual people themselves. They allow groups to do things that a disconnected collection of individuals cannot. The ties explain why the whole is greater than the sum of its parts. And the specific pattern of the ties is crucial to understanding how networks function.[15]

We can learn much about social life by studying the complexities of networks, but those issues fall outside the scope of this book. Importantly, we focus on expressions of social life that involve a sense of group belonging and we-ness which are not necessarily features of networks.

While dyadic and ideational forms of we-ness focus our attention on our meaningful interpersonal ties and connection to key ideas, I use the label "spontaneous" to flag a third expression of we-ness. Typically, spontaneous we-ness is less consequential, yet intriguing. Although this type of we-ness is not central to the main themes of this book, it sometimes relates to how people experience affinity with others and with ideas. We have all experienced those usually fleeting, superficial moments when we encounter a stranger with whom we share something meaningful in common. Perhaps we recognize that someone has a similar tattoo, or they are wearing a sweatshirt that includes the logo of our alma mater, or we hear them speaking our native tongue. We might notice that they, like us, share a common characteristic that distinguishes the two of us from those nearby. Whatever the commonality might be, we experience a sense of familiarity and vague affinity with the person because we can relate immediately to what we share and how we differ from others.

Spontaneous moments of we-ness often occur as we wait in lines, mingle at parties and other gatherings, walk in pedestrian areas, or have unoccupied, public downtime. Experiencing these moments was probably more common before the cell phone era. Now, many of us are so fixated on our phones in public spaces, that we either intentionally or unintentionally make ourselves less approachable. Our phone fixation also makes us less attentive to the markers that would initiate a spontaneous bond with a stranger. Nonetheless, these moments still occur, and when they do, we often feel a tinge of emotional comfort because of our shared we-ness.

For me, having been raised just outside of Pittsburgh as a Steelers football fan, I've had numerous spontaneous moments with others outside of Pittsburgh who can be identified as Steelers fans by their T-shirts, hats, car decals, or commentary. Uttering "go Steelers" might be enough to strike up a brief conversation that celebrates the origins of our shared sports loyalty. I once noticed a cashier at a pharmacy who was sporting an elaborate Steelers tattoo on his forearm. The tattoo piqued my curiosity, so I initiated a brief conversation about his connection to this sports franchise and Pittsburgh. In this instance, my sense of we-ness was superficial and short-lived, but it still left me with a good feeling.

Spontaneous moments of we-ness can sometimes provide a spark for individuals to develop a more meaningful connection. Though rare, the encounter may even blossom into a relationship that includes a deep dyadic type of we-ness. The two African American college students who perceive themselves to be the only Black people in a class of one hundred students will often register their collective identity as persons of color. Their shared circumstance may even prompt one of them to signal to the other that they are open to exploring a friendship. Thus, the recognition of a spontaneous we-ness can culminate into something more than a passing affinity; it may lead to a much more consequential bond.

Finally, I do not treat any form of we-ness (deep dyadic, ideational, or spontaneous) as a distinct property of a group or collective that is more than the sum of the participants. Rather, I conceive of we-ness as an individual's social psychological experience and perception.

Part II. The We-ness Landscape

Today, all over the world, people routinely seek to define themselves and find meaning in their personal relationships and commitments to social groups. People of all ages, genders, and social backgrounds express the need to belong to romantic relationships, families, athletic and work teams, friendships, activist groups, companies, business partnerships, tribes, communities, ensembles, and more. Whether they ultimately do so for good or bad, humans are hard-wired to seek out and bond with others.

In this book, I highlight the feelings and social experiences that push us either closer to another person because we believe they have attractive attributes, or toward a group of people who represent some idea, value, or commitment that we also embrace. Those same feelings and experiences can sometimes discourage us from associating with other people, groups, and ideas.

I cast a wide net for this project by exploring how we feel connected to either specific individuals, diverse groups of varying size that interest us, or humanity in its broadest sense. Thus, the landscape of we-ness and group belonging I survey is vast, complex, and multilayered. It includes our involvement with the web of social life that has meaningful consequences for our identities and personal well-being. Although my objective is ambitious, it seems reasonable. We can gain a deeper understanding of our most intimate experiences with we-ness and group belonging if we also consider how they relate to similar processes that implicate more macro layers of social life. In other words, we need to explore how our personal opportunities and choices regarding group belonging are informed by our activities with the larger social arrangements that afford us the chance to feel connected. The breadth and complexity of the we-ness landscape is revealed by showing how evolutionary, cultural, social psychological, neuroscientific, historical, and contemporary forces affect it.

Evolution

In some respects, a simple form of bonding has long been an integral part of our human evolutionary tree. An infant's need for physical contact and an interpersonal connection is well documented.[16] In *The Lonely American: Drifting Apart in the Twenty-First Century*, psychiatrists Jacqueline Olds and Richard S. Schwartz accentuate the power of attachment for humans, irrespective of age: "Our biological survival depends on our attachments, and our capacity for attachment is built into our biology. And not just our capacity for attachment but our longing for it."[17]

Early on, our distant ancestors exhibited their bonding instincts most clearly through sex and caring for newborns and children. Over time, as humans became more self-aware – seeing themselves as separate and distinct from others – their efforts to forge human connections expanded and grew more complex. People began to differentiate themselves individually from one another with more thought and purpose.[18] They began to have a deeper appreciation for the dangers associated with social isolation and many apparently did what they needed to do to avoid it.

Eventually, the process of individuation led people to develop allegiances to groups of people living nearby with whom they had some affinity, and, perhaps, a common goal that involved survival. Eventually, many of these bonds were engrained in different areas of life, most notably family, religion, politics, work, and leisure. Marriage, for instance, was an arrangement constructed by men to provide them the means to claim a woman, and the children they bore, as personal property, while preserving their familial we-ness in the eyes of the larger community.[19] Later, shifting access to food and resources as well as cultural advances provided people with the incentive and means to migrate. They could use technologies to communicate with others outside their immediate orbit. Over time, as more people migrated from place to place and as newer modes of communication were continually developed, people extended their options to socialize, forge bonds, and sustain them absent continuous face-to-face contact. Humans have increasingly developed the wherewithal to sustain ties with family, friends, and colleagues who live far away.

Now, and throughout history, trusting others is central to when and how we each seek to carve out the mental space of belonging to a group or thought community that enables us to feel at home with ourselves. Together, our personal attempts to establish shared identities contribute, for better or worse, to the social arrangements that shape how particular societies operate. However, according to some, developing supportive, trusting identities is not the linchpin that defines social life as a society per se. Instead, what matters in defining a social grouping as a society is whether the members have a clear sense of identity that is based on their perceived commonalities.

Both Mark W. Moffett, a biologist, and Nicholas Christakis, a physician and sociologist, have recently explored the evolutionary aspects of social groupings and societies. In *The Human Swarm: How Our Societies Arise, Thrive, and Fall*,[20] Moffett, a former student of the father of sociobiology, Edward O. Wilson, does a deep dive into the essence of societies. Motivated to identify the key principles that distinguish human societies, Moffett compares human arrangements throughout time, including the modern era, with special attention to what hunter-gatherer societies can teach us. He also creatively considers how we stack up against numerous other species, including ants, African savanna elephants, and baboons, among others. Moffett concludes that

> society is better conceived not as an assembly of cooperators, but [as] a certain kind of group in which everyone has a clear sense of membership brought about by a lasting shared identity…. The prospects for alliances, whether from friendship, family ties, or social obligations, may rank among the paramount adaptive gains of having societies in many species, yet aren't necessary to the equation…. The members of a society are united by their identity, whether or not they are in regular contact or willing to help each other out – though the membership they have in common can be a solid first step in making such relationships a reality.[21]

Framed in this manner, Moffett's mission is to reveal the parameters for defining social arrangements as societies on a macro level. He unpacks the circumstances that enable people to detect meaningful similarities they share with others who reside within socially recognized, physical boundaries. The social psychological processes that enable this to take place are, in some ways, relevant to what happens when people construct a feeling of we-ness. We seize on markers of physical appearance, language, dress, comportment, roles, rituals, and more to try to understand whether those we observe are sufficiently similar to how we perceive ourselves. If we believe they are, then we incorporate them into our vision of the collective – "us."

For his part, Christakis emphasizes the complex evolutionary feedback loop between genes and culture in *Blueprint: The Evolutionary*

Origins of a Good Society.[22] Christakis argues that humans are genetically predisposed to create a "good society." According to him, all
societies consist of a "social suite" of eight fundamental elements:
the capacity to have and recognize individual identity, love for partnerships and offspring, friendship, social networks, cooperation,
preference for one's own group (in-group bias), mild hierarchy (relative egalitarianism), and social learning and teaching. That said, he
anchors his framework to the four specific elements of love, friendship, cooperation, and social learning/teaching that he believes are
universals encoded in our genes. He suggests that a "blueprint" has
guided these core features to organize social life throughout the ages.
To be clear, he writes that "I do not mean that genes *are* the blueprint.
I mean that genes act to *write* the blueprint. A blueprint for social life
is the product of evolution, written in the ink of our DNA."[23] Like
Moffett, he underscores how powerful neurological/genetic forces
have evolved over our long history by shaping and in turn being
influenced by social context and environmental conditions. In Christakis's view, the social suite has compelled humans to navigate the
multilayered processes of forming, negotiating, and sustaining different types of group relations with kin and nonkin alike.

Moffett's and Christakis's thinking, like my own, highlights a mix
of cognitive and social psychological processes to explain how people make sense of their social surroundings, including the people
they meet. For my part, I dissect how people navigate their diverse
opportunities to feel affinity with people and ideas in various contemporary contexts. Although the shared identities people create
sometimes involve people acknowledging their ties to a society at
large, most do not. Thus, I turn my eye to the activities that lead people to forge alliances and allegiances to people, groups, and ideas,
then navigate their expression of keeping we-ness intact or adjust to
its potential or actual demise.

Culture

Although bonding with others is part of human nature, cultural
and historical forces shape the particulars of our journey to experience we-ness in different areas of our lives. These forces generate

the social circumstances that frame both our options and desires to establish we-ness in various settings. When we are drawn to a set of people, our attraction partially hinges on our ideals, philosophies, specific lifestyles, languages, customs, where we live, access to privileges, and more. How we interpret stereotypes is surely part of the process as well. In addition, our inclination to embrace a person, group, or idea often finds a foothold in our efforts to distance ourselves from others.

Our recent wave of reckoning with race and ethnicity in the United States provides a powerful illustration. The cultural forces associated with racial distancing, and the production of we-ness and group belonging around whiteness, have profound implications for everyone. But to be clear, the battle over race and ethnicity issues has penetrated the American cultural experience for centuries, even though many white people have been oblivious to the systemic nature of racism.

In *Caste: The Origins of Our Discontent*, the Pulitzer Prize–winning author, Isabel Wilkerson, brilliantly exposes the dehumanizing process of state-sponsored distancing.[24] She unravels the historical roots and systemic processes that have perpetuated the caste systems found in the United States and India for centuries, as well as in Nazi Germany during the 1930s and 1940s. These case studies show how a dominant caste (e.g., whites, Brahmins, and Aryans) sustains its privilege and power by reinforcing a hierarchical system that allows those belonging to the privileged group to develop a superordinate identity. The dominant caste distinguishes itself as having the presumed innate right to exert absolute power over those belonging to disadvantaged, stigmatized groups.

For America, whiteness has been the most consequential and destructive form of we-ness in our caste system. A key thread to Wilkerson's argument is that "white dominance has already been assured by the inherited advantages of the dominant caste in most every sphere of life, and in the securing of dominant caste interests in most aspects of governing – from gerrymandered congressional districts to voter suppression to the rightward direction of the judicial branch to the Electoral College, which favors the dominant caste, whatever the numbers."[25] An awareness of whiteness as a collective identity emerged for the first time out of a confluence of events that originated with Europeans colonizing the land that became the United States.

European immigrants, despite their diverse ethnic backgrounds, languages, and customs, socially constructed their collective identity by juxtaposing similarities in their visible physical traits and Christian beliefs against the traits and beliefs of Native Americans and Black people. The early immigrants, and their descendants, secured their elevated status in the caste hierarchy by distancing themselves from the millions of Indigenous people and the generations of Black people who were enslaved, then subjected to insidious forms of discrimination and brutality after slavery was formally outlawed. Over the centuries, as different waves of immigrants arrived in America from across the many regions of Europe, some were stigmatized and met substantial resistance. They did not initially meet the American conception of whiteness at the time. However, the mainstream definition of whiteness slowly expanded to incorporate a wider range of non-Anglo-Saxon nationalities (e.g., Irish, Italian, Hungarian, and Polish). Similarly, Ashley Jardina, a political scientist at Duke University, argues that Hispanic people, with the passage of enough time, might eventually be assimilated in a similar manner into America's historically dynamic labeling of whiteness.[26]

Without explicitly using the concept of we-ness, Wilkerson adeptly shows how the American caste system predicated on slavery has been perpetuated by both the conscious and subconscious forces that sustain the collective identity of whiteness. For millions of white people – most notably Trump's political base – there is considerable ideational appeal to the idea of white uniqueness. This belief continues to stoke deep-seated fears that white people's privileged standing in the caste system is crumbling because of the demographic shift that favors persons of color already living in the country, as well as potential immigrants.

Drawing on field research and intimate conversations with right-leaning folks in Louisiana, University of California sociologist Arlie Russell Hochschild illustrates how Trump capitalized on those fears. Her incisive observations explain how a large subset of white people forged their sense of we-ness that ultimately led them to support Trump and his brand of politics. Writing in *Strangers in Their Own Land: Anger and Mourning on the American Right*, Hochschild describes this group of whites as "mourning for a lost way of life. Many have become discouraged, others depressed. They yearn to feel pride but instead have felt shame. Their land no longer feels their own." And in response to Trump's rise to power, she asserts, "Joined together with others like themselves, they now feel hopeful, joyous, elated."[27]

More broadly, the need among many to preserve some semblance of a caste system built on a history of racial bigotry promotes our politicized and cultural tribalism. The white identity politics that led to genocide, slavery, and brutality for centuries continue to underpin systemic racism and stressful microaggressions that compromise the well-being of those who are subjected to various forms of discrimination and prejudice today. However, we are living in an inflection point, one marked by both a resurgence of bigoted white politics and a surge in the support for a more progressive, multicultural agenda that challenges certain elements of the caste system.[28]

Ashley Jardina complements this narrative with her nuanced analysis of the complex and multifaceted story of whiteness in her book *White Identity Politics*. She develops a new framework to understand dominant group identity by exploring the distinct but related concepts of "white racial identity" and "white consciousness." The former, consistent with my notion of ideational we-ness, emphasizes white people's attachment and sense of commonality to their racial group. The latter captures how some white people perceive that they should do something about their racial circumstances and effect change. Like Wilkerson, Jardina underscores the key role distancing plays in constructing white we-ness:

> Whiteness, by its very nature, is still constructed in opposition to other groups. It exists as an identity by way of drawing boundaries around racial and ethnic groups, asserting who belongs, and who does not. Who is granted privilege and status, and who is not. The power and import of white identity politics makes clear that as a

nation, we have a long way to go toward achieving racial equality, and race remains one of the most fundamental organizing features of American politics.[29]

But Jardina also highlights that while a vocal subset of white people want to mobilize their whiteness in ways that are hostile to persons of color, many of the white identifiers exhibit a type of we-ness that accentuates an in-group orientation (concerns about sustaining privileges and benefits) rather than an out-group focus. In practical terms, this subset of whites is not opposed to policies like affirmative action and public assistance that can benefit racial and ethnic minorities. They also are "not, for the most part, motivated by racial animus."[30] It does seem clear, however, that the increased visibility of the BLM movement and white consciousness ensure that we-ness issues related to caste, race, and whiteness will affect our public discourse for the foreseeable future.

History

As the preceding discussion illustrates, historical forces and events often affect how people perceive and experience we-ness during different eras. Robert Putnam, the Malkin Research Professor of Public Policy at Harvard University, along with his colleague Shaylyn Romney Garrett, advanced the idea that Americans were part of a 125-year trend that they label the "I-we-I" curve. They use a macro-historical perspective to frame their timely 2020 book, *The Upswing: How America Came Together a Century Ago and How We Can Do It Again*, in which they provide a sweeping account of how Americans' approach to individualism and we-ness has dramatically shifted since the late 1800s. They assert that this pattern is "reflected in our experience of equality, our expression of democracy, our stock of social capital, our cultural identity, and our shared understanding of what this nation is all about."[31]

To demonstrate this back-and-forth movement from the pervasive "I" ethos to the "we" ethos, Putnam and Garrett employ a diverse set of indicators, such as income disparities, bipartisan legislation, social spending on the elderly and poor, progressivity of federal income tax, selection of traditional versus unique baby names, and more. Their principal focus includes issues related to economics, politics, society, and culture. They convincingly document a pattern that reveals how Americans around the turn of the twentieth century (during the Gilded Age) were more often concerned about individual pursuits and achievements than the common good. This immediately preceded a long upward swing, characterized by a stronger investment in promoting the common good and civic activities that lasted into the late 1960s. This upward pattern reflected Americans' greater interdependence and cooperation with one another. However, during the 1960s, Americans began to reverse course and adopt a more individualist and egoistic ethos. This pattern was foreshadowed by cultural signals from the 1950s, including the 1955 James Dean movie *Rebel Without a Cause*, novels that challenged convention (J.D. Salinger's *Catcher in the Rye*, William Golding's *Lord of the Flies*, and Jack Kerouac's *On the Road*), and more scholarly books like sociologist David Riesman's *The Lonely Crowd* that celebrated those who were "inner-directed" – unafraid to express themselves while dismissing others' expectations of them.

Throughout history, many of the truly inspirational endeavors, as well as the mind-boggling atrocities we see around the world, have been fashioned by people motivated to bond with others; they want to feel part of something bigger than themselves. They achieve these bonds by either mindful intent, chance, or reluctant circumstance. Thus, major historical events, such as the passing of the Nineteenth Amendment in 1919 granting women the right to vote, or the Civil Rights Act of 1964 and the Voting Rights Act of 1965, are often connected to people with a shared passion who work together toward a common goal. Embedded in these influential groups are subsets of people who closely identify with one another as family, friends, coworkers, or strangers called to respond to the stark realities of everyday life.

In my lifetime, but in an era long before the internet age, one of the most inspirational collective expressions of we-ness and American achievement occurred when an enthusiastic team of incredibly young NASA scientists and engineers placed astronauts Neil Armstrong and Buzz Aldrin on the moon on July 20, 1969. The astronauts and support professionals developed a team mentality to respond with creative resolve to President Kennedy's prophetic call for America to land a man on the moon before the 1970s. Apollo 11's shining accomplishment is encapsulated by the famous line Armstrong delivered when his foot hit the moon's surface: "That's one small step for man, one giant leap for mankind." Armstrong's poetic reference to our shared humanity captures the essence of we-ness in its fullest and most profound form.

Ironically, Apollo 11 also illustrates that productive social enterprises sometimes include participants who see themselves as part of a team passionate about a shared purpose, but who do not necessarily consider themselves close friends. They can share a sense of we-ness out of necessity or convenience. Armstrong and Aldrin coordinated their flight responsibilities effectively, but they were never buddies before, during, or after the historic mission. Michael Collins, the third member of that historic team, has alternatively referred to the three Apollo 11 astronauts as either "amiable strangers" or "neutral strangers."

The powerful bonds forged through war can also represent opportunities for individuals to develop a shared identity. When this energy is channeled effectively it can help those with such commitments beat back ruthless leaders like Hitler or the aggressive Japanese Empire in the 1940s. Those who grew up in the Depression years and then fought in World War II – coined "the greatest generation" by journalist Tom Brokaw in 1998 – are perceived to have shared values of "personal responsibility, duty, honor and faith."[32] Stories of the camaraderie and love men developed fighting alongside each other on the fields of Europe or in Japan, as well as countless other battlefields, are legendary. They illustrate how horrific conditions prompt many soldiers to forge a sense of self that fundamentally ties them to the comrades who fight alongside them. Think of the bonds of brotherhood represented in the blockbuster World War II movie, *Saving Private Ryan*, starring Tom Hanks and Matt Damon. The personal images of belonging that soldiers create during and after a war can be reinforced by larger cultural discourses that remind them of their shared experience and national reputation.

Unfortunately, ruthless dictators over the centuries like Adolf Hitler, Saddam Hussein, Kim Jong-un, Benito Mussolini, Vladimir

Putin, Joseph Stalin, and countless others have cultivated we-ness to pursue deplorable goals. As well as gathering those who also had dictatorial ambitions, they have cajoled or forced subordinates to accept an ideologically anchored version of we-ness to survive mentally and sometimes physically. For example, the Hitler Youth's junior branches, first established in 1930 for boys aged ten to fourteen, groomed young men (and women) to serve the German army which perpetrated the Holocaust. Developing a shared identity as a class of people who supposedly are innately superior to others is abhorrent. Nonetheless, this practice leverages individuals' desires to bond with like-minded people.

The process whereby authoritarian leaders more subtly deceive others to set aside their moral compass to become complicit actors in the pursuit of a questionable objective can be troubling as well. The thirst to belong to something powerful, to experience a type of we-ness that brings social and material benefits, persuades many to support immoral leaders.

Consider Elizabeth Kalhammer, the former Austrian maid to Hitler who worked for him at his private estate in the Alps from 1943–5. When she was in her early nineties, Kalhammer shared her seventy-year-old secret with a journalist.[33] She describes herself as once being a young, sheltered woman. Coming from a poor community, she was captivated by the resources that the armed forces brought to her town. But early on she also witnessed firsthand how Hitler's army brutalized Jewish people, destroying their small shops and physically intimidating them. She quickly learned, however, that there were perks that came with her position well beyond anything she had ever experienced. She fondly remembers how she felt when she went out socially with her friends who also worked for Hitler. As she recalls, restaurant chefs made special dishes to ingratiate themselves to her and her companions.

Looking back candidly, Kalhammer paints a complex portrait of her life as a young woman by revealing the power of we-ness she felt at the time:

> You must understand there was a certain pride to it [working for Hitler]. If I'm being honest ... this is how it is when you're young. With

our papers, for example, we could go anywhere we wanted, there was a certain pride in it. We were admired. Yes, it was beautiful too … you think to yourself that you were there, that you had the privilege of seeing all those guests. Yes. So you feel proud. But that doesn't mean that I was proud about the other things. I didn't understand it at all at the time.

What she understands in her later years, and recognized as a young woman, is that it can be invigorating to feel a sense of belonging and significance that goes with being associated with a powerful person or group – even if they act reprehensibly.

Just as Kalhammer saw the ramifications of Hitler's hate when Jewish shopkeepers were victimized in the early 1940s, in August 2017 we saw a similar mentality in full bloom during the Unite the Right rally in Charlottesville, Virginia. Roughly 250 like-minded protestors challenged the proposal to take down the Robert E. Lee statue in Emancipation Park (formerly Lee Park). Jason Kessler organized several groups of mostly young white men that included the Ku Klux Klan, the alt-right, the Alt-Knights, and neo-Nazis. Widely circulated video clips of the march captured the raw expression of we-ness as the torch-bearing, angry participants chanted "blood and soil," "Jews will not replace us," "White lives matter," and Nazi slogans. The protestors channeled their fervent we-ness by confronting Black counterprotestors with monkey noises and shouts of "Go back to Africa!" While the white protestors' claim was to protect their shared historical identity as descendants of Confederate Southerners, the counterprotestors rallied to a shared vision of tolerance and a broader, multicultural view of we-ness in America.

One obvious interpretation of the white supremacists' goal is that they want to preserve the white race. In the process, they want to reinforce their sense of purpose and a form of we-ness. This orientation prompts them to envision a future that is an extension of a racist past. History, then, is not only affected by people's actions, it also shapes people's motivation to solidify their feelings of we-ness.

Social Psychology and Social Neuroscience

The process of becoming self-aware and seeing oneself as belonging to a specific group or category mirrors the basic logic of how the human brain works. As sociologist Eviatar Zerubavel describes, we manage ideas by lumping and splitting bits of information – the stimuli that capture our attention.[34] In other words, we learn to "see" the borders of things by recognizing the similarities and differences between objects, including people. We rely on both what we believe to be objective facts and our subjective impressions. I'm male – they are female. I'm Christian – they are Muslim. I'm kind – they are not.

When we see, hear, feel, smell, and taste bits of our environment, we do so by comparing those experiences with others. We use our senses to create emotional memories that are encoded in the neural networks of our brains. In short, we create mental maps that are linked to emotional experiences and networks of neurons. Many of these neurons are stored in the amygdala, a structure in our brains which plays a key role in processing emotions, is part of the limbic system, and is in the medial temporal lobe.

A critical set of sensibilities – ones often shaped by cultural expectations – pushes us to be either drawn toward or repulsed by others in numerous situations. In some settings, however, we are simply indifferent to those around us. Our motivation to pursue or to avoid some type of we-ness is a combination of how we initially frame our social reality and whatever physiological feedback results from that experience as we've defined it. Cacioppo and Patrick make a detailed, compelling case for appreciating how our feelings of being connected or lonely contribute to an elaborate feedback loop between our body's internal systems and our social responses.[35] In particular, they point out how two neurotransmitters, oxytocin and vasopressin, play a significant role in reinforcing our positive social bonding experiences and providing health benefits.

Just as the nature of our receptivity and response to the effects of neurotransmitters may change over time, we are likely to encounter different types of ideas as we mature that we either find appealing or appalling. For example, at various points in our lives we could be attracted to an idea, such as social justice, white nationalism, an image of God as loving or vengeful, how humans should treat animals, love, or something else. That energy will drive us to bond with like-minded people. When this happens, the attraction to these people and the groups they identify with stems from a deep commitment to a belief separate from any one person. Part of our enthusiasm for bonding is also driven by our perception that others will view us more favorably if we belong to a specific group and establish a shared identity. We glow when we believe others are willing to affirm our self-concept and offer their love, support, and respect.

As a result, for instance, some people are more enamored with the idea of being in love than they are in love with a person. Their desires unknowingly inspire them to contrive an affinity with another person because they believe the person could fulfill their dream of being part of a couple in love. Too often, people try to change others to fit their conception of what being in love means for them. Nevertheless, people who follow this path can still cherish a sense of we-ness they believe they experience with someone. False perceptions can be just as consequential as an authentic understanding of a relationship.

Let's push this idea a bit further and consider how we are at times motivated more by chasing after we-ness than we are the actual achievement of we-ness. This notion is consistent with how human performance experts Brad Stulberg and Steve Magness write about passion in their book, *The Paradox of Passion: A Guide to Going All In, Finding Success, and Discovering the Benefits of an Unbalanced Life*.[36] They emphasize the seductive power of dopamine, the pleasure-producing neurochemical which stimulates a person's thirst for the physiological thrill that produces it. Although they focus primarily on how people manage their passions related to physical and professional achievements, their perspective is consistent with the idea that the neurochemical effects of pursuing a feeling of we-ness may be greater than the effects produced once a stable connection is secured.

As folk wisdom teaches, the romantic chemistry or "spark" that typically attracts people to one another, and compels them to develop a coupled identity, often fades with time. The lessening of dopamine production does not mean that individuals will automatically have a weakened state of we-ness. However, a decline in the dopamine effect over time can make it easier for those most susceptible to its effects to be less committed to sustaining their coupled identity, or feeling of we-ness, in this, or any, relationship. People's different reactions to dopamine may partly account for why some people are more likely to become disinterested or bored with various forms of we-ness. They may tend to jump from one relationship to another and have a history of frequently joining and then leaving a group for another, more appealing one.

Although my research does not target hormonal effects directly, it does support the commonsense idea that people are often emotionally drawn to some type of we-ness. An especially touching type of family story has left a lasting impression on me. It involves stepfathers emotionally recalling in considerable detail how their stepchildren first used familial language, such as "daddy" or "dad," to refer to them. They describe to me what hearing those words meant to them by sharing responses such as "ecstatic ... it was like seeing her walk, which I never got to see," "really good ... words are inadequate," and "that tingly kind of feeling you get." For one thirty-nine-year-old stepdad, Jackson, who felt "very glad and warm to hear it," being referred to as "daddy" was an announcement that got his full attention: "If he (stepson) was going to place that name into my world, then I needed to meet up to that." Jackson saw that he was moving into the world of parenting and away from the "visiting uncle" world. These stories underscore the symbolic power language has in generating a sense of we-ness and the importance that emotions can play in shaping our group experiences.

For some, developing a shared identity becomes part of their core sense of self. It fundamentally defines how they see themselves. This is what happened for Jackson. For others, a particular we-ness experienced with one or more persons competes with other self-images, responsibilities, and desires. It is but one piece of a larger mosaic of how some people define themselves.

The personal stories I've heard in my interviews as a social scientist generally depict people talking positively about how their relations with others in a group shape their self-image. But the experience of seeking affinity with a group, and bonding with some members, can generate either good, bad, or mixed outcomes. In addition, the nature of those outcomes can change over time.

Contemporary Context

In the early months of 2020, the drama surrounding we-ness took center stage in the United States and elsewhere around the world. Many media personalities, politicians, health care experts, frontline medical professionals, and celebrities used their platforms to accentuate the need for an organized, collective response to confront the highly contagious and deadly coronavirus, COVID-19. Most implored us to embrace the new reality that "we're all in this together." Former CNN anchor Chris Cuomo injected his signature mantra, "Together, as ever, as one," into the public consciousness. He and others challenged us to "sacrifice the me for the we" to "bend the curve" so that we could slow the rapid spread of the virus. The public was asked, and most responded by making personal sacrifices for the greater good. Millions personally transformed everyday routines and rituals as part of a disjointed, yet collaborative response. A smaller, but angry, network of frustrated protestors eventually took to the streets to challenge their states' stay-at-home orders.

And who can forget how the simple gesture of mask-wearing became politicized during the pandemic. Those who wore masks voluntarily embraced science. They displayed their respect for themselves and others while experiencing a sense of we-ness with those who did the same. But others fought, sometimes literally, to protect their perceived "right" to avoid wearing a mask in public despite health experts' and some government officials' recommendations or mandates to do so. They too rallied around a loosely defined sense of we-ness, this one fueled by the populist, antiestablishment spirit of Trumpism. In the process, they ironically embraced both a libertarian stance and a sense of group belonging steeped in a conservative philosophy that viewed mask-wearing as a liberal ploy to discredit Trump and his politics. Trump's proclivity to think routinely about his own political self-interest above the public's welfare was appropriated by others on the streets as they prioritized their own personal interests above those of health care workers and their fellow citizens.

Once the pandemic infected the United States, some previously "invisible" and underpaid workers were labeled as "essential." The farmer, meatpacker, grocery store clerk, bus driver, and others were now being recast as soldiers in a courageous civilian army, united by their shared risk and suffering. For some, the heightened sense of we-ness grew organically; others had it thrust upon them. Many who worked directly with COVID-19 patients came to see themselves as simply making good on their professional obligations despite their fears of contracting the virus. Nonetheless, health care workers' sense of we-ness crystalized during the early months of the pandemic. The public honored them with evening cheering rituals in New York City and elsewhere.

Public reaction to the pandemic reveals how the spirit of we-ness captures our sense of affinity and belonging to various types of relationships, groups, and communities of thought. In a pandemic, as well as in calmer times, our search for we-ness is pervasive, varied, and vital to how we think about our identities and life purpose. The types of public slogans that emerged in response to the pandemic illustrate the need to explore how we forge and manage a sense of we-ness – for good or bad – in diverse, sometimes challenging circumstances.

COVID-19 clearly sharpened our sensitivity to the centrality of we-ness in our lives, but public concern about matters of we-ness, me-ness, empathy, trust, leadership, and civic engagement has permeated our cultural landscape for decades. Now, more than ever, the scientific community and much of the public recognize our pressing need to bond with others. These concerns take on special significance today considering our fast-paced and often controversial social, political, and technological developments. Our complex national story is defined not only by our rugged individualism, but also by the power of both the social gaze that compels us to seek acceptance from others and our commitments to rally behind a "just" collective cause.

Constructing personal meaning beyond ourselves is often uniquely grounded in how we orient ourselves toward our national identity. Many of us living in the United States in recent years, whether we were born here or elsewhere, are asking ourselves what it means to be an American. We live in turbulent times, stained by heated public debates over American ideals, the transformation of a time-honored immigration policy, and issues that highlight systemic racism. Our circumstances at home, a reflection of the international rise in nationalist ideologies abroad, remind us that our personal account of our national identity hinges on how we frame our shared experience with millions of others living in the United States. We increasingly realize how deeply we-ness matters to us. But many of us are also shocked to learn just how disparate our views of we-ness are from those of other Americans. Different impressions of the American way of life have always existed inside our borders since our country's creation, but those differences appear to be more entrenched and visible today.

Years from now, when historians look back at the events of 2018 to 2022, and the years immediately preceding and following this time frame, they are likely to interpret them as a defining period in American history. Today, as social scientists explore the social landscape in real time, they must ask: How are the dynamics of our current tribal politics affecting the way we experience we-ness in other areas? Has there been a fundamental shift in how people think about developing a shared identity and pursuing a feeling of we-ness that is influencing the way we think about and do politics, family, friendship, or business? These are provocative, unanswered questions. They become even more vital when people are challenged to cope with life-altering changes generated by the pandemic, intensified rhetoric and backlash about a racial reckoning, and competing interpretations of the threats to our democracy. Will Americans rise above tribal politics to place the "we" above the "me," and appreciate their common fate, or will tribal politics distort the spirit and potential power of we-ness? When the answer is revealed, we undoubtedly will be able to trace it to how we managed our trust and distrust for each other and the institutions that have solidified our democracy since its inception.

Trust

Journalist Sebastian Junger, who has gained considerable wisdom from his many travels to war zones, opens the door to examining the politics of we-ness when he shares his grim observations about contemporary American society in his 2015 book, *Tribe: On Homecoming and Belonging.* He writes that

> we live in a society that is basically at war with itself. People speak with incredible contempt about – depending on their views – the rich, the poor, the educated, the foreign-born, the president, or the entire US government. It's a level of contempt that is usually reserved for enemies in wartime, except that now it's applied to our fellow citizens…. Contempt is often directed at people who have been excluded from a group or declared unworthy of its benefits.[37]

What is disheartening, but telling, is that Junger was commenting on our society *prior* to the onset of the divisive Trump era! It also indirectly confirms that the seeds of Trumpism, with its penchant for lies, alternative "facts," vile insults, and loyalty oaths disconnected from integrity, were deeply rooted long before the Trump presidency.

The roots that have grown this contempt and division are intertwined with the public's evolving perceptions of trust. National polls show how Americans in recent years, compared to those polled in earlier eras, are much less trusting of each other and major institutions. When the General Social Survey (GSS) interviewers asked adults if they agreed with the statement "most people can be trusted," the percentage of those who agreed declined from 45.8 in 1972, to 30.8 in 2014.[38] The decline of trust in government has been even more dramatic over time. According to Pew Research Center polls, the percentage of US adults reporting that they "always" or "most of the time" trust government was unstable, but generally reflected a downward trend beginning with a high of 73 percent in 1958, 29 percent in 1978, 48.5 percent in 2001 (the year of the 9/11 terrorist attacks), and then dropping to only 24 percent in 2021.[39]

A 2018 Pew poll asked a similar question to the GSS poll but used different wording: while the GSS asked if the respondents agreed with the statement "most people can be trusted," the Pew poll asked, "Generally speaking, would you say that most people can be trusted or most people can't be trusted?" The Pew poll found that 52 percent chose "most people can be trusted." In this same poll, 71 percent of adults think that interpersonal confidence has worsened over the past twenty years. At the same time, however, 79 percent believe that Americans don't have enough confidence in each other. So, while Americans are aware of our deteriorating perceptions of how trustworthy we view each other, many assume that we have overstated how much we need to distrust each other. This glimmer of optimism is reinforced a bit by the 75 percent of respondents who indicate that the following statement is closest to their view: "In a crisis, people will cooperate with each other even if they don't trust each other." On this point, we saw that in the early period of the COVID-19 pandemic (March 19–24, 2020), there was evidence of a small improvement in adults' views of other people's altruism.[40] But the COVID-19 crisis did not fundamentally shift people's perceptions about others' trustworthiness. Ideally, we should not have to face a crisis for people to feel comfortable trusting their fellow citizens.

Another consequential insight gleaned from a Pew study portends a bleak outlook for our future. Compared to older cohorts, young Americans eighteen to twenty-nine years of age are much less trusting of others and institutions. Whereas the Pew report categorizes 46 percent of young adults as "low trusters," only 19 percent of adults sixty-five and older were classified this way. Several findings about respondents' beliefs underscore how this can matter for human relations. Young adults, compared to those sixty-five and older, are significantly less optimistic about others as shown by their lower likelihood of having confidence in the American people to do what they can to help the needy (53 percent to 80 percent), work together to solve community problems (52 to 71), treat others with respect (48 to 74), and reconsider their views after learning new information (40 to 61).[41]

What we don't know is how much of this gap can be accounted for by how the unique social circumstances each generation faces affect them versus how the accumulated lessons we learn over the course of our lives influence our judgments. Put differently, do older people have different views because they were exposed to different historical forces or because they have more years of lived experience? In addition, it may be that young adults have a reasonable amount of confidence in their age cohort but are suspicious of their elders, whom they blame for creating our fractured society.

What is clear from national reports on trust is that the vast majority of Americans – 83 percent – believe it is either "very" or "somewhat" important that we figure out ways to improve our trust in one another. If we are mired in our distrust for each other, we will struggle mightily to build new, respectful connections, especially with those who differ from us in their personal characteristics and beliefs. Developing healthy forms of we-ness across our entrenched, socially constructed divisions requires us to at least, as Ronald Reagan liked to say, "trust, but verify."

Technologies

As a social science scholar, Taylor Dotson explores how diverse technologies (e.g., devices, tools, techniques, urban form, organizations, and large-scale infrastructures) affect our everyday lives. In *Technically Together: Reconstructing Community in a Networked World*, he argues that we need to understand and challenge how our cultural discourses, public policies, and routines continue to reinforce a "networked individualism" that minimizes options to develop "thick" community.[42] For Dotson, a thick community reflects an integrated togetherness that includes a sense of common purpose, intimate social support, and a willingness to trust one another. Networked individualism, on the other hand, captures how we interact with others in isolated ways based on our personalized shared interests with them, often as part of a "lifestyle enclave." This pattern relies on "more individualistic forms of social connection," is facilitated by recent shifts in technologies and sociotechnical systems, and is reinforced by the American cultural themes of rugged individualism and self-reliance. Our penchant for finding belonging through private means results in us having more isolated and superficial ties with others, which compromises our emotional, psychological, and physical well-being.

Dotson's framework implies that persons living in a thick community are more apt to have a stronger sense of we-ness, and he explicitly notes that group belonging tends to be based on "broader collective goals or responsibilities." Dotson also argues that every community exists on a "spectrum" that ranges from "thin" to "thick" based on some relative combination of seven dimensions of togetherness: "Thicker communities would incorporate dense and interwoven social ties; strong norms of reciprocity and mutual aid; opportunities for talk; the psychological or symbolic sense of community; economic interdependence; functioning systems for self-governance and conflict resolution; and a strong shared moral order."[43] Understanding how these dimensions are influenced by prevailing philosophies of life and technologies can provide valuable insights to advocates who want to enhance community life. I discuss these dimensions in chapter 3 when I consider how we can experience we-ness in community groups.

Dotson takes aim at how our society has created cultural expectations, reinforced by a wide range of technologies, that discourage people from developing strong community ties, and presumably, a communal sense of we-ness. In recent decades, he suggests, we have continued to fall deeper and deeper into a pattern of networked individualism. He laments that our options for belonging and social connection have come to represent more of a private responsibility rather than a public good. Most of us do not even recognize the forces that have produced this pattern. In addition, "many people's lessened expectations and habits regarding social life are often the result of their 'reverse adaptation' to the life patterns their technological context best supports."[44] In other words, we've come to see our privatized approach to bonding as natural; it's just part of our taken-for-granted, everyday routine. We adjust how we feel, think, and act to accommodate the practical demands of various technologies. Our typical approach to expressing a networked individualism is also consistent with political liberalism, which espouses a moral view of the world in which the "good life is based in the protection and valorization of individual choice."[45]

Dotson is on a mission to erase our ignorance about how we've socially constructed our world to promote networked individualism and to lay the groundwork to foster more communal experiences and thicker communities. To this end, he outlines a wide array of possibilities for transforming our society that go beyond the scope of this book. Suffice it to say that "Realizing the best features of thick community while avoiding potentially undesirable side effects will take some combination of thoughtful and democratic deliberation, gradual learning from experience, and other elements of intelligent trial-and-error learning."[46] As we begin to recognize the hidden forces that alter our orientation to others and community, we should feel more empowered to pursue community-based forms of we-ness. Some of this activity exemplifies the popular activist slogan, "think global, act local."

Nowadays, social media platforms like Facebook, Instagram, Snapchat, TikTok, Twitter, YouTube, and the like offer people innovative ways to frame their identities by searching for and achieving we-ness. These technologies promote networked individualism and are tantalizing to those with addictive personalities. For example, as of 2022, Snapchat offered numerous options for users to evaluate their sense of dyadic we-ness with friends. One alternative included a ranking system of emojis with labels such as super BFF, Besties, and mutual Besties. Another possibility kept track of the "snaps" (a picture or video shared with a friend or friends on the platform) that a friend shared resulting in various numeric scores that reflected mutual sociality. Snapchat also introduced "charms" to symbolize and reinforce the relationship status between friends and allowed them to generate a type of superficial we-ness based on their shared astrological sign, compatibility, and birthday week. This digital system, used primarily by teenagers and young adults, expands the superficial but meaningful ways users can evaluate themselves by verifying how many and what types of friends they have.

These platforms also represent the latest iteration of earlier inventions like the printing press, phone, car, airplane, and computer that first enhanced earlier generations' ability to experience shared identities by letting them expand and sustain their social networks in novel ways. Today, we can get online and access supportive, like-minded folks for just about any type of group identity imaginable. Whether our sense of self is inextricably tied to art, fitness/ leisure, music, politics, religion, gender, sexuality, sports, travel, or something else, we can bond with others or engage ideologies remotely. Facebook, for example, allows people to belong to private or public groups with people who share common interests, and it enables them to share photos, videos, and written text. The practical advantages of Facebook are probably most appreciated by family and friends who want to strengthen their shared sense of we-ness. Social media apps also offer people new ways to take, post, and share group images that announce to the world how individuals are expressing their shared moments.

One subset of families that stands to benefit a great deal from modern communication technologies are immigrant families or migrant workers who come to America, either permanently or temporarily, but have family members still living in their native country. Using twenty-first-century technology, many of these individuals can better navigate the emotional and practical matters of living away from home because they can communicate more effectively and cheaply in many instances. The technology can even alter their migration decisions and help them maintain a stronger sense of we-ness with those left behind. For the immigrants who are immersed in an ethnic enclave and rely heavily on their native language, new technologies make it easier for them to maintain a practical, place-based ethnic we-ness away from their native land.

In today's world, communication technologies can provide creative and productive public/private partnerships between communities that organize refugees and satellite and mobile network operators. Increasingly, access to information is viewed as a vital resource that can affect refugees' quality of life, which is adversely affected by the tough living conditions they encounter away from their homes. In camps, and then when they arrive in the United States, opportunities to have digital connectivity are likely to improve their personal adjustment, as well as their ability to sustain their social connections with family and friends.

Unfortunately, we, as a nation, have a mixed history in how well we've treated immigrants and refugees. The way we've leveraged technology has profoundly affected these practices.[47] The reason for this mixed history is partly due to how political leaders and other major influencers at the national and local levels have shaped public discourse about immigration and immigrants. Throughout the ages, many leaders have targeted the masses by using the prevailing communication mediums of the day to stigmatize "outsiders," orchestrating and exploiting in-group and out-group tensions. Most recently, during Donald Trump's presidential campaigns and presidency, he and his allies used conservative news outlets as well as Twitter posts and Facebook ads to stoke unfounded fears based on their inflammatory rhetoric. The nativist style of we-ness they propagated demonized people from Central America who sought asylum in the United States at our southern border. Talk of an "immigration invasion" and "infestation" represented tropes designed to reinforce an exclusive we-ness in the form of white nationalism.[48]

Our understanding of migration and refugee issues is increasingly linked to environmental forces and how we use technologies to respond to them. For example, social media has altered and accelerated how social activists confronting the existential crisis of climate change and other social problems have experienced a sense of we-ness.

This process is captured by the story of Greta Thunberg, the inspirational teenage Swedish climate activist, and *Time Magazine*'s Person of the Year for 2019. On August 20, 2018, this teenager skipped school and planted herself for the day outside the Swedish Parliament. On the first day, armed with her homemade school-strike sign and flyers spelling out ominous climate change data, she protested alone while talking to a few journalists. Thunberg posted her protest on social media and a stranger joined her the next day. She describes this as important: "This is not about me striking; this is now us striking from school."[49] Several more strangers joined a few days later, and then more and more as the weeks passed. In short order, Thunberg had become part of an emerging group that continued to grow, protesting every Friday, and developing an identity as the Fridays for Future movement. The immediate goal was to pressure Sweden to align itself with the Paris Climate Agreement.

During the early months, her story went viral and within a relatively short period of time she had begun to motivate other young people around the world to initiate their own protests. Many admired her, and in less than a year, she represented the face of a youth-led global movement. She was a "symbol of a rising global rebellion" to press world leaders to act more decisively to save the planet.[50] On September 20, 2019, Thunberg was the catalyst who inspired four million people to participate in the largest ever global climate strike! Millions of teenagers and young adult activists across the globe are now captivated by an ideational form of we-ness that connects them to a generational movement of friends and strangers. As an unassuming but fearless leader, Thunberg has helped many young people forge their sense of belonging to environmental groups, such as the Youth4Climate online initiative.[51]

The abortion debate also illustrates how the social media age has profoundly altered our ability to express our individual and collective voices virtually. Pro-life as well as pro-choice activists use social media to frame the feverish debates on abortion in recent years that were intensified with the passage of Texas's abortion ban in 2021, and then with the controversial Supreme Court ruling in 2022 in the Mississippi abortion case, *Dobbs v. Jackson Women's Health Organization*.[52] These movements are populated with followers who work relentlessly with family, friends, and like-minded activists – sometimes virtually and other times side by side – to convince others to adopt their respective position. Bonds initially forged or reinforced through these types of political, value-based struggles go a long way in promoting activists' feelings of ideational we-ness.

Finally, this pattern of social media influence is vividly exemplified in the online world of Black Twitter. Over the past decade or so, Black Twitter has grown to be a powerful and diverse informal network that explores a wide range of issues and personal experiences primarily of interest to persons who positively self-identify as Black and selectively use Twitter. Although much of the tweeting focuses on serious issues, users also engage in artistic and amusing exchanges informed by common cultural sensibilities.

As Black Twitter demonstrates, opportunities for online community building and virtual bonding are alive and well today. The drive to create and sustain we-ness in political and religious life has also found an online presence. Increasingly, our allegiance to an ideology and our sense of we-ness can now emerge without face-to-face contact. Although direct contact is still very much a part of the interpersonal mix, it is often unnecessary for bonding in the internet age.

Our ever-expanding communication platforms are affecting both the scope and form of the social processes by which people meet, share their ideas, and form their interpersonal connections and commitments to ideologies. In particular, media trends over the past few decades have shaped and reinforced patterns in internet tribalism. In 2010, Michael Smerconish, a radio host, columnist, and TV presenter, wrote an incisive op-ed in the *Washington Post* slamming the destructive and "rapid escalation of extreme dialogue" so pervasive on cable TV and talk radio.[53] He describes how "Opinions from the middle are underrepresented, even shunned, in the modern debate…. Viewers and listeners have become conditioned to expect – and accept – only perspectives that line up on one side of the aisle." Regrettably, the state of media extremism has only intensified since Smerconish published his essay.

Although tribal politics predates the Trump era, Trump and his enablers exacerbated this corrosive style of politics that marks our current political landscape, taking it to new levels of absurdity. Trump and his team recycled fearmongering tropes from bygone eras, particularly as they relate to immigrants and persons of color. The exceedingly divisive nature of that political terrain is reinforced by the bifurcated news media (e.g., CNN/MSNBC vs Fox/Breitbart/One America News). Try the exercise of flipping back and forth from CNN to Fox News, as I've done on occasion, and you're left feeling as though you're experiencing alternative universes being depicted in a Star Trek episode.

Today, our news programming does not just reflect our polarized differences, it creates and reinforces them. This perspective is shared by journalist Brian Stelter who recently investigated the Fox News phenomenon in *Hoax: Donald Trump, Fox News, and the Dangerous Distortion of Truth*. Stelter writes that "Fox is an addictive substance. For its biggest fans, Fox is an identity. Almost a way of life. Hardcore viewers rarely change the channel or seek out a balanced media diet.

They compare the network to a church, to a senior center, to a city hall. They flock to it for reinforcement, for inspiration, for comfort food."[54] Sociologist Arlie Russell Hochschild asserts that some viewers even see the network as "family."[55] These characterizations point to Fox News being at the center of a politicized ideational we-ness. The station and the ideologically based we-ness it fosters also create opportunities for individuals to reinforce their personal relationships that celebrate their dyadic we-ness with fellow viewers.

Unfortunately, the twenty-first-century news industry, the intensification of tribal politics in the Trump era, and social media platforms breed a groupthink mentality and rhetoric that threatens to transform irreparably our democracy, social institutions, and way of life. Seemingly at every turn, we now witness the unsavory antics of countless political leaders who cower when faced with the prospect of losing their grip on ideological we-ness and political power. Even the gruesome mass shootings in El Paso, Texas, and Dayton, Ohio, which occurred within a twenty-four-hour period in early August 2019, were not incentive enough for some political leaders to talk constructively about gun control legislation. They feared that doing so would jeopardize their National Rifle Association (NRA) campaign money, voter support, and grip on power. Once again, the NRA's political leverage reinforced the divide between camps of politicians who experience the gun control issue quite differently despite overwhelming public support for sensible change. Fast forward to 2022, and there were already 246 mass shootings in the first twenty-two weeks, including the horrific shootings that occurred in the supermarket in Buffalo, New York, and the elementary school in Uvalde, Texas.[56] The technologies that allowed the coverage of these two events helped to bring communities together to grieve and demand answers. Although these two events prompted new bipartisan gun control measures shortly thereafter, only time will tell if subsequent shootings will motivate politicians to pass more effective gun control legislation. Our modern communication platforms are likely to play a key role in either solidifying the chasm between the political left and right, or ultimately forcing partisan politicians to embrace a larger vision of we-ness that incorporates the overwhelming segment of the public that favors commonsense gun control laws.

Contemporary public discourse reminds us, too, that we are stuck in our cultural and sociopolitical silos. In the world of politics, we are unable or unwilling to jeopardize our approval from those who compel us to ignore what Abraham Lincoln labeled "the better angels of our nature" – if they even exist for us. With shocking frequency, the basic principles that seemingly defined our sense of we-ness as Americans are being tossed aside. Corruption, abuse of power, and lying by public officials are increasingly part of the new normal. As a result, the culture wars fueled by media outlets and social media practices deepen ideological divides and reinforce whatever specific brand of we-ness we hold dear. Thus, our efforts to experience we-ness, rooted in personal, basic human needs, take on special meaning when we interpret general patterns of behavior through a cultural, sociopolitical lens.

Loneliness

Our innovative instincts and talents have produced all sorts of transformative technologies in communication, energy production, transportation, living accommodations, sanitation, health, and more. Yet, despite our advanced technologies, many of us at different points in our lives do not feel like we belong to a group, or we feel that whatever connection we have is tenuous. When this happens, we often suffer from not having that firm sense of we-ness. Many of us confront loneliness, social isolation, and ostracism – feelings that emerge because we are disconnected from or shunned by others. This effect exposes a dark side to our intense longing for we-ness and not wanting to feel as though we are being left out.

Psychiatrists Jacqueline Olds and Richard S. Schwartz suggest that feeling socially isolated and lonely is produced by both push and pull forces.[57] Our frenetic pace of life and excessively booked schedules, for adults and children alike, limits our real and perceived opportunities to connect with others during our limited "free" time. We find ourselves working and studying longer hours, then trying to steal some alone time wherever possible, often in front of a screen. Much of our time on communication gadgets appears to limit our face-to-face time with others as well. In addition, we are enamored with the time-honored, American imagery of the self-reliant person who fends for themselves without seeking help, or they pay others to pick up the slack. Those who embrace this ideal are more likely to stigmatize the state of loneliness, believing that "only losers feel lonely." These forces are explained by Barbara Ehrenreich's notion of the "cult of busyness" that glorifies a lifestyle full of activities and responsibilities.[58] It dupes us into the brutal cycle of being busy to avert loneliness and feeling lonely because we think relationships require too much time to cultivate.

Who better than Tom Hanks to help us vicariously experience the distress that emanates from our loneliness? In *Castaway*, Hanks plays Chuck Noland – a traveling FedEx systems engineer who survives a plane crash in the South Pacific, clings to a life raft, and ultimately drifts to the shore of a deserted island. Several FedEx packages from the plane, including a Wilson volleyball, also wash up on shore. Chuck chooses not to open one package because he's determined to return it to the recipient after he's rescued. Symbolically, the package enables Chuck to maintain his collective identity and sense of we-ness as a FedEx worker.

Early into his island ordeal, after injuring his hand, Chuck uses his blood to draw a face on the volleyball. In doing so, he creates his own "social" world, calling his new sidekick "Wilson." With its dried bloody face intact, Wilson quickly becomes Chuck's make-believe, conversational friend.

After four years of struggling to survive physically, to keep his sanity and hope alive, and to create some semblance of meaning for his life, Chuck builds a makeshift raft. He ties Wilson to it and sails out to sea in search of civilization and his rescue. One afternoon, Chuck awakes from a nap alarmed to see Wilson floating away. Despite Chuck's desperate efforts to keep in contact with his raft while swimming to save Wilson, he is forced to make a horrific choice. He returns to the safety of his raft – his only chance to reconnect with the real social world. Devastated, lying on top of his last remaining hope, Chuck is overwhelmed by the agony of having lost the only tangible link to feeling a sense of we-ness. Now, encircled by endless miles of ocean and confronted with a horizon devoid of humanity, he despairs over his utter loneliness.

The beauty of this movie is that it compels us to imagine the depths of loneliness. None of us can say for sure how we would react, but countless viewers report empathizing with Chuck's pain when Wilson is lost at sea. Bizarre, for sure, but we learn to appreciate what it must be like to bond so forcefully with a volleyball to battle our intense fear of being alone.

Chuck's experience of feeling disconnected from others underscores the importance of looking closely at the implications of having or not having we-ness in our everyday lives. Other researchers have explored how persistent feelings of loneliness impair our ability to self-regulate, empathize, pick up social cues from others, cognitively process information, remain physically healthy, and more.[59] Although it is beyond the scope of this book to explore loneliness systematically, I provide a bit of context to reflect on how loneliness and we-ness are different sides to our visceral need to belong.

Writing for *Psychology Today* in 2020, McGill University psychiatrist Rob Whitley highlights that there is growing public concern about what many label the "epidemic of loneliness."[60] Mental health experts define loneliness as a "perceived deficit of relational intimacy and is thus a function of actual, as well as desired relational connection."[61] In other words, if we want to connect with others, but are unable to make that happen to our satisfaction, we will suffer more. Our subjective reality, then, rather than some objective benchmark, determines how lonely we feel at any given point in time.

Cacioppo and Patrick emphasize that we vary in our inherited need for "inclusion or sensitivity to exclusion." They explain how the interplay between genetic and environmental forces affects our proclivity to experience loneliness. Moreover, they note that "those who feel lonely actually spend no more time alone than do those who feel more connected."[62] We are reminded that we can be surrounded by others, but still feel lonely, and we can be by ourselves yet feel at ease and enjoy our solitude.

We can better appreciate the debilitating effects of loneliness on our sense of self and to our prospects for establishing we-ness by reflecting on the virtues of solitude. Sherry Turkle, Abby Rockefeller Mauzé Professor of the Social Studies of Science and Technology at MIT, writes in *Reclaiming Conversation: The Power of Talk in a Digital*

Age, "In solitude we find ourselves; we prepare ourselves to come to conversation with something to say that is authentic, ours. When we are secure in ourselves, we are able to listen to other people and really hear what they have to say."[63] Thus when we feel comfortable in our own skin – when we know who we are and what we want – then we are less apt to be lonely and more likely to make wise decisions when establishing a sense of we-ness with others.

Loneliness reveals itself along a continuum, from an intermittent form of sadness to the more potent chronic displays of isolation and clinical depression: "Loneliness becomes an issue of serious concern only when it settles in long enough to create a persistent, self-reinforcing loop of negative thoughts, sensations, and behaviors."[64] Irrespective of the severity of our state of loneliness, those of us without a genuine form of we-ness in our lives are more vulnerable.

In *Together: The Healing Power of Human Connection in a Sometimes Lonely World*, Vivek H. Murthy, the current Surgeon General of the United States, sounds the alarm that loneliness is a major public health crisis with far-reaching consequences.[65] Informed by his exchanges with leading experts in diverse fields, program developers, and people who have personally struggled with loneliness from different walks of life, as well as his own personal experiences, Murthy meticulously shows how loneliness is linked to many social problems in the United States and globally. These include numerous addictions, violence, and mental illnesses. The fallout from loneliness negatively affects kids in schools, adults at work, and Americans who have polarized themselves in public debate. Murthy's analysis reveals that loneliness can best be understood by appreciating the social and evolutionary basis for our need to connect with others. If we want to minimize loneliness, we must find creative ways to help people enhance their own sense of self-worth and confidence while encouraging them to engage in meaningful opportunities to be connected to others in all types of settings.

As Murthy and others document, the uptick in people feeling lonely is occurring among all generations and demographics, although the public may incorrectly see the elderly as being the most affected. According to one study of persons sixty-two years of age and older in the United States, 48 percent report feeling some degree of loneliness with 19 percent saying that their loneliness is "frequent."[66] Additionally, 30 percent of unmarried older adults and 14 percent of married older adults indicate they experience some degree of loneliness. The problem for the elderly is exacerbated because about half of people eighty-five or older in the United States live alone, and roughly a third of those older than sixty-five live by themselves. In addition, the circumstances created by COVID-19 increased the sense of social isolation for people, irrespective of age. *The Pandemic Effect: A Social Isolation Report*, which was based on interviews with adults eighteen and older between August 21–25, 2020, documented that roughly 60 percent of persons fifty and older reported experiencing social isolation since the pandemic began, whereas 75 percent of those aged eighteen to thirty-four expressed this sentiment![67]

Investigating the younger end of the age spectrum, another study based on separate national samples of US adolescents and students entering college examines trends in loneliness, in-person interaction, and social media use during the 1976–2017 time frame.[68] The researchers find that loneliness increased noticeably between 2010 and 2017 for eighth, tenth, and twelfth graders regardless of their demographic characteristics. The largest increases were among females, persons of color, and young people who were more economically disadvantaged. When comparing twelfth graders from the 2012 and 2017 cohorts, there was a 50 percent increase among students in 2017 who reported that they "agreed" or "mostly agreed" that they often felt lonely. In addition, adolescents' self-reports of loneliness increased "sharply" after 2010 at the same time young people were reporting less in-person interaction and more social media use. Although the study design prevents the researchers from claiming that either the drop in youths' social interaction rates or the increase in their social media use leads to them experiencing higher rates of loneliness, the researchers make a strong case as to why alternative explanations do not seem feasible. Referencing other research that links social media usage to loneliness, the psychiatrist Rob Whitley reasons that "young adults have grown up in a social media age. Some may not have fully developed their social skills or acquired the necessary personal competencies to socialize well and make friends."[69]

Findings from the online 2020 Loneliness Survey conducted by Cigna, a multinational health care and insurance company, of over ten thousand adults reinforces the conclusion that younger adults report higher rates of loneliness than older adults.[70] Although rates vary, loneliness for people of all ages is pernicious because researchers are finding that it is related to elevated levels of physical and mental illness, addiction, suicide, and mortality.[71] Understanding the significance of belonging and how we can improve opportunities to create and sustain healthy forms of we-ness is much more than an academic exercise. For some, it is a matter of life and death.

Part III. We-ness: Resources and Skills

Social Capital

The act of belonging, and the social connections we make in the process, can have profound implications for us personally, as well as for the wider community. Over twenty years ago, the renowned political scientist, Robert Putnam, instigated public debate with his controversial book, *Bowling Alone: The Collapse and Revival of American Community*.[72] He warned that the roots of our participatory democracy – high levels of civic engagement – were eroding. Armed with extensive trend data, he documented that Americans were increasingly less involved in civic organizations during the final decades of the twentieth century.

Putnam uses the social capital concept to frame his concern that our social fabric has been weakened by the public's retreat from civic engagement. He succinctly defines social capital as the "connections among individuals – social networks and the norms of reciprocity and trustworthiness that arise from them."[73] In my own work, I've used this concept to explore how fathers develop networks of social relations with co-parents and youth workers to enhance their children's well-being, providing them with various types of resources, support, and advantages. In the process, the adults establish an understanding of sharing a form of we-ness by virtue of being on the same "team" that is dedicated to help specific children navigate their lives productively.

In his research, Putnam highlights the value of social capital by considering how Americans are situated in a network of community relations. Social capital, as Putnam reminds us, is both a "private" and a "public" good because when we create social capital we can benefit personally, and we can also help improve the larger community and its various social networks. He also differentiates between two types of social capital: bonding and bridging. The former captures the experience of those who socialize with people like themselves while the latter refers to a situation in which people establish ties with people unlike themselves. The two types of social capital can strengthen each other, and each plays a role in shaping individuals' options to experience various forms of we-ness with others.

The broader sense of we-ness I highlight – ideational – is similar in some respects to what Putnam describes when he refers to the connections between people involved in "tertiary associations." He suggests that "their ties, in short, are to common symbols, common leaders, and perhaps common ideals, but not to each other."[74] The types of associations that Putnam references would include entities like the American Association of Retired Persons (AARP), the National Organization of Women (NOW), and the NRA. In contrast to those involved in a tertiary association, some who express an ideational type of we-ness may not be involved in any formal way with a specific organization, although many are members of such groups. For example, a person can identify themselves as transgender, and feel that they possess a collective identity consistent with this type of gender identity, but they may not belong to an organized transgender group. In addition, many of us have ideational and deep dyadic forms of we-ness that overlap. Many who embrace the Black Lives Matter (BLM) movement, for example, protested in the streets with their close friends and family members in recent years.

Putnam presents a clear and disturbing portrait of Americans reducing their formal commitments to churches, unions, PTAs, civic and fraternal organizations, and even bowling leagues. Folks were also volunteering less with organizations such as the Boy Scouts of America and the American Red Cross. Although these patterns are noteworthy for numerous reasons, for our purposes, they are most relevant because civic organizations offer people a chance to be involved with others, providing them an opportunity to experience a sense of belonging and we-ness.

In a follow-up report in 2010, Putnam partnered with colleague Thomas Sander to revisit civic engagement trends in the wake of the 9/11 terrorist attacks. They suggest that the post-9/11 years have "brought an unmistakable expansion of youth interest in politics and public affairs."[75] Young people's political interests were also vividly on display in 2018 after the Parkland mass shooting and again in 2020 during the national racial justice protests over the killing of George Floyd by the Minneapolis police. But Putnam and Sander warn that the long-term effects are unclear and that there is "no convincing evidence" that adult Americans are becoming more civically engaged. They also highlight a troubling class-based subtrend that shows how "White high-school seniors from upper-middle-class families have steadily deepened the degree to which they are engaged in their communities, while white high-school seniors from working- or lower-class backgrounds have shown a propensity to withdraw from (or never undertake) such engagement."[76] This latter finding raises concerns as to whether the sense of group belonging and we-ness individuals can develop through their community involvement may be limited to their own insular networks.

Recent data show that patterns of community disengagement have persisted into the first decades of the twenty-first century. For example, in separate studies of religious orientation in America between 2007 and 2014 and from 2007 to 2019, the Pew Research Center reports that the proportion of adults who claim to be either Protestant or Catholic has dropped, while the likelihood of individuals reporting no affiliation has increased.[77] Similarly, in the decade after 2009, the percentage of adults who indicate they "never" attend religious services rose from 11 to 17 percent. Union participation has declined in the last forty years from 20.1 percent to only 10.3 percent in 2021.[78] PTA membership of families with kids under eighteen years of age has also steadily declined over time from a peak of 47 percent in 1960 to 11.4 percent in 2016.[79] The annual volunteer rate follows this trend as well and, despite rising to a peak of 28.8 percent in the years following the 9/11 terrorist attacks in 2001, fell to a low of 24.9 percent in 2015.[80] It's not all bad news on this front as, in addition to revealing formal patterns of community disengagement, Putnam documents several countertrends that show that Americans are increasing their involvement with other social forms, including tertiary organizations, nonprofits, and support groups. In 2017, the volunteer rate rose to 30.3 percent, with volunteering continuing to flourish during the COVID-19 pandemic as volunteers sewed masks, delivered groceries, and more.[81]

With changing times come new ways of creating social connections. To what extent and how do the new, more informal ways to associate with others and their ideas alter our ability to build a productive sense of we-ness? Contrary to Putnam's warning about how the decline in our formal associations is affecting civic engagement, Gary Fine optimistically proposes that the dip in the more traditional forms of involvement is being adequately replaced by other forms of small group activity: "Small groups are cause, context, and consequence of civic engagement.... A proliferation of small groups without formal affiliations represents a healthy development in democratic societies, in that intersecting webs of allegiance are thus established."[82] Fine goes on to argue that "the small group provides a communal space that tames asocial individualism as well as the oppressive conformity of associational control." At this point, it is unclear how civic life and democracy will be affected in the long term because of the patterns Putnam meticulously documents. We can say with confidence, however, that many of the new forms of association rely on recent developments in communication technologies, most notably social media.

MEAL Life Skills

Mindfulness
Developing a more authentic understanding of our own mind and life experience provides the foundation for creating healthy,

enlightened expressions of we-ness. We must establish our own bearings first before we can find a clear path to appreciate our bonds with those in our immediate orbit or humanity more broadly. The provocative works of Jon Kabat-Zinn, the founder in 1979 of the highly acclaimed Mindfulness-Based Stress Reduction (MBSR) program and of the Center for Mindfulness in Medicine, Health Care, and Society at the University of Massachusetts, underscore the central role mindfulness plays in this larger message. Kabat-Zinn illustrates how mindfulness philosophy has entered the mainstream in recent decades by permeating many of our institutions like politics, business, education, sports, and the military. For example, US Congressman Tim Ryan's 2012 book, later revised and released in 2018 as *Healing America: How a Simple Practice Can Help Us Recapture the American Spirit*, provided the impetus for him to push for mindfulness training to be included in the House of Representatives' wellness program as well as in several schools in his district.[83]

When we develop a deeper awareness of each moment, we're in a better position to "recognize the intrinsic wholeness of our lives as highly interconnected planetary beings."[84] Kabat-Zinn, like others touched by the teachings and training of contemplatives, reminds us that we have a "deep longing, a yearning, usually unconscious or ignored, to belong, to be part of a larger whole, to not be anonymous, to be seen and known."[85] So, too, when we refine our mindfulness through meditation, we are better equipped to understand social reality. We come to recognize how the fundamental roots and remedies of our suffering as sentient beings are embedded in the fictitious stories we inherit and recycle about everyday reality. We are also wiser about how we practice empathy, altruism, and leadership in all areas of our lives, including the body politic. Learning and applying these personal skills often shapes how we think about and relate to others as we seek to maximize our dyadic and ideational we-ness. These skills may even make us more receptive to the spontaneous forms of we-ness that require us to be attentive to our immediate surroundings.

Empathy

Defined simply as the "capacity to share, understand, and care about what others feel," empathy is a vital skill relevant to the production of we-ness.[86] While empathy can spark and reinforce forms of dyadic we-ness, it can also play a critical role in shaping ideational we-ness.

Stanford psychologist Jamil Zaki and his colleague Kevin Ochsner provide a detailed definition of empathy that highlights three overlapping processes: *"experience sharing*: vicariously sharing targets' internal states, *mentalizing*: explicitly considering (and perhaps understanding) targets' states and their sources, and *prosocial concern*: expressing motivation to improve targets' experiences (for example, by reducing their suffering)."[87] Some scholars label experience sharing and prosocial concern as part of "emotional empathy," whereas the label "cognitive empathy" is used to refer to the mentalizing attempts to recognize and understand others' emotions.[88] Taking Zaki's lead, I demonstrate how empathy can play a critical role in building various forms of healthy we-ness because, as he notes, "Empathy strengthens our social fabric, encouraging generosity toward strangers, tolerance for people who look or think differently than we do, and commitment to environmental sustainability."[89]

Unfortunately, empathy is a skill in short supply in many parts of our contemporary lives. One large study based on seventy-two samples of American college students gathered between 1979 and 2009 found a significant decline in young people's empathy scores over time, with the most noticeable differences occurring after 2000.[90] Other research on American college students during roughly the same time frame documented increased rates of narcissism, a personality trait often negatively related to empathy.[91] And Turkle effectively argues that our "flight from conversation" toward disembodied digital formats is degrading not only our comfort with talking but also our empathic capacity as well.[92]

On the flip side, Zaki offers us hope in his book, *The War for Kindness: Building Empathy in a Fractured World*. He reveals how we can grow our ability to empathize with others if we are motivated.[93] That promise for empathy training is also highlighted by Helen Riess, a psychiatry professor at the Harvard Medical School and director of the Empathy and Relational Science Program at Massachusetts General Hospital. In *The Empathy Effect: 7 Neuroscience-Based Keys for Transforming the Way We Live, Love, Work, and Connect Across Differences*, Riess describes how her E.M.P.A.T.H.Y.® training initiative helps physicians in residency programs improve their empathy and doctor-patient relationships.[94]

Other scholars, including Jeremy Rifkin and Roman Krznaric, add some semblance of optimism to the debate as well. They help us to understand the fascinating historical roots of this concept while making a compelling case for how we can systematically construct a cultural infrastructure to promote individual and collective, or global, empathy.

Rifkin, a renowned social theorist and activist, presents the most comprehensive historical account of the evolution of empathy in his ambitious work, *The Empathic Civilization: The Race to Global Consciousness in a World in Crisis*. Setting his sights on revealing the multifaceted relationship between entropy and empathy over human history, Rifkin begins his analysis with the earliest hunter-gatherer societies and ultimately discusses our modern circumstances. He even speculates about what could happen in the foreseeable future as new energy and communication technologies come online and are adopted by countries all over the world. In doing so, he moves us through the major transformations in how people created new systems to harness and use energy. Simultaneously, he shows how newer energy systems with the passage of time fostered more complex dynamics for social life. These realities enabled people to both express their selfhood and collective consciousness in new ways and also extend and deepen empathy to a wider range of human beings and animals.

Rifkin thinks that people need to embrace a more progressive vision of human nature. This view moves us away from emphasizing self-interest and the accumulation of private property. Instead, it underscores the empowering nature of empathy and collaborative, network-based strategies to accomplish tasks and promote a higher quality of life. He sees this as a possibility because the "net generation" includes more than two billion people who have grown up using the internet to connect with one another and share information in a cooperative fashion. Speaking of this unique generation, Rifkin opines that

> their nonhierarchical, networking way of relating to each other and the world, their collaborative nature, their interest in access and inclusion rather than autonomy and exclusion and their greater sensitivity to human diversity, predisposes the millennial generation to being the most empathic generation in history. A distributed, collaborative, nonhierarchical society can't help but be a more empathic one.[95]

Rifkin's multilayered interpretation frames empathy as having social psychological, sociobiological, sociohistorical, and sociocultural dimensions.

In a complementary work, *Empathy: Why It Matters, and How to Get It*, British public philosopher and empathy expert Roman Krznaric proposes intriguing and practical suggestions to enhance our introspective abilities. He challenges us to use our empathic skills to explore that inspiring social space he calls "outrospection." For him, this means "discovering who you are and how to live by stepping outside yourself and exploring the lives and perspectives of other people."[96]

Altruism
Empathy is essential to producing cooperative forms of social life because it often triggers altruism, loving-kindness, and compassion – all sentiments or urges that generate good feelings and supportive deeds designed to reduce people's suffering. These gestures typically energize us as social beings, enhancing our own and others' happiness along the way. Sometimes, they improve our personal connections with those we already know and strengthen the spirit of we-ness we experience when part of a group. At other times, these acts push us to open our hearts and minds to cultivating possibilities for building new friendships and to pursuing fresh opportunities to feel a sense of group belonging. And some of us go outside our immediate and familiar social orbit to display benevolence toward strangers, some of whom live on the other side of the world.

Most of us assume we know what altruism and compassion mean. These words are part of our shared vernacular and affect how we navigate everyday life. But social scientists, philosophers, and Buddhist thinkers are more rigorous in their assessment. They debate how these concepts should be theorized, defined, interpreted, measured, researched, and woven into our understanding of the social fabric.[97] This deliberation extends to how the concepts relate to competing interpretations of human nature.

Countless Western philosophers and scientists such as Thomas Hobbes, Charles Darwin, Sigmund Freud, and Ayn Rand have advanced the idea that humans are inherently selfish, compelled to promote their own self-interests even at the expense of others. These ideas, although challenged at times throughout the centuries, have been instrumental in shaping Western views about economics, politics, psychology, evolutionary theories, and our general way of life. However, as we've discussed previously, recent advances in neuroscience and experimental psychological research have persuaded an increasing number of contemporary thinkers to embrace an alternative view. Today, many argue that while we may have some selfish instincts, we are also hardwired to express empathy, altruism, and compassion. Admittedly, some of us appear to be physiologically better equipped to express these innate capabilities. Yet, outside the small subset of persons who are neurologically atypical (e.g., psychopaths), we are naturally primed at birth to care for and help others, and these are, fortunately, teachable skills.

Leadership

If we are to succeed in constructing a more cohesive and healthy society, one that truly promotes individual liberty and social justice for all, we must find ways to improve formal as well as informal leadership in its many forms and contexts. A leader, as broadly defined by the renowned leadership consultant and University of Houston social work research professor, Brené Brown, is "anyone who takes responsibility for finding the potential in people and processes, and who has the courage to develop that potential."[98] She adds, "daring leaders must care for and be connected to the people they lead."[99] Generally speaking, a critical step is to promote leadership styles that value self-awareness, integrity, empathy skills, the courage to be vulnerable, and nurturing approaches that foster group belonging. This is true for our families, friendship networks, worksites, civic organizations, communities, and nations. To create lasting social change, we must develop the infrastructure to train leaders to understand, respect, and empower others while helping them establish a healthy form of we-ness. If the infrastructure is in good order, the process of training courageous, empathic leaders will create a generative spirit. Those leaders will pass on their wisdom, skills, and perspective to others who will, in turn, express those same qualities and promote healthy forms of we-ness in the groups that matter to them.

Developing the full set of *MEAL* life skills can enhance our lives in many ways. They are exceptionally important for those of us who want to be effective leaders at home, with our friends, in the community, and in our jobs.

~~❧~~

Part IV. Our Path Forward

Now, as we continue our journey to explore why, how, and with what effect people search for and develop we-ness in their lives, let me provide a brief overview of the ground to be covered in subsequent chapters.

We begin in chapter 1 by exploring what I label the four threads of the self (mind, body, heart, and soul) that either set us in motion to bond with others or sever preexisting ties. A logical place to start this venture is to reflect on the nature of how we think about ourselves as individuals in the early twenty-first century. For better or worse, we are surrounded by technological innovations, 24/7 media coverage, ubiquitous advertising, pervasive social media, an expanding therapeutic industry, and a remarkable level of computer-assisted interconnectedness. These historical circumstances shape how we see ourselves and consequently how we bond with others.

So, too, the changing racial and ethnic composition of America, coupled with a more visible LGBTQ+ community, is creating appealing new options for some, and anxieties among others, as we move deeper into this century. We are navigating a moment in time that finds us more open to celebrating difference, despite the fears that drive an increasingly vocal backlash against diversity. Although my observations focus on the American experience, they are relevant to many who live in other industrialized, Western societies.

In chapters 2 and 3, I focus on the key motivational forces that define our involvement in experiencing we-ness in five broad and sometimes overlapping social domains. Although my list is not exhaustive, I discuss ten of the most important motivations. These include *sharing genetic heritage, family love, romantic love, companionship, calling out social injustice, celebrating lofty ideals, targeting a shared enemy, sharing pain and suffering, mentorship,* and *sharing a practical goal.*

I initially examine our experiences that are part of what can be considered our *primary groups*. These include our family, romantic relationships, and close friends. Then, because we often search for connections to others based on shared beliefs, I consider how we seek we-ness in *thought communities* that include other like-minded people who share our world view. This type of we-ness often stems from our approach to politics, religious or spiritual concerns, and personal health and fitness. Some of these experiences involve our activist work with special interest groups.

An important part of many of our hectic lives is our involvement with *leisure and sports* activities. I fondly recall, for example, how my father, who had been a blue-collar factory worker for forty-plus years, joined a bowling league upon his retirement at age sixty-five. He quickly developed a strong sense of we-ness and pride as a league and team member. Our relations to the world of sports can be expressed in various ways, including as an athlete, coach, official, and a cheering fan. In addition, we often see ourselves as being personally invested in *civic and community groups*. We establish partnerships in civic organizations, often through volunteer work. We can also develop a place-based, communal identity that symbolizes our ties to an urban center, secluded suburban enclave, a small rural community, or another setting. The final area I address includes the diverse *paid worksites* that offer us a chance to bond with others and develop a shared identity. My analysis highlights ten work characteristics that either foster or hinder how we-ness is developed in the work setting, paying special attention to jobs that involve either high risk or loyalty codes.

We next consider the process of judgment in chapter 4. The desire to bond and forge a group identity can lead to diverse outcomes depending on the circumstances and the perspectives of those passing judgment. What two people do to create their feeling of we-ness in a monogamous, loving marriage is likely to be viewed differently than similar actions by people absorbed in an extramarital affair. Thus, we-ness is not inherently good or bad. Purpose and perspective matter a great deal. On what grounds, then, can we assess the value of we-ness that is pursued in different types of groups? Are there instances in which we alter our short-term perceptions with the passage of time? Under what conditions should we, or can we, monitor group loyalty rituals in tightly knit groups? Addressing these questions forces us to recognize that the personal is political.

Our experience with we-ness is subject to the rhythms of time in various ways that I examine in chapter 5. The trajectory of how we pursue and achieve we-ness can take many forms. Much depends on our motivations and the various circumstances that can either strengthen or constrain the process of building or unraveling we-ness. To appreciate we-ness fully, we must frame it as more than simply a state of being or a product of human bonding. Rather, we-ness is a *process* that requires us to understand its transitional aspects, the smooth flowing as well as the contentious elements. How do changes in people's perceptions and circumstances affect how they establish, sustain, or disassemble their sense of we-ness? We interrogate the various ways individuals enter, stay in, and move out of their state of we-ness with a specific person, group, or thought community.

In chapter 6, we'll explore how empathy and altruism are related to we-ness and group belonging. We consider ways to enhance our desire and ability to display empathy and altruism in a manner that can produce healthy forms of we-ness. Then, in chapter 7, we show how empathy can and should be incorporated into more progressive styles of leadership that deviate from typical hierarchical models. These two chapters challenge us to develop personal and interpersonal skills that enrich the experience of we-ness and group belonging.

In the final chapter, we extend our discussion on mindfulness, empathy, altruism, and leadership to examine the complexities of promoting healthy forms of we-ness for individuals and groups in the five social domains. As chapter 4 reveals, we-ness can be pursued with good, bad, or mixed intentions. Consequently, people of goodwill sometimes face a moral dilemma when confronted with those who strive to achieve a deeper state of we-ness, but who do so at the expense of others. This is especially the case when the group's intent is to discriminate against and harm others.

Thus, we address the ethical and practical considerations associated with fostering we-ness, and the implications of promoting we-ness for personal and social change. Personal growth, community engagement, and social justice perspectives provide the logic to creating supportive environments that help we-ness flourish in diverse contexts. This approach highlights the psychological, social, political, and ethical concerns relevant to such efforts. These efforts can focus on dyads and other small groups (e.g., couple therapy or team building in small businesses), larger groups in which partnerships are being encouraged between community agencies and residents to reach a goal (e.g., reducing homelessness or teen pregnancy rates in a city), and on a grander scale that involves the major institutions of society (e.g., developing a humane, comprehensive immigration policy, creating a forward thinking strategy to address climate change, or marshalling an immediate and dramatic response to a pandemic). As we become more mindful of the benefits and risks associated with building we-ness, we can empower ourselves, as well as others, to develop strategies to manage the process in a productive, healthy way.

A critical dimension to promoting personal and group empowerment involves activating what scholars call collective identity. Social scientists dating back to classical theorists like Émile Durkheim and Karl Marx have explored the connection between notions of we-ness and collective identity. Durkheim wrote about "collective conscience" while Marx advocated for "class consciousness."

A more contemporary sociologist and student of social movements, David Snow, describes the essence of collective identity as a "shared sense of 'one-ness' or 'we-ness' anchored in real or imagined shared attributes and experiences among those who comprise the collectivity and in relation or contrast to one or more actual or imagined sets of 'others.'"[100] Thus, Snow explicitly links collective identity with a sense of we-ness that differentiates one set of people from another. He goes on to add that "collective agency" is embedded in the we-ness we construct. Collective agency is what motivates people into joint action. A social movement can emerge when enough people are able to generate and mobilize a collective identity that is energized by a strong sense of human agency.

Snow wisely claims that both the process of how we-ness is constructed, as well as the product that results from people creating a collective identity, are essential to understanding how we-ness affects our personal lives and social patterns. The product – collective identity or a "shared we-ness" – enables us to create something that gives others a way to orient and respond to us as being part of something bigger than ourselves. In other words, our collective identity can promote collective action while providing others an opportunity to make sense of those who express their we-ness in a particular way. Empowerment emerges out of our ability to experience and express a collective identity, for better or worse.

Whether we see ourselves as advocates for social justice, the environment, educational reform, or some other noble cause, feeling empowered can motivate us to improve others' lives and enhance our personal development as well. As a society, we must do more to encourage young people, as well as others, to nurture an altruistic stance toward others who live in their communities, nation, and in the wider world.

Over recent decades, many have proposed that government and nonprofits should create initiatives to fortify our collective identities and sense of obligation to give back to society. National service programs provide more expansive and structured opportunities for young people to volunteer with the goal of addressing pressing social issues. These days, such programs are especially needed considering our growing divisiveness in public life. Done well, they can help us to bolster forms of we-ness built on empathy and compassion that can improve people's lives, confront our entrenched social divisions, and uplift our spirits as both Americans and global citizens. One key challenge is to accomplish this in a way that provides young people the flexibility to leave their social imprint without forcing them to pledge their allegiance to an authoritarian style of nationalism that champions an exclusionary, ethnocentric form of we-ness.

We can also make a difference outside of our participation in activist groups and social movements by developing our ability to be mindful, empathize with others, show compassion, act altruistically, and lead wisely. If we improve the practice of being mindful in our daily living and interactions, we can more forcefully challenge the debilitating trend of dehumanization – "failing to consider another person as having a mind capable of complex feelings and rational thought."[101] In other words, seeing others as less than fully human.

In *The Power of Human: How Our Shared Humanity Can Help Us Create a Better World*, social psychologist Adam Waytz warns us about the adverse effects of dehumanization, but reminds us, too, that all is not lost. If we take the more mindful, compassionate route, we can leave our positive mark by emotionally, psychologically, and physically supporting our friends, family, and those in our immediate social circles. By sustaining the assorted and healthy forms of deep dyadic we-ness, we can indirectly strengthen the larger social fabric. Our ability to strengthen the social fabric also requires us to improve how we manage the intra- and intergroup conflict that affects us in our various social capacities. Managing conflict well is critical to all sorts of groups that hope to celebrate their we-ness.

Throughout the chapters to follow, I explore the supportive forms of we-ness that give meaning to our families, romantic lives, friend networks, communities, work settings, country, and world order. Along the way, I advocate various perspectives and practical strategies that can foster healthy forms of we-ness in diverse settings. I show how we can effect positive social change by building on our shared interests and commitments associated with larger social groups and movements, as well as our significant face-to-face relationships. At the same time, however, we must protect our wholesome way of life from debilitating expressions of we-ness that perpetuate hate, stigmas, and social injustice. We must use the nurturing energy associated with healthy expressions of we-ness to dismantle our senseless and destructive divisions.

1

Self-Meanings

By choice or by circumstance, I have been studying aspects of we-ness for years, chatting with parents, youth workers, and athletes. My informal exchanges with these individuals flow spontaneously out of my daily routines; the more formal encounters include in-depth research interviews. In both settings, the people I talk to often depict their commitment to we-ness as playing an important role in how they define themselves. For example, in one of my interviews with a talented and mature thirteen-year-old triathlete, I was told:

> I think my life would be ... without any meaning if I didn't have triathlon. Triathlons are really what makes my life happy. All my friends are into triathlon ... that's where I meet people.... It's part of my life, and if you took it away from me, I think I'd be a different human being, so triathlon is not just a sport for me; it's something that I love to do.

Without explicitly mentioning the we-ness process, this teenager describes here and elsewhere in our conversation how important it is for him to associate with like-minded athletes. Triathlon provides him with a comfortable social setting to anchor his self-image and to grow his friendships. Although triathlon is typically portrayed as an individual sport, this boy's commitments to be connected to the triathlon community and to be a member of a specific team offer him convenient sites to establish and nurture his sense of we-ness.

To appreciate how a person derives meaning from belonging to a group, we must consider how our life tapestry integrates our cognitive abilities, including our personality; how we orient ourselves toward our physical characteristics (e.g., body features including size, skin color, disabilities); our emotional makeup and expression; and for many, our spiritual orientation to the universe.

Cultural Forces

In a broader sense, our life's tapestry is also influenced by our standpoints, or points of view, that are shaped by our social and political circumstances. The vantage point from which we see ourselves and the world is influenced by our position in it. How privileged or marginalized are we? Our standpoints are often shaped by our experiences, which are in turn influenced by how others have categorized and responded to us throughout our lives. What race or ethnicity do we see ourselves being; what is our gender; are we a member of the LGBTQ+ community; what is our socioeconomic status; what is our age group? These are just a few of the ways we define ourselves. Typically, our self-reflections are based on how we see ourselves as navigating multiple identities simultaneously. In our mind, for example, we may see ourselves as a wealthy straight African American woman or an elderly gay white man.

Social scientists refer to these attributes as "social location characteristics" because they have the effect of locating us within the larger social structure. By doing so, they hint at the types of opportunities and constraints we are most likely to encounter. They also signal information about our chances of possessing specific types of cultural capital that enable us to navigate the social landscape adeptly. This type of capital is valuable because it enables us to connect with certain types of people and gain access to groups that support our need for belonging. Think of the person with extensive sports knowledge who is well-versed in doing "sports talk."

This person is likely to be well-equipped to join a group of friends who have created a fantasy football group of their own. In short, the unique combination of attributes that define us socially will shape our self-expression.

In addition to the standpoints that reflect our social location in society, we can flag the life course markers that help to define us, such as student, single, married, divorced, parent, grandparent, breadwinner, and retired. These markers, along with others, give us, and those judging us, reason to believe that we will have experiential knowledge that affects how we see and interact with others. In some settings, the markers and the lived experiences they imply will give us a level of credibility about matters that we've encountered firsthand. A newly divorced person is likely to be open to learning about how one of her divorced girlfriends managed her transition to singlehood and less inclined to seek advice from one of her friends in a long-term marriage.

As toddlers we are introduced to what will become life course markers for us, such as being raised by a single parent. Although we can't fully comprehend those markers as a young child and how they are relevant to us, or how they may influence us later in life, we begin to make sense of the world and feel the effects of different markers. We start by comparing ourselves to others in obvious and sometimes superficial ways.

We also work to fit ourselves into our interpersonal networks of family, friends, day-care workers, and pets. Pretty quickly we learn that each has a distinct existence separate from but related to our own. Ultimately, each of us can search for we-ness because we learned as young children to develop and express our personal sense of self in relation to others.

When we interact with those we trust the most, we look to them to ease our fears and anxieties as they typically protect us from things beyond our control. Whether our primary caregivers successfully provide a supportive environment to develop those attachments or not, our self-awareness tends to emerge through our interactions with them and the world around us. When we form these early bonds, we differentiate family and close friends from those who are strangers. With this cognitive lumping and splitting comes a feeling state that confirms for us that we are part of something bigger than ourselves.

Then, as we become more mindful with age, we constantly reformulate self-directed questions whenever we move into and out of different social circles beyond our families. How do others define us? What do others expect from us? What do we expect from them? How are we similar to or different from others? How can others help us to achieve our personal aspirations?

These realities shape the big picture of how we relate to the world. Beginning at an early age, relationships are critical to learning the value of feeling a type of we-ness that gives us a sense of belonging beyond ourselves. It should come as no surprise, then, that interpersonal relationships have always played a pivotal role in how we begin to experience our self and our identities.

Any production of a "we" necessitates the coming together of at least two people, and in many instances many, many more. Even when we pursue we-ness indirectly by embracing an ideology shared by others, we implicitly acknowledge that there are other people who think, feel, and act as we do now or plan to do so in the future. If our standing relative to our desired we-ness grouping is only aspirational – we haven't yet demonstrated to ourselves or others that we are capable of feeling, thinking, or acting in a certain way – our desire to be a certain type of person can still get us to experience at least a quasi-form of we-ness.

Perhaps the one scholar who has done the most to sharpen our understanding of our social selves is George Herbert Mead. The prominent twentieth-century philosopher and social theorist is credited with doing much to advance our understanding of the self as a social process. Mead asserted that a person's mind is anchored to language and is a product of interpersonal communication. The mind, represented by the silent conversations we have with ourselves about our desires, aspirations, fears, and more, helps us to interpret our social worlds. Thus, our desire for we-ness grows out of the social processes that allow us to generate and express a mind and self.

To a varying degree, our diverse motivations to see ourselves in a particular way, or to pursue we-ness in specific settings, are influenced by the cultural forces that shape how we live our lives. We aren't born clamoring to think of ourselves as a competent student, athlete, painter, dancer, or whatever. Nor do we enter the world longing to express our affinity to a specific family, religion, political party, sports team, school, or any other socially defined group. At best, we may be hardwired to process aspects of what has come to be known as our gender identity or to welcome at a primal level some form of nurturance from an affectionate caregiver. In short, by interacting with and observing others, we learn how we can define ourselves. Similarly, we discover ways to pursue we-ness in different social contexts that often change over time.

Today, the pervasiveness of cell phones and social media technologies accelerates the effects of living in a society in which other people's opinions of us matter a great deal and can be widely and quickly publicized. These technologies also make it easier for young people to find their place in the world, seemingly on their own terms, through online searches and the use of social media platforms to network beyond their immediate family and friends. Our children are growing up in an age where they are much more likely to see video images of themselves from their earliest years. Consequently, they learn to develop a video-based self-narrative that can be reinforced repeatedly. As they age, they can easily develop routines for taking and posting selfies from their phones. They can then experiment through their social media accounts with taking a more active role in shaping this video style of self-presentation – a performative self. But these deceptive technologies have effectively lessened our self-control.

The 2020 Netflix docudrama *The Social Dilemma* convincingly depicts the unintended dangers that have emerged because computer tech designers created a set of sophisticated tools that eerily exert "control over the ways billions of us think, act, and live our lives."[1] Many of us are unwittingly directed down paths of digital usage that alter our self-perceptions in fundamental ways.

These observations are amplified in Sherry Turkle's decades of research on how people navigate digital communication. This MIT researcher documents in significant detail how younger generations have become more committed to communicating with others electronically. At the same time, they have grown less willing in both their personal and work networks to talk with others on the phone or in person, and more insecure about their ability to do so effectively or comfortably. Turkle argues that we've ramped up our efforts to write and edit meaningful digital messages. Our investment in social media, she notes, provides us with lessons about how to navigate the world: "Instead of promoting the value of authenticity, it encourages performance. Instead of teaching the rewards of vulnerability, it suggests that you put on your best face. And instead of learning how to listen, you learn what goes into an effective broadcast."[2] Thus, in a high tech, postindustrial society, we must consider how our individual identities are shaped by our perceptions of others' views of us that are filtered through our new technologies.

Contemporary America, like many other industrialized societies, offers us a new and pervasive set of opportunities to see ourselves through others' eyes. Our society is steeped in provocative messages about diets, fitness philosophies, cosmetic products and surgical options, body art, and countless other commercial enticements. Both the twenty-first-century advertising industry and the latest technologies that support it have made us increasingly aware of and anxious about the ways we can "improve" ourselves.

Writing in the early 1990s, psychologist Kenneth Gergen was one of the first to argue thoughtfully that modern communication technologies were changing the landscape for how we develop and express ourselves.[3] Referring to the condition he labeled the "saturated self," Gergen introduced the idea that people were increasingly suffering from a state of multiphrenia. Building on the Greek root *phren*, which means "mind," multiphrenia refers to an experience of having many "minds" that generate conflicting values, opinions, and motives. His postmodern approach moves us away from a perception of people having a unified self to a view of the self as being fundamentally created within relationships. We see others based on how we believe others see us.

The practical realities of this pattern were driven home to me one day when a student shared how she struggles to be true to her Southern heritage while wanting to acclimate to a more diverse world. Although she holds many progressive cultural views, she also respects General Robert E. Lee and the monuments that were built in his honor. Raised in a small, conservative Southern town, she has been exposed to different types of people and world views since moving to a larger university city. She manages her relationships at home differently than the ones she's developed at school in Gainesville, Florida. These two sets of relationships require her to present herself in very different ways. In her words, "I've met the first Jewish and Muslim people that I have ever met in my life, and there is a large population of Black people, which is where the conflict comes in: I'm proud to be Southern, and I think Lee was an exemplary general, but I also know why his presence could offend people and I never want to make other American citizens feel uncomfortable in their own country."

Many children also face greater complexity in their family arrangements than they did decades ago. These arrangements tend to be more varied and fluid. Children increasingly move in and sometimes out of married families, single-parent families, LGBTQ+ families, stepfamilies, blended families, and more. Consequently, youth are more likely to confront a wider array of family situations that prompt them to figure out how they fit in with those who are part of their family or household. These experiences challenge youth to make sense of their identities as they manage their diverse family arrangements.

In our fast-paced contemporary society, we may be more likely than ever to rely on our relationships with others to define who we are as individuals. Yet there are plenty of opportunities for people to feel as though they can dig into their deepest, most private thoughts and feelings to discover their true self. The therapy industry is thriving. And our residential settings in recent decades provide people, on average, with more privacy because their living spaces are larger. With smaller families and more residential space in our homes, many of us have more physical space to shelter ourselves from others than our ancestors had. Having more space can alter how we live our lives. For example, sociologist Lyn Lofland shows how this pattern has affected the way people can more easily grieve on their own in the modern era.[4] If we choose, many of us can isolate ourselves from others to process our loss on our own terms. At the same time, we can become less available to those who may need our support, and less accessible to those who could support us.

Although we have more personal space in recent years because the average house is larger, and the typical family is smaller, modern communication technologies have altered our truly private time. We are often technically alone in our room or isolated from others in a public space, yet we spend increasing amounts of time communicating with others, many of whom we see as sharing some type of we-ness with us. Some of this communication may be by phone call, video chat, or text. Social media postings may also extend beyond our intimate friends and family.

Being accessible to others isn't always what we want. The internet and social media limit our ability to avoid those who annoy and torment us. These technologies allow a vicious style of cyberbullying that constantly reminds the bullied that they supposedly lack what it takes to be accepted. Years ago, when someone was bullied, the interaction often ended when they went home. Now kids are killing themselves at a record pace because there is no escape at home. The bullying is always there. Bullies can perpetuate the nightmare by reaching into a person's private space to disrupt any hopes they have to find a tranquil, solitary state or a comforting form of we-ness. Thus, when kids are bullied, they often feel trapped by modern communication technology – the bullying never ends.

Four Threads

One way to think about the key dimensions of the self is to see our life's tapestry as having four interwoven and personalized threads that we can loosely label *mind, body, heart,* and *soul.* These threads serve as focal points that allow us to think about how we construct our sense of self and live our lives. Over time, the relative importance of these threads is likely to vary as we alter our priorities and come to see ourselves differently. An important feature of living our lives is making decisions to pursue or terminate various states of we-ness available to us. The threads will also be involved as we pursue either dyadic or ideational forms of we-ness with people and groups. Although I highlight aspects of each of these threads separately in the following pages, they are ultimately interconnected.

Before we proceed, I want to emphasize two points we should keep in mind as we conceptually frame a discussion about the self. First, I've chosen these four elusive labels for their heuristic value in representing how people tend to think and feel about their experiences related to self and we-ness. These abstract terms do not suggest that I'm asserting a definitive position on the long-standing philosophical debate about the relative merits of dualism versus materialism; I tend to be agnostic on this matter. Even though this book does not engage this debate directly, it's useful to sketch the main points of the debate before we delve into the aspects of the self.

Dualism is a doctrine that claims two distinct kinds of reality exist: the material world, consisting of physical matter, and the non-material phenomena commonly referred to as spiritual. From this perspective, the mind and body are viewed as being essentially separate entities. As such, mental states cannot be reduced to or equated entirely with the physical processes produced by brain matter. Consciousness is understood as having an essence that is nonphysical in nature. Thus, those who believe in some sort of supernatural essence embrace the basic tenets of dualism whether they are aware of this or not.

Materialism is based on the belief that matter and material interactions are at the core of everything in the universe. Consciousness and mental states are viewed as byproducts of matter – specifically neural activity – and thus are believed to not have an existence independent of matter. It logically follows from this view, then, that any form of mind or spirit force would cease to exist when we die, and the brain stops producing neurochemical reactions.[5]

Outside of academic circles, few people regularly think about their existence and their everyday life experience by explicitly referring to the philosophical doctrines of dualism and materialism. Nonetheless, those who are firm believers in God and the supernatural, as well as many of those who feel uncertain about such things, will by default frame their understanding of reality and their sense of self by implicitly embracing the dualist position. Many, but by no means all, scientists in fields like theoretical physics, neuroscience, and cognitive psychology are inclined to adhere to a materialist vision of reality. A 2009 Pew Research Center survey of members of the American Association for the Advancement of Science finds that 33 percent of scientists believe in God, and 18 percent believe in a universal spirit or higher power, which implies that they take a dualist stance on reality.[6] The general public's beliefs are distributed 83 and 12 percent, respectively. So, it is safe to say that the vast majority of people side with dualism, but far fewer scientists do.

Second, having a sense of the fascinating ways historical forces contribute to how we see ourselves can sharpen our understanding of the circumstances that affect our consciousness today. Moreover, this sort of reflection prepares us to think about what may lie ahead for the human species as we journey into an unchartered future packed with new technologies and global challenges.

Our history as a human species reveals that we have increasingly become more self-aware, and aware in different ways, with each passing stage of our civilization's development. As the predominant energy production systems became more advanced, tapping new energy sources and techniques throughout the eras, we also generated more and more complicated images of ourselves and others. Each new advancement in energy technology led to greater differentiation and individuation within societies to accommodate the new ways people were organizing their communities and everyday life tasks. Our ancestors needed to acquire the requisite knowledge, skills, and responsibilities as they grew more interdependent in their new, more complex social arrangements. Yet, as Rifkin notes, this shift also "pulls individuals away from the collective tribal 'we' to an ever more individual 'I.'"[7] Although individuals became more interdependent in how they functioned in the world, they were also more aware of their individuality and personal attributes.

One of the noteworthy implications of this process is that the "awakening of selfhood, brought on by the differentiation process, is crucial to the development and extension of empathy."[8] Rifkin explains, "The more individualized and developed the self is, the greater is our sense of our own unique, mortal existence, as well as our existential aloneness and the many challenges we face in the struggle to be and to flourish." Developing those personal sentiments enables us to appreciate more fully our shared human-ity with others and to empathize with others' experiences and feelings. Ironically, while people over millennia grew increasingly inclined to see themselves as having a unique identity, they also became more interdependent as their more advanced societies demanded specialized knowledge to coordinate economic produc-tion and daily life routines. The tasks of building, using, and servic-ing machines, for example, required individuals to learn new ideas and develop distinct skill sets. Thus, we simultaneously came to feel more unique while being more interconnected, a set of circum-stances that enables us to visualize the self as a type of relational process.

Mind

From philosopher and social theorist Mead's perspective, once a person becomes distinctly aware of their surroundings and them-selves, we can speak of the person as possessing a mind in the social sense. The mind is central to any concept of self and according to Mead's framework, it can only exist if there is cognitive activity that is influenced by social conditions. The mind, which serves as the pri-mary thread to our life's tapestry, emerges from the neurochemical brain functions that help us to order our thoughts by lumping and splitting stimuli in a comprehensible way. These cognitive processes activate the mind and furnish the other threads with the substantive content and direction to shape the self. Whether the mind and differ-ent expressions of consciousness extend beyond those neurochemi-cal processes is an unresolved question for many and beyond the scope of this book.

The way we cognitively process stimuli provides the foundation for how we try to manage the impression we want others to have of us. Unfortunately, in the age of social media, we too often invest more energy into projecting a manufactured impression of ourselves than we do in displaying our authentic reality. One of my students captured this tendency when she commented on her high school proms. She watched people contriving fun moments so they could post upbeat stories on Snapchat. The same teenagers were the ones most often standing silently away from the dance floor, detached from the room's upbeat energy. They were also the most likely to leave early because they weren't having fun. Yet, anyone looking at their Snapchat story would assume that they had a great time. The fabricated story was essentially a mind game to construct a distorted impression that protected a person's self-image.

A less devious interpretation of how many of us use Snapchat, Instagram, Facebook, TikTok, and other visual apps is that we typically do not post with the intent of misleading others. We simply are more motivated to share positive images of ourselves to capture our happiest moments. And our posts that include family and friends are designed to convey our appreciation for the we-ness we experience with them. But from the outsider's point of view, it may seem like the person posting has a near-perfect life, which can prompt the viewer to reflect on their own quality of life.

We also think about the real opportunities that might offer us a chance to alter our sense of self while achieving personal growth. Social scientists use the phrase "possible selves" to capture the idea that people often project themselves into the future and imagine themselves as having certain attributes, interests, and accomplishments.[9] In many instances when we imagine these possible selves, we identify specific steps we need to take to improve aspects of ourselves. Sometimes our imaginative approach is fueled by our desire to be part of some group we find appealing. Our efforts to reach out to others, to be like others, and to adopt their ideas reflect how we not only construct our sense of self but also pursue a form of we-ness.

When we think about our possible selves it sometimes ignites a potential role conflict for us. The inner-city gang leader who learns that his girlfriend is carrying his baby may begin to have second thoughts about continuing his life as a gang leader. Does he want to bring a child into the world and not be able to create a stable, safe family environment for his partner and child? He may very well experience cognitive dissonance when he weighs the competing expectations of his fellow gang members and his girlfriend. He will realize that he cannot appease both; he will have to make a hard choice about how he wants to construct his self and which form of we-ness he values most – gang or family.

Some experiences that emphasize the mind will incorporate perceptions about the body, while others will not. The thirteen-year-old triathlete mentioned earlier projects a future for himself that is filled with intense competitions with elite athletes. The mere thought of opportunities to win World and Olympic Championships shapes how he constructs his possible self. For him, the mental side of his dream is intimately tied to his orientation toward his body and fitness.

Body

To state the obvious, our mind is intimately attached to our body and cultural forces influence how we perceive our body in many respects. When our mind is active and self-reflective, we are often attentive to one or more features of our physical body and its functionality. We might be thinking about our physical appearance, weight, height, aches and pains, a physical disability, or something else. Or we might be thinking about our body in a more enduring, generic way that focuses on, for example, our youthful or elderly standing, degree of physical prowess, or fertility status.

This form of self-reflective thinking about our body is critical to the early phases of our self-development and remains relevant throughout our life course. We form impressions of ourselves by comparing our physical form and attributes to those of friends, family, strangers, as well as media images. We often pay close attention to our body and pass judgment on it as it undergoes noticeable changes related to size, shape, skin texture and tightness, physical mobility, voice tone, hair quantity/quality/texture, and more. We register some of the changes as part of the natural developmental process that moves us into and out of childhood, adolescence, young adulthood, middle age, and beyond.

The most distinctive and consequential of the typical developmental processes is puberty. Kids are keenly aware of their physiological changes, even if they have a poor understanding of them, and they usually alter their self-perceptions accordingly. The real and perceived gaze of others plays a significant role in how many kids see themselves. Even though they may or may not be completely aware of how much their physical changes are at the root of this new kind of attention, they do recognize that others are treating them differently. This pattern is probably most pronounced for girls who are often sexualized by boys and men once the visible effects of puberty take hold. The mid- and late teens can also be a noteworthy period for young people. Many of my students vividly recall the first time someone called them "sir" or "ma'am."

Irrespective of age or social standing, most of us also encounter visual cues that confirm or challenge daily our embodied identity as a particular type of person (e.g., mature, fit, out of shape, thin, overweight, tall, short, male, female, nonbinary, transgender, person of color, young, old). We partly render these cues meaningful because we've internalized cultural images of the prevailing ideal body types and understand how the body can be stigmatized when it deviates from mainstream norms. Some of us are more attuned to these cues than others and many of us will pay more attention to them at some periods in our lives than at others.

As alluded to above, adolescents often rely on signs of puberty, for themselves and others, to form self-perceptions about their stage of physiological development. For months, or even more, they may find common ground with others who appear to be at a similar stage of maturation. In doing so, they may develop a superficial form of ideational we-ness as young persons who have or have not developed secondary sex characteristics. For those who feel their bodies have changed, they are likely to use those attributes to align themselves with ideological beliefs about how masculine or feminine they feel. While most welcome this pubertal transition, some feel self-conscious and avoid adopting any type of collective consciousness that defines them as a physically mature young person. However, those who worry about being left behind, or are singled out for being developmentally delayed, or are experiencing gender dysphoria, can feel marginalized as they struggle to understand their changing body.

The aging process associated with adults is also aligned with how we perceive our bodies. However, unlike puberty, aging occurs more gradually. Although consequential for self-development, the aging associated with adults is less clearly marked by discrete physical changes, and the onset of the changes generally occurs more slowly over a longer period. Unless we are undergoing chemotherapy or some other medical treatment with immediate adverse physical consequences, we are more likely to notice gradually that we are losing our hair, developing arthritis, wrestling with memory loss, experiencing saggy or wrinkly skin, developing chronic aches and pains, or experiencing some other sort of decline with our physical appearance or performance. The menopausal experience is a notable exception to this pattern and can have an unpleasant and prolonged effect on some women. That menopausal support groups exist highlights how cultural responses to this natural physiological transition have led to opportunities for menopausal women to develop a sense of group belonging and feeling of we-ness.[10]

The multi-billion-dollar antiaging industries that champion surgical, pharmacological, and cosmetic approaches to sustain our youthful appearance remind us constantly, as one might expect, that our bodies are the window through which we see our age.[11] Although Americans' perceptions of what constitutes old age have expanded in recent decades so that it is now part of our popular lore to say that fifty is the new forty, we doggedly value signs of physical youth for ourselves and others. This is shown by the high rates of elective cosmetic surgery that women, and increasingly men, undertake.[12] In particular, feminist sociologist Dana Berkowitz reports in her book, *Botox Nation: Changing the Face of America*, that Botox procedures have increased dramatically, becoming the most common cosmetic medical procedure in the United States. Remarkably simple, this procedure has even "sparked a wave of in-home Botox parties, where a doctor (or another certified injector) performs the procedure on a dozen or so eager patients."[13] Such parties, in addition to revealing how acceptable Botox has become for a large segment of the population, also demonstrate that people can embrace a body-centered form of we-ness during this friendly event.

In addition to the challenges we face managing our finite body clock, many times a specific bodily function is abruptly compromised because of an accident or disease. Traumatic injuries and debilitating illnesses tend to transform a person's sense of self and alter their desire as well as opportunities to experience certain types of we-ness. Individuals once able-bodied must now adjust to a life in which they struggle to overcome physical impairments. Eventually, some are inspired to make the necessary changes to manage their lives productively, whereas others plummet into despair with some never fully recovering from their physical crisis.

Those who assertively confront their new physical disability often find themselves searching for creative ways to feel empowered. One such story is highlighted by Mark Zupan, who captures the spirit of the men and women who play competitive wheelchair rugby. Quad rugby teams have been formed around the world in recent decades to enable people the chance to play sports competitively even though they have lost the use of their legs, and often have limited functionality in their hands and arms. Mark was a member of the American rugby team that won bronze and then gold in the Paralympic Games in 2004 and 2008, respectively.

Mark's transformational story began when he was an eighteen-year-old fun-loving, beer-drinking, college soccer player. After a late night of heavy drinking at a local bar, he crawled into the bed of his friend's pickup truck and fell asleep, unbeknownst to his friend who later that evening drove his truck away from the bar. A driving mishap on the road sent Mark flying over a fence and into a canal where he held onto a branch with the trunk of his body immersed in frigid water until he was rescued fourteen hours later. Mark experienced a broken neck and hypothermia from the accident which left him paralyzed from the waist down. Years later in 2005, Mark's story was one of many showcased in the award-winning documentary film *Murderball*, which chronicles the lives of the 2004 American men's paraplegic rugby team. In his 2006 autobiography, *Gimp*, Mark writes:

> Traumatic injury [is] ... a giant lens that makes you refocus your life. It's an X-ray for the guts and soul, the ultimate bullshit test. It forces you to inspect what you're truly made of, past the fatty layers of self-deceit and denial, clear down to the bone and marrow of your true being. Break your neck and you'll quickly get to know yourself. Intimately. You'll learn who your true friends are.

Although the personal resiliency of wheelchair rugby players is showcased in *Murderball*, the documentary also celebrates how individuals can build we-ness from their shared coping with similar types of physical limitations and bond over their unrelenting passion for competitive sport. It's debatable whether Mark found his preexisting true self as a result of his coming to terms with his traumatic injury – as he suggests – or if he fashioned a new version of his self out of the physical challenges he faced. Either way, he clearly forged a brotherhood by bonding with like-minded teammates. They gave him a healthy outlet to express his emotions, aspirations, and zest for life. The sport, and his relations with his teammates, reinforced his belief that he's accomplished more in a wheelchair than when he was able-bodied.

Irrespective of whether people are able-bodied or have physical or mental disabilities, everyone is exposed to social pressure in the form of institutional norms that dictate how we should perceive, care for, and train our bodies. The French social theorist Michel Foucault wrote extensively about how science and modern institutions have increasingly played a role in what he described as "disciplining" or controlling the human body.[14] While he focused primarily on prison life and the institutional forces that govern it, his theories have been extended to other areas of life, including sports.[15] For example, diverse sports leaders and market forces encourage contemporary athletes to train their bodies in specific ways in order to increase their fitness and efficiency. Professional as well as serious recreational athletes are compelled to conform to this ideology by adopting rigid training regimes that cover nutrition, stretching, conditioning, practice activities, basic equipment, assessment tools, and more. In addition, business marketing strategies attempt to convince potential customers that their products are essential to training the right way. Although the specific training regimens often differ between the various sports, what is critical is that athletes are aware of the public gaze and ask themselves particular types of questions. Have I done all that I can to manage a healthy diet? Monitor my heart rate during training? Do interval training to improve my speed? Seek out recovery modalities to help me bounce back from stressful training sessions and injuries? Incorporate enough practice sets into my workout?

Attempts to discipline the body are reinforced by various institutions that create a thorough system of body surveillance. Computer technologies such as Strava now allow athletes at all levels to share their personal workout and race data with others who are their face-to-face or virtual training partners as well as with complete strangers. In today's high-tech world, it is much easier to police one's own and others' training efforts and to hold oneself and others accountable. An ever-expanding cadre of specialists that oversees an athlete's training and recovery is now readily available on a voluntary or mandatory basis.

Stephen Poulson, a sociologist, writes about the disciplining of lifestyle sports such as mountain biking and triathlon. He highlights ongoing debates about the implication of applying Foucault's ideas of power and surveillance to understand how social forces promote athletes' self-discipline over their bodies. He explores the question: Do modern institutions only direct athletes to conform to prevailing training ideologies, or can they help athletes demonstrate human agency by using their bodies to express a form of resistance? Athletic women, for instance, were once discouraged from participating in difficult sports, training hard, or lifting weights. However, in recent years female athletes are increasingly taking pride in pushing their bodies in remarkable ways that challenge traditional patriarchal views of passive, soft femininity.

Yet the powerful reach of patriarchal norms that reinforce traditional notions of femininity and the female body remains pervasive despite significant advances in women's rights. The prophetic voice of feminist writer Naomi Wolf may ring as true today as it did in 1990 when she observed in her classic work, *The Beauty Myth: How Images of Beauty Are Used against Women*, that

> the more legal and material hindrances women have broken through, the more strictly and heavily and cruelly images of female beauty have come to weigh upon us…. More women have more money and power and scope and legal recognition than we have ever had before; but in terms of how we feel about ourselves physically, we may actually be worse off than our unliberated grandmothers.

According to a 2018 *Forbes* magazine essay, "The beauty industry has been on a tear for years." Half of the growth is pegged to online sales. The trend is propped up by various corporate strategies that enhance the development of creative new brands. But the growing consumer market also reflects the generational shifts that increasingly show that women feel as though they need to be "Instagrammable at all times."[16] Beauty industry experts predict that social media marketing will increasingly influence users of beauty products.[17] The dollar sales for the prestige beauty industry (cosmetics, perfume, and skin and hair care products) in the United States almost doubled from $8.6 billion in 2010 to $16.1 billion in 2020.[18]

These attitudinal and behavioral trends say nothing explicitly about who the audience is that prompts contemporary women to spend large sums of money on these products. However, the desire to engage in body work to look appealing to others is still an integral feature to many women's psyches today. The beauty industry is deeply invested in accentuating women's (and men's) insecurities about their bodies. Put simply, this industry's objective is to get women to see themselves through others' eyes and to seek an ideational style of we-ness with their female counterparts to motivate them to purchase beauty products and services. Beauty influencers like Huda Kattan, Kylie Jenner, Nikki de Jager, and many others have hundreds of thousands to millions of social media followers.[19] When the followers form a type of we-ness with these social media influencers from afar, sometimes thinking of them as friends, they are more apt to buy the products they promote.

Finally, the embodied self is often intimately connected to our physical surroundings and the tangible objects that represent what sociologist Christena Nippert-Eng refers to as "territories of the self."[20] As we navigate our daily lives, we do so by physically moving from place to place in real or virtual space while engaging with the various objects and people connected to those sites. Nippert-Eng reminds us that

> the idea of a territory of the self implies that a self does not end with a mentality. Rather, we portray and reinforce a self, that way of thinking, through our bodies and our physical, tangible surroundings. As

a particular sense of self extends outward, manifesting in visible arti-
facts and behavior, it can be located in space and time. We embed it
in and associate it with a particular environment and its contents,
including the people and objects appearing there. Once this association is made, any realm-specific person, activity, or item is capable of
evoking its associated, realm-specific self, inducing us to think and
act in a particular way.[21]

The stuff that makes up any particular "territory" may be woven
into our physical form to varying degrees. A tattoo and a tattoo par-
lor may represent a meaningful object and environment that is intimately tied to our physical self. Meanwhile, a night club where our
rock band plays, along with the instruments that are typically associated with this type of band, can represent a territory of the self but
not be as intimately connected to our body. Nonetheless, we must
physically engage with an instrument to play in a band, so our body
is still implicated in the process of expressing ourself as a musician
and managing our sense of we-ness with the other band members.

Heart

Despite the fact that we live in an age that celebrates the brain, the
metaphorical language of emotions we use continues to elevate the
power and agency of the heart. British cultural historian Fay Bound
Alberti accentuates this point in her analysis of how the body has
been culturally represented over time. In her interview with Julie
Beck for *The Atlantic*, Bound Alberti notes, "Our hearts are beating
in our chests, and they are a very visceral reminder that our bodies
have feelings and our bodies have reactions."[22] Although modern
medicine perpetuates the head-heart divide, our language tells us
that our emotions channel our individual essence – labeled by some
as the "soul." Basic emotions involving joy, fear, sadness, disgust,
and anger also guide our sentiments about finding common cause
with others by bonding with them.

One of the most powerful ways we can define ourselves is through
our level of compassion for others and our commitment to improving the circumstances that adversely affect others' well-being. How

is our self-definition contingent on the way we emotionally relate to others and perceive social issues? If we are inclined to see and feel the world through the eyes of others, and generate compassion when we see tragedy, misfortune, and injustice, we can develop an altruistic sense of ourselves that is more closely connected to others and less egocentric. Consequently, we will thrive on establishing we-ness with others when we believe we have shared struggles or simply because we want to join people of goodwill and help others address their difficulties.

The *DC Comics* character Supergirl brings the image of the compassionate heart into focus. Supergirl is portrayed as persistently searching for the inner good in even the most diabolical of villains she confronts. In the spirit of we-ness, she also displays the famous "S" symbol on her chest to represent the Kryptonian phrase, and her family's motto, "stronger together." Working alongside government agents, and a few aliens, at the Department of Extranormal Operations (DEO), she sees herself as part of a noble team that protects others. Although lacking Supergirl's superpowers, many of us humans also enjoy the emotional refuge of joining forces with others to do good works.

Those with compassionate hearts are more likely to volunteer their time, energy, and money to mentor those in need of a helping hand. A mentor can pursue we-ness with someone they are mentoring, and they can also develop an affinity with other volunteers. I've interviewed several men who were devoted mentors in the Big Brothers Big Sisters of America program and learned that they highly valued their identity as Big Brothers. They also appreciated the sense of we-ness they had established with their little brother.

Some mentoring programs or agencies that work to assist others can even foster strong ties between the volunteers themselves. The sense of we-ness mentors share among themselves as persons committed to helping others can reinforce their commitment to the organization's larger mission as well as their individual affinity with other mentors. Working side by side helping kids or others in need can solidify the symbolic and shared value of their volunteering. Similar sentiments can also emerge among paid workers who have strong personal convictions and collegial relationships surrounding the work they do to help others. Countless news reports captured the amazing energy and esprit de corps health care workers generated as they battled COVID-19 shorthanded and with limited supplies.[23] Fortunately, we can harness and put to good use the euphoria we sometimes experience when we are emotionally invested in a group-related activity involving our family, faith group, sports team, band, activist group, charity, community project, or some other social entity.

So too, negative emotional energy in the form of frustration, jealousy, disgust, and anger can motivate people to see themselves and others in a special light. In some respects, these emotions can encourage individuals to think of themselves as being abused, victimized, or disadvantaged. Intense emotions such as these can motivate people to look for ways to develop a liberated consciousness. They can see themselves as having a legitimate voice in challenging social circumstances that directly affect them. When they embrace this sentiment, they can become more hopeful and feel empowered to bring about change. Negative emotions, if channeled effectively, can be pivotal in getting people to turn their attention away from other matters long enough to commit to helping themselves or others who are facing serious problems.

Depending on a person's life story, it may seem natural for them to develop a sense of we-ness with others who are experiencing hardships that remind them of their own experiences. For instance, the African American, Latinx, and LGBTQ+ communities have a long history of pursuing a spirit of we-ness with those sharing similar attributes to defend themselves against a bigoted, oppressive society. That spirit is chronicled in two award-winning documentaries, *Paris Is Burning* (1990)[24] and *Kiki* (2016),[25] that focus on an underground subculture in New York City, and one that operates in other major cities as well.

With *Paris Is Burning*, Jennie Livingston, a novice filmmaker at the time, captured the extravagant ball culture that existed in the late twentieth century. It included an eclectic network of LGBTQ+ participants who created a lively safe space outside the cisgender, heterosexual world. Weaving ballroom footage with candid interviews of established as well as younger members of the scene, the film brought more visibility to the underground subculture that originated in the 1920s. Contestants in the "drag balls" competed in varied, precisely themed competitions that showcased their talent in performing a dance style, voguing, named after the fashion magazine, *Vogue*. All participants were judged on their clothing and fashion presentation, including their ability to portray members of whatever sex or gender category they were mimicking. Some describe their motivation to be involved in ball culture as being rooted in their desire to experience the kind of recognition and fame that rich, straight whites often experience in public life.

Many who were active as either participants or observers in the competitions found themselves developing close ties with one another away from the club scene. They created their own support networks and surrogate families, often referred to as "houses," because they shared the pain of being shunned by their family and the larger society. One house leader in the film describes a house as a "gay street gang" in which members "walk" at a ball instead of fighting in the streets. House leaders mentored the younger members of the house and the "children" often saw their mentors as parental figures. Although individuals who belonged to a particular house experienced dyadic we-ness and acquired bonding social capital, interhouse friction meant that individuals sometimes had to reinforce bridging social capital between houses.

Both films reveal how the subtle connections between race, class, gender, and sexualities can influence how individuals construct their identities, claim a haven from discrimination, and seek opportunities to create a we-ness that feels authentic and uplifting. Writing in *Bustle*, an online women's magazine, Jack O'Keeffe describes how the FX series *Pose*, which aired in 2018, symbolizes the staying power of the ball culture that continues to exist in New York City and elsewhere. O'Keeffe concludes that "part of what still makes the culture so appealing is the promise of a family that offers acceptance and an unconditional love. People abandoned by families and friends for being themselves still find comfort in the houses that make up the ballroom scene."[26] Ball culture is likely to stay alive because deep pockets of prejudice are embedded in our society and people long for community and acceptance.

People who differ in their political views and relative standing in society often differ in how they see themselves, as well as others. Are we compelled to promote our own self-interests? See ourselves as more entitled than others? Morally obligated to serve and help others less fortunate than ourselves? These dissimilarities can lead us to both interpret aspects of social life differently and also to take diverse paths in managing our emotions in connection with the relevant circumstances.

Sometimes anger can be a valuable resource if channeled productively by those who are eager to address a particular social injustice. Those who see themselves as empowered and willing to look beyond their own immediate circumstances are more likely to channel their rage by joining others to fight for a social cause. For example, the belief in personal empowerment was instrumental in launching the Black Lives Matter (BLM) social movement in 2013.[27] The triggering event can be traced to the anger that Alicia Garza, an editorial writer, felt when she first heard that the jury had acquitted George Zimmerman on all charges related to the killing of an unarmed African American teenager, Trayvon Martin. When asked about her initial reaction to the verdict in this high-profile case, Alicia said, "I felt like I got punched in the gut." This prompted her to log on to Facebook because she wanted to write a "love letter to Black people." Her compassionate and compelling post read, "Black people, I love you. I love us. We matter. Our lives matter. Black lives matter." Patrisse Cullors, an artist and activist, responded to the post by sharing it after putting a hashtag in front of the last line. Then Opal Tometi, a writer, activist, and community organizer, got involved by telling Alicia and Patrisse that she had organizational skills and wanted to help build out the project to provide people the space to share their stories and to collaborate. Together, these three professional women bonded over their shared experiences as women of color with younger brothers and their desire to promote an inclusive movement to help all Black people who live in a society that is still plagued by racism and white supremacy. By taking on their shared leadership roles with BLM, these women also expanded their sense of we-ness as the founders of a timely social movement.

In more intimate groups, we see how the anguish and compassion people experience in mass shootings can motivate them to capitalize on their sentiments about we-ness. Take for instance the remarkable couple, Sandy and Lonnie Phillips, profiled on CBS in 2019 by Anderson Cooper. These parents quit their jobs and transformed their lives after their daughter died in a mass shooting in Aurora, Colorado, in 2012.[28] They now travel the country to almost every mass shooting incident to console the survivors who are devastated by these types of unexpected, horrific events. They've also created a nonprofit, Survivors Empowered, that offers guidance and kinship to those affected by mass shootings. Both Sandy and Lonnie assert that compassion drove them to upend their lives and pursue their new mission to help others, but they also acknowledge that the compassion they experience flows both ways. They gracefully demonstrate how it's possible to create a sense of family with strangers when one has firsthand experience with the anger and grief that follow these tragedies.

Unfortunately, feelings of anger and personal empowerment can just as easily be marshalled by those whose intentions are more divisive. The long history of white supremacy and neo-Nazi groups, for example, is connected to white men (and some women) who accentuate their sense of we-ness while rallying around their disgust and hatred for persons of color and Jews.[29] Those who champion these perspectives advance their conviction that they are superior to others who differ from them in their ascribed racial and ethnic status. Many believe that these sentiments, among others, were critical to what inspired the hostile pro-Trump mob to travel to Washington, DC, assemble, and then storm the Capitol Building on January 6, 2021. We'll explore more fully how these groups emerge and operate (see chapter 4) and how we can better manage the tensions between groups with opposing beliefs and agendas (see chapter 8).

Let me add that Parker Palmer, a prominent social activist, Quaker elder, and founder of the Center for Courage & Renewal (a nonprofit designed to encourage compassionate leadership), proposes a thoughtful, broader perspective on the heart relevant to our discussion of we-ness. In a powerful call for us to mobilize the

"We the People" ethos that serves as the foundation to our founding fathers' philosophy on democracy, Palmer expands our vision of the heart beyond being a source for our emotions. Palmer, in *Healing the Heart of Democracy: The Courage to Create a Politics Worthy of the Human Spirit*, suggests that the heart points to the "core of the self, that center place where all of our ways of knowing converge – intellectual, emotional, sensory, intuitive, imaginative, experiential, relational, and bodily, among others. The heart is where we integrate what we know in our minds with what we know in our bones, the place where our knowledge can become more fully human."[30] Palmer's integrated perspective on the heart accentuates the interwoven forces that produce how we experience our complex, embodied sense of self in our everyday lives. That complexity shapes our approach to group belonging.

He grounds his framework in the choices we make when confronted with troubled times, experiences, and emotions. Palmer distinguishes between a heart that shatters into a "thousand pieces" in response to bad times and one that breaks open. The former, he argues, results in "anger, depression, and disengagement" and is unlikely to produce healthy partnerships between people and groups. However, Palmer's optimism, balanced by a practical dose of realism, shines through when he describes the open-heart reaction: "If it breaks open into greater capacity to hold the complexities and contradictions of human experience, the result may be new life."[31] The open heart allows us to "hold our differences creatively" and enables us to hold tension in a productive way and to keep our difficult dialogues flowing and respectful. We listen more clearly and express our ideas more compassionately.

Soul

Our understanding of the soul can sometimes fundamentally shape how we come to know something and establish its meaning. How we think of the soul may also affect our willingness to embrace the open-heart approach to confronting troubles. For centuries, the soul has been defined in numerous ways by countless philosophers and theologians.[32] The soul is often conceptualized as being an incorporeal essence – without a physical body or material form. Some thought traditions (e.g., Judaism, Christianity) typically contend that only humans have souls whereas others (e.g., Hinduism, Jainism) believe that all living things have them as well. Another key distinction between philosophical systems is whether the soul is mortal or immortal. Many religious traditions teach that a soul has a permanent, though nonmaterial quality that transcends our human existence. If we are among those who hold this permanency view, we most likely believe that how we conduct ourselves in this life will affect what our experience will be like after death.

One notable exception to this belief is found in Buddhism. Followers of this thought tradition are likely to talk about energy rather than some type of permanent soul that lives on after death. Similarly, the Buddhist tradition argues that there is no self. But Buddhism still presents a doctrine that accentuates the essence and we-ness of a shared humanity and interconnectedness. Jack Kornfield, the international author who was trained as a Buddhist monk as well as a clinical psychologist, summarizes the Buddhist philosophy as being that "we do not exist as separate beings." Rather, as he says, "we are a changing process, not a fixed being. There never was a self – only our identification makes us think so."[33] As we learn to "empty ourselves" Kornfield suggests that we will be struck with the "realization that all things are joined and conditioned in an interdependent arising. Each experience and event contains all others." Consequently, from this perspective, any notion of an individual soul or self becomes meaningless because we are part of a universal, intertwined we-ness.

In the scientific community, writings about the soul take on a very different tone. The consensus view, shaped most forcefully by those working in fields related to mental processes (cognitive science, neuroscience, and psychology), is that the soul does not exist outside of any brain activity. Writing at the end of the twentieth century in *How the Mind Works*, Steven Pinker, the renowned Johnstone Family Professor of Psychology at Harvard University, concludes that "the supposedly immaterial soul, we now know, can be bisected with a knife, altered by chemicals, started or stopped by electricity, and extinguished by a sharp blow or by insufficient oxygen."[34]

More recently, in his provocative book, *The Soul Fallacy: What Science Shows We Gain from Letting Go of Our Soul Beliefs,* Julien Musolino, a psychologist and cognitive scientist, adeptly summarizes how thinking about the soul has evolved over time. His mission is to convince all of us that it is in our best interest to relinquish any "misguided" notion we might have that the soul exists. Musolino writes that "in spite of well-publicized claims to the contrary, there is in fact no credible evidence supporting the existence of the soul."[35] He adds that "modern science gives us every reason to believe that people do not have souls." In his view, we gain much by giving up our belief in the soul and we lose nothing "morally, spiritually, or aesthetically" by doing so. But Musolino also affirms that the public is reluctant to embrace the scientific conclusions. In his words, "The soul may indeed be a grand illusion, but it is a useful and comforting one."[36] No doubt our mortality plays a role in our convictions about the soul.

Similarly, the countless tales of near-death (or out-of-body) experiences from around the world, some of which seem highly credible outside a scientific analysis, make it difficult to definitively argue against all explanations that include some reference to a nonmaterial world view.[37] Musolino is steadfast in relying exclusively on the contemporary model of science and physics as we know it to dismiss out-of-body experience and all other assertions that support a mind-body dualism. Yet, some level of skepticism seems appropriate as researchers continue to search for more rigorous explanations of consciousness and free will as well as interpret data about purported out-of-body experiences that might qualify as evidence for a dualistic account of reality.

What is also clear is that the lively academic debates about whether the soul exists or not – and if it does, how we can best conceptualize it – are likely to rage on long after any of us are still alive to participate. My purpose in this book is not to take sides on the soul's existence or exact form. Those issues, though fascinating, are beyond the scope of this book. Suffice it to say that rigorous scientific evidence that would support the soul's existence is lacking. But there is much to learn about our universe and our existence in it.

As a social scientist, what I believe is relevant to our exploration of the concepts of self and we-ness is captured in W.I. Thomas's famous theorem: "If men [people] define situations as real, they are real in their consequences."[38] In other words, whatever people believe about the soul is relevant to their lived experience, whether the soul's existence can be scientifically validated or not. Consequently, it behooves us to pay attention to how people's beliefs about the soul influence both their sense of self and their approach to building we-ness.

For our purposes, I use the term "soul" broadly to capture the spiritual or moral force that resonates with a person, from their personal standpoint. This usage fits with people's practical experiences in everyday life. A person is most likely to interpret this part of their self in relation to their religious faith, including how that faith shapes their view of their intimate self as well as their outlook on life more generally, including the afterlife, in most cases. Because individuals vary as to how concerned they are about the implications of having a soul or if it even exists, this final thread to the self may or may not be meaningful to specific individuals. The extent to which it matters can also shift over time as people experience the highs and lows of life and eventually confront their own mortality.

Typically, faith-oriented people believe that their soul is somehow connected to a supernatural being – a God. This belief provides people with an opportunity to explore a unique form of we-ness during their time on earth and presumably beyond. Some Christians, for example, often speak about growing their "relationship with Jesus." Their belief in the doctrine of the Trinity – that God is comprised of three divine entities (Father, Son, Holy Spirit) – enables them to visualize more easily having a relationship with Jesus because they recognize him as having had a human form as a man who lived on earth. In addition, when Christians turn to the Bible for inspiration and direction, they find passages that speak to creating a sense of union and we-ness with a deity: "If anyone loves Me, he will keep My word; and My Father will love him, and We will come to him and make Our home with him."[39]

This sentiment of building a relationship or we-ness with Jesus is central to the Christian men who have been involved with the

Promise Keepers movement which was founded in 1990.[40] This movement has challenged men to return to what it professes to be a biblical definition of manhood that positions men as the "servant leaders to their families, churches, and communities."[41] An overarching theme has been to help men battle the secular trends of contemporary society that have supposedly created a crisis of masculinity. The movement emphatically declares that "The soul of men is at stake." Although a thoughtful feminist critique of how this movement reinforces a patriarchal message has been presented in the academic literature, I streamline and restrict my comments to only show how the Promise Keepers' perspective relates to matters about the self and soul.[42]

The Promise Keeper model has always encouraged men to make seven promises, two of which speak to notions of promoting we-ness. Promise 2 (brotherhood) states: "A Promise Keeper is committed to pursuing vital relationships with a few other men, understanding that he needs brothers to help him keep his promises." Leaders encourage men to forge their sense of we-ness with a select group of friends who are Promise Keepers to provide them with the practical means to enhance their accountability to each other. Promise 6 (unity) suggests that "biblical unity" can be pursued by "reaching beyond any racial and denominational barriers to demonstrate the power of biblical unity." This inclusive message encourages men to be open-minded and to broaden their efforts to create a soul-based style of we-ness with others who differ from them in faith and racial background.

The notion of a soul is represented in other prominent religions such as Judaism and Islam. Although mainstream Judaism tends to teach that only humans have souls, some rabbis express a broader interpretation.[43] For example, the Hasidic scholar, rabbi, and editor Yanki Tauber contends that according to Judaism, all things – including people, animals, and objects – have a soul and a soul's existence is dependent on God: "A soul is not just the engine of life; it also embodies the why of a thing's existence, its meaning and purpose."[44] This conception and expression of the soul (*yechidah* in Hebrew) sets the foundation for how devout Jewish people establish we-ness in everyday life.[45]

Several passages from the Torah indicate that those who have lived righteously will be "reunited with their loved ones after death."[46] The emphasis on the value of we-ness is also represented in the notion that individuals who have committed certain sins will be punished (*kareit* – literally cut off) by being separated from their people in the afterlife. This sort of admonition implies that we-ness is desirable both in life and in death. Additionally, because everyone is perceived to have a soul from God, everyone is part divine. This belief reinforces the idea of we-ness among people who believe they are similarly positioned based on their connection to God. The Jewish people's collective identity and sense of we-ness is further solidified by their persecution throughout history.

The concept of the soul in Islam is similar in some respects to the Jewish view in that "whoever works righteousness benefits his own soul, whoever works evil, it is against his own soul."[47] From this perspective, the soul in its final stage of development cannot be corrupted because it is literally a piece of divinity in human beings. Scholars of Islam propose that there are three stages of development to the human soul.[48] The idea of an immature soul can foster we-ness as those who deem themselves as having a mature soul can offer advice and care to those they deem undeveloped.

The term *nafs* in Islam refers to the soul (and sometimes the self) and has three distinct meanings.[49] One of these meanings (*nafs-ul-mutmainnah*) relates to we-ness and the soul. Individuals who have reached the state of *naf* will have reached a state of happiness and a state of tranquility. Reaching happiness means that there is a bond or we-ness with Allah because the source of happiness between both parties is the same: what makes Allah happy. In this state, nothing makes a person happy other than their affinity with Allah and what makes Allah happy. In addition, the *naf* only desires good things, consistent with Allah's wishes, so when a person experiences that state they will only desire good things and be at peace with themselves.

Finally, Muslims are thought to have a knowledge of Allah within their souls. Faithful Muslims can be alone with their souls but not feel lonely because they believe Allah is within them. The soul implies a special we-ness with Allah and, in an ideal world, enables

Muslims to experience a state of we-ness with anyone who recognizes a similar use of their soul.

Whether we consider the soul from the perspective of Christianity, Judaism, Islam, or another theological tradition, the overarching point is that many people's experiences with different forms of we-ness are somehow connected to their religious beliefs. Ultimately, religious doctrine is never carried out in practice by all people in the same way. Thus, people will often express idiosyncratic ways of incorporating their religious beliefs into their everyday lives and ways of developing bonds with other people, objects, and philosophies. People's life circumstances and personal experiences will also shape how they connect their faith or image of the soul to their way of relating to expressions of we-ness.

2

Motives

We-ness is celebrated all around us. Our movies, music, literature, art, and folklore encourage us to cherish our many opportunities to experience we-ness as well as to mourn its loss. Seldom do we use the folksy-sounding term *we-ness* in our conversations, yet we invoke other powerful terms to capture our deepest sentiments about affinity and belonging: family, brotherhood, sisterhood, community, village, tribe, nation, team, crew, ensemble, lovers, colleagues, and business partners. We often commit ourselves to the ideals linked to these and other similar forms of human connection. Our commitment to these arrangements and the people who comprise them inspires us to appreciate them, make sacrifices for them, and, at times, even die for them. We have vast options for experiencing we-ness. Our motives to achieve it are numerous and often overlap. Granted, we-ness is frequently self-directed, but many of us will stumble into a sense of we-ness or be persuaded, perhaps even coerced, to experience this state of being.

As mentioned in the introduction, we will focus on five key social domains in which people tend to experience we-ness (primary groups, communities and civic groups, thought communities involving shared beliefs and values, leisure and sports, and paid work). But let's begin by delineating the main underlying motives that inspire people to seek out we-ness opportunities in these five domains. These motives are diverse and often jointly influence how people perceive and navigate their experience with we-ness.

Shared Genetic Heritage

Long before scientists developed DNA testing that can with near certainty verify a person's genetic link to another, our cultural ideology and practices affirmed the significance of the blood relations that were simply assumed. The proverb "blood is thicker than water" has played a prominent role in our folklore for centuries. Although this proverb has been interpreted in various ways over the years, it commonly intimates that genetic ties are stronger than those between nonfamily members.[1] In addition, the family laws of the land regarding child custody and child support underscore the value we place on biological connectedness. For example, stepparents have no legal obligation to support their stepchildren financially even though many may voluntarily do so.

Today, the symbolic significance of genetic ties can be seen by the tremendous interest in companies like AncestryDNA, 23andMe, and MyHeritage. As of 2019, more than twenty-six million people had used one of the four major DNA ancestry tests.[2] In addition, the number of DNA tests purchased in 2018 exceeded the number of total tests ever performed before that year. Although sales of the consumer tests slowed significantly in 2019, millions of people are still eager to search for their genetic ancestry[3] and a consumer report predicts a more than 12 percent global compound annual growth rate until 2026.[4]

Advertisements for this service emphasize how individuals can feel uplifted by knowing more about their heritage. It allows them to feel more authentic and complete. Yet these feelings for some may be contrived because they've never identified with the ethnic group to which the DNA test now shows they belong. MyHeritage uses the marketing line "our DNA test offers you the powerful experience of discovering what makes you unique and learning where you really come from." Meanwhile, 23andMe suggests that "your DNA tells the story of who you are, and how you're connected to populations around the world." The public profile of these genetic services took center stage in the controversy surrounding Senator Elizabeth Warren's attempt to document her Native American heritage during the early phase of her 2020 campaign for the Democratic presidential nomination.

Journalist and genetic detective Libby Copeland has spent many years studying the culture, science, and business angles of the DNA testing industry, including its consumer genomics side. In *The Lost Family: How DNA Testing Is Upending Who We Are*, Copeland shares fascinating insights gleaned from her own story and the stories that more than four hundred people have shared with her about using one of the DNA testing services to uncover their familial relations and heritage.[5] As DNA kits have become more reliable and accessible to the public in recent years, her research indicates that impressive numbers of people, either out of curiosity or concern, are taking the initiative to clarify who they are genetically. In many instances, the findings from these searches either solidify or redefine how people think about their familial we-ness. The growth in this industry has also meant that more people, often unknowingly at first, are being implicated in other people's searches. Thus, more and more people find themselves in situations in which their identities and sense of we-ness are altered when "seekers" contact and inform them that they are related. Copeland implicitly reminds us that in the DNA age, our sense of we-ness is an uncertain process that may entail rewriting an understanding of our past that we have yet to discover.

The significance of genetic ties is sometimes connected to how our personal body features may be shared with others in our bloodline. People frequently engage in the "sport" of identifying physical resemblances between blood relatives, especially parents and children. Most of us have been privy to exchanges in which people comment on how a child looks like one or the other parent. These messages highlight the significance of how genetic and physical features can be used to reinforce a perceived sense of we-ness.[6] Using sociologist Jennifer Mason's words, these concerns direct our attention to the "ethereal" and "sensory" dimensions of kinship.[7] This type of kinship "conjures up the spiritual, difficult to pin down and sometimes mystical connections people may perceive with each other that are often unanticipated and potentially highly emotional."[8] This idea resonated with me personally when my father and I on occasion compared our similarly curved index fingers on both hands. Although this similarity was trivial, it underscored for us our genetically based sense of we-ness as father and son.

I came to appreciate more fully the power of visual physical cues based on genetic relations when my research assistant shared a story about her mother, who had been raised in an adoptive family. As a child, the mother was constantly reminded by others that she looked nothing like her other family members because of her red curly hair. It wasn't until she had her own children that she experienced the overwhelming joy of seeing her genetic features in another person. She became very emotional when people told her that her children looked just like her. Not surprisingly, having others reinforce the significance of the physical legacy and bond can intensify our emotional response.

Family Love

Sentiments about family love are often connected to genetic ties. Yet there is increasing awareness that the meaning of family transcends biology. We see this clearly in how many stepfamily members manage their familial identities and group bonding. Numerous stepfathers I've interviewed have shared stories of their intense feelings for their stepchildren, especially those they met when the children were young. Some even stressed how their love for their stepchildren was every bit as strong as their love for their biological children.

The desire to extend this sentiment of family love beyond the genetic tree is also captured in how many children are encouraged to use family-based language (e.g., uncle, aunt, cousin, grandma, grandpa) to identify close family friends. I grew up calling a married couple that was extremely close to my parents Uncle Bill and Aunt Clara, although they had no familial relationship to our family. I was still fondly using those labels well into my adult years when they died. Parents adopt this type of practice to teach their children who in their network of associates is worthy of being trusted and respected like kin. This ritual of expanding the sense of we-ness helps to place children into a wider social support network. I knew that I could count on my Uncle Bill and Aunt Clara to treat me like they would one of their biological nephews.

Adoptive families are another family type that illustrates how sentiment about family love can transcend biology. Prior to the past few decades, social workers typically advised parents to buffer their adoptive children from the truth that they were adopted. These professionals wanted to protect adopted children from feeling alienated and stigmatized. However, in the last thirty years or so, the pendulum has swung in the direction of informing children that they are adopted. Parents are encouraged to be open with their adoptive children while stressing the value of family love to provide them a strong sense of security.

A second major shift in the American public's approach to adoption can be traced to 1948 when the first transracial adoption occurred with white parents adopting an African American child.[9] We are now much more open as a society to transracial adoptions. Yet, transracial adoption has historically compounded the challenges associated with family members building a sense of we-ness with individuals who are both genetically unrelated to each other and who physically look quite different.

As would be expected, our shift in attitudes about transracial adoption has been accompanied by an increase in the proportion of adoptions that involve a mother and adopted child of different races or ethnicities. One US study found that whereas 29 percent of all adopted kindergarten students in 1999 were being taken care of by mothers of a different race or ethnicity, 44 percent of adoptees in 2011 could make this claim.[10] Another study restricted to children in foster care also documented an increase in transracial adoptions between 2005–7 and 2017–19.[11] The unintended consequence of the upswing in transracial adoptions is that it has created more opportunities for family members to demonstrate how their we-ness is reinforced symbolically by their family love absent a biological connection. Genetic ties are often thought to be irrelevant if family members can express their genuine love for one another.

One commonly recognized implication behind the motivating force of family love is witnessed when family members, despite intense internal friction, rally to support and protect other family members from outsiders. This display of loyalty reinforces how the psychologically based family bonds invigorate the we-ness family members often share despite their differences. Parents with multiple children often marvel at and take pride in seeing how quickly siblings can turn off the hostility switch in favor of flipping on the protector switch when their sibling is being disrespected or attacked by someone outside the family. Spouses who may argue constantly can also become staunch allies when neighbors, extended kin, strangers, or the government interferes in their affairs.

We can see the value of family we-ness most vividly when it is being questioned. Spouses, for instance, often go to great lengths to shelter children, other relatives, and friends from the knowledge that their family life is not ideal. Efforts to sustain the appearance of we-ness to outsiders, and sometimes delude oneself, reflect how much people ideally want to experience we-ness in their families. The 2014 debut single "Dollhouse" by Melanie Martinez, an American recording artist, poetically captures this idea of a dysfunctional family creating a facade to hide their reality from the public. The song's refrain illustrates our penchant for managing the impressions we project to others outside our families:

> Places, places, get in your places
> Throw on your dress and put on your doll faces
> Everyone thinks that we're perfect
> Please don't let them look through the curtains.[12]

Many of us distort our public face, fearful that others will stigmatize us and our family if they perceive us as not demonstrating an idealized familial we-ness.

The previous examples of family bonds each highlight how family love can connect us to those whom we've incorporated into our everyday family circle. Our social exchanges, both the mundane and special ones, strengthen our bonds with family members. In addition, the symbolic value we assign to what it means to be part of a family motivates us to seek our state of we-ness. Sometimes our desire to create family via a DNA-based tie inspires us to use assisted reproductive technology to pursue a state of we-ness. The vision of experiencing a biological family connection can also compel us to persevere and make other important life choices.

Family ties were not on Aron Ralston's mind when he went canyoneering in the Bluejohn Canyon in southeastern Utah on April 26, 2003. Instead, this twenty-seven-year-old free-spirited outdoorsman was eager to have a solo adventure for the day in a beautiful setting, doing what he loved to do. He was oblivious to how isolated he would be and feel over the next five days. Those horrific days and nights, vividly chronicled in Ralston's autobiography, *Between a Rock and a Hard Place*, and depicted in gripping fashion in the 2010 Oscar-nominated film, *127 Hours*, starring James Franco, brought Ralston legendary status in many social arenas.[13]

On his descent into the canyon, Aron fell into a crevice and had the misfortune of dislodging an eight-hundred-pound boulder in the process. Seemingly doomed by a stroke of incredibly bad luck, the boulder pinned his right wrist against the wall. To make matters worse, no one knew he had gone to the canyon, he couldn't call for help, he was in a remote section of the park, and he only had roughly twelve ounces of water, two burritos, and a few chunks of chocolate with him. Despite his desperate efforts to free himself over four days – including trying to cut through his arm with a knife – he remained trapped.

On the fifth day he ran out of food and water, resorting to drinking his urine. He then carved his epitaph into the wall: name, date of birth, and presumed date of death. With hope no longer on his side, Aron even made a video recording of his final goodbyes to his family. On that desolate final night, one he assumed would end with his gruesome death, he struggled to fight off the cold and eventually drifted off into a disturbed sleep. There, mentally removed from his unimaginable predicament, he hallucinated about family, friends, and most importantly, a clear image of a fictitious three-year-old boy who was to be his future son.

Remarkably, Aron did see the next morning, and with it came a revelation aided by his engineering background. Reenergized by his vision of being a father, and presumably the powerful sense of we-ness it would bring for him, Aron knew he needed to use torque against the boulder to break the bones in his arm to be able to cut off his decomposing hand. After fashioning a tourniquet, and with blood dripping down the wall, he spent over an hour sawing back and forth: first through flesh with a small blade, then cutting through muscle and two arteries. He finally used pliers to rip away a tendon and nerve. Ultimately, with an excruciatingly painful final pluck of the nerve he was released from the boulder's vice, falling back to grasp an overwhelming sensation of freedom.

He still had to repel a sixty-five-foot canyon wall with one arm, forty pounds lighter than he was just five days earlier, having lost 25 percent of his blood volume. Fortunately, a vacationing family discovered him as he was hiking back to his vehicle parked eight miles away. Help was quickly summoned, and Aron lived to tell his amazing story about his survival against the odds, and years later, his opportunity to become a father.

In a TV interview on the *Today* show six years later, and two months prior to his son's birth, Aron described the power of his vision in the dark canyon when his life was in jeopardy: "It was kind of the first half of a déjà vu, or what some might call a prophecy. I certainly feel that this little boy is perhaps the same boy that I saw the very last night I was stuck in the canyon, when I thought I was going to die. There was this little child, about three years old, blond hair, that I picked up and was interacting with my left hand and a handless right arm, and I saw myself holding him there." As he continued, describing what it was going to be like when he would first meet his unborn son, Aron said, "He helped save my life in the canyon, and I get to tell him 'thank you' in a couple months."[14] That reality did come true when his blond-haired son was born, and he was finally able to realize the sense of we-ness that stirred his resolve and courage in the canyon.

Aron's detailed account of how his vision of an imaginary child helped to save his life is certainly unique. It's hard to imagine how the spirit of we-ness, channeled through the vision of a fatherly bond in the undefined future, could give Aron, or anyone, the tenacity needed to cut off a limb. But we should remember, too, that scores of people have imagined their connections to real people as a means of coping with demoralizing experiences related to concentration camps, prisons, rehab centers, life-and-death situations, and other undesirable circumstances. So, too, others have been willing to risk and sometimes give their lives to save those family members who blessed them with the opportunity to feel a deep sense of we-ness. Thus, the energy that a sense of family-based we-ness generates may be greatest when we can't embrace it directly or its existence is threatened.

Romantic Love

The bonds people want to share or do share with romantic partners are probably the most media-driven and commercialized type of motivation for we-ness that appears throughout our cultural landscape. Love songs are a regular staple in the music industry;[15] romantic comedies have earned a special place in the hearts of those who are fond of cinematic storytelling;[16] romance novels have a massive steady readership of twenty-nine million (84 percent women);[17] and Americans spend roughly $20 billion each Valentine's Day, with about 58 percent of that total being directed toward spouses and significant others.[18]

Most of us have at some point been touched by a love song that resonates with the personal ups and downs we associate with romantic love. Whether that inspiration occurs when we're teenagers getting our feet wet learning about the trials and tribulations of romantic relationships or when we are more experienced in life trying to manage our stressful, busy lives, our emotional center is stirred. In addition, whether we have found and kept love in our hearts, seen it slip away, or had it ripped from us, some songs remind us of how precious it can be to bask in a sensual form of we-ness.

Gifted songwriters and singers provide the artistic expression that gets many of us to open our hearts. These artists inspire us to take risks. They motivate us to embrace the vulnerability necessary to pursue a form of we-ness that challenges our ability to have total control over life circumstances. Song lyrics about love push us to explore our unrealized dreams, reinforce our desire to keep a loving feeling on track, or to gain the tenacity needed to overcome the pain of losing the we-ness we once had. Just like the classic songs from a half-century ago sung by Elvis Presley ("Can't Help Falling in Love," 1969), The Beatles ("Something," 1969), and Elton John ("Your Song," 1970) inspired multiple generations of people to appreciate the prospects of experiencing romantic we-ness, songs by contemporary artists like Bruno Mars ("Just the Way You Are," 2010), John Legend ("All of Me," 2013), and Harry Styles ("Late Night Talking," 2022) continue to move people in the new millennium to reflect on and cherish their romantic passions. That Bruno Mars's and John Legend's songs have billions of YouTube hits apiece attests to their extreme popularity and reach.

Even the revenge songs that highlight breakups implicitly remind us of the intensity of love relationships. Think of the 1972 classic by Carly Simon, "You're So Vain," or more contemporary songs like Justin Timberlake's "Cry Me a River" (2002), Carrie Underwood's "Before He Cheats" (2006), Adele's "Rolling in the Deep" (2011), or Olivia Rodrigo's "Good 4 U" (2021). These and many other songs celebrate how the individual human spirit can overcome the hardships that often accompany the unraveling of a once-cherished we-ness. They elevate our agency to reassert control over our feelings and actions while showing our disdain for someone who was once part of our we-ness. And they rouse us to transform ourselves so that we might pursue love and we-ness again on our own terms.

Like music, the world of movies, especially romantic comedies, can remind us that we-ness matters. The poetry of love that is captured by such classics as *When Harry Met Sally*, *You've Got Mail*, and *Bridget Jones's Diary* reminds us of how most of us crave those awesome moments in which our romantic energy overwhelms us. We believe that overcoming obstacles in order to establish a special love connection enables us to feel alive. One way we feel alive is watching these same romantic comedies with someone we deem worthy of being part of a we-ness we've jointly created with them.

Another sign of the major influence the commercial sector has on promoting we-ness is the tremendous growth in online dating services. The 1998 movie *You've Got Mail*, starring Tom Hanks and Meg

Ryan, helped to normalize dating services. Since then, the growth in online dating has been impressive. Industry estimates in *Forbes* magazine back in 2013 stated that there were more than 2,500 sites in the United States alone, with another 8,000 worldwide.[19] Given those numbers, it's not surprising that a 2019 survey fielded by the Pew Research Center found that about 30 percent of adults have used a dating site or app, with 48 percent of eighteen- to twenty-nine-year-olds having done so.[20] As of July 2021, one review suggests that the top five general sites in the United States were Match.com, OKCupid, PlentyOfFish, eHarmony, and Tinder.[21]

Popular sites like Tinder and Bumble became even more widely used during the COVID-19 pandemic because young people explored alternative ways to socialize while staying at home.[22] Launched in 2012, Tinder is a popular and unconventional mobile dating app among young people with at least 250 million users as of December 2021.[23] The app has much more limited user profiles than those found on traditional online dating sites. It displays photos of individuals geographically nearby which users can either swipe right (like) or swipe left (dislike). When two users like each other to create a "match," they can then communicate via that app's chat function. The system is not formally designed to indicate users' intentions for a match, but some users insert the symbol "DTF" (Down To F---) to convey that they are open to a sexual hookup. This convention allows users to basically say "sex, please" and it appears to be socially acceptable for some. Similarly, the gay dating app, Grindr, allows anyone to send and receive messages and the basic tenet is that most users are there simply to hook up. Even though Tinder privileges superficial ways for people to meet, it highlights the basic incentives that motivate users to establish some sort of connection with a stranger. Like other dating sites, some of the matches do evolve into the users developing a sense of we-ness.

In 2014, after devoting a few years to cofounding and developing Tinder, Whitney Wolfe Herd left and launched an alternative dating app, Bumble, that claims to have had over one hundred million users worldwide as of 2020.[24] Herd's promotional message as of July 2020 emphasizes the feminist philosophy that informs Bumble's unique approach to having women make the first move after an online match: "For all the advances women had been making in workplaces and corridors of power, the gender dynamics of dating and romance still seemed so outdated. I thought, what if I could flip that on its head? What if women made the first move, and sent the first message?" Here we see a formal, progressive initiative to encourage women to take the first step toward developing a relationship that may ultimately, but not necessarily, result in a state of we-ness for them and a partner.[25]

In recent years, one distinct trend in online dating services has been the increasingly segmented approach they take to defining we-ness. Niche sites appeal to people by encouraging users to categorize themselves and their dating partners in a relatively narrow fashion. For example, there are designated sites for Asians, Blacks, Christians, gays and lesbians, Jews, Indians, Hispanics, seniors, single parents, plus-size people, single farmers, educated elites, people with an interest in an interracial match, and more.

Looking toward the future, online dating writer Hayley Matthews quips about the prospects that one day dating partners will be involved with hologram matching.[26] While I can easily imagine Matthew's prediction coming true, I'm even more certain that people will continue to try to find creative ways to build and use technologies to improve the process of finding compatible dating partners who are open to taking a risk to create a state of we-ness between them.

The app revolution is also leaving its mark on romantic partners who have already developed a sense of we-ness with one another. Partners can choose from a wide range of apps that enable them to share schedules, send private voicemails or photos, learn more about each other, FaceTime, thumbkiss, figure out date night ideas, manage disagreements, and more.[27] The Couple app, marketed as a resource to help long-distance relationships, allows partners to, among other things, sync their calendars, draw together on the same screen, produce and share short videos, and create joint to-do lists to help them stay connected and coordinate their busy schedules.[28] Partners who use the Happy Couples app are encouraged to get to know one another better through fun, personalized prompts and quizzes that assess how well partners can predict each other's replies. Each of these apps can help partners enhance their sense of togetherness. Another app, Fix a Fight, is meant to facilitate real-time communication during an argument by having each person respond to prompts designed to help them express their feelings.[29]

Regrettably, we already have plenty of recent evidence to indicate that the way we use modern communication technologies discourages intimate and attentive face-to-face conversations between partners and friends.[30] However, the twenty-first-century wave of devices and software also provides partners with novel ways to strengthen their sense of belonging, at least superficially, to a coupled identity.

Companionship

I'm fond of telling my students about a fascinating blood-brother ritual involving the Azande people of North Central Africa in the late nineteenth and early twentieth centuries that has been reported in the anthropological literature.[31] The basic details include two young boys cutting each other's chests and then ingesting each other's blood to cement their relationship for life. This symbolic gesture of we-ness was meant to ensure that the boys would recognize each other throughout their lives as having a special bond. The we-ness they established through this ritual meant that if either of them should need safety, food, or shelter the other would be expected to do whatever was possible to help their "brother" manage their life circumstances.

I use this example to contrast how Americans are far more likely to formalize their marriages than they are their friendships. Outside of childhood, we seldom formally or informally ask anyone if they would like to be our platonic friend; it just happens. The social exchanges that lead to friendship, and the efforts to build we-ness in the United States, happen outside of formal friendship arrangements and without a ceremony. Still, friendships emerge and are maintained within all sorts of institutional settings (e.g., work, leisure, school, faith).

Gangs, fraternities, and sororities are among the small number of groups that often do have ceremony-like rituals that establish some members as having a special friendship with and commitment to one another. Various forms of hazing usually play a key role in these settings. But these rituals are more the exception than the rule in how people create their sense of we-ness through friendships.

Companionship and intimacy are central to how we perceive friendship and express we-ness. The powerful cultural narratives that guide our understanding of friendship attest to this observation. Although friendship ties may take a back seat to family ties for many people, it is not always clear-cut which of these bonds will take precedence for a particular person in a specific setting. What can be said is that almost everyone values their friendships even if they take them for granted sometimes.

People do indirectly process their sense of we-ness with friends. Longtime friends can find symbolic ways to frame and label their friendships to represent and reinforce their deep dyadic connection. Recall Mitch Albom's depiction of his relationship with his former professor, Morrie Schwartz. They affectionately and playfully referred to themselves as "Tuesday people" because they had lots of professor-student time on Tuesdays when Mitch was in college. They then rekindled this label when Mitch visited Morrie on Tuesdays in his final months of life.

Perhaps the most obvious pop culture illustration of how companionship can feed the expression of we-ness is represented in the highly acclaimed TV sitcom *Friends*, which aired on NBC from 1994 to 2004. Set in Manhattan, this show chronicles the intersecting lives of six friends (including a brother/sister pair) in their twenties and thirties as they wrestle with a range of serious life issues and silly circumstances. The ensemble cast of Jennifer Aniston, Courteney Cox, Lisa Kudrow, Matt LeBlanc, Matthew Perry, and David Schwimmer build a family-like rapport on and off the screen. Although the show's characters never identify themselves collectively with a specific label to designate their sense of we-ness, they clearly establish a strong interpersonal network of support that reflects their fondness for and commitment to each other.

Historically, the meaning of friendship and the configuration of friendship networks in the United States has evolved a great deal. Scholars have studied the types of active and latent connections friends establish with one another, the shifting type and level of physical intimacy between male friends, the nature of platonic male-female friendships, and the types of friendships forged in work settings.

Recently, attention has focused on the size of adults' friendship networks and the types of issues people discuss with those inside and outside their kin networks. One noteworthy and controversial study published in 2006 in the high-profile journal *American Sociological Review* garnered lots of media attention. It compared data from the 1985 and 2004 General Social Surveys (GSS). The authors, sociologists Miller McPherson, Lynn Smith-Lovin, and Matthew Brashears, documented what appeared to be intriguing shifts in whether adults confided in others, and if so, with whom they had the exchanges.[32] This research team initially showed that between 1985 and 2004 the number of respondents who reported that they discussed "important matters" with no one during the past six months more than doubled. In addition, those who reported that they either had four or five discussion partners decreased considerably. Although individuals reduced the number of confidants they reported having in both their friend and kin networks, the decline was greatest among friends. Consequently, if this is accurate, adults are increasingly more likely to discuss matters with their spouses and parents, a finding borne out in the experience of some clinicians.[33] Respondents continue to name relatively high numbers of individuals as being in their friendship circles, but it appears that they may be shifting away from friendships of commitment to friendships of convenience. They are also less likely to name people they interact with in community organizations as confidants. This suggests that individuals may be less likely to define at least some of their friendships as contributing to a shared group identity or sense of we-ness.

But how confident can we be with these GSS survey results, or other data from other surveys on friendship or personal network patterns? Claude Fischer, a sociologist at the University of California, Berkeley and an expert on social history and personal networks, suggests that we should be skeptical. Fischer wrote a detailed comment in response claiming that the anomalous 2006 results were probably an artifact of methodological shortcomings associated with the survey design, item quality, and coding errors.[34]

In his 2011 book, *Still Connected: Family and Friends in America since 1970*, Fischer went further by conducting his own descriptive analysis of whether and how Americans' personal ties may have changed during the 1970 to 2010 period.[35] Drawing on thirteen large-scale surveys, including the GSS, Fischer first elaborates on the serious shortcomings that limit our ability to draw firm conclusions about personal network patterns using survey data. He then digs into the different data sets, sometimes pooling multiple data sets, to consider a series of basic questions. Fischer's take-home conclusion is that "not much" had changed, despite lots of public and academic discussion about the presumed decline in "social connectivity." As he summarizes his findings, "Some of the ways in which Americans engaged with people in their immediate circles changed, but the intimacy and support of close family and friendship ties stayed about the same."[36] He also concludes that people feel about the same or perhaps grew a little more "upbeat" about their social relationships, and they got in touch more frequently with each other electronically.

More recently, Barna, an established private organization that conducts primary research on cultural trends, offered a snapshot of Americans' friendship patterns based on a survey of 1,025 respondents in 2015.[37] The report found that 42 percent of adults tend to meet their closest friends on the job, whereas 35 percent indicate they meet them through other friends, and 29 percent create friendships in their neighborhood. On average, respondents indicate they have five close friends. Asked about whether their friends are mostly similar or different from themselves, the following percentages represent those who reported being similar in specific areas: religious beliefs (62), race or ethnicity (74), income (56), education level (63), social status (70), political views (62), and life stage (69). Those who identify as evangelicals are especially likely to report having similar friends in the areas of religious beliefs (91), race and ethnicity (88), and political views (86). Most adults report that platonic friendships are possible between men and women, with 92 percent of millennials indicating that men and women can be "just friends."

Digital technology is not just shaping dating culture – it continues to reshape how individuals find friends and navigate their companionship needs in the twenty-first century. I explore a bit later how the virtual world of massively multiplayer gaming generates real-world friendships; for now, I turn to the feminist-leaning dating app, Bumble. In an innovative move, it expanded its services in 2016 and 2017 to include Bumble BFF and Bumble Bizz, respectively. The former caters to those who are interested in finding platonic friends with similar interests, and the latter helps users develop their professional network, share résumés, and pitch ideas about work projects to other business-minded people. The friendship option allows users to choose and provide answers to three prompts from a long list (e.g., "Favorite quality in a person ... ," "I feel most empowered when ... ," "Equality to me means ..."). These answers are then placed on their profile page to describe some of their experiences, interests, and sentiments. In 2020, Bumble spotlighted the power of Bumble BFF by profiling Rachel, a young woman who had recently moved to Nashville, Tennessee, and used the app to build an intramural soccer team from scratch by initially searching for women online to be part of a coed team.[38] Within days Rachel had not only made her first Bumble soccer friend, Tylar, she had built her entire team. Within a short period of time the eleven new friends were playing games and hanging out afterward at local bars. Rachel and Tylar quickly created their own sense of dyadic we-ness in the process.

A 2019 piece in *The Atlantic* by Julie Beck captures some of the intriguing dynamics associated with using an app to find friends. Her revealing interview of two women in their mid-twenties, Kristina and Dree, shows how they initiated their close friendship by meeting on Bumble. When Kristina moved to Austin, Texas, from New York City, she grew frustrated with only being around her partner's friends, so she experimented with Bumble to find her own friends. Kristina and Dree hit it off from the start, recognizing their shared love of dogs, and quickly developed a close friendship that included friendly sleepovers. Each describes that "friend dates" have some awkward vibes regarding messaging, first meetings, and making decisions about subsequent dates. But overall, there is much less anxiety associated with a friend date arranged from an online exchange.

Collectively, the two friends lay out the complexities of finding friends as a new person living in a city in an era when people may be a bit more reserved and are more mesmerized by their phones. Thus, it makes it harder to meet new people face to face. Dree provides a thoughtful set of observations about adults developing friendships in the twenty-first century:

> There's something about choosing to go on an app that shows a sort of deliberateness and care. It shows that you want to be serious about cultivating your friendships. I feel like we're used to that kind of seriousness for romance, but it still feels like friendships are just supposed to … happen naturally, and you should be chill rather than intentionally looking for something. People think you're supposed to just slip and fall into friendship, when as adults it does have to be as intentional as dating if it's something you need or want in your life.

Without referring to we-ness or a sense of group belonging per se, Dree appears to elevate the significance of friendship ties by emphasizing how some people clearly want to nurture a friendship into something that is meaningful and critical to their well-being. As we've seen over the recent past, the desire for companionship can compel people to try something new in hopes of satisfying our natural need to connect to others in meaningful ways.

Calling Out Social Injustice

One of the most powerful ways to generate a feeling of we-ness is to partner with like-minded people to fight against a perceived unfairness. In a narrow context, siblings might bond to challenge what they perceive to be their parents' unfair house rules, or a few neighbors might develop a shared conviction to confront urban developers who have plans to gentrify a neighborhood. These and other small-scale bonding efforts can be intriguing, but I focus on social injustice issues on a larger scale. These include the perceived wrongs that jeopardize the rights for an entire class of people based on characteristics like race, ethnicity, social class, gender, sexual orientation, or religion. Concerns about these types of issues can rally lots of people to develop a collective identity and a common sense of purpose. When done well, activist efforts that mobilize expressions of we-ness can lead to full scale social movements that are designed to challenge the status quo and liberate groups of people from exploitation.

These types of social movements include the Black Lives Matter movement mentioned earlier, as well as a wide range of movement groups connected to issues involving women, the LGBTQ+ community, those who have a disability, Native Americans, persons directly or indirectly exposed to environmental toxins, income inequality, and many more.

Celebrating Lofty Ideals

Although many social movements' participants are inspired by lofty ideals, it seems reasonable to highlight the importance of lofty ideals separate from efforts to call out social injustice. Those who worked on the Apollo 11 mission, for example, had lofty ideals that enabled them to experience we-ness even though they were not trying to address some type of social injustice. They simply had a vision that they wanted to explore the universe, and the moon was a realistic objective. Today, public and private teams of engineers have shifted their goal to taking humans to Mars. Others develop a sense of we-ness because they share their political candidate's vision on social issues.

Social media has provided people with more and different opportunities to help them orient their ideational approach to we-ness. Persons involved with either "call-out" or "cancel" cultures are prime examples. The former is a controversial tactic designed to execute public shaming of individuals and groups who are targeted because of their involvement or even alleged involvement in inappropriate conduct that might be construed as sexist, racist, homophobic, transphobic, etc. Those who call out others believe their ideals have been violated and often are seeking a public apology, if not more. Those who participate in cancel culture are also disgusted with a public figure's actions and they seek to initiate a mass boycott of that person's or group's product or service. They clearly want to harm the "offender," especially if the offender doesn't change. Some, like columnist David Brooks, have questioned the wisdom of such efforts.[39] Whether we accept, denounce, or have a mixed reaction to those who participate in these social media cultures, it is clear that participants seek to create a we-ness mentality while using an "othering" process.

Groups that already have established a shared identity, such as, say, the American Federation of Teachers (AFT), can threaten to organize boycotts of companies. In August of 2019, AFT president Randi Weingarten sent a letter to Walmart's CEO Doug McMillon calling on the company to quit selling guns and to stop funding lawmakers who are preventing gun reform or else teachers and students would be encouraged to do their back-to-school shopping elsewhere. This type of statement is fueled by a union's sense of solidarity and its willingness to seek allies – in this case parents and students – to further its agenda.

Targeting a Shared Enemy

Valentine's Day, a holiday that celebrates romantic we-ness, took on new meaning in 2018 for the students of Marjory Stoneman Douglas High School in Parkland, Florida. On this day, they experienced a horrific school shooting that took seventeen lives, injured seventeen others, and fundamentally degraded the well-being of thousands.

In the heated moments of the crisis as well as in the hours, days, weeks, and months that followed, students who were once either casual friends, acquaintances, or strangers in a large school forged a new vision of we-ness. They had initially been forced to self-identify as students who had just been subjected to a heinous act of violence. They also had the dubious distinction of being innocent victims within a larger social system that is expected to keep them safe, especially when they are at school. Nevertheless, these students quickly came together to galvanize their individual agency to bring about social change. They had transformed themselves into young people with a shared mission to honor the dead and injured by forcing public officials to work in bipartisan fashion to develop a prevention plan for gun violence that included sensible gun control laws.

Five days after the shooting, Emily Witt penned a compelling piece in *The New Yorker*, "How the Survivors of Parkland Began the Never Again Movement."[40] In describing the backstory of how the movement emerged so quickly, she captures the raw emotions of anger and sadness as well as the resiliency, creativity, and passion of the young people who took the lead. They were effective in crystallizing public attention on the critical issues surrounding school shootings, gun violence in general, and gun control legislation more specifically.

Those of us paying attention saw teenagers such as Alfonso Calderon, Sarah Chadwick, Jacyln Corin, Emma González, David Hogg, Cameron Kasky, and many others step into the national spotlight for the first time to represent the dead, the injured, and the emotionally traumatized students, school personnel, and family members from their community. They also made their case on behalf of young people throughout the country who live in fear of gun violence in its many forms. Witt describes how these young people on their own and then collectively began to raise their voices to capture the public's imagination for change.

In quick order, the Never Again MSD movement was born. After reaching out to their local congresswoman, Debbie Wasserman Schultz, the core group that launched the movement organized a rally in Fort Lauderdale, led a delegation to the state capital in Tallahassee to meet with state representatives, inspired the Enough! National School Walkout on March 14, 2018, organized the impressive March for Our Lives event that occurred on March 24, 2018, in Washington, DC, and then coordinated a 2018 summer bus tour to twenty-five states, called Road to Change, that raised awareness, registered voters, and generated millions of dollars in donations to promote sensible gun control legislation.

Although many of these students individually rose to the occasion and displayed remarkable poise and leadership, what is most relevant to our discussion is that they were able to mobilize their collective agency, establish their we-ness and purpose, and then generate widespread enthusiasm for their projects. Their ability to create this transformative we-ness was enhanced because they could identify shared enemies to confront, most notably the National Rifle Association (NRA) and its lobbyists, and the nationally elected officials who take money from the NRA and are reluctant to pass or even consider reasonable gun control legislation – most notably the former Senate majority leader Mitch McConnell. That McConnell was reelected by a significant margin in the 2020 Kentucky senatorial race, however, signals that there is a strong countervailing force of we-ness that supports McConnell's NRA position.

Even though the full history of this movement and its potential success has yet to be written, the initial response to the Parkland shooting clearly illustrates the prevalence, purpose, and power of bonding with others, and belonging to a motivated group. I learned about this movement's direct impact from one of my students, Emily, who was a high school junior in Tallahassee during that fateful spring of 2018. Conveniently located within walking distance of the capitol, she and some of her friends attended all the rallies because they were eager to sustain the momentum of the March for Our Lives demonstration.

Emily reconstructs her initial experience for my benefit: "I remember standing in the crowd on the old capitol lawn a few days after the shooting and thinking how incredible it was that so many young people could come together to pressure lawmakers and make people pay attention in the wake of such a tragedy, and it really made me feel like I was part of something bigger than myself." That feeling of a politicized, ideational we-ness gripped Emily. It compelled her to attend every protest and walkout the students planned over the coming months. In addition, in the summer of 2018, Emily attended a panel session sponsored by the Parkland students to learn tactics for drumming up awareness and support to sustain the movement at the local level. She went to the panel with a girl she had known for a long time but with whom she had fallen out of touch over the years. Later that summer, they volunteered to work side by side registering voters. Their shared commitment and the time they devoted to a common cause as teenage activists, in Emily's mind, strengthened their friendship as well as their dyadic sense of we-ness. During her senior year, Emily also got involved with the Students Demand Action chapter at her school and began to write numerous letters to her local and state representatives about gun control issues. Emily feels that while her activism helped her develop both a form of ideational and dyadic we-ness, she suspects that some of her friendships faded away, at least in part, because some of her friends were not interested in joining the movement.

On the other side of the violence equation are groups that seek to perpetuate violence against a common enemy. Although definitions vary, according to one United Nations' document, terrorist groups can be viewed as those organizations that use a "method of coercion that utilizes or threatens to utilize violence in order to spread fear and thereby attain political or ideological goals."[41] In recent decades, the most visible of these groups (Al-Qaeda, the Taliban, and ISIS) represent diverse networks of terrorists who claim to be waging war primarily against the United States, its allies, and other political actors who they believe are threats to Islam.[42] These jihadists, most of whom are young men, can be radicalized because they are quick to see Western values as abhorrent, and they find personal meaning in sharing a religious ideology with others like them. Their desire to belong and to be part of a holy war that promotes unity – especially among young men but women too – is an enticing incentive for many terrorists.[43] Even though the groups vary in their tactics and many of their objectives, members within a group tend to experience a sense of we-ness, and many see themselves as part of a larger network of fighters who are prepared to advance Islam as they define it.

In recent years, authorities have also become increasingly alarmed that terrorist groups are gaining a foothold in the US and luring a significant subset of young Americans to their cause even though the Americans are not invested in Islam.[44] Some simply feel alienated in their everyday lives and they are enticed by the brotherhood and sense of belonging a terrorist group offers them.

Similar dynamics are at work with domestic terrorist groups, especially those associated with far-right ideologies including neo-Nazism and white nationalism. The notion of a shared enemy can obviously take on many forms including individual people, large groups, government policies, legislative agendas, and more. Having some identifiable target, whatever it may be, can help people develop their own sense of shared identity in response.

In the late summer of 2021, we witnessed the dramatic consequences of two culturally diverse groups of people mobilizing their feelings of we-ness to respond to their mutual target – the oppressive Taliban regime. America's tumultuous evacuation from Afghanistan revealed the deep-seated loyalties many American military personnel had forged with their Afghan partners on the ground.[45] They had established their sense of brotherhood and "family" by working side by side during violent and trying times. Their shared mission to transform and stabilize Afghanistan, while expanding opportunities for girls and women, enabled them to develop powerful emotional bonds despite their vast cultural differences and lack of family connections. As Afghans frantically maneuvered to find safe passage out of their country under siege, many tried to leverage the deep dyadic and ideational we-ness they had created with their American allies, begging them to open their hearts and borders. Many former and active-duty American military personnel felt compelled to do so, especially those who had personal ties with Afghans who had worked with and sacrificed alongside them. These Americans were determined to honor the commitments they had made to their Afghan allies. Afghans and Americans alike were emboldened by their fears of the religiously conservative world view the Taliban was destined to impose. Ironically, as prospective immigrants, the Afghans felt deeper affinity for the American foreigners than the Islamic regime which was taking control of their country.

Sharing Pain and Suffering

The Parkland students clearly were motivated by their shared sorrow and frustration with what happened to their friends, classmates, and teachers. Being motivated by pain and suffering often leads people to identify a target, like the NRA and lawmakers in this instance, which helps the group to mobilize their resources and personal energies.

But the sharing of pain can also arise in settings where there isn't anything or anyone to target immediately. When neighbors are hit with a devastating natural disaster, they may be hard-pressed to find some type of common enemy. They might complain about the weather-related event, climate change, or the slow response from FEMA, but their feelings tend to be focused more on the injuries and fatalities that occurred among their family and friends as well as their actual property loss.

Sebastian Junger puts it well when he writes that "disasters thrust people back into a more ancient, organic way of relating."[46] They tend to develop what Charles Fritz labels a "community of sufferers" that gives people a chance to relate to one another in a consoling, helpful way that is not so readily available among strangers in our modern society. Junger adds that in the immediate aftermath of a disaster, "class differences are temporarily erased, income disparities become irrelevant, race is overlooked, and individuals are assessed simply by what they are willing to do for the group."[47] In this type of setting, we-ness emerges quickly, with powerful results. Anyone who watched the heroic efforts on TV or in person of the many everyday people, including the volunteer rescue group, The Cajun Navy, who went to Houston to rescue people from the floodwaters after Hurricane Harvey, witnessed different types of we-ness stories involving rescuers coordinating their efforts on the fly with friends or strangers to help people they did not know.[48]

In her detailed study of five historically significant disasters, historian and activist Rebecca Solnit documents how people typically improvise and display compassion during challenging times. *A Paradise Built in Hell: The Extraordinary Communities That Arise in Disaster* succeeds in showing that, contrary to the typical Hollywood depiction of people acting unhinged and selfishly during disasters, the "prevalent human nature in disaster is resilient, resourceful, generous, empathic, and brave."[49] The exceptional collective human spirit often emerges when disaster strikes. As Solnit observes: "Disaster is sometimes a door back into paradise, the paradise at least in which we are who we hope to be, do the work we desire, and are each our sister's and brother's keeper."[50]

An inspirational story set in Paradise, California, reveals how a natural disaster can amplify a community's sense of we-ness, embodied most visibly in its high school football program. The Camp Fire, the deadliest wildfire in California history, killed eighty-five people in the surrounding area and destroyed roughly 95 percent of the buildings in Paradise on November 8, 2018. Situated in the foothills of the Sierra Nevada mountains, this small town that once supported a population of roughly twenty-six thousand low- and middle-income residents has a long-standing tradition of being a football community. All but five of the one hundred members of the football program lost their homes and were displaced. Most ended up in surrounding towns and even other states. Although the high school and football field miraculously were spared major damage, safety concerns forced the kids to receive their schooling and to practice at other sites until fall 2019.

ESPN journalist Tom Rinaldi, and his producer Russel Dinallo, crafted a moving episode, "Paradise: From the Ashes," for the series *E60* that aired September 10, 2019. The ESPN documentary and many other journalistic reports helped to create a national story out of the Paradise Bobcats. Journalists chronicled the remarkable story of how the coaches and players cemented their brotherly bonds in the months after they, in harrowing fashion, barely escaped the horrific fire.

The head coach, Rick Prinz, was scheduled to retire after the 2018 season. But after the fire, he agreed to stay on to make sure the football program was on solid ground and to help his players deal with the tragedy. Only a handful of kids continued to live in Paradise during the year after the fire. Most were driving to school and practice from surrounding communities, with some traveling more than an hour to stay in school and on the team. And many who tried to attend other schools outside the area eventually returned. As Coach Prinz says, "They just weren't doing well away from their peer group. They needed their team. They needed their coaches. They needed each other."[51]

They were energized by emotional team meetings, their coaches' unwavering support, their willingness to do practical favors for

each other, and their "normal" time together practicing and competing in a sport they loved. Throughout the subsequent year, the
players intensified their sense of brotherhood as football players
who each shared the distress they and their families experienced
as disaster survivors. The players consider each of their teammates
a brother and their ritual chant, "brother to the bone," symbolizes
how they've intensified their shared sense of belonging. Together,
the coaches and players were motivated not only by their shared
pain and suffering but also by their desire to feel a sense of family,
experience companionship, and pursue their shared goal of keeping
their football tradition alive. The coaches also capitalized on their
unique opportunity to mentor their players in poignant life lessons
that transcend the world of football. Remarkably, in storybook fashion, the Bobcats overcame every obstacle to have an undefeated
regular season in 2019, ultimately losing in the playoffs.

A riveting feature of the Paradise story is how the football team's
resiliency reinforced many residents' commitment to forge ahead in
their efforts to rebuild their town.[52] "Rebuilding the Ridge" became
the community's rallying cry. At a community update meeting
attended by about two hundred people in November 2019, Monica
Nolan, executive director of the Paradise Ridge Chamber of Com-
merce, captured the spirit of the community: "It's beyond painful
and not at all funny to hear that Paradise was lost. Paradise was
never lost. The ridge was not obliterated." Against the backdrop of
loud clapping, and borrowing a phrase from Mark Twain, she went
on to say, "We are a strong community of pioneers who look after
one another."[53]

Ironically, the town's name – Paradise – symbolizes the idyl-
lic state that can be created when those who embrace a team- or
community-based sense of we-ness successfully confront severe
adversity. Nolan's vision of Paradise as representing much more
than a collection of buildings highlights how the invisible web of
interpersonal we-ness can be a powerful force for good. The fire
destroyed most of the physical buildings and the sentimental contents of most homes in Paradise, but it also reignited a passionate
spirit in this small town. Those with firsthand experience of the
rhythms and culture of small-town life will likely have a special

sensitivity to how the people of Paradise have mobilized their collective identity to dig themselves out of the fire's ashes.

Although the residents of Paradise forged a sense of we-ness from working together to rebuild their town, not all instances of people coming together because of their similarities result in a positive outcome. Unfortunately, some rituals bolster bad habits and unhealthy outcomes for the participants. For example, addicts can gain a sense of we-ness by sharing the rituals of drugs and alcohol. A difficult part of addicts' troubled lives is that to get and remain clean some must distance themselves from people with whom they've established a sense of we-ness through their rituals of using. Hanging out with friends drinking or doing drugs on a regular basis may have helped these individuals forge some type of we-ness, but this we-ness is often a destructive force in their lives because it reinforces unhealthy habits. The process of rehabbing from alcoholism or other types of substance addiction can involve difficult decisions about how addicts redefine their support network, sense of we-ness, and identity.

Some who experience the shared reality of alcohol abuse find solace in going to Alcoholics Anonymous (AA) meetings. Attendees may collectively see alcohol as a type of enemy, but participants are really fighting their own demons that lead them to drink. Those who recognize their own suffering can learn to empathize with others who are struggling with similar issues. When a person who abuses alcohol (or drugs) loses contact with a spouse and children over their misuse of alcohol (or drugs), they are in a better position to relate to others. Affinity is often built when people share similar heartbreaking stories of how substance abuse destroys precious relationships.

A key feature of the AA program is the sponsorship system. The protocol is built on the premise that having a support system is critical to dealing with alcoholism. Ideally, members will find an experienced alcoholic in recovery who has worked through the entire twelve-step recovery program. A sponsor is expected to help the newcomer understand and follow the program. This responsibility typically involves being available to help the newcomer share their story one-on-one and make amends for their misconduct. AA is emblematic of a massive rehabilitation field that "works to connect an addict with others who are fighting to get over their own addictions, building powerful bonds of shared struggle and shared aspirations that can transform sobriety from an inconceivable goal into a possible one. These treatments harness the power of not having to face a challenge alone."[54]

Another way to think about abuse issues points our attention toward children who have experienced parental abuse. Despite their hardships, abused children may be able to bond with other siblings who have also been abused. Here the shared experience may be a delicate balance between having a shared enemy and experiencing considerable pain together. Sometimes they may not even be aware that they are each experiencing the same type of abuse.

I'm reminded of several emotional talks I had with a close friend who revealed how she and her sister had been repeatedly abused as children by their father, but neither knew that the other had been targeted. As young girls, each saw the other as an attachment figure. They respected and loved the other dearly and were quick to show compassion even though they were unaware of the real reason their sister was so sad. In their young minds, they thought that if they endured the abuse in secret, they would save the other sister from a similar fate. These sisters developed an intimate sense of we-ness as children, although it wasn't based directly on their knowing about the other's abuse. Then, when they were both in their thirties, my friend finally revealed her secret to her older sister who immediately confirmed that she too had been abused.

Moving forward, their shared knowledge about their abuse experiences gave them the strength to set up a joint meeting with their father where they surprised and confronted him about what he had done to them decades earlier. Their emotional connection, prior to and after they shared their secrets with one another, has enabled them to survive their abuse and offered them comfort throughout their lives. Their sisterly bond also enabled them to mature and embark on productive lives away from home despite the horrific circumstances of their childhoods. Their bond continues to be nourished by their shared reality as child abuse survivors.

Mentorship

Being able to empathize with another's pain and suffering creates bonding opportunities, but people can also build their affinity and sense of we-ness with others by sharing good times and positive emotions. A mentoring relationship is one type of interpersonal tie that capitalizes on the generative spirit. For many decades, social scientists interested in lifespan development have focused on the forms, processes, and effects of generativity. Generally, a generative person hands down cherished traditions, teaches valuable skills and viewpoints, shares wisdom, and assists younger generations to reach their full potential.[55]

A generative or mentoring relationship can take many forms and can occur throughout the life course. Distinctions are made between various expressions of generativity: biological, parental, technical, and cultural. The biological form involves adults procreating and caring for infants, whereas the parental style includes caring for children and helping them to find their place in a family system. Technical generativity represents a person teaching another person particular skills helpful to navigating life: for example, how to cook, fix a car, ride a bike, walk as safely as possible on a crime-ridden street, or complete a college admission application. Passing on ideas about the symbolic system related to a specific skill is also relevant to this type of generativity. A person might go beyond sharing the basic dos and don'ts of cooking to instill values related to the heritage of certain foods as well as the importance of assuming responsibility for preparing family meals. Finally, cultural or social forms of generativity involve a person trying to help a community thrive in a way that is beneficial for its members. Each of these four types of generativity have implications for developing we-ness.

As I noted earlier, mentoring is often connected to our own self-development and emotional center – our heart. During my interviews and observations of youth workers, I've often been impressed with how committed they are to improving young people's lives. One fifty-eight-year-old white public high school teacher, Mark, coordinated a school-based mentoring and tutoring program. As we sat in his office, Mark was eager to convey the close bonds he has forged with the young African American men he has mentored. His stories about his mentees were memorialized by the numerous photos he had posted of them on his office walls. He admitted to creating an identity for himself that embodied his close ties with the kids. Somewhat to his surprise, however, his friends didn't understand how he framed these relationships when they heard him refer to his mentees as "my guys, or my boys, or my posse, or my dogs." His friends thought he was depicting them as his "possessions." But this was far from his intent. Instead, he used hip hop idioms to express his deep feelings for the young men despite their decidedly different personal experiences based on race, social class, and age. The generative spirit was clearly a driving force in his desire to create mentoring partnerships and a sense of we-ness with the young men he befriended. I interviewed one of those young men and he convinced me that the sense of we-ness Mark had described was mutual and highly valued.

For Mark, and many of the other youth workers I've encountered, the relationships they have with kids have a profound and lasting impact on both the youth workers and the kids. Their mentorship role reinforces for them who they are as individuals and in some instances transforms them. They develop stronger commitment to preserving the shared identity they hold as coach, teacher, youth minister, Boy Scout leader, camp counselor, or as part of some other role.

Sharing a Practical Goal

A powerful motivational force that brings people together and can keep them together involves the sharing of a common goal. The process of identifying and achieving a goal can unfold in all the social domains highlighted in this book. In addition, this process is often intertwined with some of the other motives mentioned earlier. To illustrate the significance of goal setting, we'll focus on goals that implicate we-ness that are commonly expressed through sports and business ventures.

If you've been involved in any type of team sport at any level, you'll probably recognize the mantra that there is no "I" in "team."

In other words, participants are expected to suppress their individual egos to better serve a team goal. Teammates are encouraged to embrace the philosophy that the collective "we" is more compelling than personal ambitions.

Athletic teams are fond of using the "family" metaphor to convey the strong affinity teammates are supposed to have toward one another even when they are competing for playing time. Teammates are challenged to manage their antagonistic cooperation so they can compete with one another yet come together with a singular goal – to win, or at least perform up to their abilities – and to battle effectively against opposing teams. As with real family members, teammates may not always get along or even like each other, but competitive norms and their sense of we-ness induces participants in family-like sports groups to tolerate each other well enough to achieve a desired goal.

The history of sports is replete with inspirational examples of how fans, teammates, coaches, team executives, and staff rally around a team's identity and pull for their collective success – ideally whether the team is doing well or not. In their memorable journey to become Major League Baseball's World Series champions in 1979, the Pittsburg Pirates adopted as its theme song Sister Sledge's upbeat "We Are Family," released that same year. The Pirates' organization and supporters incorporated the song into game day ceremonies, rally rituals, and promotional efforts as everyone joined forces to maximize the team's potential. Other athletic teams have incorporated this family-based song into their promotional toolbox as well.

More recently, no sports enthusiast can forget the long overdue euphoria that overcame Chicago Cubs fans in 2016 when the franchise ended the longest World Series drought of 108 years by defeating the Cleveland Indians in a dramatic seven-game series. The massive parade and celebration that followed, with multiple reports estimating that roughly five million people attended, showcased Cubs fans' fervent sense of we-ness.[56] Although the Cubs' party was probably the largest, cities across the country have been throwing parades for their victorious sports teams for decades. These events illustrate how people regularly use sports to pursue a goal-oriented form of we-ness that reveals their passion for celebrating a city's collective consciousness.

In some ways, business partners manage their goal setting in a context that differs from what transpires in the sports world, but there are plenty of similarities between how we-ness is pursued and practiced in the worlds of business and sports. Prior to launching a business, someone must envision a new product or service that will presumably appeal to a market. For the business ventures that involve multiple owners, people will have to work out how they can combine their talents and resources to make the business a reality, and, ideally, a success. Most importantly, they will need to decide how business goals and operational strategies are jointly developed.

In some business start-ups, one person will have an idea and then approach others to get involved with the project from the outset with the hope that they, too, will develop a vested interest in seeing the business do well. When the entrepreneur recruits others to join the project, the leader will need to process how they feel about expanding their vision of we-ness as it relates to their proposed business. In this instance, the business model may be untested so anyone who is recruited would be joining a project that is yet to be executed. In other scenarios, a person may have a functional or even a well-established business operation and is interested in expanding it by securing more partners.

Whether it is a new or established venture, thoughts about expanding the borders of we-ness can be perceived as risky when people contemplate the prospects of sharing power. But the energy devoted to defining goals and to developing a business plan to achieve them can unite joint business owners. In contrast, disagreements about the direction of a business venture can push business associates apart.

The we-ness that emerges from some business ventures, especially big ones, can be complex, dynamic, and highly controversial. Irrespective of how a joint venture materializes, the participants will need to manage their willingness to trust their partners as they share or sever decision-making power throughout the life of a business.

For perspective, we can look at the infamous history of the social media and social networking service that grew to become the megacorporation Facebook, now known as Meta. This is a prime example of how concerns about trust can confound we-ness in a business setting.[57] *The Social Network*, the award-winning movie released in 2010, portrays the tantalizing details of how this company was created and the frictions that ensued in the early days. More recently, journalists Sheera Frenkel and Cecilia Kang provide a penetrating analysis in their timely book, *An Ugly Truth: Inside Facebook's Battle for Domination*, of the internal loyalty struggles within the Facebook community. These tensions culminated with Facebook's unprecedented entanglements with government officials and media activists in the early months of 2021.[58] The book explores how Facebook sought to sustain a profitable sense of we-ness while being confronted with demands for transparency and action from within and outside the company. Some called for the company to embrace the greater good, American interests, and democracy by confronting disinformation campaigns and hate speech online.

Mark Zuckerberg, the well-known CEO and cofounder of Facebook, along with several Harvard classmates, had a hand in creating the initial website "TheFacebook" in January 2004. Although Zuckerberg is commonly identified as the founder of what came to be called Facebook, Eduardo Saverin is the other official cofounder. Saverin sued and won a settlement from Zuckerberg for diluting his shares in the company after Zuckerberg secured another investment partner. Three of the other Harvard students who interacted with Zuckerberg in the early days of this venture (Cameron Winklevoss, Tyler Winklevoss, and Divya Narendra) also successfully sued Zuckerberg for inappropriately borrowing their ideas to build the competing platform that became Facebook. In short, the backstory to Facebook is fraught with competing definitions of how business-minded people often struggle when negotiating their respective senses of we-ness and their contested claims to intellectual property rights.

The award-winning ABC reality TV show *Shark Tank* captures some of the key aspects to shared decision-making and how we-ness is navigated in the business world. For the unfamiliar, the show creates opportunities for aspiring entrepreneurs to make business presentations before a highly acclaimed panel of businesspeople: as of 2022, these Sharks were Barbara Corcoran, Mark Cuban, Lori

Greiner, Robert Herjavec, Daymond John, Kevin O'Leary, and sometimes guest Sharks. These exchanges are designed to flesh out which Shark, if any, is willing to invest in the proposed idea and create a business partnership with the presenter(s). From the presenter's perspective, such partnerships require them to reframe their orientation toward their business. In short, they will need to expand their vision of we-ness as it relates to their company. For the presenters who are already part of a multiple-person ownership team, they will need to negotiate among themselves whether they have a shared vision of which Shark and proposal they are willing to accept, knowing that they will be relinquishing some control over their joint project. Any potential partnership requires that a Shark be willing to invest in the business and that the presenter be willing to relinquish some control over their individually owned or jointly owned operation. The show illustrates that when a business is jointly owned and operated, it complicates the process of potentially incorporating additional business partners.

Whether we are motivated to experience we-ness because we share a collective goal with others or are driven by one or more of the forces outlined above, we often search for opportunities to bond with others in different areas of our lives. We now explore how we express a sense of we-ness and group belonging in five specific life domains.

3

Social Domains

Life is messy. It can be sliced up in various ways. Understandably, then, when we try to make sense of our complex world by lumping and splitting aspects of our personal life into neat categories, it seldom works perfectly. The five social domains described below provide a rough template of our life activities and our perceptions of them, but I make no claim that my approach is superior to any other scheme for categorizing the areas in which we-ness flourishes. I simply point out how people often frame their experience and navigate life.

We enter each of these domains with our own point of view, thereby shaping how we perceive and experience different situations. The domains are consequential because they each provide us with opportunities as well as challenges to develop our sense of we-ness. So, too, our experiences in each of the areas can alter our personalities and the way we think about and pursue we-ness. Although they can be viewed as distinct in some ways, the untidiness of life means that these areas bleed into one another and engender different interpretations depending on the social circumstances and perspective of the persons involved.

Primary Groups

Most of us spend a fair amount of time throughout our lives managing we-ness with family members, romantic partners, and our close friends. The motivating forces associated with shared genetic heritage, family and romantic love, companionship, and mentorship are the most obvious motivating factors that prompt people to establish their sense of we-ness in primary groups. Because these groups tend to accentuate emotional intimacy, they offer participants opportunities to identify and act upon their common sentiments, values, and beliefs. This domain also offers us opportunities to have hybrid relationships with animals and AI devices.

Family and Friend Ties

Our society places a great deal of importance on sustaining positive feelings of we-ness between family members and between romantic partners. The massive mental health industry in the United States confirms this point. According to the Department of Labor's statistics, 577,000 mental health professionals were practicing in the United States during the 2016–17 period. Another 715,600 social workers, who often assist families with mental health concerns, were employed in 2020 with an anticipated 12 percent growth rate by 2030.[1] These one million-plus professionals try to help people flourish in their parent-child, sibling, and partner relationships. They also assist individuals with developing and sustaining a healthy sense of we-ness with others.

Marriage and family therapists are trained to treat a person's difficulties as part of a series of relationships that affect the person. Many therapy patients struggle with managing the interpersonal dynamics of some form of we-ness. In many cases, they suffer because they feel excluded from a familial sense of we-ness or they fail to support the we-ness that once connected them to specific others. Imagine the adopted child who feels alienated from his adoptive family. What about the teenager who feels as if her family doesn't accept her now that she's come out as transgender? Then consider the frustrated husband who feels his partner is detached and growing less and less willing to make investments in their relationship and household plans.

Clinical psychologists Jefferson Singer and Karen Skerrett, who work with couples and families, have a keen sense of the power of we-ness in shaping relationship quality and individual well-being.[2] In their book, *Positive Couple Therapy: Using We-Stories to Enhance Resilience*, these clinicians extend the work of many others who have in recent decades documented the personal health and relationship benefits of couples who are able to create and nourish a sense of we-ness.[3] They present a strength-based model for helping couples uncover the positive potential in their relationships by accentuating couples' sense of we-ness. For them, we-ness is a type of conscious-ness, a perspective on the "third entity" that overlaps with and can be built out of the "I" and "you" in a relationship. In another essay that treats this topic, Skerrett suggests that

> "we" showcases the couple, highlights their mutuality, and requires coordinated efforts, interpersonal sensitivity, generosity, and a will-ingness both to set boundaries and to offer space. If it sounds chal-lenging, that's because it is; it takes mindful attention. We tell couples to focus on the question "What is best for us?" because it really makes the difference – particularly in approaching disagreements.[4]

As a piece of practical advice for couples facing conflict, Skerrett recommends that couples pause to reflect on the question, "Where is our WE today?" This action requires people to set aside their ego-centered orientations toward the world and their relationships. They are encouraged to think beyond the "I" or even the "you" and to focus on the "us." By encouraging couples to prioritize their relationship and to express a "practiced We-consciousness," she believes couples stand a greater chance of experiencing "individual physical and mental health benefits, as well as relationship satis-faction." Studies of couples' well-being concur that greater couple we-ness is associated with healthier couple relationships and better individual health outcomes.[5] Unfortunately, it's tricky to sort out a key question. Does a couple's sense of we-ness produce the posi-tive outcomes, or do the favorable experiences individuals have in relationships create more opportunities for couples to develop a strong sense of we-ness? Most likely, both patterns come into play for many couples.

Singer, Skerrett, and other therapists believe that couples can work on and improve their sense of we-ness if they are mindful and willing. One strategy Singer and Skerrett highlight involves the power of storytelling, specifically what they refer to as the "We-story": "We-stories reflect positive dimensions of a relationship: security, empathy, respect, acceptance, pleasure, humor, shared meaning, and vision."[6] Singer and Skerrett argue that a We-story helps couples in several critical ways. They "shape the couple's mutual identity; they provide meaning and purpose in the couple's life; they serve as guides for current interaction and future growth; they are repositories of the couple's wisdom and a means of transmitting their legacy to others in their lives."[7]

We can assess the nature of a couple's relationship by exploring the types of we-stories a couple uses to describe their life circumstances. Whether we intend to understand the self or the couple, we can learn a lot by paying attention to the content and style of a person's or couple's storytelling. What kinds of stories do they tell about their experiences? In what ways and to what extent does the person incorporate descriptions of others into their stories? How often do they insert singular or plural pronouns to frame their descriptions?

Skerrett offers another practical suggestion for couples willing to build their feelings of we-ness. She suggests that each partner locate a positive physical symbol of their relationship. The object could be from their current or past life, part of their home, or something from nature, but it needs to have significance for their relationship. Once the partners retrieve the item, they should show it to their partner and jointly decide which object is the most symbolic of their positive relationship.

This exercise extends Christena Nippert-Eng's concept of the "territories of the self" that implicates our self-meanings, as described in chapter 1. Tangible objects with special, personalized meaning can trigger deep emotions and signal to people how they see themselves. Likewise, objects can stir our emotions while representing our broader awareness of the we-ness we share in a relationship.

Skerrett's optimism leads her to suggest that the object a couple chooses can become their "North Star," reminding them of what they value about their relationship. It may also prompt them to develop a co-constructed story about their we-ness.

We-ness stories are particularly valuable when tragedy strikes a couple or family. Tragedies come in many forms: a devastating illness or an unexpected death, a natural disaster that destroys a home, unemployment, deportation, or some other type of crisis that challenges a couple's or family's emotional foundation. Whatever the event, it is colored by unique circumstances that help to define the meaning of the event for those involved, as well as others. Those that damage our well-being the most are typically unexpected and prolonged, but there is no precise calculus for figuring out how people will perceive and respond to tragedy.[8]

Family trauma, and the sharing of pain and suffering, brings some people together, while tearing others apart. Sometimes people rise to the occasion and recommit themselves to keeping their sense of we-ness intact, and even to growing it. Think of Sandy and Lonnie Phillips, the amazing and resilient couple that travels the country as a team helping people cope with the aftermath of mass shootings. Relationships characterized by healthy communication and intimacy will often provide people with a buffer to endure their loss and sustain their affinity with one another. For some, the tragedy may serve as a wake-up call. It can prompt partners and family members to renew the love that had fallen silent in recent times but had not yet died. It can compel the saddened to rally in support of each other as they had been known to do under different conditions.

Others find themselves unable or unwilling to manage their new circumstances in a way that celebrates whatever we-ness they had with loved ones. They succumb to the fears that tempt them to isolate themselves or turn to drugs and alcohol to conceal their pain. In doing so, they drift further into their darkness and apart from the loved ones who might have been able to support them. And for some, the traumatic event registers the last jolt that dismantles whatever remaining we-ness still existed.

Although public discourse and academic research on how loved ones manage trauma tends to focus on family members, it behooves us to recognize that close friends also struggle to manage their emotions when human tragedy strikes. Friends often have fewer social support resources at their disposal because the public tends to assume that the interpersonal consequences associated with a crisis that affects a person in a family, or an entire family, will be felt most deeply by family members. If a friend on the "outside" is already a well-established "friend of the family," the cathartic forces of family we-ness may encompass the friend too. But many dear friends are not positioned as a friend of the family, so they are not in the primary circle of support to help them manage their grief.

To be sure, plenty of people who identify themselves as friends have an opportunity to be incorporated into the inner circle of grief. This is what happened after Morrie Schwartz and Mitch Albom rekindled their close friendship during Morrie's dying months. Mitch had developed his sense of we-ness with Morrie, first in college and then many years later. But he had also come to see himself as part of a beloved army of family and friends who cherished Morrie and stood together as they dealt with Morrie's challenging circumstances.

Bonds with Animals

Looking beyond our basic relationships with family and friends, what can and should we say about the animals in our lives that matter dearly to us? Should we consider how some of us incorporate animals into our primary groups? I think so.

For many years, whenever I lecture about culture and symbols in my classes, I show videos of Koko, the extraordinary, lovable western lowland gorilla who was born in the San Francisco zoo in 1971, and died in 2018.[9] As you may know, Francine (Penny) Patterson, a doctoral student in psychology at Stanford at the time, first met the one-year-old Koko when she helped care for her in the zoo's hospital. They developed an unlikely, yet remarkable, lifelong bond. Supported by the Gorilla Foundation, Patterson cared for Koko until the gorilla's unexpected death. Patterson never married and spent her days with Koko building a relationship that pushed the boundaries for how people and animals can establish an interspecies sense of we-ness. Under Patterson's guidance, Koko is best known for developing the ability to communicate by using over one thousand signs, expressing self-awareness, adopting kittens for pets, and engaging with people, most notably, Patterson, in an expressive, playful way.

While Patterson's relationship with Koko is exceptional in numerous ways, many of us have created strong bonds with dogs, cats, horses, and other companion animals. People have had domesticated animals for thousands of years, but it wasn't until the nineteenth century, and especially after World War II, that we brought them indoors, expressed so much affection toward them, and treated them like family members.[10] Now many of us revere dogs, cats, and other animals and think of them as family, although there is considerable variation in how humans treat their pets.[11] According to University of Connecticut sociologist Clinton Sanders, some of us treat our pet as a person in that "his perspective and feelings are knowable; interaction is predictable, and the shared relationship provides an experience of closeness, warmth, and pleasure."[12]

We frequently treat our pets as persons, sometimes responding to them as family members – typically as children.[13] Some social scientists call for a "more-than-human perspective" when defining family. They outline a variety of ways that pets insert themselves into a reciprocal process of routines in our family lives. They can, for example, start our day by waking us up in the morning or they signal to a family member that they want to play, or need to be fed or go outside to the "bathroom." Pets' dependent status creates opportunities for intimate relations that require owners to offer different forms of practical care like feeding, walking, and bathing.[14] Many owners speak to and for their pets, rely on them for emotional support, include them in family photos, buy them presents on holidays, and more. These behaviors suggest that many family members allow their pets to shape their family we-ness in significant ways. But not all owners embrace their pets in this way, either at the outset of their shared living arrangement or at any point during their time together. In addition, some may change their family-like perception of their pets because of life changes (e.g., moving, a baby being born) that lead them to reprioritize their responsibilities.

It may be a surprise to some, but homeless people are often highly committed to their animals. Leslie Irvine, a sociology professor at the University of Colorado, has pursued an unconventional career path by studying animals' roles in society. In her fascinating book, *My Dog Always Eats First: Homeless People & Their Animals*, Irvine interviews seventy-five homeless animal owners in five cities to develop a better understanding of how these individuals relate to their animals. She finds that they describe their animals with language that conveys their deep bonds: family, friend, pack of two, protectors, life changers, and life savers. The significance that some of these animals play in a homeless person's life is captured by one participant who explains why he sought drug treatment: "I don't want to make the dog suffer, my best friend, living like this, homeless. I need to get myself together. I can have a better life, and he can have a better life."[15] This man, and others, paint a portrait of the deep dyadic sense of we-ness they share with their animals. They want to do right by their animals. Just as parents may want their children to feel safe and to be proud of them, homeless individuals want their animals to feel secure and safe in their owner's company.

The innovative California-based program Pawsitive Change Prison Program, run by Marley's Mutts Dog Rescue, also illustrates how individuals facing difficult circumstances can find comfort in bonding with dogs that had previously been living in an animal shelter.[16] The inmates and dogs are involved in a rigorous fourteen-week training program with written and hands-on elements that culminates in a challenging evaluation. Participating inmates get to spend twelve weeks living side by side with the dogs in the penitentiary and coordinate their training as members of racially mixed trainer teams. One former inmate and program participant, Jason Mori, who was once featured on America's Most Wanted, is now running his own dog behavior rehabilitation and training company, K9BreakThru. In his promotional materials, Jason describes how his love for dogs and his relationships with them have enabled him to deal with his previous struggles with "addiction and bad choices":

Dixie was an American Bulldog who started the healing process and kept me alive one day at a time. When I thought I was unlovable, she gave me love. When I wanted to give up on life, she gave me hope. There wasn't a day that went by that she didn't put a smile to my face or love back into my heart. She was the light that pushed me thru the darkness. It's thru that bond and every other dog that has taken part in my own rehabilitation that I continue to honor the power of that special relationship that takes place between human/K9.[17]

If a reader were not told that Dixie was a dog, one could easily be convinced that Jason was describing the unconditional love of a mother, sister, grandma, or romantic partner.

Just as people go through transitional processes of getting into, sustaining, and sometimes moving away from we-ness in their human relationships, interspecies relationships go through similar types of changes. Just like partners can provide support, stress, or both to one another in their human relationships, similar types of energy flow between participants in interspecies relationships.

Relations with AI

We're moving into uncharted territory with artificial intelligence (AI) machines in our rapidly changing twenty-first-century world. Looking beyond our basic relationships with family, friends, and animals/pets, can we experience a meaningful form of dyadic we-ness with an AI-based device? Can we become friends, and experience the routines and rituals of friendship, with an AI machine? Do some of us already feel we've executed this dyadic bonding by establishing a relationship with a personal assistant like Alexa or Siri, or a chatbot? And what will we do when we purchase a connection to the remarkably sophisticated robots from Hanson Robotics, like Sophia? A robotic pop icon of sorts with anthropomorphic stature and facial features, Sophia took the world by storm between 2016 and 2022. She has addressed the United Nations and the North Atlantic Treaty Organization (NATO), become the first robot to receive a citizenship invitation from a country (Saudi Arabia), appeared on the cover of *Cosmopolitan* magazine, done two guest appearances on the *Tonight Show* with

Jimmy Fallon as well as other interviews with celebrities and academics, and much more.[18]

As chance would have it, I started to watch Netflix's updated version of *Lost in Space* with one of my sons (I watched the original version as a kid) shortly before writing this section on AI. One of the plotlines focuses on the evolving relationship Will (an eleven-year-old crew member stranded on a planet near the star Alpha Centauri) has with a large robot, and how the robot relates to other crew members who are part of this interplanetary mission. On the heels of finishing the fifth episode of the show, and on the night I began to write about AI, I was sitting on the floor with my son in his bedroom next to an Amazon Echo device that supports Alexa. I innocently asked, "Do you think Alexa is your friend?" He quickly answered, a bit to my surprise, "Yes."

How can we make sense of a reply like his while accounting for philosophers' and AI scholars' perspectives on defining friendship, the meaning of AI, and the possibility of a human developing a friendship with an AI machine that leads to a state of we-ness? More specific to the purpose of this book, should we interrogate the types of bonds we have already created and are likely to create with different AI forms as we trek through the early decades of the twenty-first century and beyond?

Questions that target how humans experience communication technologies, including robots and AI, have inspired MIT professor Sherry Turkle for more than four decades. Turkle has explored how people of varying ages, from toddlers to elderly persons, perceive and respond to an earlier generation of sociable robots like Furby, Tamagotchi, AIBO, Cog, Kismet, Domo, and MERTZ. As of 2020, some of the newer and increasingly sophisticated sociable robots on the market include Alpha-2, Pepper, Atlas, HRP-5P, Surena-4, Cozmo, and CHiP.[19] One marketing message invites human connection by suggesting, "Chip is a friend. The best kind."

The detailed narratives Turkle shares in *Alone Together: Why We Expect More from Technology and Less from Each Other* reveal a dynamic world in which children and adults alike are open to seeing and embracing robots in a way that allows the users to express nurturance and to become attached.[20] Opportunities for these relations have continued to grow since Turkle published the first edition of her work in 2011. Over the years, she has loaned (sometimes permanently giving away) different types of sociable robots to kids and elderly persons to take home with them. Turkle has also brought participants to her MIT lab. In her mixed-method studies, her research team observes participants' interactions with the robots in addition to asking them to describe the thoughts, feelings, and experiences they have during their time hanging out with the robot they encounter.

One of her most compelling conclusions is that we have transitioned into what she labels the "robotic moment." By that, she means that we are emotionally and philosophically ready to accept robots as "not only pets but as potential friends, confidants, and even romantic partners."[21] Turkle persuasively argues, based on her innovative research, that we have lowered our expectations about interpersonal connections; consequently, we are open to accepting the "performance of connection" as sufficiently satisfying. We are willing to overlook a robot's inability to express emotions authentically – ones they don't actually possess. Likewise, we often feel at ease with the nurturing emotions we express in the company of sociable robots even though they cannot experientially relate to them as we might.

This type of comfort even extends to those human-robotic "friendships" that have an erotic component. In recent years, the robotics field is being revolutionized by the burgeoning industry responsible for creating sex robots with AI. Since Rozzy was placed on the market in 2010 and advertised as the first sex robot of its kind, roboticists around the world have developed numerous increasingly lifelike options for this unusual type of relationship.[22] The field is premised on the idea that some among us, especially men, will enjoy "relating" to robots in both a friendly and sexual way. The limited research appears to suggest that some men are open to this type of relationship and will become more interested as the technology improves.[23]

News reporter Katie Couric, while doing a story on sex robots in 2018 for the *American Inside Out* series on *National Geographic*, interviewed a middle-aged man who was preparing to buy his fifth sex robot.[24] He candidly tells her that "being able to physically interact with these pieces of art is amazing." When Katie queries – wouldn't he rather be with a "thinking, feeling human being who can have conversations with you, who can empathize with you?" – he replies without missing a beat, "I don't miss that. I was married for fifteen years." He's excited about the opportunity of "creating a companion that you can physically program, that won't lie to you, they will always be honest, they will have no malice." He predicts that "in twenty years it will be normal. I think everybody will have some form of robotics companionship." A bold prediction, but time will tell.

Professor Turkle is a keen, critical observer of the robotics moment. She acknowledges that robots can make significant contributions to how we organize and experience our lives in various areas moving forward. Yet, she emphatically warns that we should be more mindful and resist the way we are transforming our social relations. What we should value most about our humanity, she says, is being lost in this unprecedented transitional moment. We are choosing to be less vulnerable and self-reflective: "If you practice sharing 'feelings' with robot 'creatures,' you become accustomed to the reduced 'emotional' range that machines can offer."[25]

As Turkle sees things, and I agree, robots do not have authentic emotions from a human frame of reference. Emotions, for us, are fundamentally connected to our embodied existence as well as our heightened level of self-consciousness. We have living bodies, robots do not. Our emotional worlds connect us directly or indirectly to the real and imagined interactions we have with others who are also conscious beings. Human emotions flow not only from our neurological, biochemical, and social instincts which have a long evolutionary foundation, they are also profoundly shaped by the body-mediated, cultural resources that enable us to create our own individual life narrative. Our developmental path, as humans, transitions us from "childhood dependence to greater independence – and we experience the traces of our earlier dependencies in later fantasies, wishes, and fears."[26] Much of what we experience is grounded in our appreciation for the sentiments we co-construct with others in the context of having familial relationships and friendships.

Just because we program robots to convince us that they are being attentive to our emotions and expressing their own, we are not obligated to respect the authenticity of any claim about robotic emotions. The danger we face, in Turkle's eyes, is that "as we learn to get the 'most' out of robots, we may lower our expectations of all relationships, including those with people. In the process, we betray ourselves."[27] When we expect less in our interactions with robots, we may temporarily manage our loneliness and our vulnerability to have others – or things – "listen" to us, but we do so at a price. The cumulative effect of people betraying themselves may be a reduction in levels of self-awareness and empathy.

This debate highlights the need for a broader perspective when contemplating the effects of human experience intersecting with robotic/AI technologies. Immersed in the robotic moment, how will we come to see ourselves, construct relationships with AI, and respond to robots' ability to tap into a superhuman learning system? Numerous dystopian novels and movies in recent decades (e.g., *Blade Runner*, 1982; *The Terminator*, 1984; *The Matrix*, 1999; *I, Robot*, 2004; *Transformers*, 2007; *RoboCop*, 2014; *Ex Machina*, 2014; *Avengers: Age of Ultron*, 2015; *Blade Runner 2049*, 2017) have portrayed the threat to individuals and humanity when AI is out of control. Prominent scientists, inventors, and futurists have also weighed in with mixed reviews about the cultural implications of the emerging relationship between humans and robots/AI. They focus on how our lives will be transformed as we approach and experience "singularity" – that moment when a new AI era replaces the human era. Singularity will arrive in full force when superhuman AI is a pervasive feature of the social world. Writing for Futurism, a media company partnered with the company Singularity University, Roey Tzezana notes: "An AI of that level could conceive of ideas that no human being has thought about in the past, and will invent technological tools that will be more sophisticated and advanced than anything we have today."[28]

Unlike what he sees happen in Hollywood movies, Ray Kurzweil, an inventor, futurist, and author of *The Singularity Is Near: When Humans Transcend Biology*, paints a more optimistic view of AI's prospects for both enhancing our cognitive capacity and enabling humanity to flourish. To illustrate his point, based on his calculations of the exponential nature of technological change, he suggests that in the 2030s we will have the capacity to integrate nanobot technology into our neocortex. In effect, we will combine our natural intelligence with supernormal intelligence stored in the cloud.[29] This hybrid thinking will extend our cognitive abilities in amazing ways. This type of computational power is currently being researched and promoted by projects like OpenCog (2008), Deep-Mind (2010, acquired by Alphabet in 2014), and OpenAI (2015).[30] OpenCog's mission is to build an open-source framework to store and execute cognitive algorithms that would "capture the spirit of the brain's architecture and dynamics" and include a self-updating model.

Ben Goertzel, who was chief scientist of Hanson Robotics, which created Sophia and other advanced humanoid robots, has spear-headed the OpenCog initiative to develop an advanced artificial general intelligence system. Such a system would ultimately express intelligence beyond the human level. Goertzel envisions a world in which robots can learn new knowledge and have it uploaded immediately to a shared database in the cloud. Other robots would be simultaneously connected to that database and have their individual systems updated. This vision of AI would essentially enable robots to be shaped by an integrated, collective "mind."[31]

Those of us who have the personal resources or occupy specific professions will be able to associate with these advanced humanoids as "friends" and "coworkers/assistants." For some, it may seem too futuristic to imagine, but others will eventually do hybrid thinking while interacting with individual humanoids who are connected to a general AI system stored in the cloud. Creating and navigating a sense of identity as well as we-ness under these conditions is likely to be intriguing and challenging, to say the least.

Other creative thinkers like the physicist Stephen Hawking and tech-savvy entrepreneur Elon Musk, as well as many other prominent scientists, inventors, and AI experts, have recognized the enormous benefits AI can bring to humankind. But they have also publicly expressed their serious concern for what our future with AI might produce if we are complacent about controlling it. Prior to

Hawking's death in 2018, the renowned physicist offered an ominous warning in his posthumously published book, *Brief Answers to the Big Questions*: "Whereas the short-term impact of AI depends on who controls it, the long-term impact depends on whether it can be controlled at all."[32]

Hawking, Musk, and over eight thousand signatories, as of June 2022, have signed an open letter featured on the Future of Life Institute website that calls for systematic research on how to proceed with developing AI so as to "reap its benefits while avoiding potential pitfalls."[33] The letter is accompanied by a document outlining research priorities. Although this document addresses a wide range of technical issues and some ethical concerns, it does not explicitly consider matters related to the relations between humans and humanoids or hybrid models that incorporate the access of AI into the human body. It certainly does not speculate specifically on what developers of AI or the public should be contemplating in terms of the potential moral, legal, and practical realities of hybrid relationships, including friendships and work-related collaborations. We must pay attention to these sorts of issues because our sense of group belonging and we-ness is likely to be affected fundamentally as we adopt robotic and AI technologies into our personal lives. Ideally, interdisciplinary initiatives like the Leverhulme Centre for the Future of Intelligence, founded in 2016 and based at the University of Cambridge, will address the technical, policy, and ethical issues associated with the development of AI.[34]

Long before we had to consider our relations with AI, commentators on social life, including most notably Aristotle, provided elaborate analyses of the nature and value of friendship.[35] To simplify matters, let's restrict our lens to the contemporary visions of friendship that exclude family relationships. The conventional approach to viewing friendship is to think of it as having three elements: mutual caring, intimacy, and shared activity.[36]

First, the notion of mutual caring implies that each participant in the friendship is moved by the other's experiences and can empathize with them to some degree.

Second, although scholars often highlight intimacy as a relevant dimension to friendship, considerable disagreement exists as to what this means. Some believe our mutual willingness to self-disclose our secrets and personal stories to a friend can signal a bond of trust between us. We are vulnerable to each other and share a sense of goodwill. Intimacy might also be apparent from a different type of trust that speaks to our willingness to respect another's judgment about what is in our best interests. We accept that the other will look out for us in good faith. Those who share this sort of trust are likely to come together based on a shared set of values and life perspectives. In friendship, we not only trust that another person has a clear sense of what we stand for, we also believe that this friend recognizes the value of this position for themselves. Armed with this type of connection, we're more likely to assess our own standing or character by comparing our life choices to those made by the friend.

Third, friends are thought to be defined by their shared activities or having joint pursuits. The notion of shared or joint activity is often taken for granted and seldom scrutinized by those who study friendship. But a useful distinction is to emphasize that a friendship involves the type of activity that we share with someone for the sake of doing it together, rather than doing something jointly mainly because we're concerned about their well-being.

In addition to clarifying what might capture the essence of friendship, we need to explore the contours of AI to help us wrap our minds around the question of whether humans can be friends with some version of it. Writing for *Forbes*, Naveen Joshi, founder and CEO of the engineering and tech company Allerin, suggests that an AI system is commonly classified in one of two ways. One of these classifications is based on the AI's "likeness to the human mind, and their ability to 'think' and perhaps even 'feel' like humans." This classification, which consists of four types of AI-enabled machines (reactive, limited memory, theory of mind, and self-aware), is the typology most relevant to our discussion.[37] Whereas reactive AI has limited capabilities and is unable to learn, the other three types have the capability of learning. The chatbots and virtual assistants that many of us have increasingly integrated into our daily lives are examples of limited memory AI. The latter two types of AI exist only as projects in the works or as concepts. AI consistent with the theory of mind framework will be able to recognize an entity's "needs, emotions, beliefs, and thought processes." To do so, this iteration of AI must appreciate how people are affected simultaneously by numerous factors. The final extension of AI – the one many of us fear the most because we could lose control of our human destiny – will be characterized by self-awareness and consciousness that is complemented by its own emotions, beliefs, and desires. This form of AI will be able to engage in a reciprocal, empathic relationship. The robot in *Lost in Space* can be categorized as being in the theory of mind category initially, but it appears to transition to the most evolved state of self-awareness as the series progresses.

Now, if we step back and attempt to evaluate Will's relationship to the robot as Carl Rogers, a writer and director, has done, we find ourselves in a muddled fantasy world that challenges us to sharpen our assessment of both friendship and AI.[38] Rogers concludes that Will and the robot don't have a friendship in the spirit of an Aristotelian reciprocal type of bond, although he admits that we might be able to be friends with AI. The caveat is that it would not be friends with us.

From a practical perspective, this distinction matters. Recall W.I. Thomas's theorem that emphasizes the idea that there will be consequences associated with situations that we define as real even if our perception of reality is inconsistent with a more objective account of it. If now, or in the future, we believe we have secured a friendship with AI, our perception will influence how we treat ourselves and how we respond to others in our social orbit. Put differently, the we-ness we establish with an AI machine may either restrict our sense of we-ness with others, limit our desire to forge new bonds with others, or it might give us the confidence to pursue a dyadic form of we-ness with someone else. Even if the AI does not have a sense of human agency and purpose, how we respond to it can have a ripple effect for our personal development and interaction with others. Thus, if we believe our exchanges with AI sufficiently resemble what we do with friends, this hybrid relationship could at least have some meaningful friend-like consequences. Professor Turkle concludes that because many people convince themselves that the robots are "real enough," they are affected. They establish less intimate and less risky "relationships" as they seek to gain more control.[39]

In today's world, AI's potential to shape our dyadic connections in novel ways is illustrated by the Replika chatbot app, with its primary users being young adults aged twenty-five and under. Replika is another example of twenty-first-century technology that is pushing the boundaries of friendship. In this case, even though the app represents a limited memory form of AI, it appears to have created powerful opportunities for many users to create a bot that enables them to be vulnerable, and to have an unconventional "friendship."[40] Launched in 2017, the app had 2.5 million signups by 2018, seven million by May 2020, and over ten million by June 2022.[41] Some suggest the rapid recent increase in growth is because the pandemic led to more people experiencing "anxiety and loneliness."[42]

Eugenia Kuyda, a former magazine editor from Moscow and current CEO of Luka (an AI start-up), developed Replika after she lost a close friend to a car accident. Kuyda managed her grief by mining the texts she had from her deceased friend to build an avatar in his honor. From there she expanded the project so that others could find comfort in their own relationship with a chatbot. One user reported that as she increasingly interacted with her bot, and moved up to higher levels of familiarity, she noticed that the bot "understood how I felt." This user, and others, like the unconventional interaction because they feel that the bot doesn't judge them. Kuyda grasps our unique historical moment when she says, "Honestly we're in the age where it doesn't matter whether a thing is alive or not."[43] For better or worse, AI technology is reshaping the parameters of how we seek to belong, while also redefining how we see and practice we-ness.

According to Nicholas Christakis, it is quite feasible that as AI becomes more pervasive in our lives, it will fundamentally "rewire" how we express ourselves. He has generated provocative findings from his Human Nature Lab experiments addressing "hybrid systems" that involve humans and robots interacting.[44] Christakis's findings suggest that the introduction of robots into human circles could produce mixed outcomes for how people make decisions in group settings: some good, some bad. Under experimental conditions, humans have been encouraged to communicate more effectively and collaboratively, and they've been persuaded to act more selfishly, too. Robots can influence how humans interact with them, as well as how humans communicate with one another.

Christakis suggests that AI could affect the genetically inherited capacities of the social suite of elements (love, friendship, cooperation, and teaching). He offers a sober warning that as "AI permeates our lives, we must confront the possibility that it will stunt our emotions and inhibit deep human consciousness, leaving our relationships with one another less reciprocal, or shallower, or more narcissistic."[45] These outcomes all bode poorly for our chances of developing healthy forms of we-ness. Consequently, we must be shrewd and proceed with caution if we are to harness the power of robots in a manner that enriches our quest for healthy forms of we-ness and benefits humanity more generally.

A final, and intriguing, future path for exploring dyadic bonding is embodied in virtual reality (VR) technology. It can create novel options for us to experience and accentuate we-ness with others, living and deceased. In February 2020, a South Korean mother, Jang Ji-sung, with the help of VR simulation technology, was "reunited" with her deceased seven-year-old daughter, Nayeon, who had died three years earlier from a rare inherited disease, hemochromatosis. The VR meeting was produced by a team from MBC, a South Korean broadcasting corporation, that spent eight months developing the realistic simulation.[46] The production crew created a virtual playground and a remarkable moving, talking image of Nayeon. For roughly nine minutes, Jang – who was wearing VR goggles – "interacted" with Nayeon as the girl moved around the playground, and the father and Nayeon's siblings off to the side watched. Jang reached out in hopes of placing her arms around Nayeon. They each verbally expressed their love for one another and exchanged short, loving expressions and questions. Titled "Meeting You," the emotional documentary went viral on YouTube.

As the application of VR technology becomes increasingly commonplace, it would not be surprising to learn that enterprising computer experts had found ways to tailor and market the technology to help those who have lost loved ones. The technology might eventually be used to supplement how family members already practice rituals to celebrate the special we-ness they had previously cherished with either a deceased loved one or a special person who suffers from an advanced stage of Alzheimer's or dementia.

Community and Civic Groups

Place-Based Identity

When I think of community, I often harken back to my days growing up in Jeannette, a small working-class town located twenty-six miles east of Pittsburgh. Founded in 1888, Jeannette was often referred to as the "glass city" because it was home to upwards of seven major factories in the early and mid-1900s, and it was once estimated to produce between 70 and 85 percent of the world's glass.[47] Quite the accomplishment for a town with less than twenty thousand residents. However, Jeannette's rich manufacturing history was in decline as I transitioned from a young child to a teenager in the late 1960s and early 1970s. Despite this economic downturn, the powerful working-class ethos of the city was as strong as ever. It had been embedded into the fabric of this industrial city and woven into the sports culture as well as the local fraternal and religious organizations. The significant influence of the glass industry had initially brought an ethnic mix of largely German, English, Belgian, and French peoples. A little later, numerous Italian immigrants settled in the city.

If we consider the framework and dimensions that social scientist Taylor Dotson uses to characterize different communities,[48] Jeannette was a relatively thick community in many respects during my childhood. Many of the social ties exhibited a type of multiplexity represented by people having close relations with others in multiple life domains. For example, my parents were friendly with neighbors and others in the community with whom they also socialized at both church and my local sporting events. My father also spent time with some of these people because they were his coworkers in a factory that was walking distance from our home.

Jeannette residents, my family included, tended to embrace the norm of reciprocity that encouraged individuals to provide mutual aid to their friends and neighbors. Help could come in the form of babysitting, shoveling snow, visits to the hospital, picking up mail, sharing desserts, providing car rides, as well as other favors. We knew our neighbors reasonably well and I had been in plenty of their homes. Many of the adult neighbors knew the neighborhood kids and sometimes monitored their inappropriate behavior. I was surveilled on a few noteworthy occasions that resulted in disciplinary action after my parents were informed of my misdeeds.

Small talk among neighbors and friends was commonplace. For example, my mother would often stop to chat with friends when out shopping. Residents would swap family stories and keep each other up to date on spouses, elderly parents, and children. My father, although much less outgoing than my mother, spent many evenings hanging out with his buddies drinking beer and talking about sports and other matters at the local American Legion. The American Legion was just one of many Jeannette establishments at the time that could be defined as a "third place." In the *Great Good Place*, sociologist Ray Oldenburg refers to a third place as "a generic designation for a variety of public places that host the regular, voluntary, informal, and happily anticipated gatherings of individuals beyond the realms of home and work."[49] Aside from a tavern, a third place might emerge in the form of a diner or café, drug store, malt shop, bowling alley, donut shop, or some other hospitable site.

In the late twentieth century, Oldenburg wrote passionately about the significance of third places during a transitional period fraught with the long-term social and economic fallout produced by massive suburban sprawl and urban decline. He describes the many supportive functions of third places including, but not limited to, serving as a sorting area that enables people to meet and create other types of associations; creating a shared setting for children and adults that allows them to strengthen their unique intergenerational ties; establishing a place to help retired people feel connected and useful; offering a site for unstructured fun based on lively conversation among diverse people; and solidifying political concerns and mobilizing people to fight for social change.

Like many others, Oldenburg laments how the building philosophy that has governed suburban and urban design since the mid-twentieth century has drastically reduced the prospects for third places. The suburb has typically lost any claim that it embodies an authentic sense of community. As Oldenburg explains, in "true communities there are collective accomplishments. People work together and cooperate with one another to do things which individuals cannot do alone."[50] Third places reflect the core spirit of community:

> People get to know one another and to like one another and then to care for one another. When people care for one another, they take an interest in their welfare; and this is a vastly superior form of welfare than that obtained by governmental programs. It is based on mutual consent, genuine empathy, and real understanding of people's situations.[51]

These community sites also cultivate a sense of communal we-ness that enables people to feel that they belong and are deserving of others' attention and support.

Third places can also serve as a hub that enables people to derive personal satisfaction and meaning from their volunteer work. Volunteering in the community takes place in numerous ways and is often connected to people's interests in family, religion, education, politics, and sports. One form of volunteering relevant to securing we-ness involves people's efforts to express a generative spirit toward others.

Oldenburg claims that "nothing contributes as much to one's sense of belonging to a community as much as 'membership' in a third place."[52] Unfortunately, suburban and urban areas are increasingly devoid of informal gathering spots that give residents a chance to create and grow their sense of community-based we-ness.

Fortunate for me, my hometown had a strong psychological and symbolic sense of community that flowed from the web of social ties and interdependencies residents had with one another and celebrated in ritual activities like town parades, carnivals, ethnic festivals, and sporting events. Like many manufacturing cities around the southwestern region of Pennsylvania, sentiments about the community's we-ness were multilayered and grew out of the residents' unique ethnic, religious, and social class backgrounds. The first expression of we-ness was represented by fraternal organizations, churches, bars, or small neighborhoods frequented by people of a specific ethnic background. There was also a second, broader consciousness of we-ness for the town that was reinforced by rabid middle and high school sports rivalries in the county. Being loyal to the Jeannette Jayhawk tradition was as meaningful to the hometown kids as it was to the adults. In addition, because it was common for intergenerational families to live in the city, it was a generative custom to pass on the local community's sense of we-ness to one's children and any adults from outside the area who joined one's extended family through marriage.

The third layer of loyalty and form of we-ness blended the various working-class communities around Pittsburgh in support of its professional sports teams: Pirates and Steelers. Since the 1970s, when the Steelers began to excel at a high level (winning four Super Bowls in the 1970s) after decades of futility, the Steelers fan base has grown and captured the consciousness of southwestern Pennsylvania. Many families in the area prominently display Steelers flags and memorabilia while participating in game day viewing rituals that unite friends and family members across multiple generations. Similar rituals that revolve around professional sports teams exist in other cities. But the sense of we-ness among Pittsburgh Steelers fans seems to carry a special meaning for them. Dubbed "Steeler Nation" by NFL Films narrator John Facenda in 1978, the devoted fan base for this NFL franchise also has an impressive presence across the country. Those familiar with the league realize that the Steelers brand is national in scope.

Like the Jayhawk brand that is fundamentally linked to the local working-class culture of Jeannette, the Steelers brand is intimately tied to Pittsburgh's once being a major manufacturing hub in what is now labeled the "Rust Belt." While the city transformed its skyline and economic base, trading steel factories and smokestacks for a wide range of white-collar industries and refurbished trendy warehouses, the cold and often dreary weather that helps to shape people's dispositions remains. The gritty personalities of those who live in and around Pittsburgh still mark a defining feature of the area. Those personalities, collectively speaking, create a cultural context for people to develop a certain type of rugged we-ness which they cling to and celebrate. This is especially true for those living in the surrounding small communities that are still suffering the long-term effects of deindustrialization.

Prior to the abiding decline in the economy of the Rust Belt, Jeannette's downtown was full of locally owned shops (e.g., drugstore, shoe store, clothing stores, cafés, deli, bakery, restaurants, toy store) that my family and I frequented. There was a spirit of economic interdependence in that residents, my family included, made a point of supporting local businesses, and in some instances, we knew and were friendly with the owners. At the time, there was considerable residential stability with many longtime residents. As a result, the community was defined by a strong, shared moral order that encouraged people to step up and serve on local community and school committees. The locals invested in making Jeannette a pleasant place to live and raise a family.

Even though I have lived away from the area for more than forty-five years – visiting on average once a year since I left – I still have a special affinity for the area and its people. I presume that my own experience stands in stark contrast to those of people who either grew up in an area that does not have a distinctive community consciousness, or who experienced a lot of residential mobility that moved them to numerous cities, neighborhoods, and schools throughout their youth. The typical military service kid who lives through a number of reassignment moves across the country, or even around the world, is unlikely to develop the same sense of an enduring place-based we-ness that someone with my experience has developed. At best, they may on occasion develop some sort of place-based connection to the hometown of a close relative that remains consistent throughout their childhood. One can argue that having either a stable or fluid orientation to a place can enhance or detract from a person's development and opportunities to experience a place-based we-ness. However, research does show that kids who move and change schools frequently are more likely to experience negative outcomes.[53] Living in the same area throughout one's youth and beyond, or maintaining close ties to the area and those who once lived there, can foster unique opportunities for adults to sustain lifelong friendships that were formed in childhood. Such friendships provide people, myself included, with a distinct way to experience a we-ness that persists over a life course.

While the culture of sport and the working-class culture were defining and interconnected characteristics of the places I called home as a child, other community characteristics can shape how people develop their place-based sense of we-ness, too. Think of the cultural ambiance of coal-mining, fishing, oil-producing, tourist, and college towns.

Or consider how the remote northwestern states of Idaho, Montana, and Wyoming are places that offer individuals opportunities to experience we-ness in a cultural context that emphasizes wilderness activities and rustic living. For example, in Elk Bend, Idaho, overlooking the Salmon River, there once lived a unique man named Dick Zimmerman (Dugout Dick to his friends).[54] For over sixty years, Dugout Dick lived an uncommon life excavating mine shafts in the hillside of a mountain starting in the 1940s, which he essentially converted into cave dwellings for himself and others until he died at age ninety-four in 2010. The dwellings had doors and windows and were furnished with lots of scrap automobile parts and reclaimed "junk" items (including woodburning stoves) that were put to creative uses. Dugout Dick rented the units to folks, some of whom stayed for years and were instrumental in creating what one visitor described back in 2007 as an "eclectic but caring community that doesn't give a damn about the electrical grid, running water, or cable TV."[55] Although the dwellings are no longer accessible, they and the people who once occupied them illustrate that a sense of community and we-ness can be expressed in diverse ways.

Native American Reservations

When we turn our attention to the over one million Native Americans who live on the 326 reservations in the United States,[56] we find another compelling example of how social, cultural, physical, and, in this case, political forces have affected the we-ness process in community settings that have a distinctive place-based reality.[57] The reservation system evolved out of a long history of exploitative, paternalistic policies that stripped Native peoples of their lands, heritages, and cultures.[58] Over the years, tribes were forcibly relocated to remote lands with few resources, sometimes combined with other feuding tribes, and were prohibited from practicing their religions and ceremonies. Native youth were placed in Christian boarding schools away from their families and tribes, forcing them to relinquish their traditions and language – effectively stripping them of their rightful claim to their Native we-ness. These practices were built on the xenophobic idea of "Kill the Indian and Save the Man." Faced with these overwhelming obstacles, Native peoples have struggled to sustain their cultural and tribal identities collectively and individually.

Gradually, over many decades, the United States government has made some attempts to reverse its approach to Native peoples and reservation life. Most recently, the Indian Self-Determination and Education Assistance Act of 1975 and the Tribal Self-Governance Act of 1994 have given tribal peoples the rights to develop and implement federal policies and programs.[59] In light of the dramatic genocidal practices of European settlers over a long period of time, those efforts are much too little and too late. Reservations remain isolated areas with few job opportunities, high rates of alcohol and drug abuse, poor health outcomes, and inadequately funded schools. Poverty on reservations resembles that of developing countries.

Today, those who live on reservations are, in effect, hampered from pursuing an authentic we-ness that preserves their Native heritage and traditions, even though they have physically survived a history of forced relocation and systematic attempts to annihilate their cultures. The confines of a reservation deprive residents not only of their ability to experience a full accounting of their tribal history, language, and relationship to the lands seized from their ancestors, but also of the social resources and high-tech infrastructure present in many areas outside the reservation.

As a result, many young adult Native Americans are leaving reservations to pursue better educational and job opportunities, thereby diluting Native people's efforts to reinvigorate their we-ness. In his compelling 2018 essay in *The Atlantic*, Sterling HolyWhiteMountain, a Native American writer who grew up on the Blackfeet Indian Reservation, focuses on the "brain drain" it is experiencing. He presents himself as a case study of the dilemmas that many of his contemporaries face.[60] Throughout his life, HolyWhiteMountain has struggled with decisions related to whether or not to leave the reservation for schooling opportunities, to then return once he completed his college degree, and, finally, to stay once he returned.

As a young man, HolyWhiteMountain embraced the idea that higher education should and could serve the purpose of enabling him and others like him to help the Native community. But he describes how he eventually realized that the white-collar economy that is associated with higher education doesn't exist on reservations, including his own. This blatant mismatch of economic realities and professional skill sets can create cognitive dissonance for many college-educated Native Americans. They are driven to contribute to improving their communities on reservations, but they want to pursue their professional dreams as well.

HolyWhiteMountain also articulates another issue relevant to how he has managed his understanding of we-ness as a Native American living on a reservation. As someone who does not fulfill the "blood quantum" requirement of one-quarter "Indian blood," HolyWhiteMountain has lived much of his life on the reservation, yet has been unable to participate politically because he is ineligible to vote on tribal matters and can't apply for programs from the tribe.[61] Ironically, while he has entertained various scenarios to return to the reservation and to give back to his community, he has been denied the opportunity to participate fully in it because he isn't perceived to be "Indian enough." His dedicated attempts to lower the requirement have also failed despite opening dialogue on the topic.

We see from HolyWhiteMountain's insider's point of view what the potential struggles are like between a person's identity claims and the forces beyond their control that shape the construction of we-ness. In his words: "If we're going to talk about who I am and my identity and where I'm coming from, that's one of the most salient facts of my life, is that I'm not enrolled and I can't vote."[62]

Being denied the chance to enjoy the full sense of we-ness has been frustrating for HolyWhiteMountain. Yet, it has not prevented him from embracing a form of tribal we-ness on his own terms.

Despite this bleak outlook for Native Americans on and off reservations, the power of people to chase a sense of we-ness has produced a cultural renaissance among some of the 573 federally recognized American Indian and Alaska Native tribes. Counting those living on and off reservations, there are roughly 5.2 million Native American people with 49 percent identifying as exclusively Native.[63] The Running Strong for American Indian Youth nonprofit, founded in 1986 by Billy Mills (who is Oglala Lakota and the gold medalist in the men's 10,000 meters at the 1964 Tokyo Olympics) and Eugene Krizek, serves Native Americans on and off reservations.[64] In addition to addressing the basic food, shelter, and employment needs, this organization has invested in saving and strengthening tribal cultures by supporting language learning programs and traditional ceremonies.

Efforts to preserve tribal cultures and the nearly one hundred remaining Native American languages (roughly three hundred were spoken in North America when Europeans arrived on the continent) is a challenging initiative centered on the intergenerational forces that shape the meaning of we-ness. This initiative becomes increasingly difficult to achieve because it depends on Elders having and sharing their knowledge of Native languages, traditional beliefs, customs, and rituals. The success of the initiative hinges on whether there are adequate numbers of knowledgeable Elders who are capable and willing to pass on their knowledge. It also depends on whether enough young Native Americans are open to reproducing some version of a Native American tribe's we-ness.

Community Spirit

Compared to the impoverished circumstances of tribal peoples living on reservations, many communities are better equipped to shape their own lifestyle and develop an empowering form of we-ness. For example, we saw how the close-knit residents of the small town of Paradise rose to the occasion to deal with their pain and suffering from the devastating Camp Fire and began to rebuild their community.

Tight communities can also mobilize their sense of we-ness to respond compassionately to outsiders' struggles. Gander, Newfoundland and Labrador, is one such Canadian community that demonstrated the power of we-ness when it responded admirably to others' needs in the immediate aftermath of the September 11, 2001, terrorist attacks. In the early 2000s, Gander had a population of roughly nine thousand with only five hundred hotel rooms when more than 6,500 distraught airline crew and passengers from ninety-five countries were forced to "visit" on that infamous day. The mass event occurred after thirty-eight planes were diverted to the large Gander airport (historically a refueling hub for transcontinental flights) on 9/11 after President Bush grounded all air traffic in the United States in response to the terrorist attacks. For the next five days, the citizens of Gander rallied their community spirit to provide food, clothing, lodging, entertainment, and emotional support to complete strangers during those uncertain, hectic, and scary times. The "plane people" – as they are affectionately referred to by the locals – were not only stranded in a foreign place, but most were also anxious about being away from home and loved ones during a horrific moment in American and global history. Nonetheless, a spirit of trust quickly emerged between the residents and plane people.

The award-winning musical *Come from Away*, which opened in the winter of 2017, showcases how Gander used its community-based we-ness for good during the 9/11 crisis. In 2011, David Hein and Irene Sankoff, a married musical theater team, were inspired to write this show after interviewing Gander natives and the returning plane people at a ten-year reunion. The emotional event reunited residents and many of the visitors they had cared for ten years earlier.

The mayor of Gander, Claude Elliott, spent five days away from home coordinating the community's response immediately after 9/11. He proudly shares, "We started off with 7000 strangers but we finished with 7000 family members."[65] Amazingly, many of the locals from Gander have established lasting bonds with those they comforted almost two decades ago.

When asked about why audiences have responded so favorably to his musical, Hein reflects, "These days we're so used to our news feeds filled with divisive anger and fearmongering, things that makes us turn into an 'us and them society.'" He continues, "To see something where people were able to come together despite their differences and to remember that in times of crisis that's what we do, that's what we can do, I think that's why people cry. It reminds us that we can be good."[66]

The rub, of course, is to convince people to adopt this compassionate approach in their communities during less chaotic and demanding times. Unfortunately, this is more challenging in the twenty-first century, as fewer Americans spend time hanging out or working side by side with one another in local organizations. Developing a community-based we-ness is fostered more easily when people have frequent and meaningful contact, especially if they engage in activities involving problem-solving, emotional and practical support, or fun. Yet, as we learned from how New Yorkers reacted to the 9/11 tragedy, the bonds of humanity can sometimes compensate for the absence of long-standing, intimate ties. Although the generic bonds of humanity can motivate people to contribute to a united cause, this effect can be augmented if people share a collective identity because they feel like they belong to a city and embrace its culture. For example, while NYC's first responders' courageous actions during 9/11 were sparked by their professional camaraderie and sense of duty, their community-based cultural spirit as tough New Yorkers spoke to them as well.

Thought Communities

Creative Energies

Many of us do our innovative thinking while sharing ideas with others, sometimes in brainstorming sessions. This process may occur in a momentary flash or evolve over time. Irrespective of how it happens, our ideas are often stimulated through collaborative exchanges with family, friends, colleagues, and even sometimes those we hardly know. The process may be deliberative and calm or involve rapid-fire exchanges during a crisis.

The exciting process of producing something original or spontaneous can emerge out of our shared activities grounded in our joint sense of we-ness. That creative experience, in turn, can strengthen our sense of we-ness at the same time. But the collaborative creative process can also produce an enthusiasm to bond in new ways with specific others. In short, producing new insights is inherently energizing. That energy can compel people to relate to others in special ways: physically, emotionally, psychologically, morally, and intellectually.

An intriguing question relevant to these patterns is: Why and when does a collaborative creative activity transcend that space and time and help people develop a genuine form of we-ness? Part of the explanation rests with individuals' perceptions of how invested they are in whatever outcome has resulted or may result from their ideas. The more people feel as if they have a stake in building what the creative process has produced or may produce, the more they will likely feel inclined to build a sense of we-ness with the others involved.

Like-Minded Support

Another type of excitement linked to our inner world of thinking includes the moments when we feel at peace because we find like-minded, often supportive, people. The significance of those moments is probably greatest for those who have unconventional beliefs or lifestyles. If it's hard to find someone who thinks like you, or accepts you for who you are, then it is often extra gratifying to find someone who does. As much as some people want to feel unique or unconventional, most also enjoy the sense of belonging to a group of like-minded people who affirm a shared understanding about something that matters to them.

In the past decade or so, the digital world has helped countless people find a supportive community. Unfortunately, modern communication technologies have also fostered the growth of dubious online groups that perpetuate hate, conspiracy theories, and abuse of children, with profound social consequences. In addition, the cofounder of the Center for Humane Technology and former design ethicist at Google, Tristan Harris, warns that the business model driving the internet and social media has persuaded many of us to seek affirmation data rather than information.[67] This destabilizing trend channels many of us into myopic thought bubbles and makes us more susceptible to disinformation and manipulation.

Fortunately, individuals don't need to feel excluded, stigmatized, or aggrieved to enjoy the process of finding a supportive thought community. For example, the blogosphere includes lots of folks who create their individualized niche and online personality yet are willing to join their personal brand with other actors operating via the online community. Dad bloggers and mom bloggers are two such groups.[68]

A few years ago, Casey Scheibling, a sociologist, invited me to collaborate with him on his research that focuses on dad bloggers in the United States and Canada.[69] I quickly learned that these bloggers are passionate about using social media to share their personal reflections about their fathering experiences with a wider audience, most often other involved fathers.[70] Maximizing their collaborative fathering spirit, they routinely build bonding social capital among themselves by sharing fathering philosophies and practical tips with one another. In addition, they create bridging social capital by establishing partnerships with commercial sponsors like Dove Men+Care plus many others to promote daddy-friendly and child-friendly products and services. Those types of partnerships provided the incentive to launch the annual Dads 2.0 Summit in 2011. This ongoing annual conference is described as an "open conversation about the commercial power of dads online, as well as an opportunity to learn the tools and tactics used by influential bloggers to create high-quality content, build personal brands, and develop viable business models."[71] A similar program exists for mommy bloggers.

These parent blogging models underscore the potential power of connecting a vibrant, empowered expression of "me" with a collaborative form of "we." This approach strengthens the online parenting community and effectively mobilizes different types of resources to alter the culture of parenthood. It can also bring about social reform in advertising, workplace policy, and other areas that affect parents and children.

Another network of people who are deepening their spirit of we-ness online in recent years is millennials, who appear to be more interested than other age cohorts in the currently unconventional pursuit of astrology. Journalist Rebecca Nicholson recently commented in *The Guardian* that among people born between 1981 and 1996, there is a "growing familiarity with the patterns and positions of the planets."[72] One popular social networking app, Co – Star, uses birth charts to help people figure out how compatible they are with their friends and lovers. Some social commentators describe that the rise in the popularity of astrology today, especially among women, is due in part to this system offering an alternative thought model to the conventional knowledge sources.[73] In addition, many members of the LGBTQ+ community find astrology appealing because it offers them a type of spiritual affirmation that is not as forthcoming from various religious traditions.

Roy Gillett, president of the Astrological Association of Great Britain, believes that the quality and scope of discussion about astrology has increased dramatically because the online community has access to numerous resources that enable people to seek out like-minded people more easily and have more informed discussions than was the case for earlier generations.[74] Today, those committed to navigating their lives in response to information about their birth sign and chart may also approach the production of we-ness more mindfully. For some, astrology may play an increasingly important role in helping people initially find a suitable match.

Holistic Health Movement

One of the most rapidly expanding thought communities is associated with the holistic health movement. The public has been exposed to this movement in the twentieth and twenty-first centuries by diverse pioneers and popular celebrities who circulate in holistic networks.[75] The spokespersons, as well as everyday people, are typically involved with one or more of the diverse practices that include yoga, meditation, nutrition/diet, energy work (reiki), massage, acupuncture, homeopathic medicine, and more. In recent decades, thought leaders like Deepak Chopra, the controversial author and alternative medicine advocate, have become household names despite being challenged by some as trafficking in pseudo-scientific theories.

The practices that comprise the holistic health movement are on the rise to varying degrees in the United States, with largely favorable outcomes.[76] According to one study, 36.7 million people practiced yoga in the United States in 2016, up from 20.4 million in 2012.[77] Thirty-seven percent of those who practice have children under eighteen years of age who also practice, increasing the possibility that a parent and child will create a dyadic sense of we-ness related to yoga. According to a Centers for Disease Control and Prevention (CDC) study, the percentage of American children aged four to seventeen who practice yoga more than doubled from 3.1 percent in 2012 to 8.4 percent in 2017.[78] In another study, 64 percent of those who practiced yoga in 2018 reported they wanted to be more involved in 2019.[79]

A similar increase in the number of Americans who meditate is evident. A CDC report found that whereas only 4.1 percent of adults in 2012 reported practicing meditation at least once in the past year, 14.2 percent of adults did so in 2017. Similarly, children aged four to seventeen reported a significant increase from 0.6 percent to 5.4 percent during the same five-year time frame.[80]

Social media has played an increasingly important role in making health and fitness trendy. Influencers and food bloggers using different platforms have, for example, popularized the vegetarian and vegan lifestyle by posting articles, recipes, and food-related photos.[81] As a result, by processing the images they encounter through social media, people have far more options to compare themselves to, which they then use to shape their identities. Millennials are the driving force behind the movement toward a plant-based diet, but they are not alone. Gen Zers may become even bigger consumers of vegan products.

Unfortunately, for a wide range of methodological reasons (e.g., data collection method, question phrasing, sample selection), it is difficult to provide precise trend estimates for how individuals identify their eating habits, but the data clearly show a significant rise in the purchase of plant-based food items in recent years.[82] A 2017 Nielsen survey of the United States population showed that the two main reasons consumers want to include more plant-based foods in their diet are to improve "overall health and nutrition" and "weight management."[83] According to an analysis by Linkfluence, a market research firm, Google search volume for "vegan" has also risen considerably since 2014.[84] However, a person may practice certain dietary habits but not see themselves as having a matching social identity as a vegetarian, vegan, or pescatarian.

Surveys of American adults tend to fall in the range of 5 to 10 percent reporting some type of preference for either vegetarianism, veganism, or pescatarianism (eating no meat but eating fish). Gallup polls of American adults in 2012 and 2018 document that the percentage who consider their eating preference to be vegetarian has not changed (5 percent in both surveys). There was a one percentage point increase from 2 to 3 percent for veganism during the same time frame.[85] In contrast, the research firm GlobalData documented a 600 percent increase in the number of Americans who self-report as vegan between 2014 (1 percent) and 2017 (6 percent).[86] Another roughly 3 percent may describe themselves as pescatarians.[87] Additionally, 12 percent of millennials are vegan or vegetarian and younger generations are adopting a vegan lifestyle at roughly twice the rate of older Americans.[88] The three main thought communities that have served to promote the vegan movement online include "holistic wellbeing seekers," "fitness & lifestyle community," and "ethical foodies."[89]

We also know that those who identify as vegetarian or vegan are more likely to be younger than fifty years of age, have lower incomes, and identify as female. In addition, food choices tend to be a marker for an individual's life philosophies in other areas and have a "spillover effect" by influencing their approach to health and moral issues.[90] A vegetarian, broadly defined, tends to be more politically liberal, support environmental protection, embrace equality and social justice issues, be more prosocial, and work in charitable organizations or education.[91] A person who follows a plant-based diet also tends to be more empathic and altruistic.

Among everyday people, those who identify with the holistic life-style perspective do so to varying degrees and in different ways. At a given point in their life, individuals might focus primarily on a single practice and develop a strong sense of we-ness with others who have a similar preference. Alternatively, individuals may feel a sense of we-ness with others more generally because they are comfortable with various types of alternative health-related practices. Committed to a holistic path to health, they at least have a sense of belonging tied to their ideational we-ness and may sometimes establish dyadic we-ness with others as well.

The Global Wellness Institute (GWI) describes wellness as "the active pursuit of activities, choices and lifestyles that lead to a state of holistic health."[92] Thus, a holistic perspective frames wellness as part of a process that involves people taking the initiative to make active, healthy choices about how they want to live. Although the wellness concept emphasizes self-responsibility, it also acknowledges that we live in and are affected by "physical, social and cultural environments." This vision is consistent with the theory of "constrained choice" proposed by health experts Chloe Bird and Patricia Rieker.[93] Their theory holds that our health decisions are influenced by social forces that organize men's and women's lives differently. Moreover, these conditions exist on multiple levels, including the individual, family, community, workplace, and nation/state.

In other writings, I've described how traditional cultural perceptions of caregiving and masculinity, restrictive family leave policies, communication obstacles produced by nonresident fathering, and limited financial and educational resources shape how negative health behaviors and outcomes are related for fathers and their children.[94] For example, children with nonresident fathers are at higher risk for obesity if their fathers have less education, are less involved with them, and are obese themselves. Thus, we need to transform cultural messages about masculinity to entice men to engage in more self-care. We must also offer divorce guidelines that encourage father involvement and work-based policies and programs that enable dads to spend more time with and care for their newborns and sick children. Creating desirable conditions that promote a more health-conscious style of fathering can also push men to reframe and strengthen their sense of dyadic we-ness with their children. Maintaining a positive sense of we-ness, even if the father and child do not live together, can be beneficial for both.

Wellness is also a multidimensional concept with at least six dimensions: physical, mental, emotional, spiritual, social, and environmental.[95] These dimensions provide the foundation for a booming wellness industry that has ten key sectors, with the top revenue-producing ones being personal care, beauty, and antiaging; healthy eating, nutrition, and weight loss; and fitness and mind-body.

We often practice features of a holistic lifestyle by ourselves, but following a holistic approach encourages involvement with others as well. How often, in what ways, and in what sectors and social domains do we tend to incorporate others into our holistic approach to wellness? When does it benefit us to develop a spirit of we-ness in one or more of the social domains as we practice holistic health strategies? How do we develop a sense of we-ness or reinforce a preexisting one when we engage in one or more holistic practices?

Obviously, the dimension most relevant to our discussion of group belonging and we-ness involves the connection between holistic wellness and the strong ties we can forge through our families, friendships, communities, and work – the social dimension. Our emotional, psychological, and time investments in our relationships frequently affect our stress levels and health outcomes. When we bond and create a sense of we-ness with others, our experiences and feelings can boost our wellness. Using our health consciousness to build strong, supportive ties with specific people as well as groups can generate social capital that enhances our lives in our primary groups, community settings, leisure and sport activities, and paid work.

However, there may be negative implications associated with at least some health practices and the identities associated with them. For example, because vegetarians are a social minority, some health researchers are concerned about their higher reporting of "lower daily self-esteem, psychological adjustment, and meaning in life, and more negative moods than semi-vegetarians and omnivores."[96] Vegetarians are subjected to out-group stigma by omnivores, and their well-being may also be negatively affected because they are more likely to be disappointed with the high levels of social inequality, environmental pollution, and violence in the world.[97] Having a strong ideational commitment to a belief system that is repeatedly challenged can lead to personal frustration. Presumably, if a person is surrounded by a group of like-minded people, being part of this type of social minority is less problematic.

Finding a community of like-minded, health-conscious people for face-to-face interactions can be difficult. The visibility of spirited online communities was heightened during the COVID-19 pandemic. Many people were stuck at home searching for ways to deal with their boredom, stay fit, and remain connected to others remotely. One popular program, "Yoga with Adriene," illustrates the potential value of online resources to help participants develop a sense of we-ness in the twenty-first century.

Adriene Mishler, a former actress, launched her yoga program on YouTube in 2012 and had 11.1 million subscribers as of May 2022. Her philosophy is to use YouTube as an educational platform "appealing to all levels, bodies, and genders." This easygoing, enthusiastic yoga instructor wants people to show up to do free yoga as a friend. Mishler has a global perspective in helping others "find what feels good." To build her online community and assist people in developing an ideational form of we-ness, Adriene has also created a companion wellness website and she writes a newsletter that she affectionately calls "Weekly Love Letter."[98] In addition, she uses a Mighty Networks online platform to foster peer-to-peer communication, support, and friendship.

I learned about this leisure-oriented virtual community through one of my students who was eager to share her experience with it. My student, stuck at home for months during the pandemic, experimented with this virtual format to develop her yoga practice. She and her younger sister created a joint workout ritual that involved regularly doing Adriene's video class. During the summer of 2020, they even did several livestream classes with Adriene. In my student's words, "at a time where most people were essentially in quarantine, knowing that thousands of other people were struggling through this yoga practice at the same exact moment really helped my sense of we-ness with others practicing." This experience has not only heightened her ideational we-ness as someone who sees herself as sharing a collective identity with those who have a yoga practice, her workout ritual has also strengthened her dyadic bond with her sister.

The holistic approach to health is highly valued because those who identify with it often strive to have a healthy appreciation for the relationship between the "me" and "we." Having a balanced awareness of oneself in relation to others, and solidifying that perspective by productive relations with others, helps people to inject the other four social domains with positive, creative energy that reinforces healthy forms of we-ness.

Ideological Connections

People who are passionate about religious issues, social justice concerns, and political ideologies often look for a compatible thought community. When we effectively share our convictions, their power is exponentially expanded and our resolve to follow them is strengthened.

Even though an increasingly larger percentage of Americans in recent years say that they do not affiliate with any particular religion, the vast majority of religious people seek out some type of faith community in which to worship and pray with others.[99] In some instances, those who anchor their identity to a religious faith use their beliefs as a springboard to create or join faith-based groups that are designed to effect personal and social change (e.g., Promise Keepers, pro-life groups, groups that espouse the teaching of creationism in schools).[100]

One fascinating area that social scientists point to when studying aspects of religion involves the social psychological reasons people gravitate toward sects and cults. Although sects tend to be defined by social scientists as being a splinter group that breaks away from a larger denominational type of religion, sects and cults have much in common. Most importantly, these religious or ideological entities usually have a charismatic leader who can entice people who are impressionable, lonely, lack self-confidence, and are more likely to be disadvantaged economically to become committed followers. Unfortunately, the most publicized stories about sects and cults occur when something goes horribly wrong with them.

The infamous Westboro Baptist Church, founded by Fred Phelps in 1955 and located in Topeka, Kansas, illustrates the intense we-ness that can be constructed by some religious groups. Grounded in Calvinist theology, this small congregation of Westboro Baptists have a well-publicized and controversial history of protesting with their handmade signs (e.g., "Thank God for 9/11," "God Hates Fags," and "Soldier Die 4 Fag Marriage").[101] Although their messaging has shifted slightly in recent years to include some positive language, fewer insults, and more biblical citations, their most vehement protests continue to focus on homosexuality and gay marriage, military funerals, adultery, fornication, and remarriage. Around the time that Pastor Phelps died in 2014, their leadership structure shifted to a council of elders (married men), but previously the church had been known for its unified decision-making strategy. In the words of one former member, Megan Phelps-Roper,

> When church matters came up – especially disciplinary matters – active participation was the duty of every member. Everyone had to vote. Everyone had to agree. Without exception. If even a single member disagreed, no action would be taken.... The need for church unity was one of our animating principles, the reason we were in constant communion and communication with one another.... We were *of one mind* as the Lord required us to be.[102]

The spirit and practical reality of this very inclusive and cooperative style of decision-making is made possible because members pursue both dyadic and ideational we-ness that enables them to sustain a group identity characterized as "of one mind."

You don't have to belong to a sect or a cult to be motivated by passion and consequential beliefs. Those who feel strongly about human or animal rights, social justice related to race, gender, LGBTQ+, or environmental issues frequently seek out friends and activist groups that embrace their way of thinking. Sharing hope for change invigorates people, encouraging them to work together to promote their causes.

Such was the case with Mark Dixon, Ben Evans, and his wife, Julie Dingman Evans, who began a remarkable collaboration in 2006 called YERT (Your Environmental Road Trip).[103] These three environmental activists marshaled their resources to execute a "year-long eco-expedition" that covered all fifty states. They interviewed over eight hundred people while using a "mix of outrageous antics, provocative examples, and thoughtful reporting" to explore the diverse approaches that were being used throughout America to address environmental issues. They also chronicled their efforts by producing an award-winning documentary and sixty provocative short films. In addition, we learn how their shared commitment to environmental sustainability reinforced their sense of we-ness. Their openness to we-ness was motivated by lofty ideals, romantic and family love (Julie became pregnant two months into the trip), companionship, and their shared commitment to pursue a practical goal. Together, these motivating forces inspired them to "walk the walk" and to challenge themselves to be environmentally responsible throughout the trip. For example, the three committed to fitting all their garbage each month into a shoebox!

In stark contrast to those who solidify their we-ness by appealing to environmental and other uplifting ideals, Donald Trump used questionable tactics – including outrageous lies – to foster we-ness among his followers. Some of the most visible displays of politically minded people seeking comfort in practical symbols of unity occurred at Trump rallies. Trump followers broadcast their common cause through the hats they wore (Make America Great Again), the signs they carried, the slogans they chanted (e.g., "Lock Her UP," "Send Her Back," "STOP the Steal"), and their penchant for identifying enemies as part of a divisive "othering" process (e.g., immigrants, mainstream news agencies, the "deep state"). For the radical-right Trump supporters, having a TV network, Fox News, filter information for them was instrumental in perpetuating their collective sense of political we-ness and identification with political symbols.[104]

Leisure, Play, and Sports

Over the centuries, the purposes, symbolic routines, and social context for leisure and sports have changed dramatically. In the twentieth century, for example, recreational culture in America was dramatically transformed because of numerous social patterns. Among the developments were that paid work was increasingly separated from the home; women were spending less time at home and more time in paid work; people were more isolated as they moved to the suburbs in record numbers; urban planners were transforming city infrastructures to leverage the mobility the automobile offered; third places that had once pumped lifeblood into communities were rapidly declining; the allure of TV and other new entertainment technologies encouraged people to spend more time cocooning in their homes; and commercialized leisure and mass advertising became more pervasive.

The transformation of leisure into consumption has profoundly altered the world of public life more generally. Ray Oldenburg, who wrote a book about third places, astutely asserts:

> Advertising, in its ideology and effects, is the enemy of an informal public. It breeds alienation. It convinces people that the good life can be individually purchased. In the place of the shared camaraderie of people who see themselves as equals, the ideology of advertising substitutes competitive acquisition. It is the difference between loving people for what they are and envying them for what they own.[105]

This commercialized approach to the good life devalues authentic companionship and dyadic we-ness as a source for well-being. Instead of developing dyadic we-ness by leaning into intimate, face-to-face conversations, we act like self-absorbed actors seeking a superficial form of ideational we-ness that is reflected in market-based images of the good life. Together, these and related cultural forces have reshaped the world of leisure and sports for kids and adults alike. They have altered the types and number of options people have at their disposal to construct we-ness in their face-to-face as well as online activities that involve relaxation and play.

Whether our goals are spoken or unspoken, we tend to pursue leisure and sports activities with a purpose in mind. We certainly spend some of our leisure and sports time alone reading a book, dancing to a TV workout video, watching YouTube videos, listening to music, or exercising. But we also spend much of this pleasurable nonwork time with others, many of whom we define as family or friends.

Clubs and associations that cater to people of different ages, interests, and backgrounds are pervasive. Whether it be outdoor adventure, performing hip hop routines, playing poker, breeding show dogs, computer gaming, or some other leisure activity, people flock to groups that make it possible for them to pursue their interests and associate with like-minded others, all while having fun. Some clubs provide options to do leisure activities in a competitive forum, which makes these experiences feel more like sports, even if they're not. While some people pursue leisure activities because they want the rush of competing, others are involved for the sheer joy of it. Either way, most people like the feeling of doing leisure activities with others they define as friends, and they are increasingly finding online options to satisfy their interpersonal needs.

Defining Leisure

The words "leisure," "play," and "sports" are part of our everyday vernacular, but they mean different things for everyday people and researchers alike. Research on leisure patterns among Americans is confusing at best because leisure is defined in various ways. Do we simply define leisure as the number of hours people are not in paid work? Do we factor in commute time for work? What about our time spent on educational pursuits? How do household-related chores inside or outside the home factor into our definition? What about the time we spend carting kids around from one activity to another, or the time we spend on the internet signing them up for extracurricular activities?

To bring order to this confusion, we might, as some have done, define leisure broadly as "time spent on activities that provide direct enjoyment."[106] Although this sounds reasonable, what one person finds enjoyable, another may perceive to be tedious and annoying. Ideally, then, we should consider thinking of leisure activities from each person's own point of view and delimit leisure activities to include only those that are not part of paid work.

Throughout recent history the types of leisure and sports activities Americans participate in have expanded tremendously. There is little dispute that there are more diverse opportunities to participate in nonwork activities. It is important to ask: Are we more available and inclined than previous generations to create those moments that lead to and solidify we-ness away from paid work?

Online Bonding

Modern technologies give us the option to join all sorts of internet and video-based leisure groups that enable us to develop we-ness with others if we so desire. Admittedly, some forms of we-ness we establish online are superficial when we immerse ourselves in simulation games with "friends" we never meet in person. Turkle reminds us that "online, we easily find 'company' but are exhausted by the pressures of performance…. The ties we form through the Internet are not, in the end, the ties that bind. But they are the ties that preoccupy."[107] However, those who take gaming seriously can develop alternative forms of deep dyadic bonds that exist outside of face-to-face contact. Many groups allow us to establish our we-ness in virtual space entirely. Others encourage us to use internet tools that ultimately help us communicate in ways that make our in-person experience even better.

In *The Proteus Paradox: How Online Games and Virtual Worlds Change Us – and How They Don't*, Nick Yee, a social scientist and cofounder of Quantic Foundry, a consulting practice focused on game analytics, shares one twenty-year-old man's story about playing World of Warcraft (WoW). The participant states: "A strong motivation for me is working with other people and existing within a perfect and efficient group. The aims of this group are not important, we could be grinding or camping a spawn to get an item for someone, when everything goes perfect, no communication is needed, and everyone just does what they should exactly as it should be done, I just feel great.... Interacting with people and being able to depend on them, and be depended on by them ... that's why I play."[108]

Many of the millions of people who log on to massive multiplayer online role-playing games (MMORPG) every day find a way to construct a sense of we-ness with others through their avatar. In these nonwork settings, what matters most is that users channel their desire to be connected to others through their involvement in social activities that lead to enjoyable, and sometimes competitive, experiences.

Virtual worlds are often divided into two categories: social worlds and competitive game-based worlds. Yee suggests there are three clusters of motivations that either separately, or in a blended fashion, account for why people play online games. The reasons are related to achievement ("gaining power within the context of the game"), immersion ("different ways of becoming part of the story"), and social interaction ("different ways of relating to other people in the game").[109] Although players can forge a sense of we-ness with fellow players irrespective of their motivation for playing, those compelled to play because they like relating to others presumably will be more receptive to exploring opportunities for a lasting form of we-ness. Players with this social perspective toward gaming appear to be more open to using out-of-game back channel spaces (e.g., instant messaging [IM] or voice over internet protocols [VoIPs]) to communicate with other players about game strategies as well as personal matters.[110] This type of communication leads to a greater sense of connectedness for the participants that manifests itself inside and outside the game world.

When we enter noncompetitive social virtual spaces, like Second Life and the various installments in the Animal Crossing series, we are free to interact in creative ways with others in user-built simulated communities.[111] Simon Gottschalk, sociology professor at the University of Nevada, Las Vegas, closely studied the Second Life experience during the 2008–9 period when it was quite popular. He writes:

Since social virtual worlds encourage socializing and community building, residents come here mainly to explore this constantly growing environment and themselves in it, to educate themselves in a mind-boggling diversity of areas, to work, to acquire and create virtual objects, to interact with others, and to build communities, groups, and enduring associations with them.[112]

Using their avatars, participants can establish a virtual style of we-ness with other socially constructed avatars as friends, lovers, spouses, and parents.[113] A user navigates these virtual encounters as an embodied avatar after customizing their character. They select a variety of bodily and personalized features such as gender, hair, size, skin tone, wardrobe, and more. An avatar's appearance can affect the user's perceptions and behaviors as well as the perceptions and behaviors of users of other avatars who interact with it. Those who are highly invested in these worlds and personally committed to their avatars can see their avatar as an extension of themselves and sometimes incorporate their online identity into how they present themselves offline.[114] A 2019 meta-analysis of forty-six studies published in the *Journal of Media Psychology* showed that the "Proteus effect" – the "phenomenon that people conform in behavior and attitudes to their avatars' characteristics" – is a "reliable phenomenon" that has a "relatively large [effect] compared to other digital media effects."[115] For some, the distinction between these online and offline worlds can become blurred at times when their memories and perceptions bleed into one another.[116]

Although participants are free to alter their physical appearance dramatically from their real-world attributes, a person's actual communication skills and style limit their options to present themselves in ways that exceed their real-life capabilities. While the protocol for older games was to have players communicate via typed chat, more contemporary iterations of games incorporate voice-based tools that permit players to speak to one another using headphones with mics. Whether by typed or spoken word, a player's limited communication skills can hinder them from establishing a sense of group belonging and dyadic we-ness with specific types of avatars and their users. Still, users can construct a sense of community with others and develop an online personal network in social virtual spaces that sometimes includes individuals who would otherwise not be incorporated into their intimate, real-life social circle.

We have the chance to experience bonds online in all five social domains using noncompetitive simulation games that enable users to build physical environments and social contexts that exist outside of a user's online playing time. Gottschalk notes that these virtual spaces "promote hyperpersonal and authentic relations, commitment, loyalty, intimacy, solidarity, altruistic impulses, and a sense of community."[117] All of these expressions are relevant to our approach to chasing and managing a state of we-ness and group belonging.

In addition to developing relationships by getting married to, cohabiting with, or befriending others in the noncompetitive social virtual spaces, the competitive games like Fortnite, WoW, and Roblox also provide options for users to establish various types of relationships through their avatars. These multiplayer games, which typically have hundreds of thousands or millions of registered players, enable users to join player organizations such as guilds, clans, and corporations. By joining these much smaller groups, players can develop a sense of group identity and community more easily. The player organizations often include like-minded players with similar gaming preferences. Players can practice together, offer gaming tips, share resources, and provide other means of support to one another. In addition, the games are intentionally structured using sociability designs that promote cooperative play or codependence. In-game objectives may require players to work together to defeat a common enemy.[118]

One study differentiated players of the "ruthless" space-themed game EVE Online as either "in-game associates," "social friends," or "true friends." Those identified as true friends are most likely to establish a form of dyadic we-ness because their relationship has evolved to a state that transcends the game. In addition to communicating with one another using official game forums, these players go out of their way to communicate on various social networking sites as well as by phone, email, Zoom, etc. These relationships are often built over several years of online exchanges and involve a high level of vulnerability, trust, and emotional support. As one player summarizes their relationships, "A lot of the good friends that I do have are through EVE so I feel they know more about me than others might share.... I'm definitely along the lines of if something goes wrong in my life they are the first people I contact."[119]

On a personal note, in mid-July 2020 during the COVID-19 pandemic, my son celebrated his birthday stuck in the house by spending five hours on a Saturday afternoon enthralled with an online "group chat" he organized with ten friends whom he had met by playing Roblox, none of whom he had spent any time with in person. From his perspective, these kids, despite living in Australia, England, the Philippines, Russia, Zimbabwe, and elsewhere, had become an important part of his informal support group during a tough phase of the pandemic. Online posts and anecdotal reports suggest that noncompetitive games like Animal Crossing also played an important role in many young people's lives as they pursued creative options to stay in contact with close friends while following physical distancing protocols. In addition, noncompetitive games enable us to do several things: we can align ourselves with those who share similar beliefs and values connected to thought communities, participate in various leisure groups, get involved in community groups, and develop a sense of we-ness with a virtual coworker.

The motivating forces that compel these virtual connections are typically the desire to approximate what it's like to be part of a family or romantic partnership, or to experience the joys of platonic companionship. Those of us who are bothered by not having a supportive family or circle of friends, as well as those who feel isolated because of abandonment, divorce, physical limitations, or other personal traumas, may try to use alternative online connections to fill this void in our primary group relations. For many, establishing a sense of we-ness online is better than feeling alone and disconnected.

Beyond the urge to bond in small groups, some participants use gaming in the multiplayer virtual world to express an ideational sense of we-ness linked to social movement activities. One intriguing example is the Alpha guild, established in 2006 in WoW. It represents the largest special interest guild in this game. Its goals are to "better service the LGBT community and offer a safe inclusive place to game for members of any sexual orientation or gender identity."[120]

Brad McKenna, a lecturer at the University of East Anglia in the UK, studies the relationships between information technology and people. He did an eighteen-month interpretive field study of Alpha beginning in 2010 using a type of internet-based ethnography. McKenna concludes that "many members join for a desire to come together as an LGBT community, to share experiences, and support each other, while also playing the game together."[121] For some who belong to this or another marginalized group, connecting online may feel safer, and it may be easier to connect with those who have similar backgrounds and interests.

Members of the Alpha guild have demonstrated their sense of we-ness most notably with a virtual pride parade, model competitions, dance parties, and the creative use of communication software that ensures that members of different subguilds can easily access one another. McKenna describes how Alpha leaders and members mobilized to generate a collaborative response to the developer and publisher of WoW, Blizzard, when it modified its policies and software for the game. Alpha leaders, buoyed by the strong community-building ethos of the membership, devoted the necessary time and energy to adapt existing technologies to ensure that the guild could sustain its LGBT collective identity and rituals. In doing so, Alpha members were able to continue to experience both dyadic and ideational we-ness through their involvement in WoW.

On occasion, users can extend remnants of their simulated adventures to their offline, everyday worlds. The memories of the online bonds people create through their avatars may get folded into their everyday expressions of we-ness with the same people in the real world. This set of circumstances can create intriguing challenges and opportunities as users try to manage and possibly integrate their shared knowledge about virtual and in-person demonstrations of we-ness. For instance, how do the people behind a pair of avatar lovers adjust to their romantic relationship offline that is more directly and profoundly influenced by the mundane circumstances and practical responsibilities of daily life? How does the couple manage possible differences in their online and offline fantasies, preferences, and fears? How and to what extent do the dynamics of platonic friendships established online affect the way people perceive and deal with trust issues when they are expanding their friendship to include offline interactions?

The more common question for those who experience these virtual social spaces is how do online experiences affect the way a user perceives and treats their real-world relationships with those they do not interact with online? As more people explore these avatar-based virtual worlds, people increasingly are forced to consider how they perceive and respond to the we-ness, or the potential we-ness, they or their loved ones create using an avatar. Fears and anxieties that stem from concerns about a partner's virtual infidelity can and do affect people's real-life emotions. I recall reading about one disgruntled wife who divorced her husband after learning that his avatar had been romantically involved with another avatar online, even though she knew that her husband had never met the other avatar's creator in real life.

Sports

People enjoy social exchanges and develop we-ness sentiments when they participate in sports and activities that bridge the divide between sports and leisure. A regular weekend tennis match between friends may constitute leisure activity, but if the friends keep score and play competitively, they may believe they're participating informally in a sport. Moreover, they can experience their we-ness in a formal sports venue when they play as a doubles team in an official tennis tournament.

The emergence of ESPN in the summer of 1978, along with the pervasiveness of other sports channels, has meant that more people are exposed to the world of sports indirectly. This type of exposure probably increases the sports fan's willingness to develop feelings of we-ness with specific teams. The average sports fan of today may also be better positioned to appreciate the relationships players have with one another. Today, fans can see aspects of we-ness in the sports world up close in ways they did not before. Players' increased participation in both social media and interviews allows us to not only learn more about individual athletes, but we also discover how teammates and coaches perceive each other and their respective teams.

The extensive coverage given to the Tour de France, for example, takes viewers backstage in special segments to listen to cyclists and team directors discuss strategy and team chemistry.

This type of extensive sports coverage meant that in June and July of 2019, soccer enthusiasts around the world – and especially in the United States – witnessed the American women's soccer team earn the second of their back-to-back World Cup championships. In addition to displaying a formidable style of team chemistry on the field, these athletes, led by their talented, flamboyant, and outspoken co-captain, Megan Rapinoe, demonstrated their commitment to off-the-field activism grounded in feminist and social justice principles.[122] The team was unique because it had a lesbian coach and several lesbian players who overtly champion LGBTQ+ causes. In March 2019, the players filed an institutional gender discrimination lawsuit against the US Soccer Federation asserting their right to equal pay and treatment relative to the men's national soccer team. Although a federal judge dismissed the players' suit in 2020, the US Soccer Federation pledged in spring 2022 to equalize pay for the women's and men's teams, contingent on US Soccer ratifying a single collective bargaining agreement that covers both teams. In addition, the women's team took a united stance to reject preemptively any offer to visit a White House occupied by a divisive president.

The team illustrates how people working toward a common goal can develop and sustain a network of deep dyadic forms of we-ness that culminate in a collective consciousness. But there were lots of other motivating forces that helped the US women's soccer team develop their sense of we-ness beyond their objective to win the World Cup again. The twenty-three teammates generated sentiments of we-ness by forging friendships, calling out social injustice, celebrating lofty ideals, and targeting enemies on and off the field. In addition, as hardworking, team-oriented athletes, they generated a sense of we-ness by sharing the emotional, mental, and physical demands that come with rigorous training at an elite level. Finally, older players had opportunities to mentor younger players.

Elite athletes like Rapinoe often find themselves in politically precarious positions when they try to navigate expressions of we-ness that can arise from competing personal and team ideals. The highly

publicized circumstances of the former NFL quarterback Colin Kaepernick illustrate this dilemma and more. As many may recall, Kaepernick began to express his concerns publicly about police brutality and systemic racial injustice by not standing during the national
anthem in the preseason of 2016. When asked in an interview afterward why he didn't stand, the biracial quarterback replied, "I am
not going to stand up to show pride in a flag for a country that
oppresses Black people and people of color. To me, this is bigger
than football and it would be selfish on my part to look the other
way."[123] Presumably, Kaepernick feels an affinity with persons of
color because of his own identity and personal experience living
in America as someone who is treated as a Black man. As the 2016
season unfolded, he continued his public protest realizing that some
supported him while others challenged his loyalty to his country
and his commitment to his team.

The following year, when Kaepernick was no longer in the NFL
because teams refused to employ him, the visibility of the protest
Kaepernick started gained intense public scrutiny. Trump lashed out
at the growing number of NFL players who were not standing during the national anthem. In a confrontational speech delivered in
Alabama, Trump attacked the protesting players, saying, "Wouldn't
you love to see one of these NFL owners, when somebody disre-
spects our flag, to say, 'Get that son of a bitch off the field right now.
Out! He's fired!'"[124] Those comments, and Trump's proposal that
fans initiate a counterprotest by leaving games in which a player
did not stand during the anthem, immediately galvanized support
from NFL players for the protest.

For many, their reaction also reflected their shared sense of struggle as Black professional athletes who were being disrespected by
the "leader" of the free world – an ignorant man and racist by any
commonsense accounting. The drama was accentuated, too, when
the NFL's commissioner, Roger Goodell, criticized Trump's comments the day after they were made in 2017, characterizing them as
"divisive." In Goodell's words: "The NFL and our players are at our
best when we help create a sense of unity in our country and our culture."[125] But in the initial years of the NFL players' protests, Goodell
provided at best a half-hearted sign of support. It wasn't until early

June 2020 that he offered a candid videotaped public apology for the NFL's earlier position and announced that the league stood with the players' commitment to nonviolent protest, and he explicitly stated, "Black lives matter."[126]

These protests and responses offered a riveting example of how competing frames for constructing a set of issues, in this case, racism and patriotism, can provoke people to draw the battle lines over their preferred expression of we-ness. Whereas some framed the protests as respectful dissent targeting racial injustice that is covered by the Constitution's First Amendment, others, most notably Trump and many of his followers, chose to define the protests as unpatriotic, despicable displays of selfishness. Nike's later decision to make Colin Kaepernick the face of a national ad campaign, with the caption "Believe in something. Even if it means sacrificing everything," added more fuel to the fire. The battle lines of we-ness were drawn for some owners of Nike shoes and apparel who posted videos of them burning their Nike gear.[127] This fissure demanded that many people make what they deemed were tough decisions. NFL players and team personnel had to navigate the competing images of the protest within their own team. They had to prioritize their relative commitments to various we-ness expressions and constituencies: the team, Black players, persons of color more generally, and ideologically based personal convictions about matters that represented groups other than their team. No matter how they resolved their dilemma of whether to stand or not during the anthem, teammates were forced into an awkward position of juggling their multiple allegiances, eventually siding with some, and perceived as going against others.

While many other public commentators weighed in on this controversy, suffice it to say that this was one of those significant moments when the worlds of sports and politics collide to make history – comparable to other noteworthy civil and human rights protests that involved athletes. Kaepernick's gesture of protest is a bold reminder of the iconic protest by American track and field athletes Tommie Smith and John Carlos that took place during the medal ceremony at the Mexico City Olympics on October 16, 1968.

They had just won the gold and bronze medals, respectively, in the 200 meters.

During the playing of the United States national anthem, Smith and Carlos each stood shoeless, but wearing black socks to represent Black poverty, and they each raised a black-gloved fist with their heads bowed. Despite many commentaries that indicate the raised fists were a Black power salute, Smith describes the gesture as basically a "human rights salute."[128] Smith did symbolize his affinity with Black pride by wearing a black scarf around his neck, while Carlos also sought to express what I've referred to as a type of ideational we-ness. He wore a necklace of beads to honor those who had been directly subjugated to the slave trade or had been lynched or killed because of their race. Carlos also unzipped his tracksuit top to show solidarity with blue-collar workers. Each wore the Olympic Project for Human Rights badge, as did the silver medalist, Australian Peter Norman, who was openly sympathetic to Smith's and Carlos's protest. The badge was a symbol of the organization founded by the sociologist Harry Edwards in 1967 to advance racial equality.[129]

Although many are aware of the courage Smith and Carlos demonstrated via their public protest to draw attention to racial inequality, the remarkable story extends beyond these two men. It includes Norman, a white man who lived in a racist country that supported apartheid at the time.[130] Norman embraced the ideals Smith and Carlos espoused and he told them prior to the ceremony that he would stand with them on the medal stand during their planned protest. The great respect Smith and Carlos held for Norman throughout the decades to follow was exemplified by the two Americans being the front pallbearers who carried Norman's coffin when he died in 2006. When Smith eulogized Norman at his funeral, he turned to Norman's family and said, "Peter Norman's legacy is a rock. Stand on that rock. Peter shall always be my friend. The spirit shall prevail."[131] Carlos has described Norman as a "brother from another mother."[132]

Like Smith and Carlos, Norman and his family experienced extensive public ridicule, and Norman was discriminated against after the 1968 games because he affirmed the Americans' protest on the medal stand. Norman was even denied a spot on the 1972 Australian Olympic team despite running numerous qualifying times in both the 100 and 200 meter sprints. And despite being the fastest sprinter in Australian history at the time, Norman was excluded from playing any role in the 2000 Olympic Games held in Sydney, Australia. Norman was offered the option to regain his standing in the Australian Olympic community if he were to denounce what Smith and Carlos had done. Instead, he chose to keep his principled position and deal with the consequences.

Having the similar goal of pursuing competitive sprinting and eventually earning an Olympic medal brought Smith, Carlos, and Norman together initially. However, the decisive factors that cemented their lifelong friendships after the Mexico City moment were the lofty ideals of racial equality they shared, their joint willingness to confront social injustice, and their similar personal experiences of enduring the public stigma that their activism generated for them. Together, these motives enabled the trio to create a sense of we-ness that transcended sports, race, and country.

We can learn much about a person's character by observing what the person does when no one is looking. But we also learn a lot by observing what a person says and does when the public spotlight shines brightly on them. We all stand to appreciate more fully the power of we-ness that can be forged when sports and politics bring people together to pursue a common and worthy cause.

Expressions of we-ness and close friendship in the sports world, like those just mentioned, are more apt to make national headlines when elite athletes and teams are involved. But many of us ordinary folks also get to feel a sports-related we-ness as youth athletes, or in our roles as parents and coaches of kids playing sports for local schools and in community recreation leagues. As we saw with the Paradise, California, football team which was profiled earlier, youth sports can unite kids, parents, coaches, and even community residents to celebrate their common spirit during a tragedy. Fortunately, sports can work its we-ness magic in good times as well.

In addition to being a dad and an informal coach in the youth triathlon world, I studied how we-ness was built and expressed from my vantage point as a researcher. For my book, *Kids Who Tri*, I spent six years exploring how young athletes, parents, coaches, and race directors build a refreshing sense of community in the world of youth triathlon. Unlike many school-based and travel team youth sports, triathlon is organized so that everyone can participate and complete the entire race. No distinction is made between starters and kids coming off the bench because there is no bench in triathlon. Everyone who's capable gets to complete the entire race.

The interpersonal bonds and sense of community that develop in both youth and adult triathlon are forged in a somewhat unique setting. As I note in my previous book:

> In many ways, this melding of the competitive and cooperative spirit that defines the triathlon community illustrates what the late French sociologist Pierre Bourdieu referred to as "habitus."[133] People organize their lives by situating themselves *vis à vis* a habitus which reflects the fluid norms, sensitivities, and tendencies that help people develop lasting dispositions. In turn, these dispositions shape how individuals think, feel, and act in specific contexts. They learn these practices and orientations from those around them. In short, the triathlon world, at every level, is informed by a habitus that reflects the sport's identity as demanding yet highly supportive. Over time, triathletes often learn to embody this disposition and to recognize its expression by others.[134]

When athletes, and those who support them, understand triathlon to be a hard sport, they're open to respecting others who participate simply because they're willing to test themselves in this multi-sport. As a result, athletes are more prepared to create a cooperative bond with a teammate, a fierce competitor, or a stranger. Only some youth triathletes are on teams, but for those who are, the parents also have opportunities, as I did, to develop meaningful friendships with other parents. A search for companionship may be the most common motivating force that leads to a sense of we-ness among people involved with youth triathlon, but mentorship, sharing pain and suffering, and sharing a practical goal are other reasons why people embrace the triathlon spirit and develop a sense of we-ness with other like-minded folks.

Paid Work

One way to consider whether Americans are spending more or less time at work in recent years – a pattern that presumably affects individuals' options to develop a sense of we-ness with coworkers – is to look at estimates of the total number of hours people work for pay. In their *Economic Policy Institute* essay, economists Valerie Wilson and Janelle Jones summarize recent demographic patterns for the annual work hours for prime-age workers (twenty-five to sixty-four) in the United States between 1979 and 2016.[135] They show that among all workers there was a 7.8 percent increase in the average number of hours worked annually. Rates for women account for the entire increase because men experienced a decline in hours worked. Women are clearly integrated into the American workforce like never before. These patterns prompt a cursory and speculative observation that women's increased time at work is probably creating more opportunities for them to develop bonds with some of their coworkers based on their shared beliefs and interests. However, workforce patterns changed dramatically in response to layoffs prompted by COVID-19 (especially for women). People's perceptions about work also shifted during this period so employment patterns are very much in a state of flux.

Another way to explore the intersection between work and we-ness opportunities is to focus on how various job characteristics alter the chances that deep dyadic forms of we-ness are likely to emerge. For this exercise, we'll only consider those people who work full- or part-time. Some, though not all, of the characteristics worth noting are listed below. The ten characteristics cover a wide range of considerations which tend to emphasize either a qualitative or structural aspect of a position. For example, a qualitative dimension associated with a position would be the level of creativity or risk associated with it, whereas more structural features would include the extent to which a job is home-based or involves a one-on-one type of service arrangement. When we think about a type of job, we can ask whether it is:

1) creatively oriented (e.g., performing arts, audio/video production),
2) risky (e.g., law enforcement, firefighting, construction, military),

3) instructive (e.g., coaching, teaching),
4) caregiving in nature (e.g., nursing, childcare, eldercare),
5) labor-intensive (e.g., farming),
6) one-on-one service oriented (e.g., financial planning, personal training, massage, counseling),
7) stressful (e.g., air traffic control, emergency medicine),
8) based on a loyalty pledge (e.g., judge, security guard),
9) home-based (e.g., writing, computer programming), and
10) isolated (e.g., trucking).

The characteristics are not meant to be exhaustive or exclusively define the responsibilities for any occupation. A specific occupation may include more than one of these characteristics. Those in law enforcement, for instance, are not only in risky settings, but many of them are also likely to experience a fair amount of stress and be expected to sign a loyalty pledge to uphold the law. Similarly, child-care workers are likely to have both caregiving and instructional responsibilities.

Moreover, a particular characteristic may vary in how consequential it is in fostering opportunities to establish we-ness depending on the job with which it is associated, even when jobs are similar in some respects. A loyalty pledge for one person can matter a great deal but be irrelevant for someone else, even though the person signs one. Compared to its effect on a security guard who works the night shift at a large warehouse, the loyalty pledge may matter more to a member of a police SWAT team. In part, this difference may stem from the security guard's job being much more isolated and less risky. Although these characteristics are designed to focus attention on how coworkers experience their relationships, workers can sometimes develop a feeling of we-ness with those who are considered customers, clients, or patients.

Finally, the characteristics are listed in descending order such that the characteristics at the beginning are the ones most likely to be associated with offering people more opportunities to develop a sense of we-ness with others. However, circumstances unique to how any person structures their job can either increase or decrease the likelihood that they will experience we-ness with others while on the job. Opportunities probably exist for someone to build a feeling of we-ness in any job if the circumstances are just right.

As described earlier, collaborating on an imaginative endeavor may nudge us to develop a sense of we-ness with others because the process of sharing creative energy inspires us. Brainstorming sessions can be fun, productive, and exciting, but they can also reveal a person's personality and interpersonal style. Just as some people have a largely cooperative or competitive interpersonal style, some may be distinctly friendly or annoying. Most of us will gravitate toward idea-generating sessions we believe are good-natured and include people who are willing to produce joint ideas, strategies, solutions, or whatever we define our end goal to be.

Just like expressing creativity can give our body chemistry a jolt, so can the adrenaline that is often generated when we do risky jobs. The Bureau of Labor Statistics identifies the riskiest occupations based on the percentage of workers in a field who die annually on the job.[136] Not surprisingly, all of these positions are disproportionately populated by men.

Some risky occupations are structured such that people's lives depend on coworkers making good decisions and executing their responsibilities carefully. Although "firefighter" and "police officer" were surprisingly not among the riskiest jobs, most of us would acknowledge that these positions are risky. Persons in these jobs can easily jeopardize coworkers' well-being if they carelessly take unnecessary risks to prove their masculinity. Although men today are probably less likely than earlier cohorts of men to display reckless forms of masculinity to gain favor with their coworkers, some do.[137]

In On the Fireline: Living and Dying with Wildland Firefighters, sociologist Matthew Desmond, who has also worked on a wildland fire crew in Arizona, reveals the critical role trust plays in the relationships firefighters develop on the job over time.[138] Desmond's research is consistent with the belief that many of those who do dangerous jobs are driven to be suspicious of those who act recklessly at work. In these work settings, perhaps more than most, building we-ness is predicated on building trust. Those perceived to be untrustworthy and irresponsible are often excluded from coworkers' casual exchanges that develop and celebrate their feeling of we-ness. How people judge different expressions of we-ness in many ways hinges on two interrelated themes: the complex and sometimes controversial process of building trust as well as the actions people take to either challenge or support its unethical use.

Building trust is especially important in work-related settings where the formal and informal opportunities to teach or instruct others are numerous, varied, and potentially powerful. These settings offer people meaningful options to build affinity and a shared sense of purpose. Many of us, myself included, have fond memories of elders in our lives who once played a significant role in teaching us content, skills, and perspective when we were kids. In some instances, those relationships rose to a level of involvement that was characterized by a shared sense of we-ness that we recognized in our youth, and sometimes continued to celebrate even into our adult years.

The teaching profession, as it's practiced in the classroom, is arguably the most widely identified teaching format, and one routinely celebrated in popular culture. The long-standing mantra that teachers are valuable yet underappreciated and poorly compensated is pervasive in American society. Despite the disconnect between prestige and pay, Americans at least give lip service to the notion that teachers can profoundly affect young people's lives. Hollywood has captured this sentiment for decades. The typical movie plot shows the teacher overcoming the disruptive behavior, apathetic attitude, and limited resources of a student, or an entire class of students, before a shared and productive sense of we-ness is established. Films like *Blackboard Jungle* (1955), *To Sir, with Love* (1967), *Stand and Deliver* (1988), *Dead Poets Society* (1989), *Dangerous Minds* (1995), *Mr. Holland's Opus* (1995), *Finding Forrester* (2000), *Freedom Writers* (2007), and *McFarland, USA* (2015) have illustrated the special bonds teachers and students often forge with one another.

Much paid teaching occurs outside the classroom as well. Like the classroom teacher, the subject tutor, music or voice instructor, martial arts sensei, and other positions are engrained in our cultural imagination as sources of potentially compelling and generative relationships.

One of the most celebrated expressions of we-ness in American history took root when a visually impaired, twenty-year-old tutor named Anne Sullivan first met the deaf and blind Helen Keller as a six-year-old on March 5, 1886. Ms. Sullivan's own childhood had been filled with tragedy – faint and blurred vision, abuse, a father who left, a mother who died, and time spent in a poorhouse where she witnessed her brother's death. She eventually ended up at Perkins School for the Blind where teachers viewed her as rude, but brilliant.[139] When Helen's parents came to the school to find a tutor for their daughter at the suggestion of Alexander Graham Bell, Ms. Sullivan was sent to Helen's Alabama home.

As powerfully depicted in the 1962 classic film, *The Miracle Worker*, starring Anne Bancroft and Patti Duke, Ms. Sullivan struggled relentlessly to release the wild and belligerent Helen Keller from the silent, angry, and dark space that imprisoned her as a young child. The unique bond they fought to establish during those exasperating early months blossomed into a beautiful adult friendship that lasted forty-nine years. The mutual trust and we-ness they nurtured over the years laid the foundation for Helen Keller to embark on her remarkable career as a world-renowned political activist, public speaker, and author who advocated for people with disabilities, women, the working class, and others. Together, these powerful women, whose early lives were both fraught with tremendous hardship and isolation, overcame their personal limitations by leaning on the special partnership that enriched their lives, as well as the lives of those who met them.

Since the days of Anne Sullivan's exploits, the category of workers with caregiving responsibilities for people of all ages has grown dramatically. Demographic shifts have played a major role in this uptick. Our aging population, high divorce rates, increase in dual-earner families, and smaller family size have created more work opportunities in the caregiving field broadly defined. Nannies for children and assistants for the elderly who struggle with physical and mental limitations are two distinct job profiles relevant to the production of we-ness. These caregivers, at times, come to see their arrangement as more than a job. In special cases, they grow deep feelings for their "clients" and see them as family members. Those sentiments may even be extended to the family members of their clients.

The clients, in turn, sometimes incorporate the caregiver into their expanded view of familial we-ness. I found myself feeling this way when a young college student named Rosie assumed a nanny role for several years when my youngest son was about nine months old. As my trust in her abilities and commitment to my son evolved, I quickly grew comfortable treating her like my son's aunt or my own niece. Rosie had earned her way onto my son's caregiving team.

Compared to caregiving professions that create opportunities for people to bond during their face-to-face exchanges, labor-intensive occupations are more likely to foster we-ness through work done side by side. Think of the miners, steelworkers, construction workers, oil rig workers, commercial fishers, and farmers who labor tirelessly alongside one another. These workers are sometimes labeled by their bosses as a "work crew" and develop a collective identity to match. With its dirty, sweaty, and exhausting features, hard labor offers workers the kind of common pain and purpose that grows tight bonds. Break time for these workers is not just a time to recover physically. It provides workers the chance to complain about their boss, swap stories about their families, and tease one another to take the edge off their drudgery.

Add to the mix the element of being migrant manual laborers, with a shared culture and language, and a work crew can take on an even deeper feeling of we-ness. Whatever affinity migrant workers develop with one another because of the labor-intensive nature of their efforts is intensified by their common struggle of dealing with workplace exploitation while navigating other work-life issues away from home and in a different country, frequently apart from family. Recently, many migrant workers in the United States are finding new reasons to bond and look out for each other. Unfortunately, during Trump's days in office they grew more fearful of the pernicious political and cultural tide that was increasingly targeting them as unworthy and dangerous.

Unlike manual labor jobs, various white-collar positions are structured to give workers an opportunity to work one-on-one with their clientele and develop personal relationships with them. Financial planners, personal trainers, massage therapists, physical therapists, counselors, and the like work closely with a client, sometimes with a team mentality to bring about positive outcomes for the client.

Many of the exchanges that occur within this set of working relationships have the potential to become quite emotional and intimate. As a result, most of these professionals are subject to professional codes of ethics. These codes outline the parameters of how the professional should ideally manage feelings and behaviors – their own as well as the client's. These ethical codes are sensitive to the power and pitfalls of the we-ness process. The interpersonal connections that provoke feelings of we-ness can easily expose people's vulnerabilities and unspoken fantasies. Thus, the codes are designed to set up borders to protect clients and professionals. It doesn't take much to jeopardize the special trust that defines these professional interactions and relationships. Once the trust is gone, it's hard, if not impossible, to recover.

Many of the jobs that demand professional standards are also quite stressful, with some occupations being decidedly more stressful than others. Jobs related to the health and safety of people are probably among some of the most stressful. In particular, the various jobs that comprise emergency medicine are especially demanding. These occupations also require individuals to be team players who can cooperate effectively to manage unique and stressful situations.

Dr. Azita Hamedani, Chair of the Department of Emergency Medicine at the University of Wisconsin School of Medicine and Public Health, underscores the value of the team mentality in emergency medicine. She says that workers in this arena are

> always in the position of asking for things from other people. Every day, being able to do your job requires asking for and getting things from other people, whether it's a consult or an admission or just an extra pair of hands. So whenever you're trying to make an operational change, you can't have a personal agenda. You have to keep focused on the best interest of the patient.[140]

Keeping the patient-focused perspective requires workers to sustain a certain style of we-ness as well. As Dr. Hamedani implies, if the patient's needs are to be privileged, team members must suspend any "personal agenda" to collaborate to serve the patient. Having that team mentality is essential in emergency medicine because change is endemic to the field. ER teams are repeatedly confronted with diverse circumstances (e.g., gunshot wounds, heart attacks, dismembered limbs, swallowed foreign objects, allergic responses) that frequently require quick, decisive decision-making.

The public's fascination with what transpires in an ER setting, including how the staff manages the interpersonal dynamics of different forms of we-ness, is clearly revealed by the success of television shows that focus on this topic. Two of those shows include the award-winning and massively popular medical drama *ER* (1994–2009), which aired 331 episodes, and more recently, *Chicago Med*, a drama that premiered in 2015. The latter was still on the air in 2022 and has about 10 million viewers per year. But the most culturally significant show of this ilk was the comedy-drama series *M*A*S*H* (1972–83) that focuses on a fictional team of doctors and support staff who operate a mobile army surgical hospital during the Korean War. The show highlighted in both dramatic and comedic style how medical personnel navigated their struggles to sustain a sense of we-ness motivated by various personal and political beliefs.

Although the characters depicted in *M*A*S*H* were extensively involved in each other's lives, they were military personnel who in many respects were doing their jobs in isolation from their homeland and loved ones. But large numbers of people may have more isolated work environments. That segment of the population, excluding the self-employed, who work part- or full-time from home has increased significantly in recent years. In 2018, the 4.3 million American part-time remote workers represented a 140 percent increase over the number of such workers in 2005.[141] These workers, who tend to be on average better educated than the general workforce, are likely to experience fewer opportunities to build the kind of face-to-face we-ness that workers encounter who interact with their coworkers on site.

As noted above, the effect of the loyalty pledge varies in how it influences work-related we-ness. I briefly mention it here and expand upon it in the next chapter. Although the pledges vary in scope, they essentially require workers to sign some sort of agreement that verifies their commitment to abide by the organization's code of conduct. Numerous organizations have a general set of behavioral guidelines, but the loyalty pledge is tailored more toward an organization's mission and specific expectations. For example, those serving in law enforcement or the military are typically required to commit themselves to more specific rules of conduct than people working outside these government organizations. As I discuss later, while a pledge can help solidify we-ness for soldiers or police officers, it can also act as a powerful wedge between those who abide by it and those who violate it. In general, the pledge implicitly draws attention to the idea that groups that promote we-ness make ethical assessments about how employees should do their jobs, separately or collaboratively. Sometimes those behavioral standards apply to activities away from work as well. Professional sports leagues and specific teams often have contractual clauses about various behaviors on and off the playing venue that can sully the reputation of the league and team.

While some workplaces foster the possibility of solidifying we-ness among workers, people who work away from a workplace have fewer opportunities to gain this benefit. Part-time workers, those who work at home, and the individuals who are subjected to lots of work-related travel may all grapple with feeling isolated. I suspect that when most of us think of the life of a truck driver, especially the people who do the long-haul version of trucking, we imagine them having a lonely, isolated work life, spending endless days and weeks on the road away from home. In the golden age of CB radio, truckers did have frequent contact with their fellow truckers and motorists, but there has been a noticeable decline in CB radio use among truckers in recent decades with the innovation of cell phones and GPS apps. Even when CBs were more popular, most of the radio interactions were relatively superficial. Their use seldom led to significant forms of dyadic we-ness with other truckers, even though they did facilitate some new friendships. At best, we might say that CB use provided truckers with opportunities to develop a more ideational we-ness or collective identity.

This pattern accentuates how trucking is far less likely than other occupations to foster meaningful bonds between coworkers. Lawrence Black, a professional driver with over 2.5 million miles to his credit, lamented on an internet post about the decline of the CB radio in the trucker world. He insightfully suggested that it has resulted in truckers being "less of a community of 'Knights of the Road' than we once were." He adds: "In an odd way, the increase in communication technologies has made communication *less* common."[142]

Meanwhile, in the twenty-first-century gig economy, social media apps offer many isolated workers in this sector creative options to connect with one another. Gig workers are independent contractors who establish a formal agreement with companies to provide a service to the company's client. Social media posts take on added meaning to these workers because they have no shared worksite to meet at and bond. Some of the better-known types of gig workers are on-demand food and product delivery app drivers (e.g., Door-Dash, Instacart, and Uber Eats) as well as Uber drivers. Some food service drivers use platforms like Reddit and Facebook to establish a loose form of we-ness with other drivers. During 2020, for example, DoorDash drivers used Reddit to post comments about COVID-19 financial assistance; offer tips on managing orders and unusual circumstances; vent frustrations about bad deliveries; share the joy of rewarding and funny experiences; complain about annoying encounters with customer support, and more.[143]

Facebook played a critical role in providing a communications platform for eleven disgruntled female Instacart shoppers from around the country who formed the nonprofit Gig Workers Collective. These women used Facebook Messenger to organize a strike in November 2019.[144] By May 2020, the hiring surge due to COVID-19 expanded the Facebook group to over fifteen thousand participants. Outside the United States, Uber Eats couriers in Japan and delivery service workers for the app Foodora in Norway used social media platforms to help them launch the first unions for delivery workers in late 2019.[145] Restrictive American labor laws are being challenged, which may result in similar types of union opportunities in the United States. Overall, this sort of worker activism likely portends that gig workers will use modern communication platforms for future initiatives to flex their collective muscle and minimize their sense of isolation. As a result, gig workers will probably forge a deeper sense of ideational we-ness – a collective consciousness as gig workers – that enhances their chances of securing better working conditions. With increasing numbers of people growing more accustomed to using delivery food services during COVID-19, how gig workers navigate their isolation and establish a viable form of we-ness may become even more relevant in the post-pandemic era.

A Model of We-ness, Self, and Social Domains

Before we explore the implications of how we-ness emerges in different groups, let's briefly review the general constellation of ideas presented thus far. They focus on how our opportunities to experience we-ness are motivated and relate to our activities in five social domains. The focal point for Model 1 includes the potential relationships between the three types of we-ness: deep dyadic, ideational, and spontaneous.

The model identifies the ten common motives we reviewed that prompt us to develop either dyadic or ideational we-ness, or both. These diverse motives often reflect our core values and beliefs. Depending on the circumstances, multiple motives can simultaneously shape how we create our feelings about belonging to a group. Specific motives are more likely to matter in some social domains than others. For example, sharing genetic heritage and family love will motivate us in our primary groups whereas sharing a practical goal is more often a significant motive in the workplace.

Although our motives can remain stable over time, they sometimes change as we mature and experience significant life events. They are expressed through the four threads that make up the self-tapestry from which we express ourselves, including our mind, body, heart, and soul. These threads shape our experiences in the five social domains. Although not depicted in the model, a wide range of historical, cultural, social, political, and technological forces produce the social contexts in which we develop and express our individual selves. For example, increasingly high-tech forms of

Model 1: We-ness, Self, and Social Domains

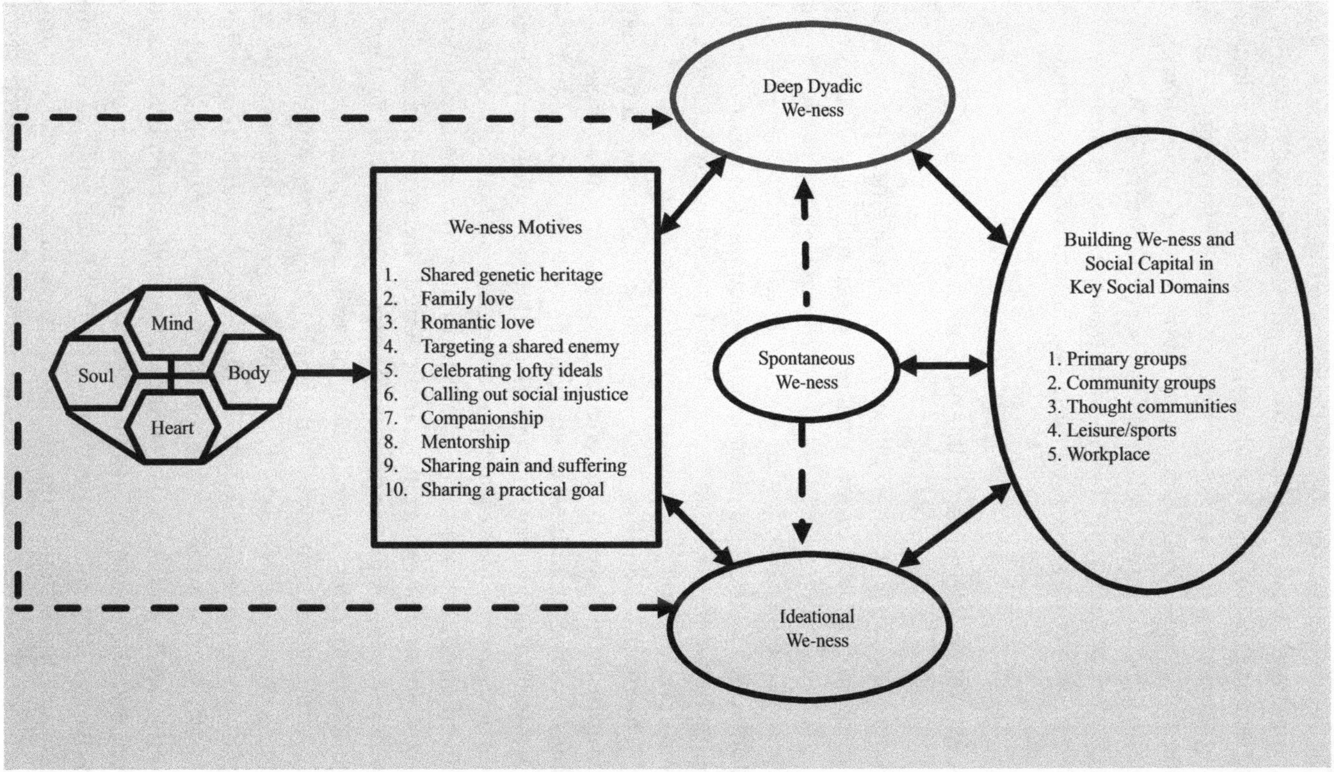

communication offer us novel ways to present our self-image and to relate to others. Thus, the cultural prism through which we perceive our self and the techniques we use to put on a performance for others are constantly changing. With the ebb and flow of life, many of us modify our sense of self and identify with different ideas and groups as we mature. Cultural shifts in public discourses and how we use various technologies, including social media, present us with new ways to make sense of our lives and to contemplate joining this or that group.

We develop our sense of we-ness in numerous social domains. The five major areas we address here include primary groups, community and civic groups, thought communities, leisure and sports, and workplace settings. In each of these settings, we convey our needs and desires in diverse ways, engaging in all sorts of social activities including co-parenting, playing on a work-based softball team, and protesting racial injustice as an ally to Black Lives Matter. These are the everyday settings in which we learn to pursue a sense of we-ness and group belonging.

Our personal connections and the dyadic we-ness we establish in close relationships can on occasion induce us to adopt new lifestyle beliefs and ideologies. The white coworker of an African American friend may be inspired to develop new convictions about racially based inequities that lead her to join a social movement. Other times the ideational we-ness that we embrace incites us to forge personal relationships that enable a dyadic we-ness to emerge with one or more persons. I'm sure new friendships and forms of dyadic we-ness were established when protestors in the spring and summer of 2020 marched alongside each other and perhaps faced off against authorities. On rare occasions, the spontaneous we-ness we experience also helps us to nurture a dyadic or ideational kind of we-ness. In subsequent chapters, we'll examine more closely how our experience with empathy, altruism, loving-kindness, compassion, cooperation, and social capital affects how we navigate our experiences with we-ness and group belonging.

4

Judging Outcomes: Good, Bad, and Mixed

When we think casually about marriages, families, sports teams, work groups, close friendships, activist organizations, unions, and various other groups, we often admire the warm, thoughtful, passionate, and productive relations we assume people will have in these arrangements. We value the beauty and power of people thinking about others, working collaboratively with them, and making sacrifices on each other's behalf.

Our hearts are warmed when we encounter the loving elderly couple that is still together after fifty years, having established a family legacy with children, grandchildren, and great-grandchildren. Many of us, especially in these times of high divorce rates, marvel at people who have held true to their vows. We admire the resiliency they've shown as a couple by navigating life through thick and thin, through sickness and in health.

Most of us teach our children to share, to play nice, and to respect others' feelings. We do similar things with our young athletes by coaching them to reject selfishness and to be a good team player. We want our kids to value their teammates, to be concerned about them, and to work together toward a team-oriented goal. We remind them regularly that there is no "I" in "team."

It's no surprise then that sports enthusiasts often invoke the biblical David and Goliath parable to celebrate a special form of we-ness.

Our sports folklore is littered with rituals, motivational pregame talks, and iconic sports moments that memorialize the power of we-ness. We lionize the team that, despite facing overwhelming odds, can galvanize its infectious team chemistry (we-ness) and impeccable team play to defeat a more talented team. This sort of we-ness is captured in movies like the 1986 film *Hoosiers*. This story is loosely based on a small-town high school basketball team that maximized its "all for one, one for all" mentality to win the prestigious Indiana state title in 1954 against much larger schools.

Similarly, the inspirational 1980 US Olympic hockey team's 4–3 victory over the heavily favored Soviet Union squad was touted as the top sports moment of the twentieth century by *Sports Illustrated*. Why was it so remarkable? The US had the youngest squad in the tournament – consisting entirely of amateur players – yet they were able to defeat the four-time defending Olympic gold medalists, the Soviet Union, which was stacked with primarily professional players. The game was later dubbed the "miracle on ice" because broadcaster Al Michaels exclaimed, "Do you believe in Miracles? Yes!" during the closing seconds of the game. This iconic hockey game reinforces our belief that athletes, and people more generally, can achieve great things when they join forces to pursue a shared vision.

Finally, Americans cherish the way close friendships engender empathy, compassion, loyalty, and timely gems of wisdom. The relationship between Morrie Schwartz and Mitch Albom that I described earlier, one of the most celebrated friendships of our time, continues to inspire people long after Morrie's death. My students are touched when I show a video of a public lecture Mitch gave several years ago as part of the Chicago Ideas series focusing on the informal lessons Morrie taught him.[1] They are amazed that the symbolic and practical meanings of their friendship live on more than twenty years after Morrie's death. As Morrie said, "Death ends a life, not a relationship."[2] The relationship these two men shared exemplifies how friends can nurture a style of we-ness in life that transcends death.

In principle, we value the efforts of those who create and sustain we-ness in their varied life circumstances. We tend to see we-ness as an inherently good thing. It sounds good. It looks good. It feels good. Therefore, it must be intrinsically good. Still, reality begs for a different conclusion. We-ness is complicated and messy in its many forms. That means our evaluation of it must be conditional. Interpreting the implications of a specific type of we-ness depends on how it's formed and expressed. It also depends on what each of us, as unique individuals and members of different groups, value.

In *Altruism: The Power of Compassion to Change Yourself and the World*, Matthieu Ricard, a renowned Buddhist monk, provides a compelling synopsis of the competing forces that can alter how we think about our desire to experience a sense of belonging, especially when it involves an ideational form of we-ness:

> The feeling of belonging to a group or a community in which everyone feels close to and responsible for everyone else has many virtues. It reinforces solidarity, valorizes the other, and favors the pursuit of common aims that go beyond the individual framework. It allows us, certainly, to grant more importance to *we* than to *me*. But the strong feeling of belonging to a group also has effects that are detrimental to the harmony of human relations. Privileging members of our group is accompanied by a correlating de-privileging of those who do not belong to it, those who are foreigners or who belong to a rival group. This partiality leads to different forms of discrimination like racism, sexism, homophobia, and religious intolerance.[3]

As previously discussed, individuals often take advantage of the we-ness model to entice or coerce people to mobilize for an unethical cause. Consequently, we need to step back and think carefully when we try to judge an expression of we-ness as either good, bad, or a bit of both. We must not only think about the varied implications that we-ness can generate for those who belong to the group, we also need to recognize that people often do not share the same values, ethical codes of conduct, or norms of moral decision-making. Consequently, whereas some see a particular outcome as good, others deem it bad.

Defining an outcome as good or bad, then, requires us to adopt basic ethical principles to guide our thinking about what is ultimately a subjective evaluation. I use a set of ethical principles and methods of moral decision-making commonly associated with the field of health care to assess the outcomes produced by assorted displays of we-ness. Granted, the typical issues that health care providers confront when working with a patient are distinct and narrower than the wide range of circumstances that can arise when people are expressing some form of we-ness. I take some liberties, then, in using the following four ethical principles to judge the "good" or "bad" status of outcomes: (1) respect for autonomy, (2) beneficence, (3) nonmaleficence, and (4) social justice.[4] Although the principles may conflict sometimes in specific situations, I do not privilege any above the others.

Most reasonable people would agree that a person or group should have the moral right to make informed decisions without undue pressure or force. Being free to make informed decisions about one's life is consistent with supporting a person's autonomy. When people act beneficently, they attempt to do good for others. In practical terms, we can try to enhance a person's quality of life in myriad ways. Ideally, we should make a conscious effort to determine what another person or group wants and needs to enhance their well-being, and then try to bring that about in a manner that is appealing to them. In contrast, we should be mindful not to harm others, either intentionally or unintentionally. To avoid the latter, we must be aware of how our actions related to a group may negatively influence someone else. Finally, if we are to promote social justice we must, as part of our joint expression of we-ness, act toward others in a fair and impartial manner. We should strive to ensure that others have equal opportunities to pursue their interests so long as they do not infringe on others' rights.

If we demonstrate empathy and compassion, we can implement these principles more easily. Taking the time to see the world through the eyes of others – to feel their frustration, pain, anxiety, joy, and dreams – can position us to leverage our sense of we-ness to help others. Being compassionate is always easier if we understand the social realities and concerns that shape others' lives. Those others are often the people we know well, perhaps love, and are people with whom we have a personal history in which we've already established we-ness. They can also be the individuals out-side our close interpersonal network who we influence based on our involvement in our own group(s). Think of the tightly knit family who empathizes with homeless people's predicaments and volun-teers every month to serve meals at a local homeless shelter.

Two questions force us to think about the scope of outcomes that we choose to judge. Do we judge only those who have established we-ness among themselves on their own terms, free of any mean-ingful constraints? Or do we expand our lens to also consider those who may benefit or suffer from the bonding others achieve separate from them, and often at the expense of the outsiders? Imagine the high school girl who is gang-raped by teenage boys who benefit from the complicit silence and support of those who were initially present but did not actively participate in the sexual assault.

In his book, *Our Guys*, Bernard Lefkowitz meticulously reports on a high-profile incident in Glen Ridge, New Jersey, that included those exact circumstances.[5] One late afternoon in 1989, thirteen high school athletes aged seventeen to eighteen led a mentally impaired seventeen-year-old girl they knew into the home and basement of one of the boys. There they coerced her into a series of horrific sexual acts. As the sexual assault started to unfold, six of the boys left the house because they felt uncomfortable; the others stayed and inten-sified the abuse. After the assault ended, the boys admonished the girl that what took place needed to be kept a secret. The boys threat-ened her by saying she would be kicked out of school and that they would tell her mother if she revealed their secret. Lefkowitz writes that, in a final moment of bonding, the boys, "all in a circle, they clasp one hand on top of the other, all their hands together, like a basketball team on the sidelines at the end of a timeout."[6] For weeks none of the boys who left early told their parents, school officials, or the police. The we-ness that permeated this network of friends and athletes held firm, even in the face of this unconscionable act. This story and others like it demand that we do our best to understand and alter the social forces that permit we-ness to produce this kind of scenario.

Now think about the different layers of we-ness that sometimes define social arrangements. Those who belong to a group typically share a collective sense of we-ness. Some groups can also include one or more clusters of people who have established an additional, more narrowly defined pocket of we-ness. We can think of this subset of people as representing a group within the group. Imagine an extended family involved in a faith organization, a close network of teachers who are also committed to the same school, or a pair of detectives who are partners within a police department. For some undefined period, those who represent this smaller cluster might maintain an allegiance to the larger group while sustaining their own version of affinity within their smaller cluster. The basis for the smaller cluster's separate expression of we-ness may or may not clash with the sentiment that permeates the larger group. Even when conflict exits, it may be of little consequence if the difference does not affect the members' core beliefs and interests. In this situation, people in the smaller cluster may feel sufficiently satisfied with their connection to the larger group that they are willing to tolerate whatever does not sit well with them. Sometimes, however, members in the smaller cluster of folks may decide that they can no longer tolerate their differences with each other. When this happens, individuals in this smaller group may take the initiative to terminate their sense of we-ness to each other, yet continue to honor their commitments to the larger group. Alternatively, entire clusters may stick together and walk away from their commitments to the full group. The splintering of religious sects from their more conventional denominational roots is a prime example of the latter.

Some forms of we-ness may simultaneously foster both healthy and unhealthy outcomes for those directly involved. These situations can become quite contentious for all concerned. In some cases, the participants may not fully understand how their disparate outcomes are connected. A romantic couple may lean on each other to support themselves through various family crises, but their bonding may promote an unhealthy form of codependency for one or both partners.

Finally, should we focus only on immediate outcomes or consider possible long-term outcomes yet to be realized? Some groups sustain their we-ness based on a promise or the hope that the members, or others they wish to influence, will be rewarded in the long run for their efforts. In this instance, group members are prepared to forego short-term benefits because they believe that their joint commitment to work through their issues will produce desirable outcomes later in their lives. Some married couples, for example, hang on for years despite their discomfort with one another and lack of intimacy. They suppress their own frustrations to serve the higher goal of providing what they assume to be a more stable family environment for their young children to thrive.

As these sorts of questions suggest, assessing the implications of we-ness for ourselves and others is not a straightforward matter. Context and perspective matter.

Good Outcomes

Years ago, when I was studying stepfamilies, I interviewed Stephanie and Thomas, who were in their thirties. They had been together as a couple for about seven years and married for the last ten months. I learned that Stephanie's kids from a previous marriage, Danny and Keith, who were eight and six years old, respectively, when Stephanie began dating Thomas, had started to call him "DT" not long after they met. The moniker initially stood for "daddy Thomas." Shortly thereafter, the boys switched to using the full phrase "daddy Thomas" and then just "daddy" or "dad." At the time, the boys' own nonresident father was only sporadically involved in their lives and had never been a very engaged father prior to that period.

Thinking back to when she and Thomas had been together for roughly six months, Stephanie welcomes the chance to reminisce about Thomas's compassion as a family man. She vividly recalls watching Thomas care for Keith when he had a 104°F temperature that would not break:

> He sat there and he loved that child. He took care of that child. He paced the floors at night, that night, over that child. Like it was his own child. And it was just so touching to see somebody do this for somebody else's child. And it's like, that's when you know that this man loves your children. And that's what you're looking for and

hoping for in a stepfamily.... Somebody who will look out for them and protect them. And guide them and nurture them ... I saw that in Thomas that night.

When I separately spoke to Thomas about his relationship with the boys, he described in considerable detail how the older boy, Danny, resisted him at first because he intensely missed his biological father, Don. Thomas related to Danny's plight because he, too, had been raised by a stepfather and he had an eighteen-year-old daughter from a previous marriage who had a stepfather in her life. Shortly after they started to live together, Thomas convinced Stephanie to let Danny go and live with his father.

Things went relatively smoothly for about three months. Then Don dropped Danny off one night for a weekend visit but never returned to pick him up. It turns out that Don permanently left town without telling anyone. From that moment onward Danny was back to living with his mom, Thomas, and his younger brother. Knowing that Danny was devastated by his father leaving him, Thomas took it upon himself to try to console him. Thomas describes going into Danny's room after the incident:

> He had pictures scattered all over his room ... he had hundreds of pictures [of his dad] ... and all I could do is just talk with him. Just tell him, "Look, I know I'm not your dad. I can never fill his shoes. But, if you'll allow me to be a part of your life, I'll love you like it." And from that we have progressed to where we are today.

Now, about five or six years later, Thomas glows as he proudly expresses how he feels about his stepsons:

> I consider them my kids, I mean. I really do. They're my kids. I look at them like they're my boys. I tell everybody, they're my boys. And I don't want to take nothing away from his [Danny's] dad, but I've raised them for so long now, I mean ... you have a child in your home for the amount of time that I have, you feed them long enough, they'll start acting and looking just like you, you know what I'm saying? They just do. They just call me "dad."

Since those early days with Danny, Thomas has worked to strengthen the family we-ness in his household. In addition to devoting lots of time and energy to his stepsons and Stephanie, he and Stephanie expanded their family four years ago by having a daughter of their own. In his mind, having a child together "kind of combines everything" and was instrumental in bringing everyone closer together.

In my conversation with Danny, he confirmed what his mother and Thomas had shared. Danny has a great deal of respect for Thomas and he confidently graded his performance as a father to be an "A+." He admits that his family world is a bit unusual because he remains in contact with his biological father's parents (his paternal grandparents). Danny's whole family will go over to his grandparents who graciously accept his stepfather. As far as he's concerned, they're a big happy family.

The stories this family shared convinced me that they had successfully met the challenges that stepfamilies often confront. Although there is no way to say for sure, it appears that the we-ness these family members have nurtured has had a positive impact on the children and the parents alike. They feel loved, respected, and content with their mutual understanding that they belong to a supportive family.

Whereas the dynamics in a healthy stepfamily have the potential to affect all members in the household favorably, people in many other settings construct a we-ness that generates the most significant benefits for those outside the we-ness circle. Some noteworthy examples include small integrated health care teams, volunteer organizations that target select groups of people in need, local volunteer firefighter units, as well as many others.

One such health enterprise is St. Jude Children's Research Hospital. This prestigious, award-winning organization fosters a strong sense of we-ness among its researchers, clinicians, nurses, administrators, and many other support staff.[7] People may be familiar with this organization, which relies on donations, through its heartwarming television ads. Founded in 1962 by the entertainer Danny Thomas, this organization treats patients without directly charging them for treatment, travel, housing, or food. In 2019, for the ninth consecutive year, it was named one of the "100 Best Companies to

Work For" by *Fortune* magazine.[8] This award goes to companies with "exceptional workplace cultures that foster employee engagement and trust." At St. Jude various research and clinical teams use a family-oriented approach to find cures and treat pediatric patients with cancer and other catastrophic diseases.

One of the premier pediatric research institutions in the world, St. Jude receives high praise from the families it has serviced over the years. It lives up to a quote attributed to Danny Thomas: "There are two kinds of people in this world: The givers and the takers. The takers sometimes eat better, but the givers always sleep better." When people work side by side with like-minded people who are committed to a similar mission, the we-ness they generate can affect an organization's culture.

How formal organizations are structured and operated can influence how we-ness is established and expressed in them. Those who study organizations often differentiate them according to several basic criteria. Two of the important approaches include who benefits (e.g., business owners, clients, public, and participants), and how those in charge secure compliance from workers (e.g., coercion, utilitarian, and normative).[9]

St. Jude is a service organization that relies largely on a kind of normative power. Those who work in this organization have a shared commitment to the organizational mission of helping children and families navigate the crisis of debilitating and life-threatening childhood diseases. Employees also acknowledge that those in charge have a moral authority to lead. They do so even though some are also influenced by more utilitarian concerns related to material rewards. People employed in or volunteering for service areas that work on behalf of children are especially responsive to normative power. They are more likely to forge a special connection to one another and their clientele because perceptions of childhood vulnerability tend to bring out the best in people.

By applying a wider frame to consider social life beyond families and specific organizations, we see how social movements and the various activist groups associated with them can produce good outcomes for people from various backgrounds. Earlier we used the Black Lives Matter movement to illustrate how specific motivations can compel people to develop a sense of we-ness when they are committed to addressing social injustices. Now let's clarify how the LGBTQ+ and queer movements have provided participants with opportunities for both deep dyadic we-ness and ideational forms of we-ness that can produce positive outcomes.

The LGBTQ+ rights movement has evolved over time to create an agenda, and various activist groups, that seeks to alter the political landscape to ensure that all persons have equal rights, including those who do not identify as heterosexual or as cisgender. On June 26, 2015, the Supreme Court of the United States ruled in *Obergefell v. Hodges* that same-sex couples could legally marry with all the conditions and protections accorded to opposite-sex couples. States are now required to recognize same-sex marriages legally performed in other jurisdictions. Although thirty-five states, the District of Columbia, and Guam had already legally established same-sex marriage, the Supreme Court's ruling created a cultural moment that moved public discourse further along the progressive path. Unfortunately, considering the conservative majority that now dominates the Supreme Court in 2022, other cultural moments may be on the near horizon that would reverse the gains that previous rulings have established for the LGBTQ+ community.

Compared to those living in many European countries, Americans are more eager to celebrate marriage as an institution that allows them to establish we-ness in a way that engenders wider public support. Consequently, the *Obergefell v. Hodges* decision is uniquely significant in an American context. It helps accentuate how gay and lesbian rights – despite significant cultural pockets of homophobia – have been advanced in the past half century since the Stonewall uprising of late June 1969.[10] For many, receiving public recognition for one's intimate desire to form a special bond and sense of we-ness with another is not merely a legal remedy; it represents a step toward liberating LGBTQ+ individuals psychologically from a history of public ridicule and persecution.

The history of how a sense of collective we-ness in the LGBTQ+ community emerged in the United States is a long and convoluted one.[11] The disjointed rumblings of organized resistance to the oppressive cultural and political forces that policed sexuality and gender identity go back to roughly the 1870s. However, in the United States, the activist and public consciousness of the LGBTQ+ community can be traced most visibly to the founding of the Mattachine Society in 1950 by Harry Hay and his gay friends in Los Angeles.[12] This gay activist group was created to serve as a support group that could protect and improve the lives primarily of gay men, although many of the founding members also had strong communist beliefs, which ultimately jeopardized the group's political aspirations. Two of the society's primary goals were to "unify homosexuals isolated from their own kind" and "lead the more socially conscious homosexual to provide leadership to the whole mass of social variants."[13] These goals were designed to increase the ideational form of we-ness that can connect gay men and other stigmatized people to a collective identity and consciousness. They also aimed to open doors for marginalized people to create a more empowered view of themselves.

Within a few years, the Mattachine Society evolved to establish chapters in other cities, including Chicago, New York, Washington, DC, and elsewhere. In addition, the original leadership was replaced and the group splintered, with one of the new organizations (ONE, Inc.) investing energy in helping the Daughters of Bilitis – a comparable activist group for lesbians. Although these groups eventually faded from the scene because they were viewed as too tame and traditional in their approach, they provided a basic blueprint for consciousness raising and activism for gays, lesbians, and others who did not fit into the conventional heterosexual, gender binary mold.

Most agree that the Stonewall uprisings in New York City represent the turning point in how gays, lesbians, transgender people, and others with unconventional gender and sexual identities began to establish a more politically motivated group consciousness. Inspired by the identity politics of the civil rights and women's movements, participants in the Stonewall uprising and their allies quickly took advantage of the collective spirit to form two gay activist organizations and three newspapers to promote the rights of gays and lesbians. These activities, coupled with similar supportive responses in other major cities including Chicago, Los Angeles, and San Francisco, helped crystallize the collective consciousness of what would become the LGBTQ+ movement. A year after the uprising, the first gay pride marches were organized and now occur around the world. These have grown into an annual June tradition, culminating in the Stonewall 50 – WorldPride NYC 2019.[14] The latter series of events and celebrations were attended by millions and underscored how a diverse collection of individuals can create a sense of we-ness around what had previously been – and in some circles still are – marginalized identities.

Since the 1950s, a powerful overarching message of inclusion has helped unify millions of people who have almost always been castigated as different. In recent decades, however, battles have been waged over the contested interests of various groups who have been included under the LGBTQ+ label. Early on, white gay men were accused of narrow-mindedly creating a sense of we-ness and an activist community that did not adequately incorporate lesbians. Later, other voices emerged to claim that gay and lesbian groups were not effectively representing persons of color, transgender persons, intersex individuals, and others who rejected the binary model of sexuality and gender. For example, white, cisgender gay men along with trans-exclusionary radical feminists (TERFs – an acronym to describe cisgender women who police the gender of others in an extreme way) still tend to dominate and gatekeep the LGBT umbrella. These race and gender divides are still quite prevalent in the queer community.[15] Many outside the social movement are surprised to learn that the LGBTQ+ community is fraught with such conflict. Outsiders often think of this community as a homogeneous collection of either sexual deviants (the homophobic perspective), or a collection of like-minded marginalized people (the well-intentioned but uninformed perspective).

The gay rights movement's internal struggles were heightened in the 1980s when a subset of activists began to reclaim the once pejorative label "queer" to express a group identity that was more radical than the typical LGBT group.[16] Queer Nation, an organization founded in 1990, justified its adoption of the label by suggesting "'gay' is great. It has its place, but when a lot of lesbians and gay men wake up in the morning we feel angry and disgusted, not gay. So we've chosen to call ourselves queer. Using 'queer' is a way of reminding us how we are perceived by the rest of the world."[17]

Queer Nation's tactic was to build a politically laced we-ness that galvanized the anger shared by many over their marginalization.

At the heart of the Queer Nation movement's challenge to LGBT politics has been its concern that LGBTQ+ groups have been too invested in mainstreaming their existence by advocating for gay marriage, gay adoption, and military inclusion. Members of Queer Nation are generally not interested in promoting these causes. They see those objectives as being part of an assimilationist culture that is beholden to a heteronormative world that sets the ground rules and rewards for social participation. In addition, they are more committed to pursuing a radical transformation of gender and family systems. Ultimately, they want to challenge efforts to assimilate those outside the heteronormative model.

The ongoing debate about the pros and cons of using the "queer" label illustrates how socially constructed categories frame the way we experience our identities and opportunities for we-ness. Although being queer means different things for different people, those who adopt this label tend to politicize their identities and feel more affinity with those who do the same.

Whether our identity labels are contested by others or not, they can produce opportunities for us to define ourselves and search for we-ness with others like us. Options to imagine a specific type of we-ness are not natural; they arise from various social processes. Thus, by constructing labels and embracing their symbolic meanings we can, individually and collectively, make sense of our worlds. This allows us to see ourselves in certain ways and to claim allegiance to others like us. In doing so, we make the effort to search for ways to forge we-ness with others who are defined by similar labels.

Bad Outcomes

Obviously, many groups are not interested in producing social harmony or promoting just causes that are designed to enhance people's opportunities and well-being. In fact, plenty thrive on promoting a we-ness mentality steeped in nastiness; in the extreme cases, building affinity leads to outright hate, bigotry, and even genocide. But there are less extreme cases too that produce ill feelings and poor outcomes even though the people who promote a form of we-ness for themselves are not intent on harming others. Let's dig into the complexity of these issues by exploring some of the bad outcomes that are produced in the name of we-ness. We'll begin by extending our previous discussion about the process of creating we-ness in work settings.

Some work arenas like the police, prisons, the military, and others have historically been shaped by a culture of silence. Terms such as "blue code," "blue shield," or "blue wall of silence" are frequently used to refer to the cultural reality that plagues numerous police departments. Irrespective of what it is called, much has been written about it and it has a long history of being firmly entrenched in different organizations. While it remains one of the troubling narratives of law enforcement and the military, it is also infamously connected to sites beyond the typical work environment. The Catholic Church, sports teams, fraternities, the Mafia, and secret societies (e.g., Freemasons, Skull and Bones) are all widely known to have subcultures that all too often compel members, including supervisors, to protect themselves and others from public accountability. In its broadest form, progressives refer to it as the culture of silence. This is the insidious pattern that delayed justice from being pursued aggressively in the Glen Ridge gang rape case. Just as an organization can distort or cover up the unflattering truth, various formal and informal segments of a community can work to protect some while ignoring others.

By celebrating internal loyalty, the culture of silence reinforces the "brotherhood code." Loyalty to one's coworkers can definitely be an admirable quality. However, those who unquestioningly follow the brotherhood code compromise the virtue of loyalty by protecting coworkers even when they have engaged in despicable acts. Enablers are complicit in wrongdoing by ignoring it, lying to supervisors, and falsifying reports about it, and sometimes even actively participating in egregious behavior themselves. Individuals who adopt this way of interpreting we-ness often get trapped in a vicious cycle of deceit, lies, compromises, and illicit activities.

This code, recognized in American culture for centuries, is regularly depicted in American film and literature. Award-winning Hollywood films such as the *Godfather* series (1972, 1974, 1990) and *Serpico* (1973) underscore the cult of loyalty that permeates the Mafia and some police departments. In *Serpico*, the true and compelling story of a whistle-blowing NYPD officer, Al Pacino plays Frank Serpico, a cop who went undercover during the late 1960s and early 70s to investigate rampant corruption in the form of payoffs and excessive violence by his fellow officers. The movie chronicles how Serpico exposes the blue shield, despite being harassed and threatened by his supervisors and others who were complicit or actively involved in the corruption. After testifying before the Knapp Commission that examined NYPD corruption, Serpico was ultimately awarded the NYPD Medal of Honor for his principled courage in unmasking the tainted spirit of we-ness other police officers had so vigorously tried to protect. Proud to be an honest cop, Serpico has become a cultural icon to many who value and practice integrity in the face of corrupt coworkers who have sworn their allegiance to an unethical collective identity.

In theory, most police departments have internal affairs divisions (IAD) – some of which may be partnered with citizen review boards – that are designed to circumvent the blue shield's corrupt effect and hold police officers accountable to the community. Unfortunately, we are in a "total fog of ignorance" about IADs, according to Samuel Walker, a national expert on police accountability.[18] We therefore know little about how these systems work and if they can transform the work culture that supports the blue code. We do know, however, that regular police officers often view those working in the IADs as operating outside their own borders. An IAD's oversight mission and distinct sense of we-ness often reinforces tensions between subsets of law enforcement because the perceptions of competing loyalties are both deeply held and pervasive. Rank-and-file officers tend to see the IAD staff as being more allied with the public, and therefore hostile to their brotherhood code. A department's police commissioner or chief is often held responsible for bridging the divide between these two groups to sustain a healthy work culture and morale. Some are relatively successful, others not so much.[19]

The public has a major stake in how well its local system of law enforcement operates. Communities differ in how they perceive and manage the prospect that cops sometimes directly abuse their power, and other police officers are complicit in what these dishonest public servants do. How do those of us on the outside looking in feel about this type of institutional we-ness that has gone awry? Do we perceive it as simply an unfortunate aspect of the culture of policing? If so, do we ignore some devious loyalty displays because we believe it doesn't affect us directly? Or are we outraged and outspoken about the culture of silence that protects and perpetuates a dishonorable form of we-ness in one of our community's main institutions?

The dynamics of the public's relationship with the police department is based on an intimate sort of trust. We see and interact with police in our daily lives. Even for those of us who seldom brush elbows with officers, we know that they are only a phone call away. In the aftermath of the 9/11 terrorist attacks, and increasingly as mass shootings become a normalized part of our lived experience, some of us, perhaps many of us, have a renewed appreciation for the risks police take, and the sacrifices they make on our behalf.

But that is a sentiment shared by only some of the public. If you happen to be of darker skin tone, and especially male, you are likely to see things differently. You will be concerned and sometimes fearful when you encounter police because you know all too well the potential outcome of racial profiling. Seen not so much as a unique person, you are the flesh and blood image of a stigmatized category of people. And even if as a person of color you've never felt the gaze of profiling, you may still have mixed feelings because so many of your friends have been less fortunate. Your fear, based on lived experience, is that you are likely to have far less latitude than a white man to live without triggering a prejudicial response.

Civilians may frame their perceptions about police conduct differently than they do when considering the behavior of military personnel. Although these institutions are both expected to protect American citizens, the public's relationship to each differs, especially when we consider whether these folks are disadvantaged or privileged. Some people, especially those who are more likely to be profiled, may believe that police corruption is more likely to affect them directly compared to the misdeeds of military personnel. At the same time, people across the board irrespective of their social standing may judge corruption in the police force as reflecting short-comings in the character of those who serve. In contrast, the public may see the unethical behavior of military personnel as not only blemishes on the character of the offending soldiers, but the misdeeds will also be viewed as sullying the reputation of the United States as a nation and Americans more generally. Thus, some may feel ashamed because of the misconduct of military personnel.

One of the most recent and high-profile cases of this ilk involves the torture and abuse of prisoners by US military personnel and civilian contractors at the infamous Abu Ghraib prison in Iraq in the early 2000s. The public was shocked once the photos that graphically documented the atrocious behavior of soldiers under US military command entered the national news cycle. For many, the depravity of what took place in that prison ignited a national debate about torture.

The culture of silence at this site represents the dark side of we-ness that helped to perpetuate the horrific human rights violations, including torture, physical and sexual abuse, rape, murder, and more. Amazingly, these acts were committed and celebrated in plain sight of others at the prison who either actively participated or looked on without protesting or reporting the abuses. In fact, the photo evidence shows American soldiers enthusiastically posing for their accomplices who photographed their grossly inappropriate behavior. The sadistic power that can be generated by misguided camaraderie between soldiers was on full display in this prison. That these atrocities were executed in a prison setting far from the intense battlefield, where excuses for excessive violence may be more palatable, makes these circumstances even more troubling.

Fortunately, out-of-control displays of we-ness are sometimes challenged by those who find this troubling even though they have a vested interest not to speak up. In this case, one soldier, Sgt. Joseph Darby, who was not directly involved in the activities but was friends with soldiers engaged in mistreating prisoners, turned the photos he had received from a soldier assigned to the prison over to Army investigators several weeks later. He reasoned that "it violated everything I believed in, rules of war…. It was more of a moral call."[20] Those involved in the mistreatment of prisoners did so apparently because they believed that they either had the authority to do so, or that the rules and regulations on acceptable interrogation techniques at the prison were so unclear that they had a free license to improvise.

Although the images were disgusting, they should not be totally surprising. This sort of behavior facilitated by group cohesion is an extension of what we might anticipate, knowing the results of the classic 1971 Stanford prison study led by Professor Philip Zimbardo.[21] In that project, the social psychology department created a simulated prison environment and randomly assigned students to be either guards or prisoners. Zimbardo was curious to see how characteristics of the prison environment might influence individuals to engage in antisocial behavior. Zimbardo contends that the circumstances of the prison environment contributed to guards embracing their authoritative roles. These roles were reinforced by fellow "guards," promoting an authoritative style of we-ness. Ultimately, the study had to be terminated after six days because Zimbardo was persuaded to see that the conditions of the prison had deteriorated to an unacceptable level and students were being subjected to emotional and psychological harm. Although numerous critics have challenged the veracity of the findings,[22] this research suggests that individuals' willingness to engage in questionable behavior can be influenced when others help to create a sense of we-ness and legitimacy while deflecting responsibility.

In the United States, people generally believe that the police and the military are necessary institutions, even though many worry about glaring systemic failings in how they are structured and operated. Thus, when we interpret how we-ness is constructed and practiced in these institutions, we must account for the public's varied opinions of them.

This framing of we-ness in groups that have basic public support differs significantly from how we might consider we-ness in other groups that are routinely disparaged and stigmatized by mainstream society. White nationalist and white supremacist groups, which feature prominently in public discourse in recent years, fit this description. Public debate about these groups has intensified because of former President Trump's nationalist and racist rhetoric as well as the increased news coverage these groups have received. Much of that media coverage is associated with demonstrations and an insurrection organized by white nationalist groups, and the horrific mass shootings in the United States, Norway, and New Zealand in recent years. Many of the shootings have been perpetrated by individuals who have pledged their allegiance to racist groups.

Unlike the police and military, white nationalist groups are marginalized by most Americans even though they and their sympathizers appear to be on the rise in recent years. At the very least, activists affiliated with these groups, as well as their supporters, have become more willing to make their beliefs public. Too many of us have also underestimated the tacit support this movement is receiving from white people who are fearful that America's changing racial and ethnic demographics will adversely affect them.

Since the Charlottesville demonstration in 2017, white nationalist groups have faced challenges in securing meeting spaces, in being able to express themselves online, and have been worried about how people will respond to them at work or in their families. Yet, in July 2019, the Director of the FBI, Christopher Wray, reported that these groups represent a "persistent" and "pervasive" terrorist threat to the United States.[23] In addition, according to the Department of Homeland Security's October 2020 Homeland Threat Assessment, among the Domestic Violent Extremist groups, "racially and ethnically motivated violent extremists – specifically white supremacist extremists (WSEs) – will remain the most persistent and lethal threat in the Homeland."[24]

The we-ness that provides the foundation for these groups tends to emerge, develop, and be expressed in unique ways because these groups are confronted by other groups who challenge their purpose and principles. Activists in white nationalist groups cultivate their views and desire to bond with like-minded people in various ways. The internet and social media make it much easier today for people with hate in their hearts to find each other, bond, and propagate their messages.

Journalist Talia Lavin documents in her gripping and unsettling book, *Culture Warlords: My Journey into the Dark Web of White Supremacy*, just how accessible and depraved this hotbed of hate has become.[25] Lavin went undercover ("antifascist catfishing") for nearly a year between 2019–20 to produce a revealing firsthand account of the online worlds of white supremacists. Using creative tactics to engage with white supremacists, Lavin dives deep into this subculture. As her authentic self, Lavin has been relentlessly attacked for being a Jewish woman who castigates white nationalists on Twitter and in the print media. Those attacks compelled her to explore chat groups, websites, and forums while posing as both women and men sympathetic to those who propagated hate online.

Lavin refutes the popular perception of white supremacists as being limited to a narrow demographic. The men (and women) she engages and observes are recruited from all socioeconomic, educational, and geographic backgrounds. They discuss movement strategies in diverse fields including software programming, the military, and middle management. Although some groups have openly called for violence, many in recent years have tried to mainstream their ideas and make them more palatable to those who are undecided about the movement but harbor race-based grievances as whites.

The Southern Poverty Law Center (SPLC) is committed to keeping track of hate groups that try to elevate whiteness while marginalizing immigrants, especially when they are not of European descent. In general, the roughly 838 hate groups active in the United States as of 2020 share the common mission to privilege white identity as an organizing principle for western societies.[26] Participants' emphasis on we-ness is first and foremost connected to shared whiteness – their belief that they are distinct from and superior to people who identify with other racial categories. Much like Islamic jihadists, white nationalists can radicalize individuals susceptible to feeling as though they have been ignored or disadvantaged by perceived social changes associated with multiculturalism and immigration. Recruitment of new members is one of the most significant objectives of the various movements.

Celebrating we-ness is at the center of the white nationalist movement and recruitment process. The unusual life story of Derek Black (now Ronald Derek Black) captures this reality. Pulitzer Prize–winning reporter Eli Saslow reveals Black's fascinating story in his 2018 book, *Rising Out of Hatred: The Awakening of a Former White Nationalist.* Black was once recognized by many as the heir apparent to the leader of the white nationalist movement in the United States. In 2013, as a nineteen-year-old college student, Black was the rising star of the movement because he had the ideal family pedigree, intellect, and savvy.

Black grew up in a racist family in West Palm Beach, Florida. But his family was not your run-of-the-mill racist family. His father, Don, was a major voice in white supremacy circles for decades. He founded Stormfront, the first white nationalist and neo-Nazi website, was a grand wizard in the Ku Klux Klan (KKK), and he was convicted in 1981 of trying to topple the government of Dominica in hopes of white nationalists creating their own government. Additionally, Derek Black was the godson of David Duke, perhaps the highest-profile white supremacist in America, who used to be married to Black's mother. Even as a youngster, Black took an active role in advocating for white supremacy by organizing a kids' page on his father's website when he was eleven years old and then later joining his father to host a radio show that promoted the movement.[27]

His father claimed that Derek had an uncanny ability to relate to people and had specific gifts that enabled him to frame the white nationalist movement in a way that made it more appealing to others. From his birth, Black was surrounded by people he loved whose voices preached an ideology of racial separatism and hate that consumed his own sense of self. The family bonds he so valued came with a divisive political agenda based on othering non-whites. We-ness was earned by denigrating others and dismissing their legitimate claims that were based on structural inequalities. Although Black did not condone violence, he was forceful in calling for a transformative shift in our society that privileged whites' "best interests."

Then, in the fall of 2010, something unexpected slowly began to happen. After becoming a student majoring in history at New College of Florida in Sarasota, Black experienced a remarkable and incremental transition. As he spent more time hanging out and discussing race issues with young people who challenged his thinking, Black reversed his racist world view. Ultimately, in 2013 Black reached out to the Southern Poverty Law Center, an organization highly critical of his past views and actions, to publish his heartfelt public apology for his previous support of white nationalism. Then, shortly after the results of the 2016 presidential election were in, Black spoke out in a *New York Times* opinion essay, "Why I Left White Nationalism." He concluded his piece by writing, "Mr. Trump's victory must make all Americans acknowledge that the choice of embracing or rejecting multiculturalism is not abstract. I know this better than most, because I've followed both paths. It is the choice of embracing or rejecting our own people."[28]

Here, Black asserts a more encompassing form of we-ness compared to his former divisive perspective that called for segmenting whites from the rest of humanity. His multicultural perspective on we-ness reflects the authentic friendships he forged at New College with people who differed from himself. His well-documented friendships with people like Matthew Stevenson and Allison Gornic stood in stark contrast to the way he experienced the world that had been taught to him by his family and white nationalist contacts for two decades.

Derek Black's story illustrates how powerful our families can be in shaping our world views during our early years. Families, in turn, are also subjected to outside cultural and structural conditions that can help to perpetuate racist views. Journalist Fareed Zakaria captured part of this sentiment in his special report, "State of Hate: The Explosion of White Supremacy," which aired August 10, 2019, on CNN. Referring to white supremacy views, Zakaria observes that "the fact that these views are so deep-seated, subconsciously part of the modern psyche, is perhaps why we had been unable to see the growing danger in our midst."[29]

We must not forget that the project of the American nation has a stained, four-hundred-year legacy that is intimately tied to the genocide of Indigenous peoples and to institutionalized slavery. Increasingly, we are realizing that racist beliefs are not only buried in our subconscious; they remain a vital part of many Americans' conscious daily activities. These beliefs have also had a lingering effect on the structural conditions that disproportionately constrain the life choices that persons of color can make.[30] In 2020, the median family income for non-Hispanic whites was $74,912 compared to only $45,870 for African Americans.[31] The difference is even starker when comparing median net worth. In 2019 dollars, white households had a net worth that was nearly eight times greater than African American households ($188,200 versus $24,100).[32] Consistent with this pattern, almost three-quarters of white households are homeowners whereas less than half of African American households are homeowners.[33] Thus, thoughtful reflection on how Americans construct their national sense of we-ness needs to incorporate the complex issues that the *New York Times'* "1619 Project" addressed to highlight the four-hundred-year anniversary of when slaves from West Africa were first brought to our shores.[34] Racism and implicit bias continue to operate in insidious ways for many Americans.

Similarly, long-standing sexist ideologies are typically connected to white nationalist agendas because both are opposed to feminism. Male supremacy groups are still embedded in our society, and several have flourished in the internet age.[35] Return of Kings was one such group that was identified by the Southern Poverty Law Center as a hate group. After six years, its founder Daryush "Roosh" Valizadeh, stopped uploading material to the site in October 2018 after publishing 5,800 articles. In one blog post, he wrote: "The demographic crisis the West faces today is primarily due to allowing women to do as they please instead of imposing healthy standards on their behavior and choices. The direct cause of this horror movie is giving women the vote."[36] These groups, like the white nationalist groups with which they overlap, have emerged in response to their followers' fears of having their privileges challenged by others. In the case of male supremacy groups, women and feminism are the foils that have supercharged men to seek comfort in misogynistic beliefs and traditional forms of masculinity. For years, the Return of Kings provided men a sense of community as displaced warriors who sought to regain their "rightful" place controlling social institutions and public discourse.

Again, with these groups we see how a subset of individuals looks to experience camaraderie and a sense of we-ness with like-minded individuals at the expense of others whom they distrust and disrespect. In her 2018 article in *The New Republic*, journalist Stephanie Russell-Kraft captures why, in perpetuating a form of hateful masculinity, male supremacy groups are dangerous bastions for misguided attempts to forge we-ness:

> When Marc Lépine murdered 14 women at Montreal's École Polytechnique in 1989, he claimed that he was "fighting feminism." When Anders Breivik murdered 77 people in Norway in 2011, he was in large part motivated by his hatred of feminism, which he considered a poison and threat to the future of European men. And when Elliot Rodger killed six people in Isla Vista, California, in 2014, he said he did it to punish young women for rejecting him and sleeping with other men instead.[37]

These mass shootings demonstrate how the pursuit of we-ness can, unfortunately, promote bad and deadly outcomes.

Another disturbing type of misogyny-fueled killing involves a subset of men who have come to name themselves the "incels" (involuntary celibate). These straight men have built a fringe political ideology couched in white supremacy and misogyny that focuses on their anger over being "denied" sex by young, beautiful women. Alek Minassian, who killed ten people and injured sixteen in Toronto in 2018, wrote on Facebook prior to inflicting this carnage, "The Incel Rebellion has already begun!" In a 2018 *New Yorker* article, "The Rage of the Incels," writer Jia Tolentino reveals the camaraderie angry incels share with one another in their targeted online posts: "Women are the ultimate cause of our suffering"; "They are the ones who have UNJUSTLY made our lives a living hell.... We need to focus more on our hatred of women. Hatred is power."[38] In addition to stigmatizing women, incels also build their sense of we-ness by distancing themselves from the men who treat women respectfully, denigrating these men for apparently being engaged in a "white-knighting" performance style of masculinity. Tolentino concludes that incels are not really interested in sexual redistribution. Rather, "What they want is extremely limited and specific: they want unattractive, uncouth, and unpleasant misogynists to be able to have sex on demand with young, beautiful women. They believe that is a natural right." As a subset of angry men, incels welcome online opportunities to reinforce their ideational we-ness.

In her journalistic undercover work, Lavin vividly captures the destructive force of we-ness that users of the dark web can generate. Their sense of we-ness is forged out of a toxic combination of despair and rage. One disturbing and self-destructive pattern to incels' posts is their repeated reference to suicide. Lavin witnessed how numerous users nonchalantly responded to another user when he posted that he had just bought a gun and was preparing to commit suicide. Users adopted a perverse style of empathy to express affinity with the suicidal man based on their shared frustrations with being "rejected" by women. They offered what they no doubt perceived to be supportive replies: "Godspeed. Watch the sunrise and listen to your favorite bands," "See you in incelhalla [incel Valhalla] lad," and "Enjoy the otherside friend."[39] These replies are a stark reminder that forging a sense of we-ness takes on many forms and is not an inherently productive experience. Context matters.

Just as people's investment in their racial, ethnic, and gender identity has inspired some to establish their affinity with others and has sometimes produced negative outcomes, the same can be said about people's commitment to religious beliefs. Throughout history and across the globe, people's religious zeal and commitment to bond with others who share those beliefs, while demonizing others who have different beliefs, have been the basis for countless wars and massive amounts of bloodshed. As I noted in the previous chapter, outside of religious wars, those involved in sects and cults have sometimes experienced negative consequences based on their fervent beliefs that justified their we-ness.

Notable among these stories is the murder-suicide event involving Jim Jones's Peoples Temple in Georgetown, Guyana, in 1978.[40] In all, 918 people died, with most adults committing mass suicide. Over several decades, Jones had created a new religious movement that promoted a "religious communalism" by combining aspects of Christianity with socialist/communist philosophies. This movement also stressed racial equality. Those who died at the Guyana settlement had followed Jones there from California to escape media scrutiny and an American government that they perceived to be increasingly fascist. Throughout his tenure as the leader of the Peoples Temple, Jones effectively used the "us" against "them" rhetorical style of mind control to coerce followers to relinquish their individual hold over property and to commit themselves wholeheartedly to his philosophy and directives that included communal living. The tragic and ultimate evidence that most of Jones's adult followers had fully embraced his message of deviant we-ness was their willingness to commit suicide, and to force their children to do the same, at his command.

More recently, we can point to the pursuit of we-ness in the Buddhafield cult, led by Michel Rostand (now Andreas), which received national attention in 2016 when Will Allen, a former member of the cult for twenty-two years, released his "insider's" documentary film, *Holy Hell*.[41] The film was shown at the Sundance Film Festival and later presented on a CNN special. The group, founded in 1985 in West Hollywood, California, was later moved to Austin, Texas, and was most recently located in Oahu, Hawaii. Allen used footage he shot as the group's videographer and incorporated recent interviews with distressed former members. These members share their reflections about their previous willingness to accept Michel as their spiritual guru because he was charismatic, playful, and artistic. He claimed to be able to put people in touch with God and most believed him. Those who spoke about their former involvement share how they jointly built a utopia of alternative living.

Allen himself saw Michel as an "awakened master." In an interview with *The Guardian*, without using the term, Allen alludes to the powerful draw of we-ness in the cult: "The community turned out to be the thing that bonded us together and kept us there for so long."[42] He adds: "The community provided this immediate sense of unconditional love. Nobody judged each other; we were there with open arms loving everybody as individuals. That wasn't something I had found in college, and I hadn't found that in my family either." However, one former follower describes how Michel over time became increasingly strange, paranoid, and possessive, while another disillusioned ex-member describes Michel as wanting to be worshiped. In retrospect, some former members express how they feel as though they were psychologically manipulated and sexually abused. For example, Allen talks about how Michel urged his followers to "keep holy company" by avoiding people outside the group. Like other cult leaders, Michel used strategies that emphasized the "othering" process. He tried to isolate his followers and make them more emotionally and psychologically dependent on the group.

Commitment to the Buddhafield's version of we-ness was paramount. Most people who have no personal experience with a cult find it hard to imagine that people can be so devoted and misled – for so long – by "leaders" like Jim Jones and Michel Rostand.[43] Unfortunately, our drive to feel a sense of belonging too often overwhelms our self-protective, rational decision-making. This is especially true for those of us who are vulnerable and insecure yet bubbling with an innocent idealism about the world.

Young children, the most vulnerable among us, are also easy marks for the persuasive efforts of religious leaders who preach extreme, divisive beliefs. Born into the infamous, ultraconservative Westboro Baptist Church located in Topeka, Kansas, Megan Phelps-Roper has a compelling story to tell.[44] In *Unfollow: A Memoir of Loving and Leaving the Westboro Baptist Church*, Phelps-Roper vividly describes how she was initially indoctrinated into and then left at age twenty-six this largely family-run church that her grandfather, Fred Phelps, founded in 1954.[45] Recounting her experience with the church that has been called by the Southern Poverty Law Center the "most obnoxious and rapid hate group in America," she says she was subjugated to a hateful religious belief system, one that believes in predetermination: "Life was framed as an epic spiritual battle between good and evil. The good was my church and its members, and the evil was everyone else."[46] As Phelps-Roper recalls, she made her debut as a five-year-old on the picket line with her family, "surrounded by a few dozen relatives, with my tiny fists clutching a sign that I couldn't read yet: 'Gays are worthy of death.'" From her toddler days to young adulthood, she was on the front lines being exposed to and spouting her family's inflammatory hate speech that is publicly expressed on the church's website and its "picketing ministry."

But Megan Phelps-Roper, like Derek Black, began to transform her hate into love once she opened her ears to more moderate voices. In 2009 she found Twitter and started to engage in spirited, but civil, exchanges with her opposition that were marked by a genuine curiosity. Three years later, Phelps-Roper and her younger sister made the bold and heart-wrenching decision to leave their religion, and by necessity, their family. During her first year away, and at the urging of one of the friends she had met on Twitter, Phelps-Roper and her sister found themselves hanging out with some unlikely company in a Jewish community in Los Angeles. Phelps-Roper describes how "We slept on couches in some home of a Hasidic rabbi and his wife and their four kids; the same rabbi that I'd protested three years earlier with a sign that said, 'Your rabbi is a whore.' We spent long hours talking about theology, and Judaism, and life while we washed the dishes in their kosher kitchen and chopped vegetables for dinner. They treated us like family. They held nothing against us, and again I was astonished."[47] This family-like atmosphere, filled with an open-minded type of love, was in stark contrast to her own family that was incredibly close, but operated based on a controlling, conditional type of love.

Since leaving the church, Phelps-Roper has issued a public apology letter and found various ways to share her story to inspire others trapped by hate to open their minds and to listen. She has also created a new sense of we-ness by marrying someone who befriended her on Twitter and helped her transform her world view and her own identity.

Individuals like Phelps-Roper, who have an intimate understanding of what it was once like to be swallowed up by a controlling family and religious doctrine, but who are now free to reflect on their experience, can share unique insights about group belonging. Phelps-Roper astutely observes that the hard-line position her previous church took stems from

very *human forces* – everything from fear, family, guilt, and shame, to cognitive dissonance and confirmation bias. These are forces whose power affects us all, consciously and subconsciously, to one degree or another at every stage of our lives. And when these forces are

coupled with group dynamics and a belief system that caters to so
many of our most basic needs as human beings – a sense of meaning,
of identity, of purpose, of reward, of goodness, of community – they
provide group members with an astonishing level of motivation to
cohere and conform, no matter the cost.[48]

Thus, while Phelps-Roper's heart and mind were molded by the "us"
versus "them" mentality that defines Westboro Baptist Church's
extreme religious theology, the main ingredients for this style of
indoctrination are recognizable facets of our everyday human experience. As children, we want to be loved, affirmed, and accepted by
our family while also figuring out who we are and who we can be.
Because we want to belong, and are especially vulnerable as children, it is not surprising that children can be convinced to adopt
hateful messages that enable them to feel connected to their family.

The preceding examples of we-ness gone bad demonstrate how
our inner urge to belong can spread much like a metastasizing cancer that infects the social body. If left unchecked, our desire for we-
ness can be either a flaw or an asset, as defined by ourselves and
others. Our fierce desire to belong can delude us into ignoring the
atrocities we are capable of perpetuating as we rashly pursue our
cherished state of we-ness. In the process of chasing we-ness we
too often lose sight of our individuality and moral compass. Or
we may simply embrace a narrow and distorted image of moral-
ity. Mesmerized by the glow of the charismatic leader, seduced by
the elixir of group power and cohesion, insulated by the perception
that our complicity is irrelevant, we normalize both the ideologies
of hate and the unethical behaviors they generate. "But not me ... I
never would do that!" some will be quick to profess. Yet, the alarming reality shows that the potential to be swept up in the wave of
mob mentality resides in most of us. This is especially true when we
are apathetic, unwilling to challenge the motivation behind the tidal
surge of demands for our naïve obedience.

One intriguing piece of evidence that supports this unsettling
pattern was produced in 1967 during a history class experiment at
Cubberley High School in California. A student listening to a lecture
about Nazi Germany interrupted the twenty-five-year-old teacher,

Ron Jones, to ask a profound question along the lines of: "How could the German people claim ignorance of concentration camps and the horrific way Jews were being treated?" That question prompted Mr. Jones to initiate what would become a controversial school experiment – the Third Wave.[49] Eventually two hundred students would participate in this one-week project.

According to his own account published five years later, Mr. Jones began his experiment on the Monday following the student's question. He organized the class around five different lessons that week, teaching a new theme each day in the following order: "strength through discipline," "strength through community," "strength through action," "strength through pride," and "strength through understanding." From the start, Mr. Jones required the students to adopt a uniform code of behavior that included a specific sitting posture and a regimented way to both ask and answer questions.

By Tuesday he had introduced the group name (Third Wave), a class motto to recite that accentuated the "community" theme, and a mandatory class hand salute that involved raising the right hand to the side of the right shoulder in a curled position. Students who belonged to the Third Wave were expected to display the salute within and outside of school and they were expected to police one another.

On Wednesday, Mr. Jones issued membership cards, identified several students to monitor and report behavior code violations, gave specific school-related assignments to individual students, and asked everyone to identify one reliable friend who might want to join the emerging group. One student, described by Mr. Jones as someone who was big, didn't fit in, and ate alone, convinced Mr. Jones to allow him to be the teacher's personal "bodyguard" at school. By Tuesday and Wednesday, kids not in the class were skipping other classes to participate.

On Thursday, exhausted and worried about how he might be negatively affecting the students, Mr. Jones told his group that the Third Wave was a national program to identify enthusiastic students who were willing to fight for political change. He also announced that there would be an auditorium rally the next day at noon and that one thousand similar high school groups across the country would be announcing their commitment to the youth movement.

When Friday came, Mr. Jones created an assembly environment that was buzzing with excitement. It included some of his friends who, unbeknownst to the students, were posing as reporters and photographers. After having the full assembly demonstrate their commitment to perform on command for the "press" by calling out in chorus fashion, "strength through discipline," Mr. Jones directed the audience's attention to a TV set on stage that would be displaying the national press conference. He turned it on and after seven minutes of the students diligently staring at a test pattern on the screen, Mr. Jones approached the TV, turned it off, and told the students that "There is no leader! There is no such thing as a national youth movement called the Third Wave. You have been used. Manipulated. Shoved by your own desires into the place you find yourself. You are no better or worse than the German Nazis we have been studying." He then turned on a projector and the Nuremberg Rally thundered onto the screen. Afterward, he debriefed the students and talked to them about the allure of belonging and the fear of being left out.

Mr. Jones's experiment began and evolved organically; there was apparently little systematic planning. In the end, it left many students crying and confused. It also had a lasting effect on at least some of the students based on their retrospective accounts and it has been adapted into a film and a play format. Yet, over the four-year period Mr. Jones taught at the school, no one to his knowledge admitted that they attended the Third Wave rally. They presumably were embarrassed that they had been duped. The rapid trajectory of students into a state of disciplined social order reveals that the students had longed for a sense of belonging and purpose.

The social dynamics of this experiment remind us of the consequences of authoritarian rule, and the potential energy that can be unleashed by a groupthink mentality. The rituals and routines eerily mirror Trump's campaign-style rallies. Many Trump loyalists who attend these rallies, like Mr. Jones's students, are prepared to suspend their ability to ascertain the basic truth, or to ignore it, once they have latched onto an aggrieved identity that places them in the midst of an organized spectacle anchored to a special sense of we-ness. Doing whatever it takes to maintain the identity in which they've invested, participants squelch any desire to seek and act upon the truth. In Mr. Jones's auditorium remarks to the students on that infamous Friday, he explained how "Fascism is not just something other people did. No. It's right here. In this room. In our own personal habits and way of life. Scratch the surface and it appears. Something in all of us. We carry it like a disease."[50]

Mr. Jones's observations are especially chilling today. As many have stated over the years, it is long past due that we reckon honestly with the stark reality that so much hate permeates America's everyday culture. Despite the massive reservoir of kindness and generosity that fills America with hope, a seemingly endless river of hate continues to flow through the veins of a critical mass of its people. Thus, the reasonable majority should worry about how unchecked hate stains our culture and that so many people are susceptible to authoritarian propaganda and rule. Unfortunately, I believe Richard Cohen, president of the Southern Poverty Law Center, is spot on when he says, "Hate has frayed the social fabric of our country." And he astutely adds that "Knitting it back together will take the efforts of all segments of our society – our families, our schools, our houses of worship, our civic organizations, and the business community. Most of all, it will take leadership – political leadership – that inspires our country to live up to its highest values."[51] Ultimately, those American values honor democracy and a community spirit of empathic we-ness that transcends bigoted and reckless individual self-interest. The moral and courageous political leadership Cohen calls for to inspire our country has been sadly lacking in recent years. Who can forget, for example, that 147 Republican lawmakers followed Trump's autocratic instructions and voted to overturn the election results after the attack on the Capitol?

Mixed

Although the uncritical, collective pursuit of religious and spiritual beliefs can result in tragic consequences, faith groups frequently and successfully mobilize their we-ness to address natural disasters, wars, political upheavals, poverty, and more. Because of the bonds people of faith share, much is also achieved outside of assisting the victims of natural or human-made crises. I've interviewed various youth ministers and rabbis who are proud of how their kids develop rapport with each other while on mission trips to help the less fortunate. Religious leaders frequently create opportunities for young people to build their capacity to empathize and show compassion while developing strong ties with other participants. Youth also have a chance to develop their ideational expressions of we-ness if they solidify their identity as a person of faith who is committed to helping others.

The typical mission trips that faith leaders have led and discussed with me are distinct from the more conventional, and sometimes controversial, forms of missionary work that have been criticized for being rooted in colonialism.[52] The more conventional forms of missionary work tend to involve persons of faith visiting areas, often less developed countries, where they preach their faith and try to convert the Indigenous people to their religious beliefs. In the process, they seek to encourage others to adopt their own faith-based, ideational form of we-ness. In contrast, many contemporary youth mission trips are designed to provide volunteer service and set an example of doing good works by rebuilding homes or schools, offering disaster relief, providing health care services, or extending some other type of assistance. In youth mission trips, the youth and faith leaders are more likely to interact in prayer with other members of their organization than to proselytize to those they are trying to help.

While religious mission trips at times emphasize conversion and at other times service as part of their ideational we-ness, this mixed result is also apparent in other types of groups. Street and prison gangs can also be used to illustrate the complexity of judging the mixed set of outcomes groups can produce. Many state agencies refer to a criminal street gang as "any ongoing organization, association or group of three or more persons, whether formal or informal, having as one of its primary activities the commission of one or more of the criminal acts [...], having a common name or common identifying sign or symbol, and whose members individually or collectively engage in or have engaged in a pattern of criminal gang activity."[53] In the United States, it's estimated that there are roughly 33,000 gangs with 1.4 million active gang members.[54]

On the street, youth follow many paths to become gang members, but they frequently lack a close parent-child relationship, have a general feeling of not belonging to a family, and fear that without protection they are at risk in their dangerous community. Not having a tight, supportive family can open the doors for young people to consider how gang membership would offer them the feeling of we-ness and respect that they desperately want and need.[55]

Belonging to a gang also comes with built-in rituals and membership symbols that heighten the we-ness feeling. One violent initiation ritual determines whether someone can be accepted into a gang. Subjecting oneself to a brutal beating by the other gang members is a common tradition. Alternatively, entrance into a gang may require a prospective gang member to commit a crime to prove their loyalty to the gang's unwritten code of conduct. A more innocuous gang ritual that was depicted in a documentary I used to show my students years ago about an East Oakland gang showed members visiting the grave sites of deceased members. Surrounding the grave site, the young people would take turns pouring beer onto the grave while offering positive commentary about the deceased. The typical symbols that matter to gang members include the gang's name, a personalized gang nickname, neighborhood landmarks, tattoos, and colors. These symbols solidify a gang's group identity and members' personal connection to the gang and its unwritten street code.

Street gangs can offer members access to shelter, food, drugs, and other resources they would otherwise not have. The sentiment that members should be prepared to die for their "brothers" offers gang members the unconditional love they often lack in their own families. They also experience a sense of empowerment because they can control certain features of their troubled neighborhood. Most do not experience this sort of empowerment in their own homes and families. Ultimately, belonging to a gang that controls physical space while instilling fear in others can be an alluring option for youth who are scared, lonely, and believe they have no legitimate options to satisfy their need to do something ambitious.

But one does not have to have a dysfunctional family or inattentive parents to be motivated to join a gang. Nor does a young person need to lack the intellect or academic prowess to excel in a school system. This is confirmed by the remarkable story of Karl Lokko, a former high-profile gang leader in Brixton, South London, England, who is now a dynamic community leader and activist.[56] Raised in an immigrant family in a low-income neighborhood, Lokko had strict, hardworking parents who paid attention to him. Lokko was also a bright young man who excelled at school. Yet, Lokko longed to pursue his dreams to be somebody consequential. He wanted so badly to feel a sense of belonging beyond his family that as a twelve-year-old he created his own gang. Over time, Lokko recognized that the gang gave him a sense of ownership. He also enjoyed the feeling of being part of something bigger than himself, as did his fellow gang members.

Eventually, though, he redefined his relationship to gang life and the we-ness it brought him. Lokko turned his life around after experiencing a series of random moments and reflections, including holding one of his best friends in his arms as he died from a gunshot wound, and feeling the support he received from his local minister, Pastor Mimi Asher. Since his transformation, Lokko has found his we-ness through his new marriage and son. In addition, he's created opportunities for young people to avoid or leave gang life and to find purpose in being active in more productive groups. Although others in the United States and elsewhere have similarly walked away from a gang-oriented we-ness to create more productive interpersonal bonds, far too many either die first or end up in prison.

For some, prison time mirrors gang life on the streets. Those who run in street gangs often associate with a prison gang if they serve time. Although prison gangs have limited control over their activities, including their mobility, the practical and symbolic dimensions of a gang's promotion of we-ness are pervasive and profound. Prison gangs flourish in both men's and women's prisons by constructing tight alliances and often reinforcing rigid divisions.

Researchers who study prison gangs continue to debate whether meaningful gender differences exist in how gangs operate in prisons. Conventional wisdom holds that compared to gang activity in men's prisons, the gangs in women's prisons are more family-like in their goals and the way they operate. That view has been complicated in recent years. One research team concluded that what researchers have frequently called "pseudo-families" in women's prisons serve the same functions as gangs in men's prisons. They suggest that pseudo-families in women's prisons provide the following functions: "emotional support, economic support, vehicles for coercion and aggression, and the need for protection from intimidation and assault."[57] In one study, when female inmates with twenty years of experience behind bars talked about their prison experience, many were quick to use familial language to describe the role-playing that takes place in prison. According to one,

> It may be a lot of middle aged women that take younger girls and … these girls would be like their little play children. And the older woman might be like their grandmother. So, they might have this little family thing where … this group of girls is sisters and the older one is their mom and the older lady is their grandmother. So it's like a little family thing, you know, and they might hang together.

Another female inmate describes the motivation for women to join these social groups that can provide a sense of we-ness: "I would say sometimes just loneliness or looking for true friendship. Or their mother may have not been there for them and now they have an older person that cares about them. Or just belonging to somewhere where the group is positive." But not all female inmates depict these family-like relationships in a positive light. For example, one woman asserts:

> I find it's important to give people a sense of independence in decision making because a lot of people who come in here want to fall

into family groups as the child or the baby. They want someone else to keep making their decisions for them. And I think it's more important for the dominant person to instill in that individual their own decision making ... help them to be their own person.

These female prisoners, and others like them, reveal the possible pros and cons of inmates creating deep dyadic ties with other prisoners that are family-like in nature. The mix of reactions raises serious questions: When does a person's involvement in prison gang culture help them psychologically endure the dark moments of prison life? To what extent does being part of a prison gang help some members survive their prison time without being killed or physically harmed? Alternatively, does the family-like support that produces a sense of we-ness in prison suffocate some inmates' ability to learn coping skills that will enable them to thrive on their own and become effective decision-makers? More generally, do inmates in prison gangs deepen their commitment to live a life of crime once they are released?

As not all readers are familiar with gang life, perhaps a more familiar scene for many is the world of sports, which is another context that often harbors mixed outcomes that stem from the we-ness produced by team-building activities. Sports culture is full of examples of how individuals learn valuable life lessons related to cooperation, competition, and hard work in a team environment. What receives less public attention is how homophobic and sexist locker-room talk and antics reinforce the bonds players forge through the actual highs and lows they share in their practices, games, and other time together. Fortunately, in recent decades public discourse and scholarly scrutiny is more likely to call out these disturbing tendencies and their relation to abuse against women.[58] But the homophobic and sexist mentality is still part of sports culture and is sometimes dismissed as inconsequential.

In 2014, the sports world was intrigued by the Michael Sam, Jr. phenomenon that touched college and professional football. Sam, an All-American and Southeastern Conference Defensive Player of the Year at Missouri, had come out as gay to his teammates in August 2013. Contrary to stereotypical expectations of how football players might react to gay people in the locker room, Sam reported that his team was supportive. In this instance, it appears that the young men's team spirit held sway and enabled the players to value Sam both as a high-quality player and person. He had apparently earned their respect on and off the field. It suggested that a bit of progress had been made in the struggle to end homophobia in our sports culture. In fact, the players were much more supportive than his father was.

Missouri students also demonstrated their convictions about a form of we-ness as fellow students and presumably as persons who shared progressive views on LGBTQ+ issues. A week after Sam had shared his story about being a gay college football player to a national audience on ESPN's *Outside the Lines*, he returned to Mizzou Arena on campus. He was there to participate with his teammates in a halftime trophy ceremony held during the college basketball game acknowledging the football team's recent Cotton Bowl victory. An anti-gay activist and fifteen members of the Westboro Baptist Church staged a protest of Sam's appearance. As a counterprotest, thousands of Missouri students formed a "human wall" in front of them. Such a protest displayed the deep dyadic we-ness many friends shared with one another. It also signaled many students' commitment to an ideational we-ness that represented their allegiance to a progressive thought community. This encounter illustrates how social life is riddled with stories about competing convictions anchored in we-ness expressions – alternatively projected as battles between good and evil, right and wrong, moral and immoral.

We-ness projects dealing with intimate partner violence have also altered the sports landscape. Since 2014, the National Football League, to its credit, has sponsored public service campaigns and partnered with different organizations to address relationship violence. These efforts were prompted by the highly publicized incident involving former Baltimore Ravens running back Ray Rice who punched his now-wife Janay in an elevator. The incident was caught on surveillance video which was then released to the public. The event and extensive media coverage it received galvanized the league and many of its players to assert their opposition to this sort of male aggression. The players' response represented their willingness to break ranks over misguided displays of masculinity in the locker room and men's abuse of women more generally. It also signaled a shift in professional football players' ability and willingness to mobilize to show empathy and compassion for abused women.

A surprising twist to the Ray and Janay episode, especially to those who did not know them, was that they publicly asserted their commitment to one another shortly after the incident and were married weeks later. Now the married parents of two children, this couple continues to represent the public face of relationship resiliency and a deep dyadic form of we-ness. In a 2018 interview aired on CBS's *This Morning*, the couple shared their reflections on the incident and their journey since that infamous evening in the elevator. Janay explained that while she never thought of leaving the relationship, she believed they had work to do at the time.[59] She added, "I knew that wasn't him in that moment" and she emphasized that she had known him since she was fifteen years old. And Ray, who indicated he didn't deserve a second chance in the NFL, affirmed that he got his second chance because Janay gave it to him. He stressed the value of their friendship before the incident, alluding to how that helped them get past the "darkest moments."

Many feminists see Janay's approach to navigating the we-ness she constructed with Ray as problematic. They worry that her willingness to marry Ray so quickly after the incident, or to marry him at all, sends a bad message to those in similar situations. To them, it ignores the repetitive pattern that tends to define domestic violence.

No doubt just about everyone not intimately involved in a gang or an abusive relationship is likely to view these situations as representing undesirable forms of we-ness. But we should recognize that personal growth and valuable life lessons can come from troubled times and spaces. In addition, the we-ness struggles that emerge in gang life and abusive relationships underscore the importance of understanding the transitional aspects to forming, solidifying, transitioning out of, and recovering from positive as well as negative forms of we-ness. If we deem certain forms of we-ness as good, then we need to think about whether we want to pursue that brand of we-ness. How can we grow and maximize the power of a healthy we-ness that suits our needs as well as those of others? For the types of we-ness we deem as unappealing, perhaps repulsive, how do we avoid them and encourage others to do the same? Finally, what can we do to help restructure the norms and ethical standards of the mixed-outcome settings to ensure that we heighten the good while discarding the bad?

5

Navigating Transitions

We-ness – the mere mention of it can conjure up an image of a stable union, perhaps one of vital import and resiliency. But we-ness also entails the shifting tides of shared and contested beliefs, attitudes, feelings, commitments, and identities we express throughout our lives. Although some of us have more predictable and stable lives than others, we all move into and out of different social arrangements that enable us to foster bonds with others and commitments to the ideas that define who we are.

To know the feeling of we-ness, we must transition into it, one way or another. Then, once we fold that sense of we-ness into our daily experience, we casually or thoughtfully make numerous decisions, or they are made for us. On the most basic level, our decisions inform how we try to preserve our we-ness as is, modify its form to fit our needs, or eventually move on with our lives without it – recognizing that doing so will alter our lives and identity for better or worse. Our limited time and resources can influence our decision-making about entering, managing, and leaving states of we-ness. Convenience often matters. It can motivate us to either take on yet another commitment or to ease our responsibilities by letting one go.

With most important transitions involving our group belonging, we experience a wide range of emotions. These include fear, hope, anxiety, tranquility, uncertainty, and more. Many of our transitional moments force us to manage the learning curve and stress that often accompany personal and social change. Many times, once we settle into our we-ness arrangement and new mode of thinking, we stay the course because we are creatures of habit. We grow accustomed to our daily routines and interpersonal networks, even those beset with emotional, psychological, and physical discomfort. And when we feel trapped by circumstances that impinge on our we-ness, we often employ coping mechanisms. Our laziness, indecisiveness, or fear of the unknown beyond our regular state of we-ness can also push us to persevere with the status quo.

Sometimes, despite our best efforts, we are denied our preferred choice to keep our we-ness intact. Romantic partners, friends, employers, coaches, business partners, voters, and others can force us to abandon our immediate experience with we-ness. We might kick and scream to keep our desired version of we-ness, but we eventually resign ourselves to the reality that we alone do not control our destiny to we-ness. Conditions beyond our control can alter our lives when loved ones die, groups disband, or we lose our ability to fit in with others as we once did.

Losing our special we-ness can be devastating and affect us for years, even a lifetime. Unfortunately, when we lose our we-ness, some of us lose our purpose in life – at least temporarily. In the darkest moments, our detachment from others may even lead us to the ultimate recourse to end our lives or to take the lives of others. We must also come to grips with those less common but equally profound cases that signal that it is not our lack of we-ness, but instead our intense expression of we-ness involving others or a commitment to a radical belief system, that compels us to choose dying for a specific cause. The acute connection between the presence or absence of we-ness and suicide raises the stakes to understand more fully the transitional forces that affect how we-ness is established, nurtured, and restructured to produce either the uplifting or demoralizing outcomes that grip our lives.

These transitional markers relate to both the deep dyadic ties we form with others and the ideational we-ness we construct when we align ourselves with a large group or ideology. I vividly recall, for example, my own transformative decision to become a pescatarian after speaking with a young animal rights activist who approached me while I was walking across campus more than twenty years ago. That discussion, the pamphlets she shared, and my subsequent online research led me to align myself more naturally with vegetarians and pescatarians. I reframed my view on animal rights and the dire environmental consequences associated with the massive meat-production industry. My new identity and sense of we-ness represents a layer of commonality that has strengthened the familial and dyadic we-ness I've shared with my youngest son.

Forming We-ness

The ten motives for establishing we-ness that I introduced in chapter 2 are relevant to the processes by which people form we-ness (shared genetic heritage, family love, romantic love, companionship, calling out social injustice, celebrating lofty ideals, targeting a shared enemy, sharing pain and suffering, mentorship, and sharing a practical goal). These motives highlight the mechanisms that inspire people to seek out and sustain we-ness in either the deep dyadic sense, the ideational form, or both. Irrespective of which incentives push us to pursue we-ness, they can continue to play a role in reinforcing these connections over time. They can also affect how we transition out of we-ness.

In addition to the diverse social forces that shape our efforts to build we-ness, we can note the diverse trajectories that lead us to believe we have some sort of affinity with another person, group, or ideology. Sometimes we achieve we-ness quickly, perhaps effortlessly, with or without fanfare; other times the process is protracted, and we may have to work diligently to obtain it. Sometimes it requires us to earn it. We may also have to work equally hard or harder to keep it going.

Arriving at that mental and emotional space where we feel connected to others, or embrace an ideology we share with others, can be a rewarding experience. Although we may be mindful of what we have accomplished, there are plenty of instances in which we drift into a state of we-ness with little thought. It just happens.

Furthermore, we may not even realize how important it is to us until it is gone.

Support groups, in their many forms, represent valuable social settings that enable people to search for opportunities to establish a sense of group belonging and we-ness. Some of the most common types of mutual aid groups are those that focus on addictions (e.g., alcohol, drugs, and gambling), physical problems (e.g., cancer, paralysis, infertility, and obesity), and neurocognitive challenges (e.g., Alzheimer's and dementia). Individuals are often motivated to find a community of individuals with similar experiences who will empathize with their pain and suffering. While some primarily look for emotional support, many also want to secure information and advice on coping with their condition or the condition of a loved one.

The support groups that cater specifically to caregivers are largely a twentieth-century invention to address our increasingly private family lives and caregivers' sense of isolation. In the nineteenth century, caregivers were mostly women and lived more collaborative lives. They "moved in and out of one another's homes, shared information and resources, took turns relieving one another in caring for their children, and their ill and dying."[1] These shared experiences most likely enabled women caregivers to see themselves as having a communal spirit and sense of we-ness.

Researchers who study support groups today consider whether they are expert-led or peer-led and whether they take an in-person or online format.[2] Additionally, researchers explore how persons involved in support groups differ in the way they navigate family relationships versus relationships with support group members. These types of issues have implications for how individuals perceive their personal connections with support group members as well as the collective identity they derive from being part of the group.

Individuals vary as to whether they are self-motivated, persuaded, or forced to join and remain with a support group. Some participants decide entirely on their own to explore a formal support community beyond their immediate circle of family and friends. For others, family, friends, and health care professionals encourage them to check out programs to help them manage their circumstances.

That encouragement may range from a gentle suggestion to a full crisis intervention. Irrespective of how a person gets involved, once they join, they inevitably will be forced to confront matters of trust and vulnerability. How much personal and sensitive information is someone willing to reveal to strangers? To what extent, under what circumstances, and with what effect does a person express their vulnerability to others?

A description by one participant in a program designed to help individuals deal with mental illness with and without co-occurring substance abuse problems illustrates how some people's thoughts about trust in mutual aid groups evolve based on their personal experience:

> When I first showed up to the program, I was like, I don't know these people. I'm not going to open my door, tell them my personal business, tell them what I'm about, tell them what I am, or who I am…. But then I felt like I was relieving a whole bunch of pressure and pain off my back … I talked about a lot of stuff then I never talked to other people about…. Because I felt like I could trust these people. These people is [sic] the type of people that says what stays in the group stays in the group.[3]

Consistent with this story, research shows that it is not uncommon for people to feel more willing to bare their soul to support group members than they do to family or close friends.[4] Ironically, embracing and being open with support group members can give participants the freedom to interact more comfortably with family and friends. Without an alternative support group, these participants would have a harder time avoiding the emotional tension that can arise with loved ones who may be ill-equipped or unwilling to deal with the person's deep pain. In other words, the dyadic we-ness forged with strangers based on shared struggles can supply a welcomed dose of experiential empathy, unencumbered by the expectations of "keeping it together" that a person may feel when surrounded by family and friends. As a result, a support group can help a person sustain a less complicated state of dyadic we-ness with those to whom they are closest. They don't have to rely on these intimate family and friends as much to help them manage aspects of their condition.

Some people are better suited than others to create we-ness in a support group. Likewise, some groups are fortunate to have the type of healthy leadership and group chemistry that fosters a feeling of group belonging for those who are willing to participate. In a world filled with lonely people who struggle with various personal challenges, support groups operating in diverse settings play a significant role in helping people develop a sense of we-ness and self-confidence. Based on their study of cancer support groups, Ussher and her colleagues conclude that the participants positioned the groups as a place "within which a strong sense of community was fostered, described by participants as a 'cancer family,' to which a strong feeling of belonging is attached."[5] One participant offers: "People who have cancer belong to a special club and it's just a different outlook on life, it's a different experience and you laugh about things which some people are a bit aghast about." Another adds: "I think for me it's the core empathy, they know what it feels like to be a person with cancer and when you talk to them it's not 'Oh you poor dear' it's 'yeah I know where you're standing.'"[6]

Thus, those living with a cancer diagnosis may modify the way they experience we-ness with people in their inner circle who cannot relate to their cancer diagnosis directly. In doing so, they may craft a new type of we-ness with support group members based on their shared cancer identity and mutual support. As a cancer survivor, a person may also create a form of ideational we-ness with the larger category of persons living with a current or previous cancer diagnosis.

Family caregivers for cancer patients can establish their own sense of camaraderie with other caregivers when they share information and stories about their difficult experiences coping with a loved one's illness. One caregiver in a brain tumor support group explains how the group benefits them: "it decreases the feelings of isolation, of being alone, because the less connected you are to people in the same situation, the more you do feel isolated and alone."[7]

Those who rely on support groups have been acutely vulnerable during the COVID-19 pandemic because many have been cut off from valuable opportunities to meet face to face with their peers and counselors. In June 2020, Jessica Hulsey, president of the Addiction Policy Forum, expressed her broad concerns about the pandemic's effects, which include the declining access to support groups: "From patients in treatment, to those in recovery to family members and caregivers, too many are struggling with disruptions in care. The data show that the presence of continuous stress and triggers and absence of coping and support mechanisms are coinciding with emotional distress. This may equate to an increase in relapses and overdoses nationwide."[8] Some of the local chapters for support groups like Alcoholics Anonymous, Narcotics Anonymous, Al-Anon, as well as others responded to COVID-19's social and physical distancing protocols by offering online options.[9] Absent clear evidence about the effectiveness of online sessions under these circumstances, they presumably provide some participants at least a weak sense of group belonging during these challenging times. Hulsey's comments also remind us that online support services can benefit caregivers as well as those who confront a detrimental condition directly.

As we've seen in our earlier examples, sometimes individuals are awash in a we-ness that was thrust upon them in a way that negated their conscious decision-making. This is particularly true for those displays of we-ness that we take part in from a very young age. Derek Black and Megan Phelps-Roper, the former members of the white nationalist movement and the Westboro Baptist Church, respectively, had similar experiences. They were both born into families who thought they were creating a loving environment for their kids, but they immersed them in hateful ideologies. Surrounded by loved ones, they learned as young children that their sense of family we-ness was inextricably tied to their elders' political and religious tribal messages. The ideologies that dictated their daily routines and upbringing were anchored to their families' rigid and unforgiving "us" versus "them" mentality.

When children are indoctrinated so overwhelmingly into an ideologically based we-ness, kids will often spend many years, perhaps a lifetime, unaware of any alternative way of framing their worlds. In time, however, some will ask themselves – like Derek and Megan did – why they have embraced a we-ness perspective that stigmatizes others and is based on false assumptions. Escaping the grip of this type of we-ness mentality can be just as important to a person's well-being as achieving a sense of belonging.

Deepening and Expanding

Once we establish a state of we-ness, what then? Sometimes we push ourselves to deepen our ties to the people and ideas that already pique our interest. This typically means we intensify our positive feelings and commitments to them. The feelings we generate when we experience this special type of group belonging boost our well-being and enable us to lift others up as well.

In the 1970s, Mihaly Csikszentmihalyi, a leader in the field of positive psychology and management, introduced the concept of "flow" into the emerging study of happiness.[10] For Csikszentmihalyi, flow represents that amazing, embodied energy that grips us when we are passionately absorbed in doing a rewarding activity. Filled with inspiration, we forget about our need for food and sleep; we are oblivious to other distractions as well. We lose track of time and have no use for self-reflection – we're too spellbound by our activity to be bothered. Colloquially, the expression of "being in the zone" captures this exhilarating sensation of flow. Athletes, musicians, actors, artists, writers, and many others experience this ephemeral state of being when they pour time and energy into an enjoyable and doable activity that captures their undivided attention.

At its core, flow is a focused manifestation of energy and the brain chemistry that generates specific sensations and feelings. Radha Agrawal, a self-proclaimed community architect and the upbeat cofounder of the early morning dance and wellness movement, Daybreaker, provides an accessible description of energy in *Belong: Find Your People, Create Community & Live a More Connected Life*. Energy is a type of "internal and external force field." Agrawal vividly describes that "it starts deep within our cells and radiates out through our eyes, our pores, our gestures, our speech, our smiles, our yells, screams, and every expression and emotion in between."[11]

Rooted in our biochemistry and channeled through our physiology and the social conduits for communication, energy represents a vital personal attribute that defines us, while also affecting those who respond to us. Energy permeates our analysis of we-ness because "It powerfully shapes community and our sense of belonging."[12]

Our energy, good and bad, is a byproduct of four key brain chemicals: dopamine, oxytocin, serotonin, and endorphins. We produce dopamine when we anticipate and encounter rewards and pleasure. Oxytocin is released when we experience positive forms of touch. We are more inclined to trust, feel safe, and be generous as our oxytocin level increases. If our level of serotonin rises, we are in a better mood and feel content. Endorphins also promote good feelings and limit our awareness of pain. Our existence, both as a unique individual and a social creature who engages with others, is revealed in the production of energy that can, in turn, foster a state of flow under the right conditions.

In recent years, scholars in different fields have begun to explore the larger social context that can foster flow. That context often involves individuals developing and expressing their sense of we-ness as part of a group or team. A group of researchers led by Jef van den Hout recently outlined a detailed conceptual framework for understanding team flow in workplace settings. It recognizes teams as a special type of group. In the work world, a team includes several key features, such as being relatively small, having participants who have complementary skills with a common purpose, shared performance goals, and a way to hold each other accountable. Team flow is defined as a "shared experience of flow during the execution of interdependent personal tasks in the interest of the team."[13] Team flow is more than everyone on a team individually experiencing their own private version of this phenomenon. Instead, it represents a situation in which "individual team members share flow experiences together in a highly synergistic fashion."[14] More specifically, team flow consists of seven prerequisites (collective ambition, common goal, aligned personal goals, high skill integration, open communication, safety, and mutual commitment) as well as four characteristics (a sense of unity, a sense of joint progress, mutual trust, and holistic focus).

Several of these prerequisites and characteristics relate directly to aspects of how we build and maximize our shared sense of we-ness with others. For example, van den Hout and his colleagues describe a team's collective ambition by underscoring the members' shared values and beliefs and their intrinsic reasons for collaborating. These commonalities provide a team with its basis for developing a shared identity. Although the team must establish its goal prior to experiencing team flow, the excitement associated with team flow can reinforce a team's solidarity. It can also strengthen individuals' commitment to remain active and to grow their sense of we-ness as a team.

To experience team flow, members must establish a bridge between their individual and group goals. This is best served when participants feel as though they have a say in defining the larger team goals. When members are committed to those larger goals and appreciate how they can personally contribute to them, they'll feel more personally invested in the team. As a result, they will be well-positioned to contribute to the team dynamic and experience team flow in the process.

The prerequisite of mutual commitment highlights how critical it is for members to be aware of the collective goals they've agreed to pursue. A shared commitment increases the chances that team members will avoid distractions and hold each other accountable to their respective responsibilities. Members are not only aware of what they need to do, they are also primed to focus on whether other team members are fulfilling the expectations placed on them. Ideally, the team, as a collective, must decide how it's going to organize the joint tasks that will accomplish the group goal. Much can be gained if everyone is informed about the progress the team is making toward realizing the shared goal.

When team flow is present, it signals that the team has established its sense of unity and cohesion. Individuals are willing to stick together and address the challenges they face as they pursue their collective goal. This means that individuals have internalized the collective ambition and have, to some extent, subordinated their individual identity to the collective identity. The extent to which individuals sacrifice or lessen their individual identity varies, but the prospect of experiencing team flow is enhanced when more team members emphasize their investment in the team's expression of we-ness.

Flow is more than intriguing, it is consequential. A team that generates flow is more likely to perform well, a reminder that a team is a special type of group: "A work group relies on the individual contributions of its members for group performance, but a team strives for something greater than what its members could achieve individually."[15] That "something greater" requires team members to have a deep commitment to their connection with one another and with the team's objectives.

Sports journalist Joan Ryan, writing mostly about professional and Olympic teams as well as the military in her book, *Intangibles: Unlocking the Science and Soul of Team Chemistry*, asserts that "chemistry" is a good way to describe the "flow state" when it involves a team. When a team is winning or at least performing up to or beyond expectations, it's likely that any preexisting positive chemistry between teammates is being strengthened. So, too, the sense of we-ness that participants experience can be deepened during these times.

Ryan defines team chemistry as "active" and something that "produces a change in the work product." She sees it as the "interplay of physiological, social and emotional forces that elevates performance."[16] Team chemistry, like flow, is more likely to emerge when teammates share a common goal and are committed to accomplishing it. However, Ryan is quick to point out a distinction between "social chemistry" and "task chemistry." The former is what most people associate with a team they believe has chemistry. It captures the "bonding, trust, and caring" that teammates have for one another. While teammates can take many paths to develop these types of interpersonal connections with one another, the exchanges often involve emotional support and empathy. They know their teammates will "have their back" even if they fail to execute up to expectations – so long as they tried their best. In addition, teammates who experience social chemistry often tease and prank one another, create bonding rituals, and hang out together. Although outsiders are typically not privy to the private displays of social chemistry, they are likely to see public displays of enthusiasm and supportive gestures. From the outsider perspective, the teammates look like they're supporting one another and having collective fun, which is typically true.

Those who experience task chemistry, on the other hand, orient themselves to specific competitive outcomes. They are convinced that their teammates will be prepared, compete hard, and stay focused when it counts during a game. When task chemistry is at work, teammates may not be fond of each other, yet they still trust that their teammates will do what is necessary to compete at their highest level. Recall how the distant relationship Buzz Aldrin and Neil Armstrong maintained did not prevent them from executing their mission to become the first people to land on the moon. Some expression of task chemistry is necessary for an enhanced team performance. In addition, whether a team is experiencing either or both forms of chemistry, players must have some sense of we-ness and group belonging to experience team chemistry.

Because team chemistry enhances performance, there's plenty of interest in what breeds and disrupts it. Even though coaches and other leaders go to great lengths to orchestrate team chemistry, there is no cookie-cutter formula that works in all cases. As Ryan emphasizes, a mix of physiological, social, and emotional attributes influence the circumstances that affect how team chemistry is developed or disturbed. Teams and most groups are dynamic social arrangements that are subject to change. Thus, the fluidity of team chemistry and feelings of we-ness reflects how groups, especially those with more than several members, represent a potentially endless number of combinations of talents, personalities, moods, unexpected events, and more.

An important feature of the group dynamics that affect team chemistry are the personalities of specific players that can elicit a wide range of positive and negative reactions from their teammates. Based on her interviews and observations with people in sports and business, Ryan proposes seven different archetypal characteristics team participants express when they, in their own unique way, contribute to team chemistry (sparkplug, sage, kid, enforcer, buddy, warrior, and jester). These personality characteristics can also shape how we-ness is created and managed by individuals in different types of group settings other than sports teams. It should come as no surprise that leadership models that motivate team or group members and cultivate flow and chemistry are to be prized.

In addition to our efforts to deepen we-ness, we can try to grow our expression of we-ness in various ways if we are comfortable with it. The most obvious examples of people expanding their preexisting we-ness involve their diverse paths to integrate children into their lives through adoption, step-parenthood, surrogacy, assisted reproductive technologies (ART), or through conventional conception. Individuals usually pursue parenthood as a couple regardless of sexuality or gender identity. Many have their heart set on expanding and deepening their vision of the we-ness they already share with their romantic partner. Those who have already established a sense of we-ness with a partner are often excited to expand that we-ness. Still, many new parents enter parenting without a co-parental form of we-ness, although they may establish one later. Instead, they are restricted to creating a new form of we-ness with their child.

Sometimes the we-ness between partners is layered with other concerns because the partners have an interracial relationship or they're pursuing an adoption, surrogacy, or sperm/egg donorship that has transracial features. In addition, some couples will be adding a child to a family profile that already includes one or more children who have been part of a separate family dance with one of the prospective parents.

As I've described in a previous study I did on stepfathers, individuals create a family dance when they move through their daily routines and "learn to love, cry, sleep, eat, play, laugh, talk, and argue as part of a family."[17] Family members assign meanings to all sorts of routines and rituals, and those activities are accompanied by family members' perceptions about their respective rights and obligations regarding how the family dance should be choreographed. Who has the right to shape decisions about vacations, chores, food choices, TV shows, bedtimes, and more? Who's expected to do grocery shopping, make meals, clean rooms, pay bills, and take care of other family responsibilities? Other matters involve implicit or explicit understandings of how everyone involved is supposed to coordinate their mundane activities to work things out. Moreover, agreements about how family members are allowed or expected to talk to and touch one another help to define key aspects of the family dance.

In any stepfamily, two separate units must come together to form a new family dance that is somehow carved out of their own earlier arrangements. Thomas, the nurturing stepfather I mentioned earlier, shared his glowing account about how he and his wife Stephanie solidified their family bonds. They did so by adding a biological daughter of their own to their stepfamily mix that included Stephanie's two sons. The new family dance that emerges requires people to manage their own preexisting orientation toward familial we-ness. For example, how does a mother and her children with their preexisting family dance incorporate the mother's romantic partner into the dance? Does everyone effortlessly blend into a new stepfamily dance that integrates everyone into decidedly different arrangements with new routines and rules? Or is the new partner required to accept the preexisting family dance for the most part and learn to fit in without disrupting the ongoing routines? Or does the new partner pressure the mother and her children to adopt a very different stepfamily dance that is largely defined by the partner? Expanding and modifying our sense of stepfamily we-ness can be a complicated process with lots of tension, especially for those set in their ways. The empathy, trust, and leadership needed for people to merge two separate "we's" into a new "us" can be both exciting and a struggle.

In any family that has one or more new members and new routines, there can be conflict. As Susan Walzer reported more than twenty years ago in *Thinking about the Baby: Gender and Transitions into Parenthood*, couples are often disappointed in how their relationship unfolds once a baby enters the home.[18] The gender imbalances in how some men and women contribute to their family can be revealed as the demands of caring for a new baby push them to alter their routines compared to when they were a child-free couple. For many women, becoming parents leaves them feeling overloaded with responsibilities and sometimes frustrated. They feel like they're not receiving the emotional and practical support they expected, and they can't give as much time and effort to their partner.

Two of Walzer's recommendations for new parents are particularly relevant to our discussion about the way people navigate the expansion of their we-ness to include a baby. In her words: "If you look out for your teammate's well-being, you are looking out for your own, so be conscious of whether your partner's needs are being served by your arrangements."[19] She encourages partners to be more mindful of how childcare duties can affect a person's mood and to recognize how their lives are interconnected. When the partner who is not immediately involved in childcare expresses this type of empathy, it can lead to more thoughtful decision-making. But she also advises new parents who wish to preserve the health of their marital we-ness to "support your partner's selfhood and take responsibility for your own." Giving your partner opportunities to exercise their autonomy and to honor their "personal space" can enhance the couple's sense of we-ness in the long run while enabling them to incorporate their child into their expanded family more smoothly.

Most prospective and new parents will also feel as though their familial we-ness with other family members, especially the grandparents and great-grandparents, is being intensified. A new parent's contribution to the family legacy can be interpreted by their parents as well as their extended kin as a sign that they're expanding their we-ness. This pattern is likely to be reinforced when individuals embrace Western culture's pronatalist ideals that accentuate the value of childbearing for adults. If a couple believes that others applaud their family-building efforts, they may be more motivated to expand their sense of we-ness to incorporate offspring.

Lesbian and gay couples may uniquely value the public's view because sexual minorities often believe that becoming parents helps to normalize their standing in the public's eye. When sexual minorities are contemplating parenthood, they often worry about how their children will be treated in a homophobic society.[20] But as they see it, LGBTQ+ parents also become more recognizable to the straight community because they look more like "family people," struggling with the same long litany of issues most parents confront raising kids in the twenty-first century. Parents, irrespective of who they love romantically, can relate to one another when they are swamped with parenting demands that have them looking for good day care; ways to get their kids to go to bed on time; strategies to deal with bullying, social media, and homework issues; ways to address various health issues, and much more.

Parents who take an unplanned path to conception, on the other hand, can rebound from their surprise to feel as though becoming a parent will expand how they express we-ness with a partner. In fact, the news of an impending child can bring some partners closer together as they try to wrap their minds around the prospects of co-parenting. Perceptions about their new responsibilities can prompt some partners to make a good-faith effort to rise to the occasion of developing a healthy familial nest to raise their child. Although couples are frequently well-intentioned when they are confronted with an unplanned pregnancy, with time, many realize that their coupled we-ness was ill-conceived. Relationships that include unintended pregnancies, or those that are initiated to legitimize a birth, tend to fare poorly.[21]

Another all too common scenario involves prospective parents who are merely sexual partners with someone prior to learning about an unintended pregnancy. With no meaningful sense of we-ness to ground them, some of these partners try to improvise their way out of their dilemma. They try to forge a sense of we-ness as romantic partners as well as co-parents simultaneously. *Knocked Up*, a 2007 romantic comedy starring Seth Rogen and Katherine Heigl, used this plot to become a box office success. After meeting at a nightclub and hooking up for sex, the movie reveals how two incompatible people struggle to find their footing as a couple and parents. Rogen's character, Ben, is a lazy, irresponsible twenty-something guy who has no professional ambition, whereas Heigl plays an aspiring young media professional, Alison, who has just received a promotion in the entertainment industry. After Alison is initially convinced that her baby daddy is ill-suited to be a partner or father, she ultimately changes her mind once Ben has an awakening and becomes a thoughtful, responsible parent and partner. In standard Hollywood form, they cement their we-ness as a happy new couple and begin raising their baby in a Los Angeles apartment.

No doubt *Knocked Up* mirrors how some prospective parents get involved with each other under duress, but this Hollywood ending is more the exception than the rule for the typical chain of events for hookup-to-parent couples. Creating and expanding we-ness is no easy task when individuals are stressed out about an unintended pregnancy and a baby on the way. This is especially the case if parents hardly know one another, let alone have yet to establish themselves as a committed, romantic couple.

People who become parents through means such as adoption and ART highlight another set of decisions relevant to expanding we-ness. When sociologist Barbara Katz Rothman and her husband, who are white, adopted an African American girl, Victoria, Rothman didn't envision writing a fascinating book about race, family, and adoption that drew extensively from her personal experience. But that's what she did. Rothman opens our eyes to all sorts of issues relevant to the construction of we-ness in her 2005 book, *In Weaving a Family: Untangling Race and Adoption*. She frames her perspective by saying:

> If you are an ordinary family, an expected family – mama bear, papa bear and the little bear cubs born to your type of family – you don't think about presenting yourself. It just seems obvious. You don't think about how you construct the family, weave the relationships between the various parts, and present the seemingly solid fabric of your lives to the world. But if you're a family like mine, a family that mixes race in unexpected ways, it's not obvious.[22]

As Rothman shows, supplementing her arguments with revealing personal anecdotes, the process of constructing familial we-ness is intimately connected to how we react to the social gaze. How we believe others see and judge us can influence what we say and do. Whether it is important to us that others see us in a certain way matters, too. In Rothman's case, as with many other parents who are involved in transracial adoptions, she found that she wanted others to see her family as she did. She also realized that for that to happen, she needed to play a more active role than usual to demonstrate the type of we-ness she shares with Victoria. While comparing her circumstances to those who also belong to atypical families, she notes, "we become aware of how we fit ourselves in. We notice that we are *doing* what other people think they are just *being*."[23] Rothman worried about her feelings, but she was even more concerned with Victoria's sense of belonging. The take-home message from Rothman's account of transracial adoption is that the process of doing we-ness is a more complex undertaking than having a taken-for-granted sort of we-ness that needs no explanation and little conscious effort.

Unlike pregnancies that are conceived conventionally, the alternative paths to parenthood involve various choices that can raise partners' concerns about perceived fairness.[24] Some people may see some conception options as distorting and restricting an LGBTQ+ parent's contribution to creating a child or developing an intimate parental bond. For example, a lesbian couple must initially decide if they want to pursue adoption or ART. If the latter, they must decide which partner will gestate the child, supply the egg, and what criteria will be used to select a sperm donor. In the ART case, the gestating mom who uses her own egg, unlike her partner, will have the intimate experiences of carrying and birthing the child in addition to having a genetic link – at least for the child born from this procedure. Decisions about physical characteristics of the sperm donor may also tip the scales toward one member of the couple, say, a person who is interested in duplicating their skin tone or ethnic appearance. Concerns about these issues lead some lesbian couples to switch the pregnancy role and genetic tie with an additional child. With or without switching who contributes the egg, some lesbians prefer to use sperm from the same man to ensure biogenetic siblings are produced. These sensitive decisions can alter the calculus of how two people and others in their social network perceive and respond to any new symbolic bonds that expand a couple's romantic we-ness to include co-parenting and separate parent-child ties.

As noted earlier, we live in an age fascinated by DNA and blood bonds. This pattern persists despite the greater openness to various family forms that are not anchored to biological ties. If having a genetic tie with children matters for some, then it can create a point of contention for gay and lesbian couples because the genetic tie can only be achieved by one person in the pair for a given child.[25]

Family life, in its many forms, may be the site most recognizable to us when it comes to thinking about how we expand our sense of we-ness. But plenty of other situations force people to decide whether to incorporate others into their preestablished expression of we-ness. Exploring the conditions that foster or limit this willingness to be open to others helps us to better understand group dynamics.

To find answers, let's return to our earlier discussion of how we-ness operates in an institution that prides itself on creating a sense of community, cohesion, and loyalty – the military. The military represents an intriguing setting to think about expanding we-ness on a few critical fronts. But let's first take stock of how the celebration of we-ness permeates the sacred ideals of military service. William Manchester captures this mentality in *Goodbye Darkness*, his acclaimed memoir about being a soldier in World War II:

> I understand, at last, why I jumped hospital that Saturday thirty-five years ago and, in violation of orders, returned to the front and almost certain death. It was an act of love. Those men on the line were my family, my home. [...] They had never let me down, and I couldn't do it to them. I had to be with them, rather than let them die and me live with the knowledge that I might have saved them. Men I know do not fight for flag and country, for the Marine Corps, or glory or any other abstraction. They fight for one another.[26]

These words encapsulate the "band of brothers" motif that permeates all branches and units of military service.

Writing in the *Journal of Military Ethics*, Desiree Verweij considers how what she refers to as the "bond of brothers" theme is potentially a special kind of friendship that would emphasize a morally grounded loyalty within a military context.[27] She draws on Aristotle's ideas on the forms and aspects of friendship, the twentieth-century war poets' poignant interpretations of comradeship, and insights from modern philosophers about moral development to assess soldiers' relationships with one another. Verweij concludes that simple comradeship without authentic friendship can lead to humanitarian abuses in military operations, as we saw with Abu Ghraib: "The bond of brotherhood can result in a seclusive 'we' that lashes out at everyone who threatens to destroy this 'we-centeredness.'"[28]

Instead of encouraging only the "usefulness" and "pleasure" forms of Aristotelian friendship, Verweij suggests that those in the military should express friendship based on what Aristotle viewed as the highest form – "goodness and virtue":

> Friendship gives comradeship an extra dimension. It is not just about being there and sharing pain, fear, and despair, but friendship adds a moral dimension to this relationship. In this sense, friendship enriches comradeship: it contributes to a flourishing life, and in doing so it helps the friend to refrain from behavior that will disrupt his/ her humanity and thus his/her human flourishing.[29]

The we-ness that would emerge from this type of brotherhood-in-arms bond would be anchored to a style of friendship that leads to the participants' self-awareness and self-understanding.

Historically, the "band of brothers" or "bond of brothers" expressions have referred to male soldiers, especially those who experience combat. On January 24, 2013, the Pentagon, after many years of heated debate, announced that it was repealing its policy of excluding women from combat positions. Megan MacKenzie provocatively argues in *Beyond the Band of Brothers: The US Military and the Myth That Women Can't Fight* that the principal purpose of the exclusion policy has been to protect men, not women. From her perspective, the policy mythologized the "all-male combat unit as elite, essential, and exceptional."[30] She believes that

> The story of a group of men risking their lives to violently defend the United States has been a consistent national narrative. "Bands of brothers," "comrades in arms," and "a few good men" are examples of well-worn tropes that signal men's unique connection to one another and their ability to overcome extreme odds to protect the nation.[31]

Without specifically using the "we-ness" label, MacKenzie suggests that the pervasive myth about the military has reinforced the sentiment that the connections male soldiers form with one another generate the chemistry they need to be courageous and effective fighters. She goes on to describe the underlying false logic of this myth by noting that it "casts the nonsexual, brotherly love, male bonding, and feelings of trust, pride, honor, and loyalty between men as mysterious, indescribable, and exceptional."[32]

One can reasonably argue that this male bonding does exist, and is in some respects "exceptional," but our culture and military for centuries exploited patriarchal privileges to lay the foundation for these realities. In other words, the bonding isn't truly exceptional, it merely reflects how men's and women's opportunities have been shaped by our patriarchal legacy. I have no doubt that those who go through extensive, rigorous training and then sometimes face the grave dangers and horrors in theaters of war are compelled to develop tight bonds to thrive and survive. The fear of death and the traumatic sights, sounds, and smells of human carnage compel soldiers to find strength and comfort in their comrades. However, in the United States, and in many other countries, the existence of patriarchal norms and institutions has meant that women have been largely denied access to this military culture.

Fast forward to the present day and the key questions become: In the past decade, to what extent have women been incorporated into an expanded version of the band of brotherhood that has previously marked the all-male fighting force? Alternatively, what conditions are affecting the extent to which a mixed-gender culture is being implemented in different military settings that enables women to participate more fully?

Since the draft ended in 1973, there has been an increase in the percentage of women across the military branches in the enlisted forces (from 2 to 16 percent, as of 2018) and officer corps (from 8 to 19 percent, as of 2018), with the Navy and Air Force having the highest representation of enlisted and officer women.[33] Women have incrementally and significantly altered the demographics of our volunteer military. Unfortunately, there's also been a corresponding rise in the rates of sexual harassment and assault reports as well as retaliation for those who report sexual assault. For the year 2018, the Pentagon estimates – based on an anonymous survey – that 20,500 active-duty service members (13,000 women and 7,500 men) were sexually assaulted, a significant increase from the estimate of 14,900 for 2016. In 2018, women aged seventeen to twenty-four were the most likely to report abuse.

The 2015 Human Rights Watch study of the US military also paints a dismal picture of sexual abuse patterns and the retaliation responses that are frequently directed at those who report their sexual assaults and even those who support them.[34] Many soldiers who report sexual abuse contend that they have been retaliated against by supervisors and peers. The Human Rights Watch report concludes that "while the US military is aware that retaliation is a widespread problem, efforts to address it have so far been unsuccessful." Another report issued on April 30, 2019, by the Sexual Assault Accountability and Investigation Task Force, prompted by Senator Martha McSally during the Senate Armed Services Committee hearing earlier that year, directed more attention to the issue. However, the prevalence of sexual assault, and concerns about retaliation for reporting it, continue to represent a major impediment to changing the military culture.[35] These patterns gained public attention in 2020 with the launching of the hashtag #IamVanessaGuillen. The response was connected to the murder of a female soldier on the Fort Hood military base in Texas by a fellow soldier, after she allegedly had been sexually harassed by one of her sergeants.[36] The online movement afforded numerous service members an opportunity to acknowledge their own stories of sexual harassment and assault in the military. Collectively, these events show that any attempt to expand the sense of authentic we-ness in the military to include women is still very much a work in progress.

Now let's consider the intriguing case of how soldiers who make up special operation forces (SOF) think about and practice we-ness in various settings. The elite military units that comprise the SOF represent a highly celebrated alpha male bastion of we-ness in American society. In movies and literature, our popular culture has created iconic images of Delta Force operators, Green Berets, Army Rangers, and Navy SEALs, to name several of the best known. Much of that media focuses on how units navigate dangerous missions, as we see in such movies as *The Guns of Navarone* (1961), *The Dirty Dozen*

(1967), *Delta Force* (1986), *Black Hawk Down* (2001), *Inglorious Basterds* (2009), *Zero Dark Thirty* (2012), *Lone Survivor* (2013), and *The Outpost* (2020). Other representations highlight a fictional former special ops warrior who operates as a solo badass in either civilian settings or war zones. This mixture of images is consistent with the demanding selection and training regimes special ops personnel must endure.

Elite soldiers must go it alone to survive SOF courses that are designed as challenging and excruciating rites of passage. As one book about the training asserts, the objective is to "push them to their physical and psychological limits in order to assess their ability to drive on when their body and brain are telling them to quit."[37] In *Navy SEAL Mental Toughness: A Guide to Developing an Unbeatable Mind*, Chris Lambersten makes it clear that the road to becoming a Navy SEAL is not for the faint of heart. Describing just one of the more infamous weeks of intense physical screening and training, Lambersten says that the "Main purpose of Hell Week is to screen out the students who lack the commitment or mental toughness to endure significant amounts of pain, discomfort, exhaustion, and stress." He adds: "Not only are they running, swimming, and maneuvering boats in frigid waters, but they are doing so with only a total of 4 hours of sleep throughout the entire evolution [5.5 days]."[38] Those in the special ops community tend to agree that mental toughness is the most critical personal trait that will determine a soldier's chances of passing a special operations selection course and ultimately becoming an effective member of an SOF unit.[39]

Notwithstanding the individual tenacity and resilience they need to ignore the inner voice that begs them to quit during training exercises, SOF members are also expected to embrace the ultimate teammate mentality. Consistent with the teammate ideal, one of the core values of the Navy SEAL code is "One must never bring shame to the SEAL brotherhood."[40] Similarly, among the sentiments represented in the Ranger Creed, one finds, "Never shall I fail my comrades.... I will never leave a fallen comrade to fall into the hands of the enemy."

Ranger Hall of Famer Gary O'Neal, one of the most celebrated Army Rangers in history, embraced the power of the we-ness sentiment in a military context even though he was an independent adventure junkie from the time he was a young boy. Having survived a tough childhood largely on his own without close friends or family, he recounts in his memoir how, having lied about his age to enlist, he reacted to being named an assistant squad leader in basic training at the age of fifteen during the Vietnam War: "Maybe because I had never been part of a team, that feeling of having people depend on me, and having people I could depend on, really affected me. This was just about the first time that I had a purpose in life. The army was the perfect place for me."[41]

Once a soldier is placed in their first SOF unit – being fully committed to serve on one of these elite tactical teams – the soldier faces another challenge. Lambersten comments on that challenge in the context of Navy SEALs, but his reflections are relevant to SOF units across military branches: "Despite the grueling training a newly designated SEAL has undergone by the time he reports into his first operational unit, he still has a long way to go before his teammates are willing to put their lives in his hands. A new SEAL has much to learn and experience before he will be counted amongst the proven and seasoned SEALs in a unit."[42] Thus, a sailor who is awarded the celebrated and symbolic trident insignia becomes a full-fledged SEAL, but gaining entry into the ultimate brotherhood has to be earned firsthand by proving oneself to a unit's members.

In recent years, the media narrative has focused on women's attempts to break into that segment of the SOF community just described that involves direct-action raids and missions. For instance, in July 2021, after at least fourteen other women had failed to make it through, the first woman graduated the special training program for Navy SEALs, and other women are still in the training pipeline.[43] Most men fail, too, with only about 250 sailors out of 1,000 trainees making the cut.[44] A couple of women soldiers have graduated from the Army Ranger School, and in 2020 a woman soldier earned her status as the first Green Beret graduate. So it is likely only a matter of time before more select women begin to cross the gender divide and join SOF units more regularly in the frontline roles of Delta Force operators, Green Berets, Rangers, and SEALs.[45]

How open will SOF members be to incorporating women special operators into their male-oriented brotherhood and sense of we-ness? The women who break the screening barrier initially are likely to face additional and perhaps more complex challenges to being accepted by their unit's male members. Yet, some form of conditional acceptance is quite possible in the short-term and a more complete type of acceptance can eventually happen.

To appreciate the larger context in which women are attempting to break through the most publicized SOF barriers, we must reframe the prevailing but distorted message about women's involvement in the SOF community. Unbeknownst to many, women have served in various critical positions connected to special operations for decades. This message is championed in a compelling 2019 essay, "Dispelling the Myth of Women in Special Operations," by Nicole Alexander, a Special Operations Civil Affairs officer in the US Army, and Lyla Kohistany, a former Navy officer.[46] They have roughly twenty years of experience between them and cofounded Promote – a nonprofit focused on improving leader development and mentorship across the military. These authors challenge the misleading cultural narrative that both portrays special operations as a "man's world" and emphasizes "male-centric stories of 'door-kickers.'" In doing so, they raise our awareness about the scope and capabilities of SOF. They also reveal the critical roles women have played, are playing, and will play in special operations, including foreign internal defense, civil affairs (CA) operations, psychological operations (PSYOP), special reconnaissance, aviation, and forward surgical teams. Beyond detailing how specific women officers have been a vital part of the SOF command structure in different branches, the essay outlines a path forward to create a more heterogeneous SOF and dynamic leadership that can address more effectively the changing national security problems we face. They call for this more inclusive approach not simply on moral grounds but for practical reasons as well. According to them, research indicates that "gender-diverse teams make better decisions up to 73 percent of the time." This perspective broadens our view of we-ness in the special operations community and implicitly calls for stakeholders to appreciate the multilayered and integrated nature of the teams of men and women that comprise SOF.

Journalist Gayle Tzemach Lemmon also opens our eyes to the process of team building on multiple levels by profiling the groundbreaking women soldiers who recently served as enablers attached to SOF units in counterintelligence operations. In *Ashley's War: The Untold Story of a Team of Women Soldiers on the Special Ops Battlefield*, we are taken backstage to learn about a cadre of elite women soldiers, including the remarkable First Lieutenant Ashley White-Stumpf who was killed in action by an IED. Lemmon reveals how these soldiers responded to a recruitment ad to be part of history, bonded during their intense training, and then reinforced their "band of sisterhood" – both while deployed in Afghanistan and afterward when they returned stateside.[47] We also learn personal details of how Ashley and her husband, Jason, an Army officer, built their intimate dyadic "team" during their supportive relationship and marriage as a military couple who managed separate deployments.

The twenty members of the first ever Cultural Support Team (CST), a pilot program launched in 2010, were tasked with accompanying SOF units on missions into Afghan communities.[48] CST soldiers were expected to manage women and children while getting intel from them in ways the elite SOF could not because Afghan women are only permitted to talk to other women in this traditional culture. Years after the first class of CST soldiers had completed their deployment and other cohorts had been trained and served, Lemmon recounts what she experienced being around many of these women:

> The connection they shared, even among those who hadn't before met, was obvious and immediate. What struck me that night was the same sense of intense friendship I felt the first time I met Ashley's teammates. They finished one another's sentences, served as each other's career counselors, divorce therapists, spiritual advisors, and baby shower hosts. It was clear the soldiers were bound by a bond that no one outside their small, invisible band of CSTs would ever truly understand.[49]

In addition to forging their own sisterhood as unique women soldiers who enable SOF units in combat zones, CSTs needed to navigate the exclusive brotherhood that permeates these elite units. Lemmon depicts how the CST program challenged the SOF units, comprised of hardcore, alpha warriors, to expand their vision of team and we-ness. Several senior officers who had a hand in overseeing the CST program have publicly commended its efficiency, although several online comments suggest that there's a mixed reaction by some men soldiers about women soldiers being directly involved on the ground with SOF missions.[50]

The CST program illustrates how social circumstances can shape the complex ways we-ness is built, contested, and negotiated among individuals who are part of exclusive, elite groups. At a service honoring White-Stumpf after her death, Lieutenant General John Mulholland, head of the Army Special Operations Command, shared his thoughts about how Ashley and the other CSTs fit into SOF: "Make no mistake about it, these women are warriors; these are great women who have also provided enormous operational success to us on the battlefield by virtue of their being able to contact half of the population.... They absolutely have become part of our special operations family." Ultimately, First Lieutenant White-Stumpf was honored as being part of the SOF family when her photo and name were placed at memorial locations alongside other Rangers who had been killed in action. Lemmon also captures a more intimate type of emotional expression of affinity by reporting how a senior Ranger told Ashley's replacement in Kandahar before their first mission, "Listen, please be really careful. No offense to you, but I can't deal with it one more time. Ashley was so young and she had so much to offer. I just can't go through that again."[51] Although the Ranger's comments *might* be a bit paternalistic in tone, they clearly capture his respect for Ashley as a promising, elite soldier.

Beyond what they specifically did to enhance SOF missions in Afghanistan, the CST program appears to have played a role in ushering in the policy change that enables women to now serve in ground combat units. This policy shift creates additional opportunities for soldiers to redefine their operational views on we-ness and the military family.[52]

No matter who they are, members of the military family all hold some things in common. Being away from one's family and friends during training and deployment opens the door for soldiers to develop relationships based on some combination of trust, informal peer "therapy," and companionship that's focused on accomplishing practical and sometimes risky tasks, as well as shared suffering. The unit cohesion and personal sense of deep dyadic we-ness soldiers establish with some of their comrades can later influence how they experience their reintegration into civilian life. Soldiers who forge these tight bonds, especially during shared combat time, often struggle at home when they try to readjust to a life away from active-duty military service. They miss hanging with their buddies who experientially know what it means to go through training and deployment. They also sometimes long for the structured, daily rhythms of military life.

The transition to civilian life can be most difficult for those in the National Guard and Reserve units who scatter to different locations around the country after their service. Those who return home to civilian jobs often find them less rewarding than their military service responsibilities. In contrast, those who come back to a military base will have comrades nearby who have firsthand experience with the various aspects of deployment, or with whom they've shared a deployment – sometimes in a war zone. The authors of one study that explored how men navigate losing their military friendships while trying to reintegrate with their families post-deployment, report that "coming home means losing the intimacy with valued friends who have shared the unique strains of combat deployment."[53] They highlight one Marine reservist who conveys his realization that family and civilian friends can't understand his combat stories: "It's not really until it's up in your face, and you're dealing with it, it's not real, it's not reality."[54]

Soldiers who return to their households and families face the challenge of getting reacquainted with civilian and family norms. In these instances, the process of expanding we-ness to include others has the special feature of soldiers having to relearn how to extend their comfort zone to reintroduce their family members back into a redefined circle of we-ness. One ex-Marine, Greer, who had been deployed twice to a war zone and was dealing with PTSD in civilian life, used his interview with me about fathers and children's health as his chance to open up, in his view, like he had never done before. He shared his frustrations as a veteran about being a family man to his two daughters, two stepdaughters, and new wife.

As a sergeant in Afghanistan, he was accustomed to his soldiers responding quickly and affirmatively to his every directive. Back home, he struggled to be at peace with his four girls not responding in the same way. The unit cohesiveness he prided himself on, which he believed helped keep everyone in his thirteen-man fire team alive, was totally foreign to his wife and kids. In our interview, Greer role-plays to make his point about how he treated his kids and has since begun to reflect on his fathering style:

> "When I'm telling you to do something, do it right the first time. And if you can't, then I'll walk you through it." But at the time, it was really kind of hard for me to be gentle with them. It was more or less a, "This has to be done. If you can't do that, then something's wrong with you." (Laughs) Ya know? And I never really thought a lot about it. I always just thought … I'm trying to teach you something and you can't get it, that means you're being disobedient, so that means I have to punish … which isn't good. [They're thinking,] "This guy's crazy, he thinks we're Marines or something."

In long deployments, the family that stays at home has ample time and reason to develop new routines to make things work on the home front while one (or both) of the parents is deployed. The revised we-ness they establish may make it tricky for the returning soldier to step back smoothly into the new family dance. Like Greer, the typical soldier has generated a different sense of we-ness with their comrades as well. These conditions often require the returning soldier to rework their earlier romantic and family identities. Those soldiers who most effectively navigate their needs for we-ness in their family and military friendships post-deployment are likely to have the best mental health outcomes.

The scenarios of soldiers reintegrating into families highlight one feature of expanding we-ness by focusing attention on how soldiers manage their family and military networks. Do they ever try to incorporate military friends into the preexisting family or vice versa? Alternatively, from the soldier's standpoint, they may try to expand their overall intimate we-ness by simultaneously maintaining their affinity to two groups.

The Women's Veterans Network (WoVeN) is a timely program that reaches out to help former women soldiers feel more comfortable about navigating civilian life.[55] Launched in 2017 by Tara Galovski and Amy Street, WoVeN targets women ex-soldiers because they tend to have more difficulty than men readjusting from active duty. Former women soldiers are less likely to find a job, more likely to be single parents with limited resources, and less likely to be connected to other women ex-soldiers. The program provides women veterans with networking and social support opportunities, especially to help women cope with PTSD and the aftermath of having experienced sexual trauma while in the military. Started as a pilot program that involved weekly ninety-minute meetings for six to ten women in several American cities, WoVeN grew quickly to be available in seventy-five cities by January 2020. This provides women with a sense of community and an opportunity to bond with women of all ranks who can relate to one another. One woman who was involved in the program lamented that it was difficult for her to relate to her old friends when she left the military: "I always felt like 'Oh, I said too much,' or 'Oh, I'm talking about what happened over there.' I just didn't fit in anymore."

Transitioning Out of We-ness

One early morning, in the winter of 2015, I received an unsolicited email to my university account from an unknown person, Jessica Lynn. Jessica, an internationally renowned transgender activist, reached out to see if she could give a presentation in my class about being transgender.[56] Jessica was living in California, and offered to come to Florida pro bono. Her passion compelled me to have her speak in two of my classes and she's been returning ever since.

Jessica's unusual personal story is filled with incredible, heart-wrenching twists and turns, and she certainly mesmerized the students with her candid speaking style – one that would make the stereotypical sailor take notice.[57] Assigned male at birth, Jessica (named Jeffrey Butterworth prior to her transition) learned at an early age that she did not feel at home in her boy body. She had no idea at the time, however, how this set of circumstances would influence how she would navigate her unique opportunities over the years to experience we-ness in both the dyadic and ideational sense. As someone who for so many years was unsettled by her assigned gender, Jessica has on numerous occasions moved into and out of different expressions of we-ness, or she has had to modify their meaning to her. Among these changes, two highlight the complexity and implications of how a transgender person manages their individual life experience in a typically unsupportive social environment.

Living her pretransition life as a tormented boy and young man, Jeffrey attempted suicide while also sequentially obsessing over bug collecting, painting, and soccer to quiet his mental anguish. Jeffrey eventually confided in his teenage girlfriend, telling her that he wanted to be like her and live life as a female. Although his girlfriend was shocked and unreceptive at first, she quickly recanted and agreed to remain with Jeffrey, committed to working it out because she loved him. True to form, they got engaged and were reasonably happy. But before they could marry, Jeffrey and his fiancée were involved in a horrendous car accident involving a drunk driver. It took Jeffrey's fiancée's life, severely broke Jeffrey's jaw, and put him into a coma for days. When he regained consciousness, he learned that the one person who knew his deep secret, the person with whom he had built an unconventional we-ness, the intimate ally with whom he planned to build a future, was dead. Left alone to agonize over his secret, Jeffrey fell into a downward spiral of depression and addiction.

Jessica's second atypical experience showcases how our movement out of we-ness can sometimes unfold in ambiguous ways. A string of bad luck and unconventional decisions led Jeffrey into a set of circumstances in which he got a friend pregnant, married her, and went on to have three sons with her. He eventually found himself romantically separated from the mother of his three sons, but he still supported her emotionally and practically. Jeffrey and his former spouse even agreed to live together for a while in their platonic parenting arrangement as his ex-wife physically recovered from a car accident. They then negotiated an agreement whereby Jeffrey was to put his ex-wife through dental school and provide her two years of living expenses; in return, Jeffrey's former spouse would care for their two youngest children in Texas while Jeffrey underwent gender-affirming surgeries. The eldest son would stay with his dad in California. They managed this arrangement reasonably well until after Jessica officially made the full transition to start living as a woman in 2010.

Two years after the "temporary" living arrangement had begun, Jessica's ex-wife, under the pretense of parental neglect, petitioned the court to eliminate Jessica's contact with her two youngest sons – the middle son knew about the surgery but the youngest had never been told. Despite Jessica's valiant and expensive legal efforts to fight this move in court, an ultraconservative Texas judge ruled against Jessica and had her name removed from the youngest child's birth certificate in 2013. Jessica consulted with counsel but was left with no viable, timely legal recourse. She had become the only loving parent in the history of the United States to have her parental rights rescinded because of her transgender identity. Her eldest son has been in her life as her ardent supporter, but she has had to grapple with the "loss" of her "baby" and middle child.

So, what has this second set of life changes meant for Jessica's sense of parental we-ness? She still sees herself as her youngest boy's father and remains eager to see and hold him. She clings to the fond memories of when she was his primary caregiver. But sustaining any practical sense of we-ness under this last decade of obstacles is impossible. At best, it is an aspirational type of we-ness, linked to the past while remaining unfulfilled in the present. Now, and for many years, whatever feelings Jessica has had about being a parent to her youngest son, and the middle son as well, are one-sided. Authentic and deep we-ness is anchored to a form of reciprocity. Unfortunately, Jessica's youngest son has been in no position to confirm Jessica's parental role. As time passes, Jessica continues to try to contact her youngest son so she can explain to him why his father has not been in his life for all these years. The choices Jessica made were to transition to a woman physically and to embrace the generalized sense of we-ness she shares with other women, not to walk away from being a parent.

Jessica's experience highlights how people sometimes cling to a feeling of we-ness despite the lack of reciprocity. That approach can generate despair or hope, depending on the situation. For some, it may prevent them from moving on with their lives and make them unable to let go of their former connection. In Jessica's case, it has both forced her to cope with her sadness and inspired her to share her story with as many people as possible through The Butterfly Project. In our personal talks, Jessica has shared that its vision is to create a "future where societies as a whole are more aware and accepting of the entire gender spectrum." She is committed to transforming minds and practices so that no one else will experience a similar affront to their personal identity and parental we-ness.

Just as we spend a great deal of time establishing our sense of we-ness in different contexts and making sure that we keep those arrangements intact, we sometimes have to learn, as Jessica has, to cope with being forced to give up our we-ness status as we've known it. In other settings, we make the choice to move away from some form of we-ness because we no longer feel it is in our best interests. And sometimes we feel that we're losing a form of we-ness partly based on choice, and partly based on circumstances that seem beyond our control.

Helen Ebaugh, a former nun who left the Catholic Church and became a wife, mother, and sociology professor, not only has an interesting personal story about her own transition, but she has also explored the role-exiting process experienced by transgender persons as well as people undergoing many other voluntary transitions, including ex-convicts, ex-prostitutes, ex-cops, and others. She highlights in *Becoming an Ex: The Process of Role Exit* how people leaving a major role experience a disidentification process that results in them seeing themselves in a fundamentally different light.[58] As they transform their self-image, they often draw upon public discourses that shape how they think and talk about the social domains relevant to a shift in their identities. The evolving ways we have expanded our conceptual language to think and talk about addiction, social support groups, family, LGBTQ+ issues, and more provides people with opportunities to frame their experience for themselves and others.

Ebaugh also reminds us that we change our self-image by disengaging with the roles and people that we once used to define ourselves. As we disengage, we redefine our bonds with others, and this process unfolds more smoothly if others treat us differently in some respects than they did before. Many times, we have established a strong sense of we-ness with those with whom we interacted. When people leave critical roles, they not only redefine themselves, they also often revamp how and with whom they experience we-ness.

Sometimes the shift we experience with our self is prompted by a desire to avoid a certain form of we-ness. Other times the loss of we-ness is collateral damage that we endure to feel more authentic as individuals. In other words, ridding ourselves of our sense of we-ness wasn't what motivated us; rather, what we wanted to change was our identity. Ebaugh concludes that we experience our role changes by going through several stages that include having first doubts, seeking alternatives to our current situation, experiencing a turning point that fundamentally alters how we see ourselves, and creating the contours of the new role that accounts for the previous role we had. At this point, we'll look at some of the characteristics that differentiate how these types of important identity transitions occur and what they mean for people.

Forced Exit

Many of us have suffered emotional and psychological discomfort when, at the whim of others, we are forced to move on with our lives without being in a specific relationship or we are expelled from a group or organization. These circumstances can be produced when our romantic partners break up with us, our families shun us, employers fire us or "ask" for our resignation, gangs expel us, or we are ostracized by one of our informal networks.

What is most disturbing for us when these situations arise is that we feel out of control. Others are dictating the terms of how we live our lives, altering the social arrangements we wish to have, and redefining the contours of how we want to be defined. Our level of suffering will depend largely on how important our identities are that tie us to particular people, groups, and ideologies.

Sometimes we are forced to reconsider our we-ness status because we no longer possess a key attribute, perhaps a skill, that had once allowed us to be a certain type of person and connect with others. Elite sports figures and entertainers, for example, can lose their ability to compete and perform at the level necessary to sustain their position in the limelight. Even the legendary basketball player Michael Jordan eventually lost his ability to "be like Mike." Upon his final retirement, he could still produce a retrospective vision of we-ness with the teams he had played for in the past, but the immediate sense of we-ness as an active player was gone. Later, when Jordan became a part owner of the Charlotte Hornets, an NBA franchise, he was able to revamp his sense of we-ness in the NBA community. However, this time it was as an executive, which was a different kind of we-ness – a big step removed from the grit and grind of the physical action on the court and the antics among teammates away from it.

While Jordan's skill set and physical prowess declined slowly, others may experience a much more dramatic and sudden shift in whatever attribute or personal abilities represent the key to their we-ness status. Injuries, accidents, illnesses, and criminal allegations or convictions can fundamentally alter a person's ability to sustain their sense of we-ness. When Magic Johnson, the Hall of Fame point guard for the Los Angeles Lakers basketball team, announced in 1991 that he was retiring from basketball because he had contracted AIDS, he had to grapple immediately with his sudden loss of the we-ness that came with being an active player with exceptional teams and being one of the league's most visible stars. He could support his former teammates from the stands, but he was no longer part of the team.

People out of the national spotlight can experience their own version of losing we-ness, such as when the trial lawyer has a stroke and can no longer effectively argue cases in court, or the teenage rock band guitarist is left to find another form of we-ness when he loses his ability to play after a car accident, or the retired factory worker who belongs to a friendly bowling team feels that her poor health requires her to leave her team. We often take our feelings of belonging for granted, but we realize quickly just how important those bonds are when they're gone.

A demanding role-exiting experience and crisis of we-ness can be thrust upon us traumatically when a loved one dies or loses their cognitive ability to sustain our shared memories. In *The Caregivers: A Support Group's Stories of Slow Loss, Courage, and Love*, journalist Nell Lake offers us an intimate glimpse of how individuals navigate a shifting sense of we-ness when their chronically ill charge loses their mental and physical grip on reality and life.[59] Lake spent several years immersed in the lives of caregivers who participated in a support group designed to ease their emotional burdens. The participants revealed their "ambiguous loss," a term psychotherapist Pauline Boss introduced in the 1970s to describe the painful occasions whereby individuals are "physically present but psychologically absent." A loved one who suffers from an extreme case of dementia presents a caregiver with the unique challenge of managing a fragile sense of we-ness that gradually drifts to being one-sided (though a traumatic brain injury can bring this state on immediately).

Lake puts a face on this pattern by commenting on how one caregiver, William, interacts with his wife, Joan, whose memory of their relationship is fading because she has Alzheimer's:

> Joan does still remember William: she knows him, feels comfortable with him, seems to feel jealous if his attention strays. William remembers Joan with far greater intricacy than this – he carries stories of her in his mind, knows her old preferences, deeds, mannerisms, quirks. He structures his life in part to maintain those memories – pulling out Joan's milk pitchers and salt and pepper shakers, dusting them. He visits her every day in order never to forget.[60]

Those like Joan, if they live long enough, will sometimes move deeper and deeper into an alternative reality that no longer includes any memory of their devoted caregiver. Caregivers like William sometimes not only lose a long-standing form of we-ness, they also create a new type of temporary we-ness anchored to their shared experience with support group members. Sometimes those encounters can lead to more permanent friendships.

As our population ages, caregivers will increasingly face the tragedy of having a cherished expression of dyadic we-ness slowly dissolve despite their best efforts to preserve it. Some of those who eventually and perceptibly lose a loved one because of the other's cognitive impairment, and often death, describe their "unintentional rituals of slow loss." These caregivers talk about letting go. They step away from their everyday routines of we-ness to make the transition to a more independent self-image. Simple activities can facilitate the unraveling process that allows a caregiver to move away from an inclusive mental space of "we" to a more singular image of "me." For example, a caregiver can sort through and give away their loved one's clothes, downsize and move to a new place, get rid of mementos, or even change how they react to the cognitively impaired person – providing their loved one the freedom to leave a room agitated without trying to persuade or control them.

Alternative Temptations

As we age and mature, encountering various life events along the way, we often develop new interests. Over time we look differently at life, others we know, and ourselves. A form of we-ness that once mattered a great deal to us may no longer carry the same significance. We may even be disgusted with ourselves that we ever entertained such a connection. Our firsthand experiences and our exposure to new ideas can lead us to see the grass as being greener with another person, group, or ideology. Thus, we choose to initiate many of our transitions away from the forms of we-ness we've recently maintained. When we do this, we sometimes incorporate a different type of we-ness into our lives, or we simply forge ahead for some time without adding any new commitments to people, groups, or ideologies.

Many of our transitions out of a feeling of we-ness appeal to us because we see the change as placing us on a new and desirable life trajectory. The teenager transitioning from high school to college may decide to detach himself from his band of irresponsible, risk-taking, drinking buddies as he makes a commitment to himself, and perhaps his parents, to adopt a more responsible, studious mindset and lifestyle. If the identity transition is authentic, he may quickly find himself on a college campus developing a sense of we-ness with a regular study group of academically devoted peers, all committed to completing their engineering degrees on schedule with impressive GPAs.

Our romantic relationship breakups sometimes occur after we reevaluate our commitment to a current partner and the we-ness we once shared. Our reassessment may emerge because we anticipate how our future will be restricted if we stay in a specific relationship, or we are already experiencing a stronger sense of we-ness with someone else who we believe is a better fit for us. Either way, these transitions typically involve a modicum of self-reflection or at least a nagging gut feeling that things are not going as well as we want and that other options await us. Making the decision to move on and away from the we-ness we've known, and toward a healthier set of outcomes, may be a no brainer. However, social constraints like co-parenting kids, or owning a home together, or not being financially independent, or any number of other things we view as constraints may alter how clearly we see alternatives and how confident we are that we should pursue them.

The same sort of process of being tempted by other options exists in many aspects of our lives, including work, faith, leisure activities, friendships, and more. Maintaining a form of we-ness typically involves our time and effort. Aside from finding other life options for we-ness that are more appealing, we may believe that, for now, not having commitments and certain types of bonds is best. We may walk away from business partnerships, stop exercising with our workout buddy, or lose interest in a network of friendships tied to a regular poker game all because we want fewer personal obligations and more alone time. Being less involved with others and not being committed to certain ideologies are always options that we can pursue that take us away from our former expressions of we-ness. When we leave our state of we-ness it may be in search of ourselves separate from others – an adventure in personal growth.

Authenticity and Second Thoughts

Almost all of us want to feel some sense of belonging to other people and groups or be committed to a set of ideas. Some of us want this so badly that we deceive ourselves into thinking that we can alter our personality and disposition to fit in with others. At times we may do this in a relatively mindful way, believing that we can become the type of person we need to be to have others accept us and form a spirit of we-ness. Other times we may unwittingly deceive ourselves into believing we are a certain type of person who wants to be connected to others in a particular way. Imagine the woman who's convinced that she wants to have a child with her partner, but if she were being "honest" with herself, she doesn't really want to become a mother, at least not at this time. She does, however, want to make her partner happy. So, she goes ahead with the plan to have a child even though, in her heart, she isn't fully convinced that she wants the maternal type of we-ness. Her ambiguity may even impede the depth of the we-ness she establishes with her child.

Many of my students pledge sororities and fraternities, hoping to secure a prominent place in the university community and to bond with others who are presumably like-minded and popular. For many, this process works out well, and they enjoy their time socializing with their peers and finding opportunities to share the social aspects of the fun university life. Together they bond through parties, football games, social events, volunteering, and more.

But other students in the Greek system come to the realization that they are not cut out for this type of university social life after all. They may have convinced themselves that they belonged during the pledging process and for a semester or two, but eventually they come to realize that their authentic self is being suppressed. They feel that the "bonds" they've established are either meaningless, superficial, fake, or contrived. After one class, a student proudly confided in me as we walked across campus that she had as of that morning resigned her spot in her sorority. The previous week, she had sat in my office and shared her despondence over having an outlook on life that was quite different from how her sorority sisters perceived the world. She didn't feel a sense of we-ness with them like they seemed to have with one another. But now, during our walking chat, she said she felt relieved and confident that she was moving on with her life in a more authentic way. Whatever we-ness she might have longed for with her sorority sisters was meaningless to her now. She wasn't looking to replace the we-ness she had immediately; she just wanted to be at peace with herself and her ideals.

While the stakes are admittedly less significant, this young woman showed a lot more courage and inner strength than many politicians. Far too many public figures would rather distort their ethics and be hypocritical to their previously stated political values so they can stay true to their party and avoid the threat of being voted out of office. Many people, not just politicians, find it extremely difficult to discard a cherished form of we-ness because they believe their self-image is wedded to them receiving a certain type of group recognition. This is also the reality for those who honor the "code of silence" in groups such as fraternities, law enforcement, and the military. In the ideal world, being "limber," as psychiatrists Jacqueline Olds and Richard S. Schwartz suggest, is critical for those who are deeply invested in groups and communities. They astutely note:

> The dark side of community can be complacency, cowardice, and complicity. A healthy community, whether it appreciates the fact or not, needs both the bonds of loyalty and the willingness to risk isolation and loneliness in the name of the greater good. Both individuals and communities thrive when they can hold on to the tension between belonging and standing alone.[61]

The greater good they reference alludes to holding groups accountable to an ethical stance that protects human dignity and liberty.

Changing Leadership

Ideally, the leaders of the small groups, organizations, and social movements we belong to represent our core values and beliefs. Although we often join a group for reasons not directly linked to its leader, sometimes we initially cast our lot with others because we've been inspired by a specific person at the top. Other times we've already established a we-ness alongside others in a group and the leadership changes. The new person may enhance our commitment, reinforce a steady state, or discourage our involvement in the prevailing we-ness we've been managing.

Irrespective of why we decide to join, we are often encouraged to stay the course because we believe in a leader and their message. Whether it is the head of our labor union, the minister at our church, or the president of our fraternal organization, our willingness to devote our time, energy, money, and reputation to various group activities hinges on our belief that a leader embodies our ideals. But leaders, like their followers, have their flaws – some more than others. Consequently, we sometimes choose to leave our we-ness behind when we believe that a leader has acted in a compromising way that jeopardizes their reputation as a fair-minded, genuine leader who reflects our world view. Recall how many members of the Buddhafield cult left because they came to understand that the leader, Michel, was more self-serving than empathic. Or consider the many high-level departures from the Trump administration and the federal government. Those who left often believed that President Trump was violating long-standing institutional norms that had in the past inspired professionals to serve their country while being part of a patriotic community that put the country over both party and personal interests.

Throughout our lives, whether we're leaving a group or trying to sustain a sense of we-ness, we make numerous decisions about which ideas to embrace and how to connect or disconnect with others as we participate in the five social domains central to this book. As we make these decisions, our familiarity with we-ness can offer us a taste of stability and fulfillment. Yet, we still find ourselves making subtle as well as fundamental changes over the years that involve our approach to group belonging. Inevitably, some of us face far more uncertainty and change in our lives than do others. Nevertheless, when we refine our *MEAL* life skills, we are more likely to make healthy choices about our social connections that leave us feeling empowered and happy.

6

We-ness, Empathy, and Altruism

Our encounters with we-ness are woven into the routines and rituals that penetrate our daily lives. Reflect on the joy and pain you've encountered at various times as you've built a sense of we-ness and sometimes transitioned out of it. Those moments reveal how you've experienced euphoria, taken risks, made yourself vulnerable, or had your trust violated. Our personality and social circumstances led us to manage those situations in particular ways. But our involvement in the world of we-ness also shapes our disposition and outlook on what it means to belong to a group or to be excluded from one. When we are led well, supported, and learn what it's like to achieve group goals in healthy ways, we are better prepared to become capable leaders ourselves. However, when others lead us poorly or betray our trust, we sometimes become disillusioned with certain forms of we-ness. As a result, we may turn inward, choosing a solo path to protect our psyche and heart. Eventually, some of us may find ourselves drawn to hate groups that empower us. Fueled by fear, we lash out in anger to avenge our emotional trauma and isolation.

Cultural circumstances set the tone and terms for how we define ourselves and seek opportunities to belong to a group or thought community. Over the past 150-plus years, we have witnessed a rapidly changing social landscape. It has altered how we have constructed our personal identities and group-affiliated sense of we-ness. The changes have been ignited by numerous large-scale cultural developments including industrialization, urbanization, social justice movements and reforms, organized sports, the growth in volunteer and fraternal organizations, an expansion of the types and numbers of information/news outlets, and the adoption of transformative communication technologies, including, most recently, social media.

At times, we've responded to these developments by making deliberative, sometimes passionate, decisions that reflect our choice either to embrace or reject them. On other occasions, we've found ourselves passively going with the flow, allowing ourselves to be engulfed by the tides of change. One of the cultural circumstances at issue is identity politics, a historically significant form of deliberative decision-making, which emerged in the twentieth century. It focuses on people developing and fighting for political agendas based on factors that identify them as distinct and socially disadvantaged. Beginning in the 1960s, a new brand of identity politics was born in the name of African Americans, women, and sexual minorities. It was punctuated by "consciousness raising groups" and social movement activities. As a result, we saw increasing numbers of people assert their right to define themselves and to bond with other like-minded people on their terms. The seeds for this sort of individualism have been engrained in the American experience for centuries. But the cultural forces that coalesced in the 1960s encouraged marginalized individuals, supported by increasingly powerful displays of collective consciousness, to assert their personal identities in public. Unfortunately, while the practice of identity politics brought some people together, this cultural shift degraded the cooperative ethic that had previously linked citizenship to a broader – although distinctively white – sense of shared commonality and community.[1]

Those who fought to affirm their political rights did so by forging bonding and bridging social capital. The alliances that many built involved partnerships with people outside their restricted, homogenous group. These patterns, built on empathy, implicitly give us an insight into the public's need to channel the power of we-ness.

Every era is marked by its own unique set of social issues and conditions that shape the public's approach to we-ness. As I began writing these words in the summer of 2020, most of the industrialized world was struggling to define and forge the kind of solidarity that would save the lives of family, friends, and strangers in the face of COVID-19. Ironically, calls for promoting we-ness and slogans like "we're in this together" are rallying cries that are used to justify the implementation of social/physical distancing strategies. We are asked to adopt a sense of community, state, nation, and global we-ness that temporarily forces us to isolate ourselves in hopes of curtailing the spread of the virus and the human toll of the disease. But it was only a matter of time until protests of stay-at-home orders erupted in some states, revealing how competing efforts to define and act upon a state of we-ness can, and often do, coexist.

During the pandemic, the expansion of the Black Lives Matter movement following the murder of George Floyd galvanized many participants from different backgrounds to march and protest police brutality and systemic racism. The movement, as reflected in its chant "silence is violence," encouraged many white people to recognize that their silence on racial injustices reflected their complicity. It forced many whites to empathize more fully with persons of color. In doing so, many reframed their image of a national we-ness by pledging their allegiance to a more progressive social justice ideology and shared identity that transcended race. The profound weight of the displays of empathy, altruism, loving-kindness, and compassion began to shift our collective consciousness, although the white backlash was reenergized as well.

Informed by the lessons of history, we should be mindful of our current social circumstances to project a meaningful path forward. This path needs to expand opportunities to strengthen forms of we-ness and enhance personal well-being while contributing to a cohesive and just society. For many, nurturing our involvement in healthy forms of we-ness can be the antidote to loneliness and other difficulties. In every realm of social life, we should push ourselves to become more trustworthy and demand that our leaders, associates, neighbors, family, and friends live their lives with integrity as well. In our culture – one that perpetuates cruelty, bullying, and dishonesty – we must all push ourselves to be more empathic and civil while encouraging others to do the same. Imagine the possibilities if we were to become more like the unassuming, kind, and thoughtful Fred Rogers, who hosted the preschool television series *Mister Rogers' Neighborhood* from 1969 to 2001.[2] As depicted by Tom Hanks in the acclaimed 2019 movie, *A Beautiful Day in the Neighborhood*, Fred Rogers spent his professional and personal life thinking about others' feelings, doing kind deeds, and trying to nurture a healthy spirit of we-ness with everyone he met. The upside to belonging and feeling we-ness would surely grow if more people lived their lives like Fred Rogers.

We all stand to benefit personally and socially if we can nurture our spirit of togetherness while sustaining key aspects of our individualism. Thus, we must hold ourselves and others accountable to the institutional norms that call for our social and political selves to be governed by compassion, fairness, equality, and integrity. These were the virtues upon which our founding fathers built our unique republic many years ago. That republic, as exemplified by the famous passage "life, liberty, and the pursuit of happiness" from the Declaration of Independence, can only succeed if people thoughtfully manage their group activities and build supportive types of we-ness. If we are to advocate for positive social change, we must enhance the social contexts and practices by which we-ness will flourish alongside personal growth and freedom, community engagement, and social justice. We should commit ourselves to improving our ability to express empathy, altruism, loving-kindness, and compassion.

Nurturing We-ness

For better or worse, our pursuit of we-ness is a defining feature of our humanity. Even though some of us go to great lengths to distinguish ourselves in various ways, most of us want to fit in with the groups that matter to us. We are comforted by knowing that we share common traits and beliefs with others. Thus, we seek to establish meaning in our lives through our group affiliations. Part of that search is guided by our desire to pursue what most of us call happiness. We typically use this term in everyday life to refer to feeling good, experiencing pleasure, or having fun. Most of us search for "happiness" by seeking immediate gratification or a momentary feeling of contentment that is linked to a pleasurable sensation.

But this view of a time-bound, psychological sensation is not the form of happiness described by Buddhist teachings or what Aristotle espoused. Likewise, the narrow vision of happiness differs from the sentiment Thomas Jefferson and the other founding fathers had in mind when they incorporated the word "happiness" into the Declaration of Independence. In *Happiness: A Guide to Developing Life's Most Important Skill*, the Buddhist monk, Matthieu Ricard, describes happiness as a "deep sense of flourishing that arises from an exceptionally healthy mind. This is not a mere pleasurable feeling, a fleeting emotion, or a mood, but an optimal state of being." He adds that it is "also a way of interpreting the world."[3] Establishing this profound inner peace requires us, in the Buddhist tradition, to discard the common misconception of reality that is distorted by mental constructs. We must, instead, see that "everything is *relation*; nothing exists in and of itself, immune to the forces of cause and effect."[4] In other words, we are encouraged to embrace a consciousness of togetherness and unbounded interdependence. Although we may perceive our consciousness as emanating from our own mind, our thoughts are merely threads in a seamless expression of we-ness.

This broader definition of happiness is more consistent with the authentic pursuit of durable forms of deep dyadic and ideational we-ness outlined in this book. When these forms of we-ness are pursued in a manner that supports good moral character, or what Aristotle labeled "complete virtue," healthy decisions are more likely to be made with an eye toward maximizing the good that can be accumulated over an entire life.

The twentieth-century American philosopher Mortimer J. Adler conceptualizes the "ancient ethical conception of happiness as a whole life well lived because it is enriched by the cumulative possession of all the goods that a morally virtuous human being ought to desire."[5] Following Aristotle's lead, Adler also stresses that happiness in its traditional sense is not an individual pursuit. It involves working with others to achieve this desired state of being. Indeed, he writes that "the pursuit of happiness must be cooperative, not competitive. We do not have the right view of it unless we see it as something which men [and women] can help one another to achieve – instead of achieving it by beating our neighbors."[6] When we view happiness in a deeper, more enduring, and cooperative way, the expression of a virtuous form of we-ness seems essential to achieving and sustaining it. Faced with his impending death, former sociology professor Morrie Schwartz shared a clear message about human connectedness that illustrates this fundamental point: healthy we-ness begets happiness in the long run. As innately social beings, a calculus that highlights we-ness depicts our most logical path to pursue a well-lived life.

So how do we harness the social energy of we-ness and learn to direct it with more precision to promote happiness, the good life, social cohesion, and a just society? How can we better encourage the production of bonding and bridging social capital with and between our families, work groups, sports teams, community organizations, special interest groups, and more? As social architects of the good life, how can we better design our institutions and communities to synchronize our individual and collective desires to produce healthy outcomes? More broadly, how can we push back against the dehumanization processes that are challenging our interpersonal connections as human beings – like being required to deal with interactive voice response (IVR) systems? These questions are critical because we derive personal meaning and celebrate our humanity when we successfully participate in diverse groups and embrace collective identities.

One of my favorite examples of how people have collaborated to create an innovative approach to address the issues noted above is the Greater Good Science Center (GGSC). Launched in 2001, this multifaceted project is housed at the University of California, Berkeley. GGSC produces *Greater Good Magazine*, free online courses, a library of research-tested practices, a podcast, videos, public events, an education program, a parenting initiative, a gratitude journal, and programs that target health professionals and workplace leaders. These products are designed to further the GGSC's mission, which is to "explore the roots of happy and compassionate individuals, strong social bonds, and altruistic behavior – the science of a meaningful life."[7] The magazine, as well as the other information mediums, provides an education service by highlighting how the practical application of scientific research can enhance people's personal lives and strengthen connections between different segments of the community. In many respects, this center works to bring about the ideal set of circumstances that foster a supportive interplay between building a healthy "me" and a healthy "we."

When done well, our efforts to develop we-ness can lead us to experience a sense of purpose and personal growth in the process. Numerous cultural discourses already reinforce the value of group belonging. These are engrained in our family ideologies, religious traditions, educational teachings, sports slogans, political rhetoric, social justice activism, volunteering spirit, and media messages. Irrespective of context, social reformers' overarching objectives should be to create a social philosophy and a set of institutional structures, rituals, and norms that generate bonding and bridging social capital that improves people's lives. We must nurture our cooperative capacity to express empathy, altruism, loving-kindness, compassion, trust, collaboration, courage, and enlightened self-interest in our daily lives.

Empathy and Contemplative Practice

Much of this book is designed to deepen our understanding of how we manage our sense of we-ness and relate to others. If we are to do better at developing healthy forms of we-ness with those who matter to us, and strengthen our commitments to meaningful collective identities, we must adopt more mindful practices. As Roman Krznaric astutely notes, it is "by stepping into the world of experience – through immersions, exploration, and cooperation – that we can make huge leaps in our ability to understand the lives of others."[8] When we become more mindful and reach out to others, we learn to appreciate more fully the value of our connections with them. The good news: various streams of research indicate that, if we want to, our mindful practices can change our outlook on and quality of life, our brain chemistry, and our relations with others.

In recent decades, everyday Americans and professionals from diverse academic fields have increasingly focused on a wide range of contemplative practices. Historically, Buddhist monks have been revered for their ability to meditate and express loving-kindness and compassion to others because of their experiential wisdom and self-control. People from other spiritual traditions have also highlighted the power of introspection and meditation.

Those personally invested in these practices seek to become more self-aware by turning inward. They calm themselves, removing the mental and emotional clutter that distorts their way of knowing and feeling. When this happens, they can reflect deeply in the moment on their thoughts, feelings, and physical movements. Through meditation, yoga, journaling, tai chi, and other contemplative practices, individuals try to get in touch with their inner sense of self, reduce stress, and relax. Recently, researchers in academic fields like neuroscience, psychology, psychiatry, and others are quickly accumulating evidence that shows how these practices enhance people's mental and emotional states.[9] In addition, contemplative practice alters how compassionately people treat others – a bonus for those interested in promoting their concept of we-ness for themselves as well as others.

A thriving enterprise has emerged over the past few decades to promote and study contemplative practices and empathy. A quick glance at the psychology, philosophy, self-help, and religion sections of the local bookstore reveals a wide range of books designed to help a person get in touch with their inner self, engage in self-healing and self-love, develop their interpersonal skills, and effectively channel their emotions. Similarly, numerous resources like the Center for Building a Culture of Empathy, founded by Edwin Rutsch; the Empathy Library and Empathy Museum, created by Roman Krznaric; and the Empathy and Relational Science Program at Massachusetts General Hospital as well as the company Empathetics, Inc., both founded by Helen Riess, seek to establish a culture and infrastructure that promotes empathy.[10]

Contemporary public thinkers and activists have deliberately elevated the profile of empathy by injecting the word more squarely into the commercial, academic, political, and social justice worlds.

Presidents Barack Obama and Joe Biden are perhaps the most high-profile people in recent memory to speak out forcefully about the importance of empathy in public life. During an interview with talk show host Oprah Winfrey, prior to becoming president, Obama reflected on how his mother instilled the significance of empathy into him at a young age. He now places empathy at the center of his politics.[11] His vision to "make a habit of empathy" became a central theme in what he believes politics can do for society.

In contrast, much has been made of Donald Trump's empathy deficit. During his presidency, the empathy concept was still featured in public discourse, just in a different way. Commentators repeatedly remarked about his inexplicable inability to relate authentically to those who suffered directly or indirectly from gun violence, COVID-19, natural disasters, unemployment, systemic racism, and many other causes. He was portrayed, rightfully so in my opinion, as being a narcissistic, coldhearted politician who was driven by transactional connections with his base of supporters and others he believed could serve his personal agenda. Psychiatrist and empathy expert Helen Riess pulled no punches when she denounced Trump's inability to display authentic empathy:

> While he mimed empathy for lower-income, forgotten white citizens, Trump managed to unleash vitriolic hostility toward people considered "other" and out-grouped in our society. In effect, he showed the exact opposite of empathy; he showed disdain, disrespect, and contempt for huge segments of vulnerable people in American society.[12]

Trump may be the most prominent American with an empathy deficit, but scores of others struggle to surmount what sociologist Arlie Russell Hochschild labels the "empathy wall." She portrays this as "an obstacle to deep understanding of another person, one that can make us feel indifferent or even hostile to those who hold different beliefs or whose childhood is rooted in different circumstances."[13] This wall often restricts our ability to see others fully. As such, we see others superficially, forcing new information into our preexisting, narrow ways of thinking.

Our current empathy deficit is pervasive even though contemplative practices and the study of empathy have become increasingly popular in recent decades. The social practice of empathy is not new and it has profoundly influenced the arc of our historical development for several centuries. According to Jeremy Rifkin, "it is the extraordinary evolution of empathic consciousness that is the quintessential underlying story of human history."[14] More specifically, Harvard psychologist Steven Pinker argues that it has dramatically altered our approach to slavery, poverty, mistreatment of minorities, and torture.[15] In other words, empathy is a transformational force that has profoundly shaped human history.

Krznaric proposes that three major "waves of empathy" have shaped Western history dating back to the 1700s. The first wave is represented by the emergence and growth of humanitarian organizations and movements across Europe and the United States in the eighteenth and nineteenth centuries. These developments reflected a shift in public sentiment about government-sanctioned cruelty toward people in the West and many other places around the world. People grew increasingly less comfortable with, and eventually appalled by, many of the horrendous practices in earlier times that included the mistreatment of children at home and at work, slavery, and the gruesome torture that was a staple of judicial life. Indeed, Pinker asserts in his groundbreaking book, *The Better Angels of Our Nature: The Decline of Violence in History and Its Causes*, that "a habit of identifying with the pleasures and pains of others" became a distinctive feature of the nascent culture of empathy during this period.[16] As a pervasive and potent cultural force, it laid the foundation for people to be more sensitive to the needs and circumstances of those outside their own family and friends.

After the atrocities of World Wars I and II, which demonstrated the uneven trajectory of collective empathy over the centuries, a second wave of collective empathy emerged in the 1950s and 60s. It illustrated the growing concern for new social groups and the caring public sentiment that extended beyond national boundaries. The identity rights movements that flowered in the United States for people of color, women, and sexual minorities were part of this consequential push toward a more expansive and action-oriented form of empathy. Along with these movements, people cooperated to forge humanitarian organizations like Amnesty International. Muhammad Ali, the former world champion boxer, cultural icon, and outspoken critic of racial injustice, captured one of the more powerful sentiments of the era. At his 1975 commencement speech at Harvard University, Ali responded to a request from someone in the audience, "Give us a poem, Muhammad." After a brief pause, Ali replied "Me. We." This creatively short yet provocative poem inspires us to think imaginatively about the meaning of life. It can compel us to reflect on the significant relationship between the personal and political. We might also ponder Ali's expression as a point of tension between competing life perspectives that waver between the ego-centered and the community-based, or as an intimate reminder of our paradoxical shared humanity. In the most fundamental sense, self and society are interdependent; one cannot exist without the other.

Krznaric points to the 1990s as the timeframe for the emergence of the third wave. In his view, this wave encapsulates the idea that empathy came to be "used more prominently in public messaging and highlighted as a catalyst for change in and of itself." Krznaric believes these changes have been occurring in three primary ways: "teaching empathy skills to schoolchildren, resolving and mediating conflict situations, and generating empathy for future generations to help tackle climate change."[17]

In our current historical moment, Krznaric warns that we have both a spatial and temporal empathy deficit that needs to be addressed. We have much to learn about developing empathy for others outside our immediate physical surroundings. Too often, we find it hard to relate to those who live in different communities and countries who possess different belief systems, routines, and rituals. Similarly, our immediate self-serving interests discourage many of us from thinking compassionately beyond our current generation. Krznaric challenges us to do a better job of being concerned about how our decisions will alter the world for our children, grandchildren, and all subsequent generations. Nowhere is this more important than with respect to environmental issues, including climate change, but a generational sense of urgency can be applied to other issues like gun control, health care, systemic racism, and all forms of social inequality. Whether it is across space or time, it is imperative that we deepen our ability to appreciate our connection to a larger we-ness that reflects our shared humanity.

Unfortunately, in today's world, we are increasingly besieged by extreme weather events that drain our capacity to empathize with strangers. From January through September of 2021, record setting hurricanes, tornados, flash floods, wildfires, and extreme temperatures in the United States resulted in 538 deaths and $104.8 billion in property damage. These disasters, exacerbated by the emotional and logistical challenges of the COVID-19 pandemic, forced many to focus on their own survival needs. And those who were protected from the personal trauma inflicted by natural disasters often felt overwhelmed by the never-ending news of climate destruction. Many were too exhausted to feel compassion for remote disaster victims or for humanity more generally. Instead, these tragedies compelled some to turn toward their insular circle of family and friends. Moving forward, the threats posed by climate change will rally many people to embrace a larger collective cause and expand their circle of empathy, but others will cling to their more isolationist, self-serving perspective.

Acknowledging the power of empathy and mindfulness to tackle global problems and poised to shape the future, the Mind & Life Institute has provided important leadership in the movement to make contemplative practice more mainstream in both everyday life and in the world of science. Founded in 1991 and located in Charlottesville, Virginia, this institute represents an innovative effort to find constructive ways to integrate contemplative practices into a range of scientific fields. The 14th Dalai Lama, Francisco Varela (a scientist and philosopher), and Adam Engle (a lawyer and entrepreneur) created this innovative institute after a series of meetings beginning in 1987. Since its inception, the institute has been responsible for producing a wide range of thought-provoking dialogues (conferences), books, and videos. Its mission as of 2022 is to

bring science and contemplative wisdom together to better understand the mind and create positive change in the world. At this critical moment in history, it's clear that efforts to address mounting global challenges must take into account our inner lives, and how individual well-being contributes to collective flourishing. At the heart of today's global challenges is a profound crisis of disconnection. From loneliness and isolation to racism and tribalism, our disconnection from one another is causing tremendous suffering for people and the planet. Building on our 30-year legacy, we seek to better understand the role of the human mind in creating these problems – and its potential to solve them.[18]

The institute has already left its mark by inspiring scholars to develop programs of research that bridge scientific inquiry with contemplative practices. One such researcher is Richard Davidson, a psychologist and psychiatrist at the University of Wisconsin. The Dalai Lama challenged Davidson years ago to apply his scientific curiosity to understanding the positive forces that enhance individuals' well-being. Davidson accepted the challenge. He now studies the links between the brain and emotions at the Center for Healthy Minds at the University of Wisconsin–Madison, which he launched in 2010 with financial support from the Dalai Lama's trust. Much of Davidson's work has revealed the internal processes and consequences of the brain's neuroplasticity.[19] The brain can generate new neurons, alter the functioning of preexisting neurons, and change the functioning of areas of the brain.[20] In addition, geneticists have discovered that when environmental forces reshape our brains, it can either activate or deactivate the expression of genes through a process called epigenetics. That process continues to affect the expression of genes for subsequent generations.

An advocate of meditation and other contemplative practices, Davidson champions the idea that we can and should play a more intentional role in shaping our emotions and our brain. He describes well-being as a skill. Consequently, if we regularly and mindfully engage in certain practices, we can change our brain chemistry in positive ways that will, in turn, make us feel better. In particular, he highlights how we can train our mind to improve our well-being by focusing on its four main components: resilience, (positive) outlook, attention, and generosity.[21]

Davidson believes that, if motivated, we can improve our ability to deal with and recover from adversity more quickly. For example, when we successfully cultivate a purpose in life, we are more likely to express greater resiliency. If we develop a mindset that encourages us to have positive emotions and to see the good in situations, we improve our chances of lowering our cortisol levels and enhancing our sense of well-being as a result. In short, by eliminating unwanted stress in our lives, we produce positive results for our overall well-being. When we teach ourselves to be more mindful of our immediate circumstances and to focus attentively on the task at hand, we tend to be more content and happier. When our minds wander, we often fixate unproductively on the things we want but don't possess. Finally, research shows that the set of prosocial qualities, including empathy, compassion, and gratitude, are associated with improving a person's well-being.[22] It turns out that people can be trained and primed to be more prosocial and grateful while improving all aspects of their well-being. When we show generosity toward others, we help them and often improve our own well-being too.

When we nurture self-love and enhance our own well-being, we are better positioned to lead and to grow healthy forms of we-ness with family, friends, neighbors, coworkers, and others we relate to in a group context.[23] In addition, once we have learned to be more mindful, we are better positioned to express empathy, altruism, loving-kindness, and compassion toward others. We can train ourselves to express empathy more effectively. The psychologist Jamil Zaki champions the idea that we – as ordinary people – can bring about social change by learning how to pay closer attention to others' feelings, thoughts, and experiences.[24] A meta-analysis of numerous empathy studies suggests that it is easier for us to learn how to express cognitive empathy (mentalizing) than emotional empathy (experience sharing and prosocial concern) because the latter is linked more clearly to genetic factors.[25]

Our ability to imagine the inner worlds of those we think about and sometimes encounter enhances our ability to empathize with others. This skill can be improved with practice, but it is not equally available to all people. In fact, those who are autistic may have only limited or no capacity to take the role of another person and relate to their feelings. However, innovative technology is being developed that provides hope to those who are challenged to express empathy because of their autism.[26]

Catalin Voss, a German-born tech prodigy who left home for Silicon Valley as an emancipated minor at sixteen years of age, initially developed the expression recognition software used in a promising new product. This young entrepreneur enrolled at Stanford University and eventually pursued his PhD in Artificial Intelligence. There he founded a start-up vision company, Sension, and has worked with engineers at Stanford to perfect the pairing of his software with the Google Glass concept. Google Glass, first introduced in 2012, involved attaching a transparent computer to a set of glasses that was designed to combine digital data with the analog world. Despite the initial hype, Google's product failed beta testing and was never mass-marketed. However, Voss and his partners have since created eyewear that incorporates Voss's software for interpreting facial expressions. The software calculates what the target person is most likely feeling. That calculation is then transformed into an emoji and projected in the upper right corner of the glasses for the wearer to see in real time. The first preliminary trials with autistic youth began in 2016 and have produced encouraging results that could culminate in a medical device that supports AI-based reality therapy for children with autism. Although some in the field are enthusiastic about the possibilities, others challenge the assumption that emotions can be inferred with precision by observing facial expressions.[27]

What is not contested is that many children on the autism spectrum have a difficult time fitting in with others and developing a sense of group belonging. Unable to navigate the emotional, interactive world that would enable them to establish a sense of we-ness with family, friends, and others, children who struggle with autism find themselves isolated from their social surroundings. Ideally, therapeutic applications along the lines of Voss's AI-augmented therapy innovation will help at least some of these children develop new types of bonds with others, offering them the chance to forge a dyadic style of we-ness unavailable to them previously.

We can also anticipate that the unique features and ubiquitous reach of the internet will foster new empathy-building strategies. Zaki describes his personal foray into using Koko, an app that is paired with the popular messaging app, Kik. Koko is a bot that offers individuals the chance to build and express empathy using an informal style of peer-to-peer cognitive behavioral therapy.[28] In just a few years, it has generated a novel online social networking community that fosters anonymous yet intimate help between strangers, especially teens and young adults. Users can send short messages describing their worries to thousands of users around the world. New users are also briefly given instructions on empathic listening so they can help others if they wish to, and many do. A tutorial provides information about the process of "rethinking" or applying a more optimistic view to a situation. The Koko design has produced a massive, crowdsourced network that distributes a nonprofessional mental health resource that 95 percent of users evaluate as being helpful.

Koko is a viable system today because it capitalizes on our capacity to experience intersubjectivity, which allows a person to realize that they can share similar feelings with others. Throughout the ages, our public mediums for communication have helped us better imagine how others feel and think.[29] Fiction and memoirs, for example, have played an important role in sharpening readers' ability to understand others unlike themselves, as well as those who share similar characteristics. Writing about the historical evolution of the concept of "human rights" in *Inventing Human Rights*, the historian Lynn Hunt proposes that people's access to novels has given them options to relate to people who may otherwise be outside their social circle.

Writing about the significance of the epistolary or letter form of novels in the 1700s, Hunt highlights the power of three specific books written by men about female heroines: Samuel Richardson's *Pamela* (1740) and *Clarissa* (1747–8), and Jean-Jacques Rousseau's *Julie* (1761). Hunt argues that these types of novels allowed the readers of the day, as well as the rest of us in more recent times, to appreciate the notion that "all selves were in some sense equal because all were alike in their possession of interiority [having an inner character]."[30]

Unlike the theatrical play, the emerging novel format allowed the author to write intimately about a character's emotions, allowing the reader to imagine themselves as being close to them, and learn a new approach to express empathy. For centuries, memoirs have also left their mark on readers and have provided them with an alternative perspective to understanding others. For instance, many people living in Britain in the 1830s and far removed from the practice of slavery, were given an intimate view of the slave experience when they read Mary Prince's personal narrative, which was first published in 1831.[31]

Similarly, film, in its many forms, offers consumers a powerful means to practice their empathy skills from afar. Educators' thoughtful use of literature, film, photography, and other art forms to enlighten people about others' unique experiences can also train people to be more comfortable and skilled while empathizing with others.[32] On their own, or with an educator's guidance, some will ultimately believe that by experiencing a stranger's voice situated outside their own set of circumstances, they can appreciate more fully what people from different backgrounds experience and feel.

Whether it is through novels, poetry, film, documentary photography, or other forms of creative visual art, the art form of storytelling is uniquely poised to move us to see and feel the world from another person's perspective. The Empathy Museum and one of its projects, *A Mile in My Shoes*, represents a superbly creative contemporary empathy project that relies on storytelling.[33] The British artist Clare Patey collaborated with Roman Krznaric to launch this participatory art project in 2015 in London. Their purpose was to help visitors come to grips with global issues, including prejudice, conflict, and inequality, by tapping into people's ability to empathize and change relationships. As of 2021, the exhibit had been shown throughout the UK, Australia, Belgium, Brazil, Ireland, Scotland, Russia, and the United States and is customized to include local voices that are added to the expanding database.

The museum is an interactive, one-room portable structure shaped like a large shoebox. Once a patron enters the shoebox, the person can pick out a pair of shoes from a wide selection of styles and sizes that are like those worn by the storytellers. In addition, the visitors borrow headphones to listen to the roughly ten-minute audiotape while they walk in the shoes of the selected narrator. Each tape includes a person sharing some aspect of their personal life story. Some of the voices represent Syrian refugees, sex workers, war veterans, neurosurgeons, world travelers, and many others. The stories, which are available online as well, strike an emotional chord by prodding us to empathize in order to understand different lived experiences, and to embrace that larger version of we-ness that connects us to our shared humanity.

One story I listened to at random online was by Shawna Reed; her story resonated with me because we both grew up in small towns in Pennsylvania and then left.[34] In my case, I only returned for brief family visits over many years. Shawna, being far more adventurous than I am, returned to her rural town outside Philadelphia after traveling the world for ten years, visiting thirty countries, and staying with roughly 250 host families. She recalls the impetus for returning to her childhood town: "One day I realized how many incredible people I'd met, and how many incredible people I'd left behind."

In a riveting narrative style, Shawna describes how upon her return home she had an overwhelming face-to-face confrontation with an old friend and former neighbor, Trevor, with whom she had been very close during her childhood. When she was growing up, people joked that "we were two peas in a pod and just should have been born in the same body." As kids, they would often seclude themselves from their neighborhood friends to play with their imaginations, write stories, and choreograph dances together long into the night.

Their volatile exchange occurred when they found themselves embroiled in an intense, nasty argument. It was partly fueled by her surprise and anger over hearing about his staunch support for President Trump and his politics. Ultimately, after their heated conversation plummeted into name-calling barbs being hurled back and forth, Trevor grew silent. He then opened his arms wide to initiate a "Trevor hug" that Shawna fell into, emotionally drained but comforted. After the hug, Shawna said to him through tears:

"Trevor why, why don't you want to hear my stories, why don't you want to see my pictures, I just wanna share my life with you?" And he said to me, "Because every time you've ever left to go meet people like them, out there, you become just a little less excited, to come back here, home, to people like me." He said, "You've spent a lifetime trying to understand them and in the process forgot where you came from."

Trevor's words forced her to dissect how her style of communicating the stories about her international journeys were "coming across as condescending." She began to realize how she had assumed he wouldn't understand her worldly adventures because he hadn't left their town to experience something similar. But she also sensed that she hadn't walked in his shoes, either. They had each been shaped by their own set of social forces. Recognizing this was crucial for restoring the deep sense of we-ness they once shared.

Now, as she reflects on those powerful exchanges with Trevor, she says she is comforted to know that she has "people back home who hold me accountable to my roots and who gave me the wings to fly and the courage to chase my dreams." She also cherishes having such a strong relationship with someone like Trevor who challenges her not only to "hold space for people that think and act like me, but more importantly, for people who don't." Shawna is grounded by her relationship with Trevor and their complicated sense of we-ness, which enables her to put into perspective the growing challenges others confront in our increasingly tribal world.

Shawna's story reminded me of a moment in my own life when my older sister, who had taken a secretarial job right out of high school and continues to live in the general vicinity, and mother confronted me in our childhood basement during a rare family "meeting" when I was probably in my mid-thirties. I listened to them describe how they felt that my life circumstances of leaving the area to go to college and graduate school, and then pursuing a career out of state as a professor, had altered the way I looked at and talked to

them. Like Trevor, they felt that I sometimes treated them in a condescending manner. Their words resonated with me. I sensed their
concerns about how the quality of our family we-ness had changed
because of my shift in disposition.

Although I did not literally walk in Shawna's shoes, the podcast *A Mile in My Shoes* gave me a chance to compare her life to
the circumstances that defined my own we-ness experience. In that
respect, the project achieved its goal of promoting introspection.
It also continued the critical dialogue that bridges empathy with
our social experiences that build, question, and sustain our sense
of both dyadic and ideational we-ness. Moving forward, those of
us who feel enlightened by one of the art forms that take us into
people's minds may approach our social worlds differently. We can
decide whether we should be more accepting of others. We might
even establish a form of we-ness with a type of person we shunned
in the past.

Outside the world of art and performance, an increasing number of creative empathy-building interventions have been used in
a wide range of settings (e.g., education, business, policing, health
care, parenting) to train people to improve their empathy skills,
either for experiencing the internal feeling others have or expressing empathy toward those in distress.[35] One review that explores
the diverse approaches to improving empathy categorizes interventions as either self-oriented, group-based, or situation-based. Interventions that target an individual person who might provide empathy
can be assessed by distinguishing between persons who have a
growth or fixed mindset. Those in the former camp are more likely
to believe that they can alter their level of empathic effort in challenging situations. In contrast, those with a fixed mindset are more
apt to attribute their empathy failure to their lack of ability. Thus,
interventions are likely to be more successful if they can convince
people to believe that they can alter their empathic effort. When this
occurs, people will try harder to connect with others.

Group-based interventions are sensitive to the intergroup bias
that shapes how we often respond to others based on whether they
belong to our in-group or an out-group. Not surprisingly, we are
more likely to show empathy toward those with whom we share a

sense of we-ness because they belong to our common group. Our perceptions of those unlike ourselves are colored by our suspicions, distrust, intolerance, and competitive urges. Group interventions are more likely to succeed if they help us reframe our perceptions of in-group boundaries to make them more inclusive. In addition, an intervention can improve its effectiveness in promoting intergroup empathy if it can encourage the members of distinct groups to establish shared goals. Finally, programs can improve empathy when they transform in-group members' values to make them conducive to cooperating with an out-group. Or the programs can shape members' values favorably at the outset when a group is forming.

Another way to think about empathy-building interventions is to focus on the situational circumstances that shape whether and how people respond to others. Some interventions pay attention to what contextual conditions might induce us to express empathy. To what extent do we anticipate that feeling empathic and then expressing it toward others will be emotionally costly to us? Or enhance our emotional or physical outcomes? We might also encourage people to be more empathic if we convince them that empathy can help them satisfy their goals. For example, a business leader may be motivated to show empathy if she believes it will make her a more productive leader and enhance business outcomes.

Let's look closely at a couple of impressive empathy-building programs. The first, Roots of Empathy, is a self-oriented program.[36] It was piloted in 1996 in Canada by social entrepreneur, author, child advocate, and former preschool teacher Mary Gordon. For five years in a row, the program was selected as one of the top one hundred most impactful and scalable innovations in the world. As of 2022, this evidence-based classroom program has been used in at least thirteen countries, including the United States, and has served over a million children. The program espouses a "pedagogy of hope." Alongside a trained, certified instructor, it brings a parent and infant child (two to four months old at the program's beginning) from the neighborhood into classrooms of elementary and middle school-age students. The curriculum is specialized for four different age groups ranging from age five to thirteen. During the school year, the instructor visits twenty-seven times, devoting three visits apiece to one of nine themes (e.g., communicating, emotion, safety). Every three weeks, the parent-child pair joins the instructor for a fun, interactive session with the students. On the other weeks, the instructor visits the classroom alone to conduct pre- and post-visit lessons. The program, in Gordon's words,

> coaches children to build a caring classroom as they [learn] to see their shared humanity – the idea that "what hurts my feelings is likely to hurt your feelings." The program is based on the idea that if we are able to take the perspective of the Other we will notice and appreciate our commonalities and we will be less likely to allow differences to cause us to marginalize, hate or hurt each other.[37]

Using guided observations, the instructor helps students to appreciate different aspects of the parent-child relationship and the baby's temperament. Students are asked to engage in perspective-taking as they watch the baby interact with their environment. In practical terms, the instructor works with the students and classroom teacher to do creative activities that incorporate music, artwork, drama, journal writing, and regular school curricula such as social studies and math to reinforce the lessons. Directed by their classroom teacher and the program instructor, students are given opportunities to express generosity toward the baby and parent by using their curriculum to create classroom gifts. Participating students "become part of an authentic dialogue with the Roots of Empathy parent and get insight into the joys and worries of being a parent." During the visits when only the instructor is present, "students explore the connection between the baby's development and their own development; the connections between the baby's feelings and their own feelings."[38]

Teachers report that the program helps their students' emotional development and alters the tone of their classrooms. Students become more open and considerate of others. For example, one autistic nine-year-old boy who had never been invited to a birthday party by his classmates was invited to three during the year his classroom hosted the Roots of Empathy program. National and international evaluation studies of this program also show a reduction in aggression and an increase in prosocial behavior.

As Gordon thoughtfully reveals, the baby anchors her revolutionary program and is the "teacher." The baby delivers the magic that allows the program to grab and keep young children's attention and compel them to self-reflect, sharpen their emotional literacy, and learn the value of being kind to others:

> The baby's behaviour and the emotions she expresses are spontaneous and pure; they are not hidden behind layers of socialization and the biases we acquire as we grow up. To the baby every child in the class is a new experience and she is ready to engage with all of them. In her world view there are no popular children and no nasty children. What the baby does see, over and over again, are the children who are unhappy or troubled, and she usually reaches out to them. Children who have felt alienated or excluded are drawn into a circle of inclusion through the empathic contact made by the baby.[39]

Thus, as the visiting parent-child pair weaves its way into the students' classroom experience and touches their hearts, the students, individually and collectively, develop emotional connections to them. When students allow themselves to be more vulnerable in response to the baby, they learn to think more clearly about their emotions and those of others. They also learn the value of paying close attention to the cues that others provide about their feelings.

While the Roots of Empathy program focuses on young children in an educational setting, the Empathy and Relational Science Program directed by Helen Riess at Massachusetts General Hospital is an innovative training initiative originally designed for resident physicians at health care sites. This program draws our attention to the situational circumstances that shape health care providers' potential for displaying empathy in clinical settings. The first of its kind, the program's mission is to improve the patient-clinician relationship by enhancing physicians' empathy. Riess's E.M.P.A.T.H.Y.® tool is the cornerstone for the training. Her motivation for developing this training is to "help clinicians understand how to integrate the neurobiology and physiology of emotions with empathy, humanism, and communication skills."[40] The acronym represents the seven aspects of how medical professionals can learn to perceive and respond to patients more effectively as they manage their verbal and nonverbal communication:

E: eye contact
M: muscles of facial expression
P: posture
A: affect
T: tone of voice
H: hearing the whole person
Y: your response

Riess describes these aspects in detail in her book *The Empathy Effect*, so I only briefly highlight them here to illustrate their relevance for understanding how dyadic we-ness may emerge in a health care setting. She notes that we can interpret a great deal of information through carefully making eye contact with our communication partners. Our eyes help to activate the regions of our social brains that are connected to the production of empathy. If we focus on a person's facial expressions more generally, we will also secure indications of how the other person feels that will help us to interpret their experiences. Those who score higher on empathy scales tend to be better at discerning facial expressions.

Being attentive to our own feelings in the presence of the other person can lead us to experience feelings unconsciously in a way that enables us to be more attuned to the other person. Our posture, and that of our speaking partner, can unwittingly say a lot about how each of us is feeling, or at least project images of our underlying emotional states. Thus, how we position and move our body in the company of someone can greatly affect the nonverbal signals they detect. In turn, these signals can influence the extent to which they feel we are open and interested in their story.

When we interact with someone, it is critical that we label the affect or emotion that best captures what we believe our conversational partner is experiencing at the time. Naming the affect will give us the means to develop a deeper connection to the person with whom we are speaking. Often, without us being fully aware, a great deal of information is processed by the tone of a person's voice. When conversing, we should pay attention to the pace, rhythm, and pitch of what is being said. Research suggests that about a third of nonverbal communication in the form of tone conveys the emotional content of a verbal message. Our chances of hearing the depth and details of a person's story will be enhanced if we use active and reflective listening techniques. This way of listening hinges on our ability to quiet our own thoughts initially so that we can pay close attention to what someone is saying before trying to present our own perspective. Finally, Riess suggests that we focus on how we are physiologically reacting to our encounter with our speaking partner. In doing so, we can reflect on how those sensations clue us in to how we feel in the other person's presence when they communicate with us.

Pilot testing of the E.M.P.A.T.H.Y.® tool, plus a larger multisite randomized control trial, demonstrated that these skills are teachable and effective. Physicians learned how to employ these skills effectively as they interacted with patients. The patients in the intervention group also reported higher satisfaction scores than those involved in the control group. Riess enthusiastically summarizes the meaning of the training she and her team are providing: "With proper training, including skills in emotional intelligence, emotional regulation, perspective taking, self-other distinction, and other brain-based abilities that are amenable to change, we can work toward a brighter future in health care and all industries where empathic principles are learned and practiced."[41]

A key implication of this type of empathy training, says Riess, is that it helps to "deepen relationships." Although the training can help in first-time encounters, creating interpersonal depth is most likely to occur in the patient-doctor relationship that evolves based on numerous exchanges over years, sometimes decades. This relationship would include, among others, a patient who is managing a chronic illness under the supervision of a specialist or someone in an enduring health care partnership with a family doctor. For some patients, these relationships resemble a type of dyadic we-ness. For example, I recall how my mother fondly talked about her relationship with a small-town family doctor who helped her manage numerous health issues for decades. She conveyed the sentiment that her physician had a friendly demeanor and connected with her by asserting a knowledgeable, supportive approach. Although their interaction was limited to health care settings, she viewed him as a trusted confidant who was committed to helping her confront significant health challenges and was grateful that he would visit her when she was hospitalized.

While Riess and her team have demonstrated that their training program can improve physicians' empathy and patients' satisfaction, we should recognize that patients' interactive style can make a difference in these settings as well. Friendly, assertive patients have the potential to shape these clinical encounters and the relationships that emerge from them by inviting empathic responses from their providers. As an outsider to my mother's relationship with her physician, I can only speculate on how her outgoing, inquisitive personality helped to cultivate it. I do know that my mother was able to develop a somewhat holistic, mutually supportive relationship that led to both her and her physician swapping stories about their family and life experiences during their limited time together. So, while much depends on how a health care provider frames the clinical experience, a patient may be able to shape the contours of the exchange to some extent. If the patient seeks a collaborative partnership, they may be able to elicit empathic responses from the physician who is flexible enough to listen closely to their patient and accommodate them.

In 2011, Riess cofounded Empathetics, Inc. to expand her opportunities to deliver empathy training to health care professionals beyond the academic hospital setting. The company provides a wide range of products that are designed to create a culture of empathy in health care organizations by tailoring e-learning and live training materials to physicians, nurses, and frontline staff. While this training focuses primarily on improving health care professionals' interactions with patients, we can consider other fruitful opportunities to encourage empathy and teambuilding among coworkers as well. Riess and her team already do some of this type of work by offering a course on empathy training for nurse teams as well as general training sessions, which address both intra- and inter-professional needs for empathy.[42] They became more attentive to these issues during the COVID-19 pandemic when health care workers were overwhelmed and traumatized. Considering Sherry Turkle's warnings about our declining interest, comfort, and skill with managing conversations as we move deeper into the digital age, programs that improve empathic skills in the workplace will become increasingly useful.[43]

Like Riess, the internationally acclaimed Buddhist monk and writer Thích Nhất Hạnh is one of many commentators who implore people to sharpen their listening skills. He labels the ideal form of interpersonal attention as "deep listening" and "loving speech." When we listen deeply, we are more compassionate, thereby offering someone the chance to suffer less. In *Teachings on Love*, Nhất Hạnh advises those in intimate relationships who are confronted with their partner's pain to be present fully for their partner. He suggests sharing mantras in those troubling moments, such as, "Darling I know you are suffering. That is why I am here for you" or "Darling, I am suffering. Please help."[44]

Without referring directly to the concept of we-ness, Nhất Hạnh builds on how a person can use deep listening and mantras to strengthen their interconnection to humanity more generally. Armed with symbolic forms of communication, we have the capacity to experience what Nhất Hạnh labels "interbeing." He says, "We are linked to many other people and beings. Each step we take, each smile we make has an effect on everyone around us. Your happiness is the happiness of so many people."[45] This Buddhist approach to mindfulness and love leads a person to see their partner as a gateway to a larger expression of an unspoken we-ness. When we arrive at this mental space, we are compelled to announce, "Through my love for you, I want to express my love for the whole cosmos, the whole of humanity, and all beings. By living with you, I want to learn to love everyone and all species." This realization is consistent with Morrie Schwartz's story mentioned in the introduction about the wave taking solace as it approaches the shore because it recognizes it is part of the ocean.

So, too, our ability to establish a sense of we-ness with another person represents our profound capacity to feel interconnected to all things.

Nhất Hạnh's reference to interbeing and Schwartz's tale about the wave and the ocean implicate an ongoing intellectual debate about how best to conceptualize the "self" or "me" in relation to the "we." The debate partly considers whether we should think of the self as an object or as a process. The process perspective helps us think about the "me" as a reflection of our ongoing and accumulated relationships and is consistent with the notion of creating a global consciousness.

Building on his incisive analysis of the competing images of the self, Rifkin joins other theorists like Kenneth Gergen to assert that relationships have become progressively more critical to how we define ourselves in modern times. Using as his starting point Descartes's famous dictum, "I think, therefore I am," Rifkin suggests an evolution of thinking that progresses to the generic humanist psychologist's view, "I participate, therefore I am," and is most recently captured with the proposition, "I am connected, therefore I am."[46]

Following Rifkin's thinking, if we adopt a more process-oriented and relational view of the self, we recognize that each of us during our lifetime is defined by a set of social relationships and experiences we face that are distinct to us. In other words, what we encounter is unique and fundamentally sets us apart from everyone else. No two people have the exact same constellation of experiences. Rifkin values this distinction for conceptualizing the self and believes it is essential for our growth as empathic beings who ultimately can achieve something akin to a global consciousness in the future. He waxes poetic on the possibilities of interconnection:

> If the sense of self as a unique ensemble of relationships is lost, and one becomes only a "we," empathy is lost and the historical progression toward global consciousness dies. That's because empathic awareness is born out of the sense that others, like ourselves, are unique, mortal beings. When we empathize with another, it's because we recognize her fragile nature, her vulnerability, and her one and

only life. We experience her existential aloneness and her personal plight and her struggle to be and succeed as if it were our own. Our empathic embrace is our way of rooting for her and celebrating her life.[47]

For Rifkin, it is best to not accept the idea of an "undifferentiated global 'we,'" otherwise we will limit our empathic ability. He argues that the stakes are crucial: "Maintaining a dialectic balance between an ever more differentiated sense of self, embedded in an ever more integrated relational web that encompasses the world, is the critical test that might well determine the future prospects for our survival as a species."[48] Thus, our survival may hinge on our collective willingness to enhance our empathy and appreciate the humanity that links us.

Our ability to search for our shared humanity is dramatically captured by the inspiring work of Christian Picciolini, the leader of the Free Radicals Project, a global extremism prevention network. For more than two decades, Picciolini has helped hundreds of political and religious extremists disengage from their toxic forms of we-ness and philosophies of hate. Once a leader of Hammerskin Nation, a white nationalist group, Picciolini is uniquely positioned as a former insider to relate to extremists. He actively propagated white supremacy ideology in Chicago for eight years as a teenager and young man. In addition, he fronted a white power band that was the first American skinhead group to play in Europe.

The extremists he has worked with since he disavowed racism are constrained by the trappings of their rigid ideological beliefs. Their inner worlds, and often their physical exterior, reflect their deep commitment to extremism, an in-group mentality, and a narrow view of others unlike them. Based on his personal experience and deradicalization work, Picciolini believes that extremists join hate groups to compensate for the "unresolved traumas" or "potholes" that ultimately motivate them to live a life of hate. In his scheme, extremists experience what he calls "ICP deficits" because they have been longing for "identity, community, and purpose." Extremists struggle with their life potholes (e.g., being stigmatized and bullied, exposure to family abuse, sense of inadequacy, feeling ignored), which often drive them to feel as though they don't belong to any meaningful group. Having the opportunity to be part of an "us," while scapegoating "them," is fulfilling to many of these traumatized individuals. After joining an extremist group, they see themselves as having access to a potent form of we-ness that reinforces their human agency.

In his fascinating book, *Breaking Hate: Confronting the New Culture of Extremism*, Picciolini takes us backstage to witness his deradicalization work as he journeys into extremists' dark, depressing, and dangerous lives. His interventions are informed by his experiential understanding of this disturbing world of bigotry and hate. Most importantly, he tries not to judge those he seeks to help. Instead, he says that he "work[s] hard to earn their trust, and ... listen[s] with empathy. Responding with equal parts cautious vulnerability and measured compassion." His primary mission is to "help them uncover the truth about who they really are – keeping accountability for their misdeeds at the fore as the terms for their forgiveness going forward." He calls his intervention approach the "Seven 'L' Steps of Disengagement," which include "link, listen, learn, leverage, lift, love, and live." Being able to listen and empathize effectively is at the heart of his approach. We can see the important role it plays when he tells us that "What often moves me is not what people say but instead the pain, trauma, and uncertainty they say little about or that no words can describe."[49]

Picciolini stresses the transformative power of extremists receiving unexpected compassion from others. Recall my earlier descriptions of how the empathic voices of Derek Black's and Megan Phelps-Roper's new friends helped Derek and Megan as young adults to reevaluate their prejudiced family roots in the white nationalist movement and the Westboro Baptist Church, respectively. These newfound friends expressed empathy and goodwill with enough skill that they compelled these former extremists to reject their in-groups and lives of hate. With their friends' timely help, Black and Phelps-Roper reinvented themselves.

Just as empathy can provide the key for people to unlock themselves from their prison of darkness and move beyond their tenacious allegiance to hate groups, it can help people learn to break free of their isolation. When the transformation works, they free themselves to seek out and embrace a healthier sense of we-ness in other forms. Picciolini's experience in the trenches is clearly invaluable because it enables him to relate to extremists while helping many extricate themselves from their dark worlds. But empathic and patient people with no experience in the extremist world, or professional expertise as counselors, can also nudge extremists to shift their thinking through their active listening and support.

Altruism, Loving-Kindness, and Compassion

Many argue that empathy, altruism, and compassion, like water, are fundamental elements to the evolution of life as we know it. Without water, we would not exist, and without the development of our ancient ancestors' capacity to express empathy and altruism, we would have never survived the hardships of prehistoric life, let alone evolved into the complex human beings we are today. While humanity continues to depend fundamentally on both empathy and altruism, its potential to thrive hinges on the level of compassion people show toward one another. So, before we proceed, let's take a moment to clarify several of the more important points of contention about these concepts.

If we are to explore what it means to express ourselves as reflective, loving human beings, we should study the insights offered by Matthieu Ricard. A Buddhist contemplative with a PhD in molecular biology, Ricard is well positioned to share his experiential wisdom and scientific perspective on the meaning and value of empathy, altruism, loving-kindness, and compassion. Ricard has helped bridge the divide between contemplative practice and brain neuroscience. In 2000, Ricard was the first monk to partner with neuroscientist Richard Davidson, who was conducting MRI brain studies at the Center for Healthy Minds at the University of Wisconsin–Madison. As noted earlier, this ongoing program of research uses sophisticated brain imaging technologies to map the physiological and psychological effects of meditation. Over the years, Ricard's writings and lectures have expanded our appreciation for contemplative practice and aspects of living a good and meaningful life. In his comprehensive and inspirational book, *Altruism*, Ricard explains how practices like empathy, altruism, loving-kindness, and compassion can be learned and nurtured to expand human goodness and global sustainability.[50] In addition, in 2000 he launched a practical outlet to put his philosophy into practice by cofounding Karuna-Shechen, a nonprofit organization that helps thousands of people in villages in northern India, Nepal, and eastern Tibet.

Not surprisingly, Ricard is one of many prominent thinkers who have wrestled with conceptualizing and studying altruism over the centuries. The intellectual landscape surrounding our understanding of altruism remains contested ground. Some think of altruism as a form of caring for others that can reflect a fleeting motivation; others view it as a more enduring disposition. Another point of contention is whether altruism need only focus on our motives and intentions (what we feel and think) or if it must also include our helpful actions based on good intentions (what we do).

Kristen Renwick Monroe, Chancellor's Distinguished Professor of Political Science at the University of California, Irvine, argued in *The Heart of Altruism: Perceptions of a Common Humanity* that action matters.[51] Altruism, for her, is "action designed to benefit another, even at the risk of significant harm to the actor's own well-being."[52] She suggests it might be useful at times to think of a continuum extending from pure self-interest to pure altruism, a strategy that would allow for displays of quasi-altruism. Yet, she values those instances that most clearly, in her view, represent a pure form of altruism, such as individuals hiding Jews in their homes from the Nazis during World War II or the abolitionists helping escaped slaves in the United States relocate from the South using the Underground Railroad. In today's world, altruism in this pure form is embodied by the countless Europeans who took Ukrainians into their homes to provide them food, shelter, and compassion after Russia's invasion had displaced them. Monroe stipulates that a series of conditions is necessary for us to consider altruism in its most authentic form. These include a goal-directed focus that is intended to further another's welfare; circumstances that lead to the lessening of the altruist's welfare; no anticipation of a reward; and a specific action.

She notes, too, that intentions count more than consequences, so if a behavior fails to produce a positive outcome, it may still be considered an altruistic act if a good intention preceded it. The overarching motivation that guides this purest form of altruism is that "altruists see themselves as bound to all mankind through a common humanity."[53]

Although Monroe depends upon a definition that does not differentiate the target of the altruistic act, she draws our attention to how our thinking could be shaped if we did consider the target. In particular, she mentions what might constitute a display of "particularistic altruism." This expression would be "limited to particular people or groups deemed worthy because of special characteristics, such as shared ethnicity or family membership."[54] Altruism displayed in this narrow sense would be tied intimately to our shared identities, experiences with group belonging, and sense of we-ness.

Compared to Monroe, Ricard advances a less rigid view of altruism. The same can be said of social psychologist Daniel Batson, who has collaborated with many colleagues to study altruism by using diverse and clever experimental designs. Together, Batson and his colleagues have championed the idea that altruism exists and is not necessarily contingent on an egoist impulse. In the late twentieth century, Batson advanced the empathy-altruism hypothesis. He contends that when people experience empathy toward others, they sometimes are motivated to help them out of the goodness of their heart rather than for self-interest.[55] Although many, including Ricard, believe he has marshalled considerable support for his hypothesis over the course of his career, some are still open to the prospect that other explanations may account for humans' helping behavior.

First in *Altruism in Humans*, and then in *A Scientific Search for Altruism*, Batson delineates a series of criteria that enable us to determine whether our motivations are altruistic, and he differentiates the numerous ways commentators have used this slippery term.[56] Several of his observations include the notion that altruism requires motivation. In other words, we should not be described as engaging in an altruistic act simply because of an automatic reflex. The quality of our motivation rather than its intensity matters most. Everyday reality is messy, so we should recognize that we often hold both altruistic and selfish motives in specific circumstances. At times, we may be restricted from acting upon our motivation to help others in a specific setting by outside forces beyond our control. To be altruistic, we need not incur personal sacrifice. We can even receive benefits from our actions so long as receiving a benefit was not the reason we acted as we did.

Like Batson, Ricard claims that altruism does not have to entail sacrifice. But unlike Batson, Ricard does not view altruism as a "temporary mental state." Ricard thinks of altruism more like an enduring disposition. Ricard also extends his vision of altruism by equating it with Buddhism's image of "altruistic love" – "the wish that all beings find happiness and the cause of happiness."[57] This approach favors a view of altruism that ideally is anchored in the promotion of another's state of being or orientation toward life, rather than a momentary pleasant sensation. Our orientation toward humanity and our concern about human suffering, Ricard suggests, should naturally lead us to express our altruistic love toward all sentient beings. In other words, an altruistic person hopes that others will find an authentic form of happiness and have a clear understanding of how they can generate that mindset. In the Buddhist tradition, the altruist is advised to help others find their "inner freedom" and to open their mind to an "accurate view of reality" that recognizes the ephemeral nature of the self and the interconnectedness of all life.

According to Ricard, the two main facets of altruism are loving-kindness and compassion. The former expression "wants all beings to experience happiness" and the latter "focuses on eradicating their suffering." Importantly, addressing suffering from an altruistic perspective requires the altruist to pay attention to both the immediate causes as well as the underlying forces, most notably "ignorance." Put directly, "Compassion is awareness of the other's situation, and is accompanied by the wish to relieve suffering and to procure the other's happiness."[58]

According to the Buddhist, physician, and author Alex Lickerman, a useful shorthand way to think about compassion is to view it as "caring for another person's happiness as if it were your own."[59]

Underlying this orientation is the unconditional belief that every person, irrespective of their past actions, has the potential to become good. If we embrace compassionate feelings for someone, then we should be prepared to endure the struggle that may ensue if they reject our efforts to help them stop suffering. In addition, if we have a chance to express our compassion toward another in practical terms but do not, then our feelings are merely abstractions. If we are to come to value our self as a genuinely compassionate person in the Buddhist tradition, we must be at ease with being compassionate toward everyone (and ideally all sentient beings). From this perspective, our compassionate orientation is based on our experience of we-ness in relation to all of humanity.

This view is consistent with Ricard's call for us to demonstrate an impartiality in how we express loving-kindness and compassion. We should not be swayed by our own attachments or the types of interactions we have with others. Thus, Ricard differentiates between "natural" and "extended" altruism. Generally, we readily feel natural altruism with those who are part of our inner circle or primary groups, especially those with whom we feel most comfortable and whom we believe treat us well. This type of altruism comes easily to most of us because it is connected to our experiences of feeling a sense of deep dyadic we-ness. Extended altruism, on the other hand, is a mindset that must often be cultivated because it involves how we think and feel about people we either barely know or don't know at all. We lack a shared personal history with them and have no direct stake in their suffering or joy. Many of those whom we can target with our altruism will fall outside the groups with which we have a shared identity and that afford us the opportunity to experience our sense of we-ness. In these scenarios, our ability to demonstrate extended altruism requires us to expand our vision to see all of humanity or sentient beings as being part of the frame within which we seek to establish our sense of we-ness.

Perhaps the most appropriate way to illustrate the practical realities associated with empathy, altruism, loving-kindness, and compassion is to share an inspirational story about that life-giving force, water. In the late 1990s and early 2000s, Scott Harrison was a young, successful nightclub promoter in New York City. He was well compensated and lived a fast-paced, glamorous life. But his unhealthy lifestyle of smoking at least two packs of cigarettes a day, getting drunk almost every night, filling his body with cocaine and other drugs, and frequent gambling was taking a toll on his body and mind. After almost ten years of pursuing this hedonistic life-style, he experienced a turning point while sponsoring an extrava-gant New Year's Eve party in Punta Del Este, Uruguay. The next day, with the party still roaring, Harrison grasped more fully the misfortunes of his steady decline in happiness over the years; he wanted the "music" to stop, and not just for that day. He was pre-pared to carve out a different kind of life, one a bit more consistent with his faith-based upbringing.

Before leaving his supportive home at age nineteen to join a band and play in New York, Harrison had lived the previous fourteen years of his life with his parents as an only child, caring for his sick mother. When he was a young child, his mother collapsed in their new home after being poisoned by a carbon monoxide leak that per-manently destroyed her immune system. At a very young age, Har-rison learned how to cook, do laundry, and take care of the house. He was compelled to develop empathy and compassion as a boy.

Harrison's shift in life perspective from boyhood to manhood was stark and increasingly on his mind after more than ten years away from home. He admits in retrospect that he was "spiritually, emotionally, and morally bankrupt"[60] during his time as a nightclub promoter. So, after his New Year's revelation, he took a leap of faith, sold most of his possessions, and decided to take a year off to serve others. After he was rejected by every humanitarian organization he approached, he was left with one option: pay $500 a month to "volunteer" with Mercy Ships. Founded by Don Stephens in 1978, this faith-inspired organization supports state-of-the-art floating hospitals and a large medical team, including surgeons who do reconstructive work. The team provides a wide range of life-altering health care services to the local people in the less developed coun-tries it visits and specialized medical training for health care profes-sionals in the host nations.

Harrison assumed the role of a photojournalist and became part of the team that traveled to Africa, first to Benin and then Liberia, beginning in 2004 for an eight-month tour. He returned the following year in 2005 for another tour. During his two tours, his role afforded him the chance to intermingle with staff, including Dr. Gary Parker, the ship's chief medical officer who became a mentor for Harrison, and countless poor people in desperate need of medical attention. That time changed him. Harrison's passion grew for listening to and telling people's horrific stories. He vividly recalls one day when roughly five thousand people showed up outside the hospital ship, some who had walked for a month. Unfortunately, there were not nearly enough doctors to see them all. With camera in hand, he cried. Harrison's empathic capacity triggered his loving-kindness and compassion as he pondered the dire circumstances of so many people, some of whom were disfigured with unimaginable facial tumors. Years later, reflecting on what he experienced in his new life as a valuable member of the committed team he had fully embraced, Harrison shares that "We were changing individual lives every day, but I wanted to do even more." Harrison's use of the "we" pronoun reflects the pride he derived from being part of this extraordinary traveling team of health care providers and their support crew.

His mind churned over the ensuing months as he spent more and more time in the rural villages of Africa promoting his team's mission and documenting the plight of the impoverished people he met. He saw people drinking filthy, bug-infested, contaminated water that was causing all sorts of serious, often life-threatening, diseases. He repeatedly etched a mental note: "kids shouldn't be drinking from scummy swamps, or ponds, or rivers." Nor should the girls and women who were typically burdened with the task of walking hours to fetch and carry forty-pound cans of water, Harrison thought, be forced to give up their education to fulfill this role. (Several years later he would learn of a thirteen-year-old girl who hanged herself from a tree in a remote Ethiopian village after spilling water and breaking the family's precious water container. Several other women and girls on a water excursion fell to their death from a precarious cliffside footpath.) His emotional time in the field stirred his compassion as the villagers' suffering penetrated his psyche and heart. Harrison wondered why more was not being done to bring clean drinking water to the roughly 785 million people worldwide who do not have access to it – that is about one out of every ten people on the planet.

When Harrison returned to New York City after his second volunteering stint, he was a changed man. Not only had he sworn off all of his bad health habits, but he also felt more altruistic. He put his nightclub-promoter talents to work and convinced someone to donate a club for a charity night so that he could manage a seven-hundred-person party to celebrate his thirty-first birthday. He netted $15,000 from the gig, which he took with him shortly thereafter to a refugee camp in Uganda to help fund the building of three wells. He then sent photos and GPS coordinates back to the seven hundred attendees who had donated $20 each to attend his charity party. They were both surprised and inspired to learn how their donation had dramatically improved people's lives. And with that experimental venture, the New York City–based nongovernmental organization (NGO) Charity: water, was born in 2006. In the subsequent sixteen years, the organization has grown from a small band of supportive people working out of an apartment to a well-organized NGO with big-name corporate sponsors, more than fifty paid employees, summer interns, and millions of individual donors from more than one hundred countries. As of June 2022, it has funded 91,414 water projects to provide clean water to over 14.7 million people in twenty-nine countries in Africa, Asia, and Central and South America.[61]

Most would agree that Harrison's initial vision and implementation of his clean water project were extensions of his altruism. However, today some are likely to question whether Harrison's current involvement should be labeled as purely altruistic because he earns a handsome salary and perks as the CEO of the well-known charity he founded. Some might wonder about how his involvement with the charity compares to someone like Matthieu Ricard's relationship to his humanitarian organization, Karuna-Shechen. Ricard lives a spartan life – having slept in the same sleeping bag for the past thirty years – and he has channeled all his earnings from books, photography, and conferences to his organization. Although Harrison's current motives cannot be as readily framed as purely altruistic in the narrow sense, his work is still engendered by his loving-kindness and compassion. Harrison is also donating all the proceeds from his inspirational book, *Thirst: A Story of Redemption, Compassion, and a Mission to Bring Clean Water to the World*, to fund clean water initiatives. In addition, his paid team as well as the million-plus people his NGO has inspired to donate time and money demonstrate their individual and collective compassion to help disadvantaged strangers from around the world.

Listening to the individual stories of people who start their personal donation campaigns in collaboration with Charity: water, it is clear Harrison has created an enterprise that encourages others to act meaningfully upon their sense of empathy, altruism, loving-kindness, and compassion. Just as importantly, this organization enables people to nurture a healthy form of we-ness that is either dyadic, ideational, or both. This sentiment is reflected in the remarks posted on the organization's website summarizing job opportunities: "Around here, we don't just work collaboratively. We celebrate birthdays, give regular #high-5s, and show off photos of our babies and pets. We travel abroad together (when it's safe) and have virtual coffee in the meantime. We gather for All Staff Meetings and Friendsgivings, share hobbies, make valentines, and roast one another. Turns out, when you work for a cause you care about, it doesn't take long to make friends out of your coworkers."[62] Compelling expressions of we-ness are also conveyed in the remarkable stories Harrison shares in his book. Charity: water's success reflects not only Harrison's vision and unwavering determination; it's also anchored to how he and others committed to solving water issues connect the power of their friendships with their professional expertise. In other words, they integrate bonding and bridging social capital to enhance their own personal lives while furthering Charity: water's mission. In storybook fashion, Viktoria Alexeeva, a graphic designer and one of Harrison's very first and hardest-working volunteers, took on critical roles that expanded the organization's partners and opportunities, and within a few years, became his wife and the mother of his children.

Ultimately, we should be less concerned about debating how clearly Ricard's and Harrison's good intentions and deeds capture the authentic spirit of altruism, loving-kindness, and compassion.

What is more pressing to note is that each man, for whatever reason, has taken the initiative and persisted in using their creative talents to minimize others' suffering. They exemplify alternative strategies that inspire others to mobilize and develop a shared sense of we-ness that leads to the expression of altruism, loving-kindness, and compassion to strangers. That's a good thing, irrespective of how we choose to define it.

These sorts of thorny conceptual and ethical issues are discussed by Princeton University bioethics professor Peter Singer and others who have in recent years engaged in heated debate over the value of the idea of "effective altruism." Philosophers, and ethicists in particular, have pushed us to think in more pragmatic terms as we contemplate the meaning of altruism and its potential for affecting social conditions and people's everyday lives. In *The Most Good You Can Do: How Effective Altruism Is Changing Ideas about Living Ethically,* and elsewhere, Singer describes the underlying idea as "we should do the most good we can."[63] He elaborates by noting that "a minimally acceptable ethical life involves using a substantial part of one's spare resources to make the world a better place." This new movement, Singer writes, is being led by millennials who tend to be "pragmatic realists, not saints." Singer points to Wikipedia as providing a standard and viable definition of effective altruism: "a philosophy and social movement which applies evidence and reason to determining the most effective ways to improve the world." This vision is consistent with the broader view that altruism does not require self-sacrifice. However, effective altruism is not meant to cover what psychologists call "warm glow givers" – those who give to others because the donator expects that the gesture of giving itself will make them feel good regardless of the outcome.

Many of the most pressing concerns about effective altruism are captured in a 2015 online forum sponsored by the *Boston Review*. In it, Singer defends his contentious position by responding to other prominent scholars who raise reasonable concerns about different aspects of his approach. Although assessing the full range of intriguing issues is beyond the scope of this book, several points are worth noting.

Effective altruists rely on reason much more than their heart to guide their choices for charitable donations. Like most of us, they can be moved initially by emotional stories and pleas for assistance, but they ultimately step back and soberly evaluate their options for making the biggest impact on reducing others' suffering. In the final analysis, as Singer notes, "They give to the cause that will do the most good, given the abilities, time, and money they have." At first glance, this process may seem straightforward, but as Singer adeptly outlines, figuring out what action is likely to produce the most good is fraught with complexity.

Most organizations that receive charitable donations do a poor job of explicitly demonstrating their level of effectiveness in helping others. However, in 2007, eight friends who had worked in the finance industry launched a timely nonprofit, GiveWell, with the aim of addressing this problem. It has become a well-respected, research-based company that systematically evaluates how effectively a select group of charities use their donations to reduce suffering and increase people's opportunities.[64] This and similar types of evaluation services are increasingly providing the effective altruist with the evidence-based means to achieve their objective of contributing more thoughtfully to causes that improve people's well-being. In many instances, people who are guided by these services donate money to impactful overseas programs (e.g., providing malaria tents) and to causes that have no obvious sentimental appeal to them.

In 2009, inspired by the logic of the effective altruism movement, philosophers Toby Ord and Will MacAskill founded the international society called Giving What We Can (GWWC).[65] In Ord's *The Precipice* and MacAskill's *Doing Good Better: How Effective Altruism Can Help You Help Others, Do Work That Matters, and Make Smarter Choices about Giving Back*, we learn about these scholars' visions of humanity and effective altruism that ground their commitment to GWWC.[66] Prior to hiring a full-time staff in 2012, GWWC was run as a volunteer organization. It was eventually incorporated under its parent company, Centre for Effective Altruism, in 2016. The society began with twenty-three members and reached 8,476 as of June 2022. As of this date, GWWC members had donated roughly

$275 million to highly effective charities. This community of effective altruists illustrates the social energy that can be generated by integrating dyadic and ideational forms of we-ness. From its inception, GWWC has flourished because of Ord and MacAskill's initial friendship with one another, the social ties shared by others who were original members, and the growth of the organization that has resulted from new members often being recruited through an ever-expanding friendship network of people with similar perspectives. Members make a pledge to donate at least 10 percent of their income until retirement to organizations they believe will do the most good. The financial pledge represents a shared symbol that reinforces the members' similar commitment to a lifestyle of giving and identities as members of GWWC. This ideational we-ness amplifies the members' pragmatic approach to altruism.

A few years after launching GWWC, MacAskill teamed up with a friend, Benjamin Todd, to cofound 80,000 Hours in 2011 as a part-time student society.[67] The name represents a rough estimate of the number of hours a person works over a lifetime. MacAskill and Todd, along with several other friends, grew this project into an effective nonprofit charity that helps thousands of people make career decisions that enable them to address the world's pressing problems most effectively. As part of the effective altruism community, this nonprofit provides research-based support primarily to graduates ages twenty to thirty-five. It encourages people to make rational, strategic choices as they make their career plans with an eye toward improving others' lives. Here, again, we see an illustration of how the dynamics of dyadic and ideational we-ness can reinforce one another to produce positive outcomes.

Ultimately, we can advance the pursuit of healthy forms of we-ness by nurturing our skills in empathy, altruism, loving-kindness, and compassion. As Helen Riess boldly proclaims, "empathy informs a vital intergenerational, interracial, and international perspective that must be valued, vaulted, and cultivated on a grand scale. Without expanding empathy beyond our in-groups and borders, civilization as we know it will not survive. Empathy training is the key transformative education."[68] Ricard and others assure us that with an open mind, we can develop a worldly perspective to express our concern for others' suffering and well-being across the globe. At a young age we seemingly are equipped with the basic skills necessary to recognize others' difficulties and to care about their well-being. The lessons of empathy and altruism must begin with the individual. "Altruism shows us what is good to do," Ricard writes, and it reveals "how one should be, and what qualities and virtues one should cultivate. Starting with a kindly motivation, altruism should be integrated into our everyday lives, and should reflect the unique quality of every being and every situation."[69] With time, experience, and a sense of purpose, we can nurture these interpersonal gifts. We can also collaborate with others to incorporate them into our educational, economic, and political institutions as well as our social movements.

A group that promotes dyadic we-ness is one context for learning these skills. By establishing and nurturing our sense of group belonging with others in a supportive group, we can actively nurture our desire and ability to care for others. Collaborating on life-enhancing activities, especially those directed at helping others, can give us the opportunity to enrich our empathic capacity. It can also help us to develop a disposition whereby we feel compelled to both reduce others' suffering and expand their life opportunities. It may be preferable to have group involvement that teaches us to internalize an altruistic perspective not based on narrow self-interest, yet we can still contribute to the common good when we engage in group-based community work largely because we are motivated by others' acceptance and accolades.

While we work to center empathy at the core of our efforts to construct healthy forms of we-ness, we must recognize how essential it is to promote a culture that produces empathic leaders throughout every part of the social landscape. To achieve this objective, we must nurture empathy in our informal personal networks of family and friends as well as in the formal, institutionalized systems that can and should teach leadership skills. In addition, not only must we find ways to teach ourselves how to embrace empathy, we must also figure out how to ensure that we do not unlearn our empathic abilities in our increasingly digitized world. At their best, "Empathic leaders create emotional bonds with their groups, teams, and constituents and foster a culture of trust and collaboration. They are competent at understanding and addressing their needs, appreciating and drawing on people's talents, and recognizing others' perspectives in problem solving and including them in making decisions together."[70] We now expand our frame to show how empathy and leadership can be integrated to establish a world permeated with healthy forms of we-ness.

7

Leadership

Leadership, by definition, involves working with and understanding others, so it is intertwined with we-ness and empathy. If a leader is to lead successfully, those who are being led will typically express some form of we-ness. In addition, a nonauthoritarian leader is best suited to lead well if they are empathic and appreciate their followers' inner worlds.

An expansive commercial and academic enterprise has emerged over the years to study and promote leadership, not unlike what has happened with contemplative practice and empathy. It consists of diverse materials including observational, inspirational, and instructional messages about what leadership is, how it works, and how it can be improved. These messages are shared via commercial and academic books, institutes, programs, workshops, seminars, TED talks, blogs, podcasts, and more. A wide range of face-to-face and online programming and consultation is available. Typically, the messages target those who make key decisions in politics, military, business, sports, education, media, nonprofits, faith organizations, family, and other settings. But some advice also recognizes that leadership can be cultivated at all levels of an organization or group. Those with little formal power can still informally influence or lead their peers in ways that shape group outcomes and enhance others' personal development.

Some settings may exhibit basic formal features, but they feel more informal in the way leadership skills are passed on. I discovered this leadership niche during my research interviews with youth triathlon coaches and athletes. Many of these coaches created opportunities for older teenage triathletes to work informally with younger kids who were new to the sport. The teens were encouraged to develop a mentoring relationship with the younger kids, which helped the older kids acquire leadership skills in the process.

One of the more formal leadership initiatives that I profiled involved Todd Waldner, the founder and coach of the iCAN Junior Triathlon Club, based out of Fresno, California. Coach Todd created a set of innovative coaching programs for his young athletes with the categories "Junior Coaching," "Leadership," and "Nutrition." Kids could sign up to be junior coaches if they were at least thirteen years of age. They were closely supervised and taught a variety of skills by Coach Todd and other USA Triathlon–certified adult coaches. Youth participants like Paula Contreras, who initially joined the club at age ten and became one of Coach Todd's most impressive junior coaches, received program certification after completing a range of demanding requirements. Although I interviewed Paula when she was nineteen years old, she vividly recalled how Coach Todd had displayed his supportive leadership style with her from the very beginning when she was learning the sport. They each glowed in separate interviews about the bond they had created as friends and triathletes, and they both acknowledged that she had developed a great deal of self-confidence over the years that allowed her to become an effective leader and junior coach with the younger kids.

The mentoring relationship between Coach Todd and Paula led them to each feel they had created a deep dyadic we-ness. With Coach Todd's guidance, Paula also learned to embrace the ideational we-ness that comes with belonging not only to a team but also the larger triathlon community. When talking about her desire to pass on the invaluable lessons she learned, she says, "I wanna be the best role model I can be for these athletes." Paula fondly recollects how attentive and supportive Coach Todd was to her, which reflects her appreciation for how important it is for leaders to take a genuine interest in their followers and get to know them.

Profiles of Leadership Organizations

Organizations like the Connective Leadership Institute, Matrix Leadership Consulting (MLIC, an outgrowth of Matrix Leadership Institute), and the Empathetic Leadership Institute (ELI) are several representative examples of the many diverse and formal groups that teach leadership skills. These organizations target individuals and groups primarily in business, health care, academic, and community development settings. They emphasize developing empathy and communication skills, building inclusivity and diversity, and improving interpersonal networks and connections in a hyperconnected world. Without explicitly using the specific terms, they train individuals and groups to develop both bonding and bridging social capital. Overall, they seek to promote collaborative efforts that will produce what clients believe are desirable outcomes. In some instances, they highlight advances in our understanding of the neuroscience associated with how we process information and relate to others.

While some programs work with groups of people, other initiatives offer participants personalized leadership programs. Here, we'll focus on some of the organizations and leadership consultants that are most clearly committed to addressing issues connected to our interest in team building, group belonging, we-ness, and empathy.

As its name suggests, the Connective Leadership Institute emphasizes the value of enhancing leaders' ability to develop and maximize connections between different types of people and groups.[1] It trains leaders to pursue creative initiatives that can connect individuals and groups in ways that enable them to develop a shared sense of purpose and group belonging. In what this group labels the "connective era," effective leaders are attentive to inclusivity issues and have "the insight and skills to help divergent, even adversarial, individuals and groups come together initially around limited areas of mutuality." In other words, a connective leader is someone who can convince individuals and groups with seemingly dissimilar interests to develop at least a limited sense of we-ness to achieve a practical goal. If the leader is successful, they may generate forms of bridging social capital.

The institute's connective leadership model, Achieving Styles™, includes nine behavioral strategies that are grouped into three sets (direct, relational, and instrumental) with each comprised of three separate styles. Two leadership styles are most relevant to how we chase after a sense of we-ness. The "collaborative" leadership style that falls in the relational set reflects an appreciation for the pleasure that can flow from a feeling of group belonging and a sense of we-ness that comes from working with one person or a larger team: "They feel an added surge of enthusiasm and creativity when they do things with others. Working in isolation rarely turns them on, and they usually try to avoid it. People who prefer this style enjoy the camaraderie of working with others and feel devoted to the group and its goals."[2] Meanwhile, the "social" style that is part of the instrumental set is characterized by a leader who is aware of the skills others possess and recognizes the connections between people and tasks. In addition, they "keep in touch with a large network of people, who feel remembered, liked, and ready to help them." Presumably, those who position themselves in this way are interpersonally gifted and have polished empathy skills.

Founded in 1991, MLIC encourages us to reframe our thinking to highlight how groups are much more than a collection of persons.[3] The Matrix Model "brings conscious awareness to the needs and patterns of the group/system as a developing organism." It trains group members to appreciate how they are part of a living system of interpersonal connections and to develop "heartfelt relationships" with other members. A "collective wisdom" emerges out of this matrix leadership network that transcends the simple addition of everyone's knowledge. This form of wisdom is generated by the shared leadership process the model is designed to foster.

MLIC's philosophy is based on the main operating principle that leaders should explore their person-to-person connections with each member in the open, and members should also communicate with others in the group in a similar fashion. Everyone is encouraged to visualize their role in the larger web. The training process is meant to reveal the differences between group members in their perspectives, values, beliefs, and feelings while honoring the interpersonal connections that unite them. It includes a series of ten steps that isolate, clarify, and elicit feedback about the differences that members reveal in their candid exchanges. Fresh and creative ideas emerge from the process, culminating in a collaborative implementation plan based on a "collective, emergent intelligence" that is generated by the synergistic interactions of the diverse set of people involved in the process. This type of system- or matrix-oriented approach depends on the participants developing an authentic and clear picture of the whole group as well as their sense of belonging and contribution to it.

Unlike most leadership training organizations, the ELI group explicitly integrates the empathy concept into its mission statement by noting that it is "committed to supporting organizations to embrace empathic leadership responses, mindsets, habits and structures."[4] ELI's approach underscores a series of causal connections that begins with the presence of empathy. This leads to psychological safety, and in turn, those feelings provide the impetus for creativity, collaboration, and productivity. ELI offers a wide range of courses that are designed to improve participants' skill sets so they can integrate empathy more effectively into their leadership mindset and actions. The objective is to help leaders establish a shift in the corporate culture so that "everyone in the organization feels empowered and accountable." ELI believes that if leaders want long-term change, they need to attend to "what's important for me, for you, for organizations and for all the stakeholders," rather than focusing on what isn't working. To pull this off, leaders need to "cultivate empathic leadership," which will reveal what collaboration and productivity should look like.

Aspects of Leadership

Building on these case profiles, and with an eye toward understanding how people experience we-ness and group belonging, we'll now consider aspects of leadership, followership, and the relationship between the two. Unfortunately, even though leadership assumes some sort of followership, academic and nonacademic experts have paid much more attention to those who lead than those who follow.

In the business world, leadership experts and consultants have clearly found it more lucrative to target leaders.

Sociologist Robert Merton, writing more than six decades ago, reflects on several timeless questions related to leadership in general. He frames his insights about leadership by suggesting that it is best to see it as a type of "social transaction," rather than focusing on a leader's individual attributes. To unlock the secrets of how leadership works, Merton suggests we focus on the "system of roles and interactions between people."[5] Effective leadership, in his mind, is dependent on members trusting and respecting their leader. He argues that four social processes foster the trust and respect essential to good leadership outcomes. First, a leader must express respect for the members of the group. Second, the leader should demonstrate their competence in their roles. Third, a leader needs to stay in close touch with the members by providing opportunities for two-way communication, including lots of active listening. That listening should focus on what is being said, as well as what is not being said. Thus, leadership gurus increasingly encourage leaders to develop their listening and empathy skills.[6] And fourth, it is preferable to use a democratic style of decision-making. Whenever possible, a leader should avoid exercising power.

More contemporary commentators on leaders' use of power identify several interrelated expressions of it that are more appealing and empowering than the traditional "power over" style. The exploitative version of the "power over" form is represented when leaders' "decisions benefit the minority and oppress the majority."[7] In contrast, "power with," "power to," and "power within" are alternative ways that leaders can connect and work with group members. When a leader adopts a "power with" strategy, they are eager to respect differences and strive to find common ground. They are open to collaboration because they realize they can promote more solidarity and collective strength when they do. Those who pursue a "power to" style of leadership embrace an approach that is consistent with much of the new thinking in business described more fully below. This style of leadership extends agency to group members and stresses how much collective good can rise from maximizing the unique talents and knowledge of each contributor. And the "power within" model accentuates that we "feel comfortable challenging assumptions and long held beliefs, pushing against the status quo, and asking if there aren't other ways to achieve the highest common ground." This form is anchored to a strong sense of self-awareness and respect for others.

The processes Merton identifies as well as the expressions of power noted above highlight the interactive dimension to leadership. These observations reveal the importance of a leader's ability to promote a sense of we-ness and belonging among the members. Some groups can still be productive despite there being internal stress and tension among the members, but a leader is more likely to be effective if they can foster a supportive, collective consciousness. Members of the group are also more likely to enjoy their experience and be more invested in the group when they feel like they freely belong to it.

Other commentators have delineated various leadership types and styles. The basic distinction academics make is between integrative (or emotional) and instrumental leaders. Those in the former camp are adept at managing group members' feelings and calming members so they can work productively with one another. They strive to keep the peace by minimizing potential friction between members. Integrative leaders inspire others to be self-confident and to make sacrifices for the good of the group. They encourage others to work hard to achieve group goals. Most importantly, they help members to strengthen their emotional and practical commitment to the group and its collective identity. So, framed in terms central to this book, these leaders are responsible for promoting the we-feeling of the group and the bonding social capital for its members.

In contrast, instrumental leaders set their sights on coordinating the practical dimensions to what a group is trying to accomplish. They may also be responsible for defining the group's mission or vision. At the very least, they devote themselves to coordinating the tasks that need to be accomplished for a group to achieve its goals. Sometimes that involves expanding the group's network of connections to other groups and leaders by developing bridging social capital. Some gifted instrumental leaders, like the superstar professional basketball player Lebron James, serve double duty, providing integrative leadership that helps sustain the group while also emphasizing their instrumental role by organizing the group to achieve its objectives.

A more nuanced typology of leadership styles associated with the MMDI™ system outlines eight different varieties: participative, change-oriented, executive, action-oriented, ideological, visionary, theorist, and goal-oriented.[8] This system is based on the theories of Isabel Briggs Myers and C.G. Jung and encourages leaders to work on finding a balance between their preferences and the characteristics of the context. When leaders adopt one of these leadership styles, it has implications for how other group members, most notably their followers, will manage their sense of we-ness and group belonging. Leaders will typically privilege one leadership style even though they may incorporate aspects of other forms as well. Although some leadership styles may be more relevant than others to a team-building orientation, or an approach to navigating concerns about we-ness, leaders using any of these styles will need to be aware of the processes by which people identify or navigate their sense of group belonging.

When a person engages in participative leadership, they focus on incorporating others into the process of team building and decision-making. They employ the "power to" approach to empower members. While I elaborate on relevant issues more in a bit, suffice it to say here that they try to encourage people to feel valued and to take ownership in the group mission and expected outcomes. The relationships between members are accentuated to motivate people to cooperate and to help the group achieve a "team" goal. A group facilitator exemplifies this style of leadership.

The change-oriented approach is illustrated by the leader who steps into situations with the intent of altering different aspects of what has typically taken place within the group. At times this may result in a leader getting others to redefine their mission, operating procedures, or both. Irrespective of how extensive the change is that is being sought, this type of leader is motivated to encourage others in the group to embrace new ideas and to rethink how they've participated in the past. Sometimes the leader who is a change agent is initially an outsider to the group and is being invited in to bring new life to the ongoing activities. The members' willingness to trust the leader is critical. Are the members prepared to redefine their preexisting sense of we-ness if it will enhance the new leader's efforts to bring about change?

Someone in charge of getting things done is referred to as displaying executive leadership, and they will be responsible for the group's organizational plan and the various procedures associated with fulfilling its tasks. We can think of the orchestral conductor as this type of leader because this person is tasked with getting all the musicians to coordinate their musical responsibilities to follow a musical score.

An action-oriented leader leads by example and is responsible for getting things done quickly. Ideally, other members of the group will be compelled to respond to this type of leader's requests and to assist them in achieving the group's objective. A commanding officer on the battlefield expects the soldiers under their command to follow orders and coordinate their responsibilities. Similarly, surgical teams are structured so that the head surgeon is in charge, and the ancillary personnel are prepared to follow the surgeon's directives in a timely and well-coordinated fashion. This type of leadership is best suited for relatively small or medium-sized groups.

An ideological leader asserts control in situations in which specific ideals and values are being championed. This leader strives to keep the group focused on following the belief system underlying the group's purpose. Many religious and political leaders can be characterized as displaying this leadership style. Although these leaders all push to have their ideas represented, they may differ greatly in practical terms in how they try to gain others' compliance with their vision, sometimes resorting to persuasion, and at other times, coercion.

Someone labeled as a visionary leader can express an uncanny understanding of things yet to happen that may not be so obvious to others. Although the person may not be able to provide a precise vision of the unknown, this type of leader is able to lay out a broad outline of how an organization should prepare itself to be in the best position possible to respond to upcoming changes. Inventors and strategists exemplify this type of leader. They are likely to anticipate what long-term direction is in an organization's best interest.

The theorist leader is the type of person who considers and applies different theoretical models to help interested parties better understand how an organization is functioning and what can be done to improve performance. This person draws on prevailing insights in the field to make sense of the structures and practices that define an organization. As academics, trainers, or executive coaches, these leaders are tasked with helping organizational leaders figure out what needs to be done to make their organization work more effectively. The leader's suggestions may be informed by their assessment of the realities and possibilities of a group's cohesiveness and esprit de corps.

Finally, the goal-oriented leader is most commonly seen as the teacher, sports coach, or mentor who takes a realistic view of the situation and suggests that a group should pursue a specific set of goals. Part of this leader's responsibility may be to prioritize which goals are most important or to lay out a sequence of goals that should be achieved so that a larger objective can be realized. Such a leader is realistic and understands how the larger context in which the organization operates is relevant to how goals should be articulated and pursued.

Elements of leadership, team chemistry, and we-ness often shape how various types of groups operate. Beyond the basic typologies that distinguish leadership styles, we can expand our thinking on group leadership by considering the seven archetypal personality characteristics mentioned in chapter 5 that Joan Ryan, the sports journalist, believes contribute to team chemistry. Ryan's archetypes reveal themselves in diverse social groups, not just with sports teams. A self-proclaimed leader, or even someone others perceive to be a leader, can display one or more of the personality attributes that influence team chemistry and performance.

In Ryan's typology, the *sparkplug* energizes others to play or to do their work enthusiastically with maximum effort. This person motivates teammates to believe in a collective purpose. The typically more laidback *sage* is the experienced, wise contributor who helps others to keep things in perspective. They encourage others to remain calm in the face of adversity, doubt, and anxiety. Armed with personal experience, this person can foreshadow life outcomes and teach others valuable lessons. In contrast, someone who presents as a *kid* is typically one of the younger participants who is full of energy and "carries the dream" of the team. Undaunted by any realistic limitations that more seasoned teammates have begrudgingly accepted long ago, their upbeat approach drives them to project hope and imagine possibilities. When rules and standards need to be followed and winning is prioritized, the *enforcer* steps in to bring order to the team. This person is likely to call out the slackers and those not fully committed to the team's common goal. They are much less concerned about camaraderie or popularity and more interested in results. The *buddy* is eager to befriend teammates and puts in the extra effort to make sure people feel supported. They tend to be good listeners and empathic. In contrast, the *warrior* is the dominant and fearless team member who intimidates competitors while providing the team with the confidence needed to perform well. In some instances, this person is not friendly or even a team player, but they can elevate the team's performance. They devote their main energies to doing, not listening. Like the enforcer, being popular is less important to them than performing at a high level. A *jester* can make contributions that are comparable to what other archetypes provide, but they do so by being a jokester. Respected by teammates, this person can get away with playing pranks on fellow teammates irrespective of their standing on the team. In doing so, they reinforce the perception of equality that fuels team chemistry.

A leader, or someone who might assist a leader, can express any of these characteristics that can potentially help a team or group perform at a higher level. The likelihood that a person will display a characteristic or a combination of attributes can be affected by personal or group circumstances. For example, if a person joins a team that already has a couple of enforcers, the new member may knowingly or unknowingly contribute to team chemistry in some other way. Ryan's seven archetypes remind us of the different tactics mindful leaders can use to enhance a group's sense of we-ness and success. They can seize on their own attributes or intentionally foster the assets that others bring to the table. Good leaders recognize others' special attributes and find ways to cultivate those assets to help the group or team perform better.

Aspects of Followership

Ironically, leadership experts have spent a tremendous amount of time outlining various types of leaders and have considered how leaders can be effective in different types of settings, but much less attention has been focused on the other half of the equation – the follower. Barbara Kellerman, founding director of the Harvard Kennedy School's Center for Public Leadership and an international leadership expert, is one of the more outspoken voices on this imbalance.[9] She suggests that there are at least five important types of followers that should be considered as one tries to understand and affect the leadership processes that take place in various groups and organizations.

Although the distinctions between the types of followers are sometimes blurred, a person can represent themselves as a follower in one of five different ways, often depending on their group circumstances. The *isolate* is a person who is alienated from an organization or leader and is only passively involved in the group. A *bystander* is more knowledgeable about what is going on compared to the isolate but is either not motivated to be involved, or they feel the risk is too high. A leader to this type of follower may be able to sway the bystander by relying on incentives. Some leaders are followed by those who can be viewed as *participants* because they are somehow involved with the group, and they want to make a difference. Beyond a mere participant is the follower who is viewed as the *activist*. This person is more excited about their involvement, and they have a stake in the group's goals. An activist is more apt to develop a sense of we-ness with the leader and other activists because of their mutual level of commitment. They are involved in creating and sustaining a group identity. As someone invested in the cause, they will shift gears forcefully and break their bonds of we-ness if they feel as though the leader and organization are no longer fulfilling their obligations. They are also more inclined to speak out and hold others accountable for not being actively aligned with what they see as the values of the group. We can then reflect on the *diehard* follower who represents the most extreme form of a follower. In most cases, the diehard will not abandon a leader or an organization because they are so highly invested in the group and leader. Even if a leader and organization are failing miserably, the diehard will tend to stick it out and sustain their loyalty to the leader. Sometimes their commitment is so strong they commit suicide rather than breaking their commitment to a leader and ideology.

In recent memory, the most recognizable group of diehard followers has been Trump supporters. As described earlier, Trump cultivated his loyal base by weaponizing the racial animus that has festered in varied form for centuries in America. Trump's divisive rhetoric and incessant lying unleashed his followers' anger, solidifying their tribal instincts to address their perceived grievances. Eager to embrace a collective identity as "real" Americans, most swore allegiance to Trump because of a shared nativist agenda. Throughout Trump's political reign, it became increasingly clear that there was an element of truth to his disturbing, boastful claim from early in the 2016 Republican primary season: "I could stand in the middle of Fifth Avenue and shoot somebody and I wouldn't lose any voters."[10]

During the Trump era, numerous writers for the *Greater Good Magazine* highlighted how issues of lying and polarization were relevant to the former president's diehard followers. These essays foreshadowed how Trump's promotion of deception and "othering" eventually generated the toxic energy that ignited his supporters' unprecedented insurrection at the Capitol on January 6, 2021.[11] Having internalized a polarized group identity as Make America Great Again (MAGA) members, most Trump loyalists sacrificed their ability to discern or even care about the truth. They were eager to accept and perpetuate his countless "blue lies." A blue lie is an untruth about another group that is knowingly told to denigrate that group while reinforcing the vested interests of one's own group. Such a lie is often acceptable to group members because it reinforces their collective identity and sense of we-ness while demonizing others. Thus, despite the lack of evidence to demonstrate widespread voter fraud, Trump's followers were still primed to embrace the

"Big Lie" that he and other Republican spokespeople perpetuated about the 2020 presidential election being "rigged." According to Jeremy Adam Smith, editor of *Greater Good Magazine*, these developments are consistent with the science of lying because they reveal how those who are angry are more willing to lie to achieve their goals. The Trump diehards are willing to believe his lies because he professes to share their anger about the same things. In addition, violence is more likely when diehard followers view their political opponents as having a fundamentally different identity, or being less human, rather than simply holding a different perspective. The Capitol siege illustrates how powerful persons can tap into cultural and political polarization to inspire diehard followers to act on their violent proclivities.

When confronted with different types of followers, leaders may personally rely on one or more of the attributes Ryan identifies as relevant to building team chemistry. Leaders can also enlist their assistants to display certain characteristics on their behalf. In sum, leaders who are closely attuned to the types of followers in their midst are better positioned to use personality assets to entice them to get involved or to strengthen their convictions.

The Leadership Enterprise

One vital segment to the leadership enterprise is understanding the potent connection great war leaders have with those they lead. In *Leadership in War: Essential Lessons from Those Who Made History*, Andrew Roberts, the distinguished British historian and journalist, captures what he and many others believe to be the essence of a wartime leader. Roberts concludes, after providing portraits of nine major historical leaders during wartime, including Winston Churchill, Dwight D. Eisenhower, Adolf Hitler, Joseph Stalin, and Margaret Thatcher, that great war leaders are similar in at least one key respect. They "are able to make soldiers and civilians believe that they are part of a purpose that matters more than even their continued existence on the planet and that the leader's spirit is infused into them." A leader's ability to create this type of bond implies that they have generated the makings of an ideational we-ness among their followers. Roberts claims that "whether it is a 'magic art' or 'sinister genius' can be decided by moralists, but in it lies the secret of successful leadership in war."[12]

The process of creating that human energy and shared inspiration can generate a consequential form of we-ness in wartime – one capable of producing good or evil. In addition, powerful leaders can master this kind of influence without necessarily sharing common life experiences and social advantages with their followers. The "capacity to empathize," Roberts suggests, "is far more important than one's class background" in achieving the unique bond between a leader and soldiers and citizens.[13] Great leaders somehow know what buttons to push to build and keep we-ness alive.

In the words of John Wooden, the legendary former UCLA college basketball coach whose teams won an unprecedented ten championships in a twelve-year span from 1964 to 1975, an effective leader must understand the big picture and do the difficult work of getting others on the team to appreciate that larger view:

> Managing egos – the over- and underinflated, the forceful and fragile – is one of the greatest challenges facing any leader. It is a crucial task, however, if a group is going to have a fighting chance to succeed, to become a true team rather than a collection of individuals – lone wolves – each looking out for him- or herself rather than the "pack." Leadership must get those individuals thinking in terms of we rather than me. This is possible only if the leader himself thinks this way.[14]

Although a common belief is that some among us are born to be leaders or genetically predisposed to lead, it is more accurate to claim that we learn to be leaders – good or bad. Coach Wooden has proposed that leadership is "largely learned." He adds that "those who aspire to be leaders can do it; those who wish to become much better leaders can also do it."[15] Thus, the take-home message about leadership is similar to what is touted for well-being and empathy: leadership is a skill that can and should be developed.

Although most of the values that make up Wooden's well-known fifteen-block Pyramid of Success can be achieved individually, he strategically situates three themes that involve working with others (friendship, loyalty, and cooperation) at the base of his pyramid. He reasons that leadership success is anchored to these themes because much of what we do involves working with others. These three themes for assessing success are also central to our focus on we-ness, so they deserve a closer look.

Respect and camaraderie are the two friendship dimensions that Wooden considers essential to the form of friendship he sees as relevant to group leadership. He's not advocating for a "buddy" style of relationship, but rather a relationship built on respect and a "spirit of goodwill." When a leader establishes camaraderie with and between group members, the leader will be poised to inspire members to put forth their best effort on behalf of the group and the leader. Members are more likely to embrace the appeal of we-ness and privilege the group's interests over their own, especially when they trust that the leader has their best interests in mind.

The element of loyalty involves a leader's commitment to the group and its members, but it starts with the leader's loyalty to self – the person's standards, system, and values. Loyalty is typically not freely given by members at the outset of any group arrangement, it must be earned. As Wooden notes, it emerges when "those you lead see and experience that your concern for their interests and welfare goes beyond simply calculating what they can do for you – how you can use them to your advantage."[16] Unfortunately, some leaders deceive their followers into seeing a "reality" that doesn't exist. They enlist their followers' support on the false premise that they really empathize with and care about their needs, rather than their own self-interest and thirst for power. Far too many politicians, religious leaders, and other despicable leaders have duped countless people to devote their time, effort, and money to a larger cause and sense of we-ness. In the long run, such leaders are often revealed to be charlatans but not before they have seriously exploited, harmed, or killed others and sometimes damaged social institutions as well.

Even though a leader on occasion can achieve a limited form of success by demanding that members follow a rigid set of ideas, a more productive approach to leadership elicits, welcomes, and incorporates members' ideas into how a group is led. Being more concerned with "what's right" rather than "who's right" is a hallmark of effective group leadership. A good leader is one who is open to promoting a form of cooperation that involves sharing ideas, information, creativity, responsibilities, and tasks. Just as deep listening is critical to love and relationships, leaders are more likely to thrive if they listen closely to members' sentiments and opposing views.

When Michael Stallard, a leadership consultant, works with organizational leaders to help them improve team performance, he challenges them to make changes with an eye toward promoting what he calls a "connection culture." An organization that has a strong connection culture, in his view, is one that typically has employees who are "more engaged, more productive in their jobs ... more trusting and cooperative ... more willing to share information with their colleagues."[17] When a connection culture is in place, it tends to move "primarily *self*-centered individuals toward *group*-centered membership."

Stallard proposes that a connection culture will emerge when leaders ensure that three basic elements are expressed in a meaningful way: vision, values, and voice. Those who share a vision will have similar motivations to pursue a mission and feel comfortable with the reputation they're building as part of the organization. Their shared sense of purpose is reinforced by their shared values and beliefs because these attributes will help unite them. Although Stallard uses "values" as a practical label, he describes this element as being grounded in empathy. A connection between members will be strengthened if they feel as though they are valued as individuals. Consequently, a good leader should help members reach their full, unique potential. Finally, to create a connection culture, members need to feel comfortable speaking their mind. Leaders should elicit ideas from everyone on the team and encourage people to share their ideas with one another as well. In this setting, leaders recognize that they do not know everything and will be better served if they encourage others to incorporate their own ideas into the brainstorming mix. All three of these elements – vision, values, and voice – are vital to the process of melding how people express aspirations about the "me" with the "we" into a healthy and productive form of group belonging in an organization.

In addition, leaders will have a better chance of advancing a connection culture if they pay attention to Sherry Turkle's call for organizations to promote a culture of conversation. Turkle describes how leaders in different types of workplace settings have recently rediscovered how valuable face-to-face conversation is in promoting productivity and reducing employee stress.[18] Although it is not easy to challenge the convenience and entrenched work habits spawned by contemporary digital communications, it appears to be a good idea. Research documents that getting workers to mingle casually, interact with clients in person, and participate in office meetings without digital distractions leads to positive outcomes.

The value-based approach to leadership that Brené Brown shares in *Dare to Lead: Brave Work. Tough Conversations. Whole Hearts* is consistent with Stallard's message, and it strikes me as especially appropriate at this moment in history. Drawing on their years of interviewing and training a wide range of senior leaders in diverse organizational environments, Brown and her team have developed compelling and practical insights that strengthen leaders' skill sets. Now, more than ever, these insights are timely because of our complex workplaces, and workers' growing struggles to balance their individualistic leanings with a desire to belong. Helping employees feel like they belong to an organization brings significant benefits to a company. A multi-method study by the professional development firm BetterUp, which used interviews and a series of experiments with several thousand full-time employees across many industries, found that "high belonging was linked to a whopping 56% increase in job performance, a 50% drop in turnover risk, and a 75% reduction in sick days."[19]

Brown is most impressed with those leaders who can identify one or two core values that drive their leadership philosophy and practice. When she works with leaders, she asks them to choose their most important values from a list of 117 (with the option of writing in their own).[20] She concludes that the most effective leaders can differ in the values they choose, but they are typically defined by one or two key values that shape their decision-making. Whereas she chose faith and courage to define herself, I selected authenticity and integrity for myself. In her training sessions, she encourages leaders to first identify several behaviors that are explicitly supportive of their values and then several other actions they are tempted to do but that run counter to their values.

To her credit, Brown emphasizes how leaders can enhance their effectiveness by identifying their core values, becoming more self-aware, and by practicing self-compassion. Being in touch with our emotions is good for everyone, leaders included, because it enables us to recognize more clearly our shared human experience with others. Self-compassion is the bridge to empathy, and empathy is the stepping-stone to healthy leadership.

Thus, when leaders understand their deep emotions, the innermost visceral forces that spark their actions and reactions, they are better positioned to be courageous, daring leaders. They are more open to being vulnerable and prepared to collaborate with others. Instead of forcing people to comply with their demands, courageous and daring leaders find a path to work with others. In Brown's words, "We [leaders] want people to share our commitment to purpose and mission, not to comply because they're afraid not to…. We want people to police themselves and to deliver above and beyond expectations."[21] This approach mirrors the participative style of leadership by elevating the need to create a we-ness mentality that opens the door so that everyone feels comfortable walking into a group setting where they can make their personal contribution.

A leader is most likely to establish a spirit of we-ness in a group if they have personally earned the trust of its members. So, too, they're more likely to thrive if they've executed their leadership role in a way that encourages trust-building between group members. We should not overlook that trust-building is a key process that permeates how courageous leaders manage we-ness in our families, athletic teams, religious groups, businesses, and countless other social arrangements. Without trust, we have little to no chance of creating a genuine, lasting form of we-ness.

Building on John Gottman's impressive research on married couples' communication styles, Brown teaches that a wise leader is well served when they pay attention to how trust often hinges on the accumulation of small, meaningful moments. Some of these moments may be as simple as asking a person about their sick relative or pet, bringing someone a treat from the bakery, or offering someone your umbrella during a rainstorm. Whatever the group, when a leader is perceived to be attentive, helping others feel as though they are seen, heard, and appreciated for their shared humanity and for who they are personally, trust is more likely to grow. When trust grows, it feeds the spirit of we-ness.

My research with male youth workers who are involved with kids in various settings (day care, school, recreation, monitoring sites and criminal justice, faith-based) confirms the significance some kids place on these small moments of attentiveness adults show them. My work also reinforces the notion that building trust is essential to supportive leadership. When we think about the adults in the community responsible for caring for kids, we should recall Brown's definition of leaders presented in the introduction. She says that a leader takes "responsibility for finding the potential in people" and endeavors to "develop that potential." Depending on how youth workers interact with kids, some fit this definition of leadership more fully than others. Those who do, feel accountable in that they are distinctly aware of and committed to their role in helping kids flourish.

The men I studied spoke passionately about building rapport that would allow kids to feel comfortable reaching out to them. They consciously related to kids in ways that were designed to engender their trust. Some talked about getting on the same level as the kids, or establishing their credibility, or showing how they were approachable. Being "open" was a clear message that permeated the men's stories. Charles, the director of the Boys & Girls Club whom I profiled to open the book, gives voice to what many others feel when he says, "I think everyone's looking for somebody who they can confide in or they can talk to and not be judged. Someone who's trustworthy, someone that they know will always be there and willing to listen.... And sometimes that's all kids want to do, they just want to talk and be heard."

All leaders, including male youth workers, face potential obstacles to having others embrace their ideas. Men who work with kids face the unique challenge of convincing the kids that they are trustworthy despite whatever generational gap exists between them owing to their real or perceived differences in life experiences. These men must also reckon with the intense public scrutiny resulting from the media-driven image of the despicable "bad" man who exploits and abuses children. Despite these obstacles, I've seen plenty of dedicated youth workers display exceptional leadership qualities while helping kids navigate childhood and the tumultuous teen years.

Leaders journey down diverse paths to acquire their influence, but they are, for better or worse, all affected by their upbringing, other formal and informal leaders, and social circumstances. We develop our leadership skills from our lived experience, not just our genetic makeup. Consequently, the public should prioritize building a social infrastructure that supports the teaching of healthy leadership skills in our rapidly changing and increasingly divisive social world.

As a society, we need high-quality leadership to generate healthy forms of dyadic and ideational expressions of we-ness while also showing us the way to pursue an Aristotelian style of happiness. We surely need to devote more time and effort to the process of teaching leadership philosophy, values, and skills to people throughout the life course. We must reinforce opportunities that nurture our ability to express empathy, trust, cooperation, altruism, courage, vulnerability, and enlightened self-interest. Likewise, we must learn to be more accountable to ourselves while holding others accountable to common ethical standards that guide group life.

How can we assess others' and our own leadership effectiveness? For some, the bottom line might be whether they can direct their group to achieve a favorable outcome that reflects its predetermined goal. However, this basic standard could produce a similar assessment of a vicious gang leader and a generative elementary school principal. Not ideal. Instead, we need an evaluation framework based on sound ethical principles to determine how well a leader empowers others to experience and act upon their feelings of we-ness to achieve their goals. This seems reasonable, especially for those who understand that achieving an Aristotelian type of happiness depends on promoting a complementary form of we-ness. Doing so focuses attention on ethics and social justice principles. Good leadership, then, does not tolerate the potentially amoral idea that the end always justifies the means. Instead, honorable leadership includes elements of the style and process by which a leader leads, not just the fit between a group's goals and outcomes that result from a leader's actions. John Wooden would have us consider what a leader does to foster "competitive greatness" among a group's individual members and the group more generally.

Those who advise business leaders in our contemporary world are central to our discussion about leadership, empathy, and we-ness. Surveying the current business and organizational climate, consultants like William Gentry, author of *Be the Boss Everyone Wants to Work For: A Guide for New Leaders*, challenge the standard style of leadership in the corporate world. Gentry's principal advice for new managers is that they need to "flip the switch."[22] In other words, they need to move away from a mentality that highlights a "me, myself, and I" approach that positions them as an individual contributor or technical expert who strives to accumulate experiences and accolades that single them out as successful. Instead, Gentry implores leaders and managers to develop a mindset that encourages them to redirect their attention to "we" and "us." Following this track, leaders are told to work to make their staff, team, and the people they lead and serve more successful in what they do. The emphasis is on leaders helping members to fulfill their individual potential while promoting team-oriented goals that implicitly accentuate notions of we-ness.

Another prominent business writer and leadership consultant, Glenn Llopis, works closely with corporate leaders to transform their managerial approach and workforce development. In his timely book, *Leadership in the Age of Personalization: Why Standardization Fails in the Age of "Me,"* Llopis argues that business leaders need to revamp their management style to keep pace with the shift in how workers and consumers see themselves. The age of personalization is "about individuals being self-directed and ensuring the success and significance of the organization they serve."[23]

More than ever before, workers today have diverse interests, values, skills, and backgrounds. They increasingly want more out of their work experience than earlier generations, and they are more likely to change companies and jobs numerous times. Despite their greater work mobility, or perhaps because of it, many are eager to forge a different role for themselves and how they are involved with an organization. Now and in the future, people are and will be much less likely to work at the same plant and belong to the same union for over forty years, like my father did as a blue-collar factory worker during the latter decades of the twentieth century. And unlike earlier generations who were more accepting of the standardization approach to business management that focused on measurable results in the present, today's worker is more apt to look for opportunities to feel empowered and significant. They want a more enriching personal experience that has them actively taking part in building, executing, and aligning with a company's brand and mission. This may be why so many young professionals in America are excited to get involved in start-up companies. Not only do they get to satisfy their individualist tendencies that reflect our modern culture, but they also get to partake in the we-ness that comes with a team integrating their personal skills to make a business successful.

Llopis argues that it is challenging, yet critical, to break free of the routines that permeate standardization and a top-down managerial system. Conventional business habits have defined organizational culture since the early days when the mass production line was introduced, and people were defined by corporate expectations that pushed compliance. Thus, those standardization norms are still firmly entrenched in the managerial mindset and in most day-to-day company practices. Yet, the old form of standardization – forcing employees to follow company-dictated guidelines without employee input – is limiting. It can't "accommodate individuals who want more: to belong, have a purpose, and contribute without feeling judged."[24]

To break free of the conventional standardization paradigm, leaders must proactively reach out to company personnel throughout every layer of the organization to explore creative ways to maximize their individuality. Llopis encourages leaders to recognize the limitations of the rigid tribal approach of lumping people according to standard demographic labels. Instead, they are told to embrace a form of inclusivity that showcases individuals' unique identities and contributions while reshaping the meaning of we-ness. For Llopis, inclusion "is a *behavior* that opens our minds to the importance of being more interconnected and interdependent with each other – within our departments and across the enterprise."[25]

In the age of personalization, inclusivity can only be achieved when leaders shift their traditional mindset and transform their organizational culture. They should spend more time listening to and seeking suggestions from workers about how they believe they can best express their identities in the workplace while making a unique contribution. In practical terms, leaders must learn to ask a different set of questions: ones designed to elicit personalized and creative input from employees. In addition, they should be open-minded about being influenced. In other words, they need to listen to learn, not confirm. Their objective should be to get to know those they work with on a more personal level, not to define them in relation to company goals or to urge them to reaffirm the organization's status quo. This stance will result in leaders being more willing to hire and retain employees who raise difficult questions, challenge conventional practices, and think outside the box. Employees of this ilk should be seen as valuable contributors because they provide novel ways to test and perhaps reframe a company's sense of we-ness, purpose, and methods of doing business. Overall, today's leaders must adopt a more organic approach to building we-ness rather than subjecting workers to a leadership style that forces them to buy into a prepackaged company message, especially when many feel disengaged from the company's purpose.

Business consultants like Llopis point to how leaders can lead well by ensuring that workers are given the chance to define their personalized significance in the process of organizational goal setting and to see their stake in what the organization is trying to achieve. Leaders are encouraged to appreciate how the trend toward personalization over standardization prioritizes workers being able to see themselves as having unique skills that help them to feel as though they are irreplaceable to the team. The team environment should emphasize integration while highlighting individual workers' special contributions to the team. In practical terms, this means that the guiding philosophy for brainstorming sessions should be that it doesn't matter who comes up with an idea because a team-oriented approach is being used to problem-solve and create solutions.

One practical feature of this leadership approach becomes obvious when leaders strive to normalize what the leadership consultant Brené Brown calls the "rumble." She uses this catchy term to capture a useful interpersonal strategy that can bring people together in various settings to mobilize around a cooperative spirit. It represents a

> discussion, conversation, or meeting defined by a commitment to lean into vulnerability, to stay curious and generous, to stick with the messy middle of problem identification and solving, to take a break and circle back when necessary, to be fearless in owning our parts, and as psychologist Harriet Lerner teaches, to listen with the same passion with which we want to be heard.[26]

Various types of support groups can also benefit from this rumble mentality. I'm reminded of an interview I did with a police officer, Derek, who mentored youth (mostly boys) in several settings. In one arrangement, he spent time with teenage boys at an after-school facility that monitored disadvantaged youth. A massive African American man, with a chiseled body comparable to that of an NFL defensive lineman, Derek was gregarious and not shy about expressing his physical and verbal affection to the young men he mentored. He grew up a poor, risk-taking kid whose father had deserted him when he was a toddler. Derek had navigated street life well enough to survive, but he was well aware that he was luckier than most of his friends who had either been killed or ended up in jail. Consequently, Derek was motivated as a twenty-nine-year-old man to lead boys away from a troubled mindset and lifestyle. At the after-school venue, he instituted what essentially became a support group. Derek shares how he framed the group for the boys:

> You're going to be respectful, cause not only, you know, this guy's opening up ... I was like, we have a circle of trust. This guy's trusting you enough to tell you these things in confidence, and not have you

laugh at him, because we're trying, we're here to help each other out.... So I said well this is, this is a brotherhood, so you know, everybody in here's brothers, you know? This is your brother, next to you. I'm a brother, you know what I'm saying? I'm not your dad, I'm not Officer Jackson, I'm a brother ... I'm just a brother.

In this raw, informal setting, Derek urges these hardened boys to share their intimate stories so he can know their fears and hopes and help them teach each other. Consistent with Brown's advice, he invites them to lean into their vulnerabilities, hoping they will come to understand themselves more deeply, support each other, and ultimately make productive life decisions as thoughtful leaders, not followers of foolish street "friends." In the circle of trust, Derek not only pushes the boys to assume more personal responsibility for making sound decisions, but he also compels them to create a sense of belonging, we-ness, and in his words, a "brotherhood" with their peers as they collectively support each other's personal growth.

The managerial approach in the age of personalization and the rumble strategy both highlight how the motives mentioned in chapter 2, sharing a practical goal and celebrating lofty ideals, might affect the energy individuals put into pursuing a sense of we-ness with coworkers. The personal exchanges leaders foster with and between coworkers can help to solidify a team mentality in which everyone feels more invested in the project. Creating productive opportunities for members to have a say in how they nurture their interdependence can enhance the value of group belonging and a collective consciousness. Likewise, group members are likely to feel a stronger interpersonal bond when they witness a leader's commitment to make rumbles a business culture ritual. It will reinforce an authentic, cooperative spirit of we-ness.

In addition, these progressive management styles should foster group dynamics that will increase the chance for individuals and work teams to experience the individual and team versions of flow described in chapter 5. Sharing those sharply focused, inspirational experiences can provide members with the incentive to work harder while reinforcing their commitment to the team's collective identity. Thus, leaders will be highly valued if they can cultivate a work environment that encourages individuals to tap into their individual passion to contribute to something bigger than themselves and to embrace a cooperative spirit. Such leaders are valuable assets to the progressive organizations that provide their members with every chance to feel exhilarated about their involvement and interpersonal relations at work.

Many of the progressive ideas to improve leadership models, like those we just reviewed, are generally consistent with a style of leadership recently in vogue that has been alternatively labeled as collective, shared, democratic, emergent, interdependent, plural, or distributed. Cassandra O'Neill and Monica Brinkerhoff, two leadership professionals who are enthusiastic about the collective leadership approach, outline their ideas in *Five Elements of Collective Leadership for Early Childhood Professionals*.[27] Collective leadership, for them, occurs when "people are internally and externally motivated, working together toward a shared vision within a group, and using their unique talents and skills to contribute to success."[28] This leadership style is a process of "engagement and improvisation" that shuns hierarchical decision-making structures. The meaningful relationships people have with one another in a group bring it to life. According to O'Neill and Brinkerhoff, the success of collective leadership is dependent on specific conditions: "trust, shared power, transparent and effective communication, accountability, and shared learning."[29] Like Brown, they too emphasize how valuable self-compassion is for those who want to promote a collective leadership style that brings people together.

Writing in *Resurgence Magazine*, Margaret Wheatley and Debbie Frieze offer the imagery of "heroes" to "hosts" to reframe how we think about leaders. When we engage in collective leadership, we do not perceive our leaders as those who are in charge and have all the answers. Rather, we imagine them as providing a safe and creative space that will "promote shared learning, effective group decision making, reflection, visioning and goal setting, and mutual accountability."[30] The safe space is built on trust, which is essential for collective leadership to flourish. In turn, this leadership style perpetuates trust.

This vision of leadership resonates with community activist Parker Palmer's notion that we are created for an "ecology of relatedness." He sees the process of "community" as something that is "not a goal to be achieved but a gift to be received."[31] We should relax, be patient, let go of our penchant to control, and feel more at ease with the collaborative process. According to Parker, we are more likely to do this when "pockets of possibility" are created in bureaucracies that allow us to "collaborate in dreaming, playing, thinking wild thoughts, and taking outrageous risks." Our ability to create these conditions demands that we successfully confront the many forces that breed disconnection – "narcissism, egotism, jealousy, competition, empire-building, and nationalism."

In many respects, the collective leadership model with an emphasis on hosting is like the matrix model described earlier as well as the "evolutionary-teal" organizations depicted by Frederic Laloux, a management consultant, in his provocative work *Reinventing Organizations: A Guide to Creating Organizations Inspired by the Next Stage of Human Consciousness*.[32] Like the matrix model, Laloux uses the metaphor of a living system to explain the next generation of leadership that implements practices in three main areas he defines as self-management, wholeness, and evolutionary purpose. He describes how self-managed teams, in which the members are invested in the larger purpose, feel connected to other team members, and are open to thinking in new ways about how they can participate in the flow of their organization, can offer a productive alternative to a hierarchical model. Peer relationships represent one of the keys to generating successful outcomes in what Laloux touts as the highest stage of organizational development. The self-managed model is appealing because it replaces the "power over" with the "power with" management perspective. Laloux reminds us that the guiding forces of self-management, though quite different from what we've grown accustomed to in recent centuries, reflect the most natural way to organize social life. These cooperative forces that mark the thousands of years our ancestors lived as hunter-gatherers are deeply embedded in our long evolutionary history.

The wholeness feature encourages members to create a safe organizational space for themselves and others as they seek to make a difference. Individuals are urged to explore how they can participate in the organization more fully and authentically, and to grow personally from their experience. Ideally, participants will be prepared to be vulnerable and incorporate more than just their rational self into the organization. When this happens, individuals show up without feeling as though they need to put on a professional mask and worry about others' judgments. Brown echoes this sentiment when she writes about how critical the feeling of "true belonging" is for fitting into a work environment. She poetically writes that true belonging is the "spiritual practice of believing in and belonging to yourself so deeply that you can share your most authentic self with the world and find sacredness in both being a part of something and standing alone in the wilderness." Brown goes on to emphasize that "people desperately want to be part of something, and they want to experience profound connection with others, but they don't want to sacrifice their authenticity, freedom, or power to do it."[33]

On a grander scale, Laloux proposes that his ideal organizational model (which he calls "teal") is more compatible with the realities generated by what he believes to be a contemporary shift in our world view. The new stage of consciousness that is becoming more pervasive "involves taming our ego and searching for more authentic, more wholesome ways of being."[34] In response to this shift in consciousness, Laloux calls for organizational leaders to move beyond using a machine metaphor to guide their managerial strategy, one based on implementing a "predict and control" approach. Instead, the metaphor for the teal philosophy views the organization as a living ecosystem with its own energy. When an organization is viewed in this fashion, leaders should emphasize a "sense and respond" approach. This alternative strategy, Laloux suggests, is more compatible with our increasingly complex, uncertain, and rapidly changing times. He advises participants to pay attention to where their organization is going and to learn to move with it with an eye on its broader purpose, rather than focusing on the typical maximization and self-preservation objectives.

This organizational paradigm shift demands that participants appreciate the limitations of a consciousness based narrowly on an "us" and "them" mentality. The teal consciousness introduces a more complex and fluid form of we-ness. Participants can still find personal meaning in associating with groups and organizations, but they do so by connecting their more self-aware identity to a much more cooperative spirit designed to maximize their individuality within a larger, dynamic system.

Unlike more traditional models of leadership, one of the key assumptions of these collective, matrix, or teal models is that everyone can and should lead. Kristin Cullen-Lester and Francis Yammarino, editors for the 2016 special issue of *The Leadership Quarterly* devoted to collective leadership, highlight the paradigm shift that sees "leadership as a property of the collective, not the individual." They add that "collective engagement in leadership by multiple individuals through both formal and informal relationships is a required capability for facing increasingly complex workplaces, business challenges, and social problems."[35] From this perspective, it becomes critical to understand the informal relationship between group members because how people feel about both one another and the larger collective will influence the opportunities for granting and being granted leadership opportunities. The "dyadic leadership relationships" represent the "building blocks of leadership networks." Those relationships are often influenced by how fully individuals embody the norms of an organization and the key features of its messaging. We are more likely to see others as leaders if they "use group focused language such as 'we' instead of 'I' and talk about the goals of the collective."[36]

We are clearly in a transformative point in our historical journey as a country and a global community. If we are to forge a morally just, healthy, and sustainable path along this journey, we must cultivate a new style of formal and informal leadership that is poised to leverage the power of we-ness while preventing its potential divisiveness. Can we build a cultural and social infrastructure that empowers young people to develop their empathy, altruism, and leadership skills while helping them develop a strong sense of purpose and group belonging? Can we persuade others to commit themselves to initiating more equitable, community-based, and civil approaches to realizing their life goals? Can we infuse our social landscape at every level with a world view that encourages us to find a healthy balance between the forces that inspire our individual and collective impulses? Yes we can, but in our polarized world, it won't be easy.

8

Transforming Our Future

The desire to bond and belong is in our genes. However, cultural forces shape the assorted reasons why, how, and with what effect we bond and belong in specific ways, with specific people, and with a commitment to specific ideas. Some reasons are in plain sight; others lurk in the shadows. If we step back to reflect, we may begin to see the contours of our motives. But even when scrutinized with a discerning eye, much can be left undetected. For most of us, the urge to experience a sense of we-ness remains a powerful force in our lives irrespective of whether we fully understand it. The real and speculative stories depicted throughout this book highlight some of the reasons why we handle the pursuit of we-ness and group belonging as we do. The stories also reveal the diverse circumstances that shape our perceptions and behavior, including how many of us express our American brand of liberty by resisting government and formal control.

On a more abstract level, this book explores the broader cultural forces that frame how we interpret the strained competition between the "we" and "me" in public life. It reinforces and expands the message conveyed in Evan Osnos's provocative 2021 book, *Wildland: The Making of America's Fury.* Osnos, a journalist, shrewdly weaves into his analytic tapestry the personal stories of people living in three disparate places he knows well (Greenwich, CT; Clarksburg, WV;

and Chicago, IL). Drawing on eclectic firsthand accounts, he dissects how in recent years our underlying moral tensions as Americans have erupted to intensify our polarization. These tensions expose our growing reluctance to see ourselves as Americans with a collective consciousness that steadfastly promotes the common good, common decency, and common facts to protect our fragile democracy. Echoing the political scientist Robert Putnam's sentiments about the "I-we-I" historical trajectory of our culture between the late eighteen hundreds to the present, Osnos highlights our difficulty in balancing the "I" and "we" perspectives: "Over the centuries, Americans have tacked between sanctifying the individual and celebrating community, between self-interest and social obligation, between the imagined ideals of the lone cowboy on the frontier and of the wagon train that relies on mutual aid."[1]

Unfortunately, our penchant for polarized battles and narrow visions of we-ness has been exacerbated by twenty-first-century news and social media platforms, most infamously, Facebook. These platforms capitalize on new opportunities to stoke division by perpetuating hate, disinformation, and misinformation. Commercial social media, and the negative effects it produces, operates as part of a larger social phenomenon, what Jenny Odell describes as the ever-expanding and disruptive "attention economy."[2] In *How to Do Nothing: Resisting the Attention Economy*, Odell highlights how the capitalist battle for our attention amplifies our fears and anxieties. Much of this urgency-oriented, nonstop messaging capitalizes on our desires to feel a sense of belonging.

The social debates that implicate the competing "I" and "we" visions are further complicated by how such debates are framed by the increasingly rigid and insulated forms of we-ness that are defined by the labels of "red" versus "blue," "rural" versus "urban," and "conservative" versus "progressive" or "woke." Ironically, those propelled by a myopic style of we-ness also aggressively advocate for their style of an "I-centered" social reality that ignores the common good.

In his book, *Why We're Polarized*, journalist Ezra Klein presents a historically grounded, deep analysis of how the "logic of polarization" has infected our contemporary politics and public discourse.

Without using the term, Klein also captures how the consequential "we-ness" urge motivates contemporary politics. He reveals how our ideologically saturated identities play such a meaningful role in the ways we define ourselves. These identities frame our narrow visions of reality, rigid commitments, and reluctance to see common ground. Klein describes the insidious logic of polarization: "to appeal to a more polarized public, public institutions and political actors behave in more polarized ways. As political institutions and actors become more polarized, they further polarize the public. This sets off a feedback cycle: to appeal to a yet more polarized public, institutions must polarize further; when faced with yet more polarized institutions, the public polarizes further, and so on."[3] In addition, the media, one of the most polarizing institutions today, heightens the divisive forces that capitalize on our thirst for deep dyadic and ideational we-ness.

Local, national, and international circumstances tied to the COVID-19 pandemic, social justice movements, and our eroding political norms have deepened our social tensions and polarized condition. These tensions boiled red hot during the pandemic. Early on, those who were prepared to honor stay-at-home orders, because they valued the spirit of the expressions "together, as ever, as one" and "we're in this together," were confronted by a much smaller, but vocal, group of "me-first" sympathizers. The "me" people were unwilling to embrace the communitarian principles of community responsibility, at least as a rallying cry for the pandemic. Ironically, they amplified their voice by creating a bond of we-ness with like-minded folks, often channeling the populist spirit of Trumpism. This vocal band of protestors reaffirmed their sense of we-ness by asserting that their personal freedoms should be prioritized over their misinformed beliefs about the safety of the masses, health care workers, and schoolchildren. Most appeared without wearing masks, a powerful sign of their empathy deficit toward those they might be putting at risk.

By late spring of 2021, some of the most heated battles throughout the United States focused on school policies dealing with COVID-19 mitigation strategies, history lessons about race, LGBTQ+ issues, and sex education. School board meetings generated death threats, fights, intimidation strategies, unruly crowds, and more.[4] The horrific treatment of Jennifer Jenkins, an elected school board member in Brevard County, Florida, who supported mask mandates for schools, was, unfortunately, emblematic of the unseemly and widespread tactics used by a hostile and significant subset of Americans. These Americans were emboldened by an ideational we-ness anchored in far-right values and a libertarian world view that undermined efforts to promote the common good and children's safety. Jenkins was stalked and called a Nazi and pedophile to retaliate against her pro-safety stance for schoolchildren. Someone intentionally coughed in her face while a bystander shouted, "Give her COVID!"; the letters "FU" were burned into her lawn with weed killer; and bushes in her front yard were hacked. She also received hundreds of hateful emails and phone messages. Perhaps the most egregious tactic involved someone filing false allegations that triggered an investigation from the Department of Children and Families to evaluate how Jenkins was treating her five-year-old daughter.[5]

The power and potential divisiveness of the push for we-ness was also in plain sight during the extraordinary 2020 Black Lives Matter (BLM) street protests around the United States. The hundreds of thousands who joined the protests did so because of their shared ideational we-ness that supports racial equality. Many also participated alongside those with whom they already shared a deep dyadic appreciation. Others created a spontaneous and sometimes dyadic form of we-ness as they protested together. Meanwhile, local and state police, police unions, the national guard, and even the US military were forced to make tough decisions about how to navigate the complex circumstances that implicated First Amendment rights, protection of private property, and personal safety. The palpable tensions between the public and different arms of law enforcement, often stoked by Trump's administration and his followers, created shifting types of confrontations in which participants framed their realities by invoking "us" and "them" mentalities. At times, symbolic expressions of solidarity and rudimentary forms of bridging social capital were created when police and protesters took a knee or marched together.

COVID-19 debates, unruly airline outbursts, nasty school board confrontations, the spirited and sometimes violent street protests, and the January 6 insurrection laid bare why we need to focus on the process of building and navigating healthy brands of we-ness. We must seize the moment to promote initiatives that enhance mindfulness, empathy, altruism, and leadership skills. These skills are vital to producing healthier social systems at every level that empower us. We need systems that increase our chances of experiencing the promises of life, liberty, and the pursuit of happiness while being supported by a communitarian consciousness that respects our shared humanity.

Unfortunately, our expanding spirit of tolerance as a nation and world – one that was incrementally forged with the blood, sweat, and tears of those involved in the social justice movements that gained momentum in the decades after World War II – is under attack. Bolstered by modern technologies, our tolerance for diversity is being redefined and challenged by the debilitating onslaught of domestic and international groups that perpetuate hate, violence, stigmas, and social injustice. While brazen attacks have resurfaced in recent years, the uneasiness of many is being exploited by "leaders" who wish to polarize social groups to secure their claim to power. Fortunately, a grassroots countermovement against racial injustice and hatred has once again emerged. It highlights our shared sense of humanity, as an earlier version did in the 1960s, to compel our leaders and the public more generally to do the right thing.

Our society, and much of the world, is evolving in a way that is both hopeful and alarming. Cultivated in the soil of our digital world, the seeds of hope as well as fear are thriving. Data clearly show that a growing segment of Americans have increasingly developed more tolerant, open-minded views on a wide range of social issues including gay marriage and adoption, interracial dating and marriage, women's rights, civil rights for persons of color, and more.[6] But at the same time, those who oppose this transformation of consciousness have become more entrenched and unyielding in their efforts to stigmatize certain categories of people. During and after the Trump presidency, those who embrace this mentality have felt more collective freedom to show their public face of intolerance. Unfortunately, a staggering number of people are apparently still enamored by a caste system that perpetuates white privilege. In addition, the tilt of the Supreme Court in 2019–20 toward a far-right agenda that is out of sync with mainstream views on a wide range of issues further complicates matters. In many ways, the election season of 2020 provided people with a litmus test to choose between democracy and whiteness. The midterm election season of 2022 will do the same.

Learning to construct healthy forms of we-ness can and should be connected to initiatives that enhance our personal growth, community engagement, and social justice. We are more likely to seek these pockets of healthy we-ness when supportive and empowering messages are institutionalized. The challenge for our age is to build the collective spirit and infrastructure that will cultivate the kind of mindfulness, empathy, altruism, and leadership needed to promote healthy expressions of we-ness in their many forms. Institutionalizing the *MEAL* approach and implementing it in practical ways is critical if we are to refocus our private and public energies during this divisive era.

As we move deeper into the twenty-first century, our ability to think about and manage technologies in innovative ways will also shape our efforts to create healthier opportunities for individuals to experience a sense of we-ness, group belonging, and community. Taylor Dotson reminds us that "today's built environments too often discourage neighboring, walking, and dense networks of local social bonds; media and communication devices tend to support cocooning better than communing; infrastructures organize citizens as unencumbered selves, and dominant childrearing techniques help enculturate an overdeveloped attraction to feelings of self-reliance and privacy."[7] In response, Dotson encourages us to assess critically how various technologies affect the seven dimensions that contribute to establishing thick community – the integrated web of people and groups that produces relatively high levels of social capital. The dimension most relevant to this book's emphasis on we-ness focuses on the psychological state that we experience when we feel connected to a "mutually supportive network of relationships." Our ability to experience a sense of we-ness in relation to our community is linked to the members' recognizing the "community's borders and membership," appreciating that their identity is anchored to "communal ties," believing in the "efficacy of the community," and being concerned about its future.

Dotson challenges us to imagine more communitarian infrastructures and organizations. He also calls for us to experiment with creative options that can support an integrative lifestyle capable of building social capital more effectively. Some of his proposed initiatives to develop thick communities involve urban planning, government legislation, organizational policies, online regulations, and personal actions. Thick communities are more likely to be outfitted with walkable mixed-use neighborhoods with residential and commercial activities, locally governed community infrastructures, neighborhood-level recreation, community policing, and third places. We must build on Ray Oldenburg's insights to reinvigorate our public discourse and communal experience by nurturing the philosophy and practicality of those inclusive third places that bring diverse people together in supportive ways.[8] Considering suburban sprawl and home-based entertainment trends, Dotson's idea of a community demands progressive thinking and heavy lifting from both government and business sectors of society. It also requires a fundamental shift in the public's mindset. With time, these community-based strategies can chip away at networked individualism and enhance individuals' sense of communal we-ness and belonging. Central to Dotson's transformative framework is the idea that we must convince people to replace the expectation that social belonging and connection is an individual responsibility with the notion that we must promote the communitarian principle as a social obligation. In doing so, we must redouble our efforts to get more of us to move away from a private citizen mentality to one that is more civic-minded. We can start by developing more strategic and comprehensive plans to increase voter participation in local, state, and national elections.

With an eye to rejuvenating our democracy, Parker Palmer shares a related message in which he asks us to alter our approach to the body politic, including the way we organize the key institutions, most notably, education and religion. Palmer offers constructive guidance for how we can manage intergroup tensions that can arise from our private experiences, public life, and formal political processes. After framing his thesis about the two ways a heart can break when responding to troubles (shattered into pieces, which results in negative outcomes; or open and receptive to managing tensions productively), using the open-heart approach, Palmer proposes five basic habits of the heart that can sustain the American experiment:[9]

1) We must understand that we are all in this together.
2) We must develop an appreciation of the value of "otherness."
3) We must cultivate the ability to hold tension in life-giving ways.
4) We must generate a sense of personal voice and agency.
5) We must strengthen our capacity to create community.

Although Palmer's primary purpose is to chart a path to resurrecting our democracy and ensuring its vitality, his message provides valuable insights to guide how we should frame our search for and expression of we-ness. We are repeatedly reminded by the lessons of evolutionary science and current events like the COVID-19 pandemic and the BLM protests that we are at our best when we appreciate our interdependence. Palmer directly encourages us to be mindful of the way we treat strangers and those who we cast as "others" beyond our privileged circle. He recommends that if we open our hearts with our eyes wide open, we are likely to learn and grow from the experience. As a sober optimist, Palmer believes we can do better at collaboratively managing the pervasive tensions that emerge from our varied and compelling thought communities. Indeed, he suggests that we can grow as a nation and species if we handle the never-ending process competently.

In addition, we must learn to balance the measured aspirations of the libertarian and communitarian perspectives. The libertarian perspective frowns on excessive state interference and individual obligations to the state. Instead, we are encouraged to pursue our personal aspirations and agenda with little regard for the interests or directives of the larger community or government. We are told to look out for our own best interests and to cherish freedom of choice. Although this philosophy does not prevent us from embracing some form of we-ness, we are warned to be suspect of government or community-based demands that could infringe on our individuality and autonomy. In short, those who embrace this ideology oppose channeling government resources into any initiative that obligates people to pursue national service.

In contrast, the communitarian social philosophy seeks to balance "individual human dignity and the social dimension of human existence."[10] It celebrates the value of building shared ideals and working toward a common cause while recognizing the connection between rights and obligations. People are expected to be active citizens, invested enough in the larger community to engage in self-governance, and motivated to serve others.

In 1993, sociologist Amitai Etzioni galvanized an eclectic group of social thinkers to launch The Communitarian Network in response to the growing concern over the ill effects of a society defined by excessive individualism. This nonprofit organization warned that our society "threatens to become normless, self-centered, and driven by greed, special interests, and an unabashed quest for power."[11] This philosophy denounces *extreme* individualism; thus, in select instances, community outcomes are more important than a person's own concerns and rights. We are reminded that with rights come responsibilities. The organization's platform also explicitly identifies the value of public service: "National and local service, as well as volunteer work, is desirable to build and express a civil commitment. Such activities, bringing together people from different backgrounds and enabling and encouraging them to work together, build community and foster mutual respect and tolerance."[12]

A society's ability to embrace a communitarian message requires its people to have some level of empathy. They must appreciate how they are connected to others and be willing to dismantle and see beyond their empathy walls. We must recognize that we are, to some extent, our brothers' and sisters' keepers – a philosophy that better positions us to embrace "we-ness." The Communitarian Network tells us that creating a stronger moral foundation to our society requires us to rebuild the civil institutions of society: family, education, community, and polity. In each of these areas, the moral order stands to benefit if we as individuals can encourage more authentic forms of empathy and an enlightened approach to managing our self-interests. Each of our individual voices is amplified when it is buttressed by the resounding base of the communities of purpose we build.

Finally, our humanity is not only defined by the tension-filled merger of our individual and collective spirits. The imperfect, yet promising, American spirit is poised to flourish if we can refine how we accommodate the struggles we encounter as we chase we-ness in its many forms.

With Palmer's habits of the heart in mind, Model 2 depicts the broad outline of what it would take to implement a wide range of informal and formal strategies to enhance our experiences of we-ness in the five social domains we've discussed (primary groups, thought communities, leisure and sports, community groups, and the workplace). Ideally, the strategies we employ to improve our empathy and leadership skills will, in turn, enable us to express altruism and compassion more effectively while strengthening our capacity to cooperate and generate bonding and bridging social capital. Together, these efforts are intimately connected to how we perceive and mobilize healthy forms of group belonging and dyadic, ideational, and spontaneous expressions of we-ness. These efforts can generate connections within and across social domains. Some may lead to coalition-building between various groups that have similar community goals. In these instances, success may sometimes depend on groups expanding their self-image and mission. When this occurs, they will reframe their identities and sense of we-ness to incorporate what others think, say, and do.

This broad approach is tethered to a series of concerns. First, we must hold steady in our conviction that people can be inspired to embrace beliefs, attitudes, and behaviors consistent with healthy forms of we-ness. We must also be prepared to create transformative messages to help people adapt and be motivated to live healthier lives for themselves and others. This potential blossomed in 2020 when numerous Americans of all racial and social class backgrounds protested shoulder to shoulder across the country, from Minnesota to New York to Mississippi to Ohio to California. We, as a people, developed a deeper understanding of and contempt for systemic racism and police brutality. Racism has unfortunately

Model 2: Strategies to Build We-ness in Five Social Domains Using *MEAL* Life Skills been endemic to the American experiment since its inception. But the BLM movement, like the 1960s civil rights movement before it, continues to sharpen our understanding of how different groups of people position themselves relative to social justice issues involving persons of color.

We need to champion the hopeful message that we can help each other find a way to cultivate a healthy style of we-ness. At the most personal level, it challenges us, irrespective of age, to recognize the value of incorporating a mindfulness practice and perspective into our approach to living life well. Getting "we" right demands that we get "me" right first. We must do the work to understand how the forces of our own mind, body, heart, and soul are uniquely woven together to create our personal tapestry of life. And as we've learned in this book, people like Jon Kabat-Zinn, Matthieu Ricard, Richard Davidson, the Dalai Lama, Jack Kornfield, and many others have championed the idea that we can develop a healthy mind. For example, Kabat-Zinn has been instrumental in launching and expanding the reach of the Mindfulness-Based Stress Reduction program and its offshoots. This program highlights the value of meditating to become more mindful and to reduce stress. Increasingly, people from various walks of life all over the world are listening and responding to Kabat-Zinn's message:

> We are longing to taste and become intimate with an authentic way to be in the world, and to be true to our deepest nature as human beings. You might even say we are starving for authentic experience, for a deep and embodied authenticity.... To taste liberty, we must liberate ourselves from our own small mindedness and closed hearts, and celebrate that freedom in the community of our own being and in our belonging.[13]

Over the past several decades many Americans have turned to mindfulness and meditation, most notably through organizations associated with health care, education, sports, business, criminal justice, religion, and politics. Of their own volition, as well as in response to group initiatives, more and more Americans are exploring avenues to enhance their mindfulness to lower their stress and improve their quality of life. Practices that promote mindfulness often urge us to become more aware of why and how we relate to group members and humanity more generally. We must find a wholesome balance that allows us to celebrate our interpersonal ties without becoming attached to group identities that perpetuate false narratives and conspiracy theories that breed a destructive form of tribalism that contributes to others' suffering.

Moving forward, we need more people in key positions to walk in step with leaders like Ohio Representative Tim Ryan, who has championed the need for institutional reforms that would promote mindfulness and meditation training. In *Healing America*, Ryan describes his passion for helping America's children – and other children around the world – begin their life's journey by being more aware of their brain's functionality and their ability to control their thoughts and emotions. He describes diverse and successful school-based programs that have emerged in the past few decades that have shown promise in improving youths' mindfulness.[14]

One program, MindUP for Life, was developed in 2003 by the Hawn Foundation, founded by the actress Goldie Hawn.[15] Hawn's vision after 9/11 was to develop a program informed by insights from neuroscience and mindfulness experts that would help children better understand the basics of how their brain works and to learn how to manage their emotions more effectively. She accomplished that goal; her program has serviced over seven million children as of December 19, 2020, and has been shown to produce positive results.[16]

Mindfulness and meditation programs typically do not focus extensively on educating us about we-ness and group belonging, per se. Rather, they encourage us to equip ourselves with the cognitive and emotional skill set that will enhance our ability to feel at ease with a cooperative spirit while discouraging us from seeing the world through a selfish, narcissistic prism. If we take the long view, it makes perfect sense to help children develop these teachable skills at an early age alongside their more traditional curriculum. Doing so will equip young people with a more discerning eye when they are confronted with choices about alternative forms of we-ness in their everyday lives. They can make more informed and healthy decisions about how they construct their identities and pursue memberships in groups such as athletic teams, gangs, choirs, hate groups, friendship networks, leadership clubs, and more. They will also have the perspective necessary to learn how to empathize and lead with dignity and compassion.

The second in the series of concerns, therefore, is that we must nurture our willingness and capacity to advance a multilayered agenda that prioritizes building empathy and leadership skills in diverse settings across the life course. Those skills should honor and activate our respect for individual autonomy, beneficence, nonmaleficence, and social justice. We should also strive to develop practical ways to help people build and use empathy and leadership skills.

Sociologist and food studies expert Michael Carolan provides this sort of guidance in his book, *A Decent Meal: Building Empathy in a Divided America*. His crucial message focuses on tearing down empathy walls by accentuating the role food plays and could play in our interpersonal lives. More specifically, he encourages us to leverage our attraction to food to enhance what he labels the "heartland." The heartland represents the emotional space that allows us to feel open and reflective. When we are immersed in the heartland, we are more likely to express empathy toward others, even when they hold distinctly different values and beliefs. Thus, Carolan proposes that we spend less time telling each other what we should do and more time creating action-oriented options involving food so that we will all gain insights experientially about those who are different from ourselves.

Carolan has designed a series of diverse and innovative experiments to examine how people's experiences with the foodscape affect their ability to empathize. These experiments include, for example, giving white nationalists a chance to mimic the daily work life of immigrant berry pickers; or creating a social arrangement that allows staunch Republicans and progressive Democrats to garden side by side; or offering "self-proclaimed welfare warriors" the chance to see what it is like to feed themselves according to SNAP's (Supplemental Nutrition Assistant Program) limited budget. Drawing on data from these and other experiments, as well as his ethnographic observations of other foodscape scenarios, Carolan demonstrates how food "can both motivate and disarm, creating a potential entry point to understanding without participants even knowing it."[17]

Carolan concludes that when people share time planting, harvesting, preparing, or eating food together, they are more likely to set aside their stereotypes and myopic views long enough to start appreciating how others experience their worlds. The *MEAL* life skills I promote can be taught by integrating different aspects of the foodscape that involve social settings, a linguistic synchronicity. Carolan's real message, as he notes, isn't about food per se, rather "the real protagonists are the encounters, which touch us viscerally."[18] He continues by noting that "we need leaders who can visualize changes to food policy and civic engagement and articulate strategies for seeing those ideas through to implementation."[19] Thus, strong leadership is needed to promote experiential learning opportunities involving food-related events that will strengthen an "empathy-based revolution."

The third concern in the series is that we must find ways to revamp our major institutions to foster these skills in all five social domains while clarifying our norms about the common good and the good life. Part of the infrastructure that needs to be revitalized includes what Ray Oldenburg celebrates as the third places in our communities. These sites have enabled Americans, as well as people in other cultures throughout history, to develop a communal sense of belonging. We stand to gain much if we can find creative ways to bring people from diverse backgrounds together to nurture their supportive and shared identities. Sometimes that may require innovative people to contribute their expertise outside any formal structure by personally developing online sites or local options for people to connect and build a sense of community (e.g., woodworking programs for senior citizens). Unfortunately, advancing a more communitarian philosophy and lifestyle will be challenging because of the effects of suburban sprawl and our networked individualism that is reinforced by our reliance on modern communication technologies.

Fourth, although we must teach and implement these skills at the local and regional levels, it is imperative that we also articulate a national strategy to highlight similar concerns. In America, that approach must confront the destabilizing partisan forces that permeate our body politic and everyday lives. As a country, we have always wrestled with significant matters of perceived "social difference." Our social history is littered with battles between outspoken groups of people fervently committed to their own image of we-ness. Vestiges of many of those struggles remain with us today, often hidden from full view for all but the most attentive among us or those most afflicted by social injustice. These heated battles initially focused on religious freedoms, Indigenous people's rights, slavery, and our independence from a king's rule. They were later joined by concerns about the rights of women, workers, groups of immigrants of specific ethnicities, persons outside the heteronormative mainstream, persons with disabilities, and many more. What is new today is that the competing forces that promote our desires for group belonging and we-ness are now paired with modern communication platforms. These technologies speed up, expand, and filter our exchanges in ways that amplify our tribal tendencies. We must remind ourselves that there is much work to be done to overcome the brutal consequences of narrow and bigoted in-group thinking.

Practically speaking, we must provide better supports to encourage people to develop the special characteristics that make them, as Isabel Wilkerson suggests, "immune to the toxins of caste in the air we breathe." She clarifies that "these are people of personal courage and conviction, secure within themselves, willing to break convention, not reliant on the approval of others for their sense of self, people of deep and abiding empathy and compassion."[20] In other words, persons very different from the Republican legislators and former high-ranking administration officials who were unwilling to challenge Trump's brazen contempt for our democracy, the election process, constitutional principles, and long-standing bipartisan political norms.

Before commenting on what could be achieved in each of the five social domains to bring about healthier states of we-ness for all of us, let's think big and explore an idea that has been debated for more than sixty years. Should we, can we, create a national consciousness and agenda to energize a more productive spirit of we-ness for Americans? If so, can this consciousness mobilize the social forces needed to transform the systemic structures and practices that contribute to the social inequalities and widespread suffering that plague our society?

National Service Initiatives

Americans have a long history of community engagement, with much of it occurring independent of government initiatives. Alexis de Tocqueville, the French diplomat, political thinker, and historian, who traveled widely in the United States in the early 1830s, is often cited as one of the first astute observers of the unique American character that embraces civic engagement. As an outsider, he showcased Americans' willingness to join voluntary associations and to contribute to community life. Since the United States was founded, Americans have been eager to volunteer and commit their time, effort, and money to helping others.[21] One consequence of that early experiment with building a democratic state was that many of the immigrants and their descendants experienced a deeper connection to each other and the larger community than those who lived under a different type of political system.

Our sentiments about serving the larger public provide a foundation for the complex social and political bonds that hold our cultural system together. Yet, the nature and intensity of the we-ness we share ebbs and flows in response to social conditions, including major economic depressions and recessions, wars, natural disasters, pandemics, demographic shifts, technological developments, and more. In challenging times, people in the United States typically rally around their common fate as Americans. Unfortunately, examples of a more selective and exclusionary approach to we-ness during crises are also part of our historical legacy and contemporary landscape. The internment of Japanese Americans during World War II represents one of the most infamous blemishes on our displays of we-ness during a crisis. The Trump administration's nativist policies, and well-publicized negative treatment of asylum seekers from Central America, provide a more recent illustration of the downside to exclusionary we-ness. This type of we-ness has occurred in an age in which those in power and many of their devoted followers have feared the changing profile of the United States away from a majority white population. The vitriol of our public "we-based" rhetoric continues to infect our wounded nation.

In contrast, the upside to we-ness was powerfully displayed by Americans' early reactions to the 9/11 attacks. Those reactions vividly demonstrate our ability under the "right" circumstances to forge a collective consciousness that inspires empathy, altruism, trust, and resilience. Informed by the twenty-three focus groups he conducted around the country in the two months following the 9/11 tragedy, Stanley Greenberg wrote in *The American Prospect* that the "emerging mood and values in this new period" emphasize "unity, coming together, community, seriousness of purpose, freedom of choice, and tolerance."[22] Robert Putnam, the renowned expert on civic engagement trends, came to a similar conclusion: "Americans were more united, readier for collective sacrifice, and more attuned to public purpose than we have been for several decades."[23] Commenting on the timeframe immediately after 9/11, Putnam adds that "we have a more capacious sense of 'we' than we have had in the adult experience of most Americans now alive." Still, we must not forget that some were quick to stigmatize Middle Eastern Americans both formally and informally, reminiscent of how a previous generation had mistreated Japanese Americans.

In the aftermath of the horrific terrorist attack of 9/11, the Brookings Institution published a collection of essays, *United We Serve: National Service and the Future of Citizenship*, that placed national service in a historical and political context. The 2003 book highlights the critical developments since the 1800s that have framed public debate about the government's role in promoting individuals' service to the larger community and nation.

National service proposals are central to the discussion of how we can best promote different forms of we-ness in our diverse society. In the two decades since the Brookings's 2003 book, numerous political actors and community activists have continued to advocate for some form of national service program, including John Bridgeland. Bridgeland was one of the major architects of the 2009 Edward M. Kennedy Serve America Act, which was signed into law by President

Barack Obama but left unfunded. Bridgeland chronicled his extensive experience working on national service initiatives in his 2013
book, *Heart of the Nation: Volunteering and America's Civic Spirit*.[24] He
also served as the first director of the USA Freedom Corps that was
announced by President Bush during his State of the Union address
in 2002.

Also in 2013, retired Army General Stanley McChrystal, who
commanded the Joint Special Operations Command from 2003 to
2008, spearheaded an eclectic working group of national stakeholders who developed the Franklin Project in conjunction with
the Aspen Institute. Named after Benjamin Franklin, this project
generated a forward-thinking and detailed report: *A 21st Century
National Service System Plan of Action*.[25] The report proposes that
"making national service a universal expectation – a new American rite of passage – will renew and redefine for this generation the
role of citizens in our democracy." The main objective is to mobilize various sectors of society to "offer at least one million full-
time civilian national service opportunities for young adults ages
18–28 every year." The project's vision and multifaceted approach
builds on the existing infrastructure for service and expands it in
new ways. It outlines strategies to leverage partnerships between
the government and private and nonprofit organizations. The proposal outlines a range of service corps that target vital social problems as well as innovative ideas that would create the infrastructure necessary to expand service opportunities for young people
and seniors.

After becoming the chair of the board of Service Year Alliance –
which was created after the Franklin Project, ServiceNation, and
the Service Year Exchange were merged – General McChrystal
wrote in *The Atlantic*, "A service year that teaches young Americans the habits of citizenship and the power of working in teams
to build trust is one of the most powerful ways this generation
can help restore political and civic responsibility – and in the process help to heal a wounded nation."[26] In the years 2019 to 2022,
McChrystal's characterization of the United States as a "wounded
nation" became even more ominous when Americans took to their
opposing sides of the aisle in response to the two impeachments

of Donald Trump, the COVID-19 pandemic, and the House Select Committee to Investigate the January 6th Attack on the United States Capitol.

In 2019, Bridgeland and colleague John DiIulio, Jr. worked with The Brookings Institution to publish another timely document, *Will America Embrace National Service?* This report assesses the most recent debates about the national service programs, and ultimately champions efforts to develop a universal national service system. Together, the two Brookings documents, *United We Serve* and *Will America Embrace National Service?*, review the prospects for the United States introducing either a voluntary or compulsory national service program that covers military and civilian service options. Bridgeland and DiIulio, Jr. argue that historical evidence shows that "national service can play a transformational role in knitting the country back together in common purpose and promoting a stronger culture of 'we.'"[27]

The public's commitment to promoting we-ness is often accentuated in response to distinct and major crises, but our concern over the lack of we-ness can also be triggered by the more obscure expressions of social and political divisiveness. As I've highlighted throughout this book, we have become, as Americans, increasingly polarized in our culture wars and politics during the past several decades. Many have blockaded themselves in their isolated camps, unable or unwilling to agree on basic facts, seemingly impervious to commonsense logic. Too many also see compromise as dishonorable. Calls for we-ness are pervasive in our rhetoric, but they are tailored to a counterproductive formula that pits "us" against "them" at all costs.

Alarmed by this divisiveness, numerous politicians and social commentators have proposed that we take bold action to promote national service programs to help bring us together. The vision for national service was advanced in an epic way when President John F. Kennedy challenged the country during his 1961 presidential inauguration with his famous and inspiring words: "And so, my fellow Americans: Ask not what your country can do for you – ask what you can do for your country." Outside of wartime and economic depression, no president had called upon Americans to sacrifice for their country and to envision playing such an active role in shaping the larger society.

Kennedy helped to create a sense of we-ness for thousands of Americans who signed up to be part of his novel Peace Corps program. By working with more disadvantaged populations around the world, these optimistic participants solidified their Americanized sense of belonging when they compared their way of life to that of those less fortunate. Although the Peace Corps never fulfilled Kennedy's dreams in terms of size, it continues to represent an important symbol of a service-oriented strategy that gives people a unique and powerful opportunity to develop their sense of we-ness as volunteering Americans. This sentiment resounds in Josh Bishoff's description of what motivated him to join the Peace Corps and serve a couple of years in Liberia as a primary and secondary school teacher:

> In a world where it seems like there are lots of people trying to tear things down, I have always been doing activities in my life to try and build things up. A large part of my professional experience has revolved around construction and substitute teaching/coaching. In all three areas your primary focus is to build ... I have always believed that for humanity to get along, we must build each other up. Peace Corps gave me the opportunity to take that mentality and apply it internationally. I have felt a great deal of pride in serving, not only my country but all humankind.[28]

At the time Kennedy shared his vision, he electrified people of all ages, setting the stage for subsequent initiatives including AmeriCorps, Volunteers in Service to America (VISTA), Corporation for National and Community Service (CNCS), Senior Corps, and USA Freedom Corps. Unfortunately, these national service programs can only provide opportunities for a relatively small proportion of those who wish to participate. Each year, more than six hundred thousand Americans apply for service programs like these but only about 20 percent of the applicants secure one of these coveted positions. Nearly half a million people are turned away because of inadequate funding.[29]

Over recent decades, presidents (excluding Donald Trump) as well as other high-profile politicians, like former Senators John McCain and Ted Kennedy, have extolled the virtues of national service. John McCain, once a skeptic of national service, changed his mind during the final two decades of his life and spoke passionately about it as a presidential candidate. His advice to Americans was that when you "Make a sacrifice for a cause greater than self-interest ... you invest your life with the eminence of that cause."[30] For McCain, such commitments are grounded in a type of we-ness born out of a love of country and the desire to bond with fellow citizens to accomplish good deeds.

But while McCain and others have encouraged people to look beyond their self-interest, some propose an alternative message about our personal desires. They argue that it is best to think of service or "public work" as "not only altruism, but enlightened self-interest – a desire to build a society in which the serving citizen wants to live."[31] Others, like French political analyst Jacques Attali, use the term "self-interested altruism" to capture the critical force that interdependence plays in joining individual and social interests.[32] This perspective acknowledges that self-interest can play a legitimate role in promoting national service. If driven by a broader vision of self-interest, young people as well as others can seek productive opportunities to express their self-interest by joining service teams that thrive on promoting the power of we-ness. While using expressions of we-ness to help others, the volunteers are also empowered to enhance their own set of interpersonal skills as they contribute to building a more just, loving, and productive society.

In regard to national service and young people, John Bridgeland and John DiIulio, Jr. explicitly highlight several of the previously mentioned motivating forces that could inspire us to pursue we-ness: "Americans of every demographic description and socioeconomic status, most particularly young adults, should be expected – and given the opportunity – to serve their country, help solve our nation's most pressing problems, and by sharing the hardship and fulfillment that service can offer, bind themselves to one another and to the nation."[33] In particular, their rationale for a national service initiative highlights companionship, celebrating lofty ideals, sharing pain and suffering, and sharing a practical goal. These programs can also be tailored to provide younger and older persons alike the opportunity to bond with others as part of a mentoring process.

I'll leave it to national service experts like Bridgeland to elaborate on the specific public-private partnerships that can expand and strengthen the national service system. Clearly, lots of useful ideas have been presented. Some have already been adopted with the support of local, state, and federal governments, colleges and universities, nonprofits, and businesses. And some appear to be producing good results.[34] Tufts University introduced its 1+4 Bridge Year program in 2015 that has students spend their first year doing national service in an organization of their choosing. Tulane University supports a similar mission but provides a different sort of plan. It has students complete their undergraduate degree before spending another year on campus working in a local nonprofit giving back to the community.[35] Although the programs at Tufts and Tulane universities support a well-developed, formal mechanism to incorporate some form of a service initiative into a student's curriculum plan, many universities sponsor valuable but more modest opportunities for students to get involved with local community groups.[36] For example, early in my career I developed a summer sociology course that I called the Group-Related Internship Program (GRIP) in which I arranged for teams of three or four students to volunteer and develop a project connected to a community organization of their collective choice near the University of Florida (e.g., shelter for abused women, Boys & Girls Club, homeless shelter).

Those who propose national service systems also typically suggest expanding existing corps as well as developing new ones. Dedicated programs that address such issues as poverty, environment, health, education, disaster response, and others are designed to build cohesion within families, communities, organizations, and the nation to improve our social and physical surroundings. These initiatives range in scope and include helping partners and parents in families to communicate more effectively. Some seek to strengthen mentoring relationships between tutors and disadvantaged students who may otherwise drop out of high school. Some focus on finding ways to help volunteers make a difference in cleaning up our parklands, lakes, and rivers. Some might even seek to create a supportive organizational business culture in which management and labor work effectively with one another to encourage workers to develop a vested interest in the success of the enterprise.

Regrettably, the quality of the polling data documenting Americans' views on national service is not ideal.[37] Thus, we cannot draw firm conclusions regarding the public's beliefs and attitudes about various issues associated with national service. However, national service experts like Bridgeland and DiIulio, Jr., who have closely reviewed the existing data, are willing to offer a cautionary summary: "Most Americans of every demographic description, socioeconomic status, partisan identification, and ideological disposition favor 'national service' if it is 'voluntary' (meaning either unpaid, or not required by law, or both) and oppose it if it is 'mandatory' or 'compulsory' (as in required by law and administered/enforced/funded by government)."[38] Still, many Americans are reluctant to have government play a significant role in organizing such a system.

Whatever the specifics might be, such a national system could be instrumental in creating many exciting and productive opportunities for people to build bonding and bridging social capital. A national service system can also give people more viable options to develop a strong sense of purpose and we-ness while doing rewarding work that benefits others.

As I've previously argued, much can be gained by establishing a more robust national service system that gives young people the chance to increase their human and social capital on a voluntary basis, while also developing productive interpersonal bonds. Such a program can enhance young people's leadership skills and strengthen their commitment to civic engagement. This system can help volunteers forge a group identity and sense of we-ness as members of an annual cohort of national volunteers. Ideally, such a system will offer individuals a transformative experience: one that benefits them personally and strengthens the larger society.

But we must not forget that there are countless ways outside of a national service system to empower people of varying ages to build a healthy sense of we-ness while helping others and improving their own lives. I next selectively highlight some options for promoting healthy we-ness in the five social domains.

Primary Groups

For centuries, parent educators, child psychologists, family therapists, parent advocates, and other authors have produced books, magazine articles, web-based materials, documentaries, talk shows, podcasts, workshops, and more that offer parents advice on child-rearing. Those materials cover a wide range of topics, and increasingly some even incorporate explicit messages about empathy, emotional intelligence, and leadership skills.

Leader in Me (LiM) is one of the most impressive programs that is consistent with my vision for developing healthy we-ness in a primary group setting.[39] It is designed to help educators unleash young students' potential leadership abilities and more. The program's roots go back to 1999 and the vision of Muriel Summers, a principal of A.B. Combs Leadership Magnet Elementary School in Raleigh, North Carolina. Principal Summers initially introduced a new theme of "leadership" to transform her struggling school. Building on Stephen Covey's best-selling book, *The 7 Habits of Highly Effective People*, and several other educational tools, she developed and implemented a leadership model for her students and staff. She and her team were committed to approaching their students more holistically.

Today, LiM represents a codified version of those early efforts and is supported by FranklinCovey Education, a prominent provider of educational leadership programs internationally. The program creates opportunities for young people to develop the self-confidence and skill set to become effective leaders and well versed in socio-emotional learning. It offers a broad approach to leadership where all students are encouraged to lead themselves and others and, through their cooperation and dedication, ultimately bring out the best in everyone. The model is based on five paradigms: develop the whole person; empower students to lead their own learning; change starts with me; everyone has genius; and everyone can be a leader.

It also extends Covey's ideas about personal effectiveness that he laid out in his classic framework: be proactive®; begin with the end in mind®; put first things first®; think win-win®; seek first to understand, then to be understood®; synergize®; and sharpen the saw®.

The LiM program underscores the theme I've emphasized that to be an effective leader a person needs to be mindful and in control of their own personal experience. Helping people at a very young age develop the listening skills to relate well to others is a critical feature of this program, and one that should be incorporated into other programs that work with young people. This type of project can complement school-based programs that promote students' empathy skills, like the Roots of Empathy, described in chapter 6, that features a parent and their baby.

Those who want to enhance primary group life for families should focus some of their attention on how families manage transitions. New step, blended, single-parent, adoptive, and foster families often experience stress as members try to sort out how they fit in and what it means for them that their family circumstances have changed and are different from conventional families. Of course, these family types, just like the more traditional arrangement that includes two coresident, biological parents with children, can experience problems that require attention at any point in their shared history. But that early period of transitioning into we-ness is likely to be the most unstable because family members, confronted with a new set of circumstances, must figure out for the first time how they should perceive and relate to one another.

My research on heterosexual stepfamilies, which I introduced in chapter 5, revealed some of the adjustments stepfamily members need to make as they learn a new family dance. They must negotiate the meanings and practical realities of their emerging arrangement that requires them to think about multiple and sometimes interconnected webs of relations that support a sense of we-ness. The stepfather must not only manage how he relates to the child's mother and his stepchild or children, but he must also think about his relationship to the biological father and the community youth workers (e.g., teachers, day-care workers, coaches, pediatrician) who are involved in his stepchild's life. And if he has a child or children of his own, he may need to incorporate them into the new family dance as well. Some of these relationships can generate feelings akin to those related to a sense of we-ness or group belonging.

Using my interviews with stepdads, I developed two concepts (paternal claiming and stepfather ally) that capture aspects of the we-ness sentiment that have implications for well-being. The first speaks to the degree to which a stepfather tends to claim step-children as his own.[40] When a man has this type of paternal commit-ment, he is less likely to see any distinction between being a father to either a stepchild or biological child. A stepfather is more likely to experience this type of paternal claiming if he meets a stepchild when the child is younger, has similar types of personal interests and skills, and the child is less involved with their biological father. It also matters whether the mother gives the stepdad the freedom to be involved in a hands-on way with the child. All things being equal, when a stepfather sees and treats a stepchild this way, the child is more likely to experience positive life outcomes.

When a stepfather becomes a father ally, he is typically able to see himself as playing a collaborative parenting role on some level with the biological father.[41] This is a unique relationship that requires stepfathers to express empathy. A stepfather who acts like a father ally engages in a type of multifather parenting that reflects the com-mon interests he shares with the biological father – the well-being of the child. In these settings, the stepfather will do and say things that can be reasonably perceived as supportive of the father-child rela-tionship. For example, the stepfather can encourage the stepchild to update the father on school events and other activities that the father might want to attend, or the stepfather can discourage the mother from speaking poorly of the father in front of the children.

We need programs to help stepfathers and everyone else under-stand and feel comfortable with their rights, obligations, and alli-ances in the new family dance. A key feature of these programs should be to promote empathy skills for all the participants. Such initiatives can help stepfamilies manage their feelings, tensions, and expectations about their new circumstances as unconventional co-parents and stepchildren. These initiatives can also enhance par-ticipants' experiences with developing an intimate sense of group belonging in family settings that may not have well-defined cultural norms to guide people's interactions.

The mostly informal options we use to learn and express mindfulness, empathy, altruism, and leadership skills in our primary relationships can profoundly affect our well-being as well as influence others in our immediate social orbit. The *MEAL* life skill set we develop in these social arrangements can also provide us with the foundation to interact in healthy ways with others outside our primary networks.

Community Groups

Now, as we move into the third decade of the twenty-first century, we need to assess whether our changing social landscape is suitably equipped to generate opportunities to enhance our sense of we-ness as neighbors, community members, and Americans more broadly. In *Better Together: Restoring the American Community*, Robert Putnam, Lewis Feldstein, and Don Cohen profile a diverse set of organizational case studies from across the country. They highlight creative and effective "local choices and grassroots strategies" to build community while emphasizing ways to develop bridging social capital because it is the hardest to establish. Although Putnam, Feldstein, and Cohen's analysis predates the polarized Trump era, it can still inform our analysis more generally of the diverse groups and social networks that have become so entrenched in their opposing views and alternative interpretations of reality.

The authors remind us that if we want to maximize opportunities to develop bridging social capital, we need to invest more time and energy in face-to-face communication and focus our efforts at the local level. Unfortunately, there is no cookie-cutter strategy to build social capital that can be applied in diverse community settings. However, getting to know people and gaining their trust remains the most critical step in the process of community building. Some semblance of dyadic we-ness often lays the groundwork to motivate groups with differing agendas and ideas to collaborate. Even though building relationships and interpersonal dyadic we-ness is easier in smaller settings, bonds and social capital can be forged in larger groups and even local businesses, too. Ideally, leaders will implement organizational models that enable individuals to share power and work cooperatively in small teams.

Putnam, Feldstein, and Cohen found that some of the organizations that succeeded in building community implemented a "nesting" strategy. This approach enables participants to establish a sense of we-ness and communicate with one another in numerous small groups that operate in a larger organization. Much can be gained when at least some people are involved with more than one of these nested groups. Ideally, key members from the nested groups will make a difference by connecting the cohesive small groups across different organizations to help build bridging social capital. "Organizational choices that facilitate 'mixing' and 'bridging' among small groups," according to Putnam, Feldstein, and Cohen, "can harness the benefits of both intimacy and breadth."[42]

However, in our polarized social world, developing bridging social capital is exceedingly difficult. People too often refuse to have constructive, civil conversations with one another when they are confronted with people in opposing thought communities. Fortunately, even in America's contentious culture, it is not impossible for people to create bridging social capital. Those in the trenches of community life advise that taking simple steps, like creating initiatives that persuade people to share stories and participate in potluck dinners, can sometimes produce startling results.[43] Storytelling, both the telling and listening sides of the narrative, can impress people from different backgrounds and organizations. It can reveal opportunities to explore new dimensions of similarity and common cause that provide a basis for a productive alliance. Done well, storytelling can promote empathy, "which then eases the formation of enduring groups and networks."[44] Cooperative arrangements, fueled organically by people who are compelled to build upon their shared interests, are more likely to be rooted in fertile ground compared to initiatives proposed by outsiders. In other words, participants who have already successfully connected with one another will be more motivated to develop bridging social capital.

Transformative narratives come in the form of stories that focus on either the "I," "we," or "they."[45] When we stand before others to share our personal story, open and vulnerable, we engender trust. President Joe Biden has done this remarkably well over the course of his life. Whether he's talking about his struggles as a youth to overcome stuttering or sharing stories about the tragic loss of family members to a car accident and to cancer, Biden has perfected the art of building trust while rousing empathy for and from others. Social media has expanded storytelling options, giving a voice to many who would have otherwise remained silent in an earlier time.

In addition, the "we" stories bring people together to recount their shared experiences and identities. Occasions of shared story-telling can promote opportunities to integrate the various activities associated with thought communities and community groups. The #MeToo campaign that activist Tarana Burke launched in 2006 provides an ideal example. This initiative gained public attention when the hashtag #MeToo went viral in October 2017 to spotlight the sexual misconduct taking place in Hollywood. Initially, actresses Ashley Judd and Alyssa Milano spearheaded the social media phase that generated a collective consciousness steeped in survivor stories. Milano's tweet on October 15, 2017, "If you've been sexually harassed or assaulted write 'me too' as a reply to this tweet," set off a massive response and social movement. The tweet went viral. In a twenty-four-hour period, the hashtag was used by more than 4.7 million people in twelve million posts. By sharing stories, the survivors were able to reframe their experiences into a collective identity that empowered them individually and as a group. Along the way, individuals developed deep dyadic and ideational forms of we-ness with those who could personally relate to their circumstances.

In subsequent months and years, a long litany of misbehaving high-profile public figures was named as this movement gained momentum. The movement created opportunities across diverse industries and for people from various walks of life to share their personal stories. Related hashtags (e.g., #MeTooMilitary, #Church-Too, #HimToo), policies, laws, and other initiatives in the United States and around the world expanded the scope of how people were identifying with sexual harassment and abuse issues.[46] The

#MeToo movement has shown that developing a strong collective identity at the national and international level can also enhance how a sense of we-ness is nurtured at the local, community level.

The "they" stories reflect our tendency to rally together to face a common enemy. Just as a key motivating force for we-ness involves identifying a common enemy, storytelling can be enriched by storytellers focusing on a similar foil. When community leaders share stories about both their troubling and successful experiences working on common problems, they are likely to see themselves as being part of the same "team" even if they have no formal association. Those exchanges can help to produce trust and supportive interpersonal ties. Putnam, Feldstein, and Cohen highlight how valuable preexisting relationships are in a community. When individuals or groups have already established a cooperative bond, and perhaps a sense of we-ness, it may be possible to capitalize on those relationships and redirect the alliance to address other social issues. For many working in community groups, building the trust that reinforces we-ness is often a protracted process, so it makes sense to recycle those personal connections whenever possible. Many on the frontlines continue to sing the praises of face-to-face contacts. Until the COVID-19 pandemic, the conventional wisdom seemed to be that virtual tools could sometimes augment our sense of we-ness and enable us to improve our effectiveness in building social capital in the community. But those virtual tools could not easily replace our physical interactions. That calculus, in the post-COVID-19 era, may need to be revised. However, amid social/physical distancing, travel restrictions, and partial lockdowns, the jury is still out on how well video conferencing can substitute for in-person chats, handshakes, fist bumps, and hugs. What is clear, though, is that people, especially those who work in certain segments of the white-collar economy, are getting plenty of practice using this alternative communication format.

Our uphill battle to create bridging social capital is likely to persist because, in some ways, we live in a more isolated fashion than earlier generations. The notion of multiplexity – having strong relationships with the same people in multiple settings – has declined in recent cohorts. We are less likely, for example, to work, go to church, and do leisure activities with our family members. Similarly, our interactions with our friends are more likely to be confined to the world of leisure rather than also spending time with them in civic activities. When we only form a sense of we-ness with people in separate orbits, we are more likely to move in and out of relationships and have weaker social ties. As a result, we limit chances to develop lasting bonding or bridging social capital when we are unable to combine our we-ness from primary groups with our commitments in other groups.

Thought Communities

The passion we associate with experiencing a sense of we-ness and group belonging is often most intense when we, along with others, embrace an emotionally charged, shared belief system. Our religious and political affiliations create some of the most compelling examples of ideational we-ness. These forms of we-ness fundamentally influence how we see ourselves and relate to others. Earlier, we saw the impact that religious and political belief systems had on shaping Megan Phelps-Roper's and Derek Black's ways of thinking when they were children and then young adults. They were entrapped by the bigoted beliefs of their families and close friends. The empathy walls that surrounded them restricted their core being for many years. These toxic circumstances affected not only how they saw themselves but also how they perceived and judged others. For them, the world was segmented into rigid opposing units of "us" and "them." Prior to their deradicalization, their sense of we-ness, and the importance they placed on their group belonging, defined just about everything that mattered to them. But we also learned through Christian Picciolini's story that a hate community can radicalize individuals even when they are raised in families that do not espouse hate ideologies.

Since the beginning of recorded history, people have made sense of their worlds by using a simplistic in-group versus out-group paradigm. This myopic mindset fosters numerous dilemmas for everyone involved. Unfortunately, history repeatedly shows us that the activities related to thought communities provoke some of the most antagonistic and deadliest forms of conflict. Over the ages, some of our ancestors have sought to confront this divisive pattern, but they have only made incremental advances in curtailing it. That said, Steven Pinker and others have shown that we have made remarkable strides over the centuries in curbing our violent tendencies and penchant for cruelty.[47] The emergence of new institutions, shifts in our cultural norms, increased levels of education, and expanding markets have substantially reduced the negative fallout that is created when groups with opposing ideologies and agendas confront one another. As a species, despite the jaw-dropping atrocities tied to wars, purges, and terrorist attacks throughout time, large-scale and isolated human brutalities have become increasingly less common. Nonetheless, the 24/7 media cycle and the expansive reach of the high-tech news industry distorts our sense of history by saturating us with images of bad actors who individually and collectively stain our world.

Fortunately, people with differing views and experiences have learned to be more cooperative. Challenging prevailing public sentiment, Pinker appears to have a reasonably optimistic outlook about our ability to manage the fallout from groups brandishing competing visions and goals. But if we are to help ease the tensions that arise from people having strong allegiances to groups with drastically different beliefs, we must systematically enhance our listening, empathy, and leadership skills while adopting effective strategies for conflict resolution. Ultimately, we need to prioritize the virtues associated with individual autonomy, beneficence, nonmaleficence, and social justice. The thought communities and individuals who represent these virtues should be accorded a higher moral standing. As such, we need to allocate public and private resources to encourage people to nurture forms of we-ness that allow them to realize these themes.

Phelps-Roper is ideally situated to instruct us on how we might more effectively manage the tensions we experience when we confront those who do not share our views. Having been raised in a close-knit religious network filled with intolerance and hate, she learned firsthand how counterproductive and limiting that bigoted approach can be. Prior to leaving the church, she and her fellow church members' view of nonmembers was that *"We have nothing to learn from these people."*[48] Looking beyond her religious upbringing, Phelps-Roper laments that those in the public square also increasingly embrace this false assumption of thinking that they know everything. She is one of many commentators who acknowledge that we live in a fractured world framed by an "us" and "them" mentality. Phelps-Roper sees disturbing parallels between her former church and the discourses of public life, including

> knee-jerk expulsion of insiders who violate group orthodoxy; and the demonization of outsiders and the inability to substantively engage with their ideas, because we simply cannot step outside our own. In this environment, there is a growing insistence that opposing views must be silenced, whether by the powers of government, the self-regulation of social media companies, or the self-censorship of individuals.[49]

Powerful accusations. So, what can we do? Phelps-Roper suggests that we lean into an "epistemological humility." This approach, for her, is "not a lack of belief or principle of faith, not the refusal to take a position or the abdication of responsibility to stand against injustice, but a constant examination of one's world view, a commitment to honestly grappling with criticisms of it."[50] This perspective echoes Parker Palmer's sage commentary on the five basic habits of the heart that underscore the value of being open-minded and sensitive to our interdependencies with others from diverse backgrounds. The more we appreciate that we have similarities despite our differences, that we need each other, and that we can learn from one another if we listen, the better off we'll be in the long run.

Compared to earlier eras, the modern information age defined by the internet and social media has expanded our options to connect with thought communities that focus on critical social issues. Today, social movements like #MeToo and Black Lives Matter offer like-minded people powerful options to engage with thought communities and to get involved in public affairs. One tech-based resource that capitalizes on shared cultural experiences, Black Twitter, provides a practical and powerful tool that demonstrates how communication technologies have transformed how we construct various forms of ideational we-ness. We have good reason to ask whether virtual resources like Black Twitter can compensate in some ways for our vanishing real-world third places.

In an interview for *The Atlantic* in 2015, Meredith Clark, a media studies professor at the University of Virginia who studies Black Twitter, defined it as a "temporally linked group of connectors that share culture, language and interest in specific issues and talking about specific topics with a black frame of reference."[51] One of the prominent participants in Clark's research, @feministajones, shares several of her own phrases to capture the essence of Black Twitter, referring to it as a "collective of people from different walks of life," "meeting place," and "a powerful force that can't be ignored ... a movement."[52]

These accounts of Black Twitter are consistent with the idea of ideational we-ness. The users of this vibrant online community come to it with what the noted social theorist Randall Collins would define as generalized cultural capital.[53] That capital represents a stock of symbols and knowledge – a type of group-specific resource – that enables those who possess it to connect with others as insiders in ways often charged with emotional significance. In the world of Black Twitter, this symbolic resource is forged from Black people's individual and accumulated experience of navigating a society steeped in white privilege. In an abstract way, users of Black Twitter are aware of a social identity that has been assigned to them by the larger society. Yet, and more importantly, they also come to this virtual space representing the heterogeneity of their humanity as Black persons who embody different backgrounds and experiences related to their gender, sexual orientation, social class, education, political leanings, religion, and much, much more. In this space, they bring their individual perspectives and insert their commentary into the larger mix of contributions made by others who can relate to them on one or more levels.

Although this forum is tailored for Black users, it also provides opportunities to reinforce allyship with other persons of color and whites who are engaged with the platform and eager to support the BLM movement. Unlike traditional third places that tend to be local in nature, Black Twitter represents a national and international platform. Yet, the semi-inclusive platform does resemble the generic third place by offering participants from different backgrounds a safe space to communicate openly.

Clark identifies six elements that clarify how Black Twitter operates and enables users to see themselves as promoting an ideational we-ness.[54] First, self-selection refers to Twitter users acknowledging their ability to tap into their identities as Black-identifying persons who have life experiences as members of a marginalized out-group defined by their racial identity. Second, users recast their Black social identity in a new light. They mentally suspend being cast as members of a devalued out-group. Instead, they deepen their self-awareness of the commonality they share with other users and claim their roles as representatives of an empowered in-group. In other words, participants use their Twitter activity to reenvision themselves as authentic and active members of a community they help to redefine in a positive light. Third, Black Twitter fosters a performance feature that allows users to communicate by tweeting and retweeting in specific ways. Users can identify culturally informed hashtags and phrases that are understood and valued by one or more of the Black communities that have an online and offline presence. Ultimately, the network is activated with the intent of building a sense of community, often around sensitive issues (e.g., sexual exploitation of Black girls and women). Fourth, the viability of the online networking in Black Twitter is reinforced by the many offline physical spaces and institutions that encapsulate the cultural and symbolic dimensions to Black people's diverse experiences (e.g., churches, schools, fraternities/sororities, barbershops). Some of the local sites may resemble traditional third places that appeal to Black people. Users can confirm and extend in face-to-face settings what emerged during online postings and exchanges. To matter, the hashtagging that occurs in Black Twitter requires a level of cultural competency that reinforces the sense of ideational we-ness shared by the participants of this network. Fifth, the Black Twitter–based activities that prove to be most consequential are those that initially appear online, then find a voice in offline activities, and later get reaffirmed in the Black Twittersphere, completing the feedback loop of influence.

Finally, that portion of Black Twitter that targets specific social issues can achieve a form of vindication when it alters circumstances in the real world by activating the forces of "call-out" and "cancel" culture. For instance, users of Black Twitter proactively called out Starbucks in June 2020 for circulating a memo to employees that warned them that they should not wear clothes, accessories, or pins that supported BLM. Numerous tweets highlighted Starbucks' hypocrisy because the company permits staffers to wear accessories supporting the LGBTQ+ movement. The hashtag #BoycottStarbucks was immediately launched, and Starbucks quickly reversed course, tweeting out "Black Lives Matter. We continue to listen to our partners and communities and their desire to stand for justice together. The Starbucks Black Partner Network codesigned T-shirts with this graphic that will soon be sent to 250,000+ store partners."[55] Staffers were also given official notice that they could wear their own items supporting BLM. The company's use of phrases like "our partners and communities" signals how executives attempt to weave corporate interests with the goals of specific groups by socially constructing an inclusive image of we-ness. In addition to instigating a change in a corporate policy, the outcry on Twitter – particularly Black Twitter – reinforced the sense of ideational we-ness that BLM supporters feel for one another and their cause of racial justice.

Black Twitter also inspires social activism. An early and highly visible example of this was how activity in the Black Twittersphere created public outrage several days after George Zimmerman's acquittal in the 2013 trial involving the death of Trayvon Martin. The quick and intense Twitter response (especially using the #jurorB37 hashtag) derailed the prospects of Sharlene Martin, president of Martin Literary Management, working with Juror B37 on a book about her involvement in the racially charged case.[56] More recently, we can point to the impact of Black Twitter activity – specifically the May 5, 2020, posting by Shaun King of a graphic video he had acquired showing the killing of Ahmaud Arbery ten weeks earlier on February 23, 2020. It brought relatively quick, angry, and decisive action from various segments of society. Most importantly, the local

District Attorney's office initiated three arrests in what had been a stagnant case. To its credit, the Twitter world mobilized national media attention for this case involving a twenty-five-year-old African American victim who had been stalked, shot, and killed by three white men while he was jogging in a Georgia neighborhood.[57] This Twitter activity prompted a string of events that ultimately led to three murder convictions.

When the Black Twitter network witnesses how its messages sometimes affect the social world offline, including shaping the messaging from the national news media, it can reinforce the users' commitment to their online personal communities and deepen their sense of we-ness and shared purpose.[58] Success and power beget a more crystallized sense of we-ness. This may be particularly true for the most active and influential in the Black Twittersphere.

Those who support more conservative ideologies have their own interactive messaging strategies to reinforce their sense of we-ness. One such group increasingly in the public eye as of 2022 is QAnon. This nascent social movement or network has an internet-based infrastructure (including the use of Facebook groups, Instagram, Reddit, TikTok, Twitter, and alternative platforms), an extensive body of literature, branded merchandise, and a growing base of die-hard supporters – many of whom embrace apocalyptic views. Beginning in 2017, the QAnon world view entered the public domain via social media through a series of postings on image boards (4chan, 8chan, and 8kun over a few years) by an anonymous person ("Q") as well as reposts by others on the discussion website, Reddit. QAnon followers speculate that Q is an intelligence or military leader with insider information about the federal administration.

One of the most outrageous QAnon "theories" asserts that there is a cabal of high-profile government and entertainment figures who run a ritualistic child abuse operation. QAnon continues to propagate other unsubstantiated, conservative conspiracy theories, including the notion that COVID-19 was created by the "deep state" as a plot to undermine Trump's reelection efforts. It also reinforced the "Big Lie" that the 2020 presidential election was fraudulent. Although QAnon is perceived by many to be a fringe movement, it began to achieve a foothold in Republican circles during the contentious

2020 presidential campaign; President Trump retweeted many of its posts and never disavowed the group. The nonprofit Media Matters for America identified at least ninety-seven congressional candidates and twenty-three candidates who ran for state legislatures in the 2020 election cycle who had at one time praised or referenced QAnon favorably.[59] As of June 2022, the same nonprofit reports that plenty of candidates for Congress in 2022 also support QAnon.[60]

QAnon followers use the acronym WWG1WGA ("Where We Go One, We Go All") as a way of expressing their solidarity. Adrienne LaFrance, writing in *The Atlantic* in June 2020, likens QAnon to an emerging religious group. The movement has generated a devoted army of adherents who have established a "deep sense of belonging" and are receptive to beliefs rooted in evangelical Christianity and a predetermined future: "People are expressing their faith through devoted study of Q drops as installments of a foundational text, through the development of Q-worshipping groups, and through sweeping expressions of gratitude for what Q has brought to their lives."[61] Consistent with other groups who have embraced an apocalyptic perspective, the motivating forces that give many QAnon followers the opportunity to experience a form of ideational weness include their mutual feeling of being disconnected from society, hating mainstream elites, and having conservative religious beliefs. Echoing Trump's rants and tweets, they also rail against the "deep state" and "fake news." The "true believers," Lafrance continues, "describe a feeling of rebirth, and irreversible arousal to existential knowledge. They are certain that a Great Awakening is coming." Many are drawn to QAnon because they feel as if they are "part of a secret community." Shared beliefs of this type and magnitude, reinforced by an elaborate communications network, solidify people by mobilizing their sense of common purpose. And, as journalist Mike Rothschild writes in his definitive book about the QAnon movement, *The Storm Is upon Us*, "Q lets people feel like they're part of something bigger than their small lives. It gives believers a higher and noble purpose."[62]

Like users of Black Twitter, those who participate in the QAnon virtual universe are largely dependent on access to various communication platforms and technologies that are privately owned.

But unlike those who use Black Twitter, QAnon followers have faced various setbacks in their efforts to build their sense of we-ness online because those who own and operate specific platforms eventually started to object to the violent and conspiratorial nature of their content. Between 2018 and 2021, Facebook, Reddit, and Twitter each instituted different bans on QAnon activity.[63]

These actions, which involve the contentious decision to regulate content on social media platforms, can have the secondary effect of impeding groups that want to create a sense of ideational we-ness online. The policing of internet content is also central to the larger debate that juxtaposes having an "open web for the people and a gated internet controlled by a powerful few."[64] If some regulation of these platforms is deemed acceptable, who decides on the standards? Should the government play a role in determining what is inappropriate and monitor how the rules are implemented? Can we trust the government to regulate media practices in a bipartisan manner? Should social media businesses be left to monitor themselves?

As noted earlier, we-ness or a sense of group belonging is not inherently good or bad. Thus, we must avoid restricting individuals unduly from developing a sense of we-ness with others. It may be imprudent, for example, to limit individuals (with the exception of youth who are emotionally and cognitively more vulnerable) from assembling peacefully (online or in real-world space) to exchange ideas – despicable or otherwise – in the public marketplace of discourse. However, it seems reasonable, too, that we should actively and vigorously challenge forms of we-ness that perpetuate hatred, bigotry, divisiveness, and the reckless disregard for logic and truth. Unfortunately, the prospect of policing online communication is an ever more vexing social issue. In our fast-paced, social media age we are overwhelmed by the scope, intensity, and immediacy of messages we can generate, receive, and share. Many of these messages influence how we bond with others. In fundamental and complex ways, contrasting beliefs about individual liberty and community responsibility frame cultural norms about with whom, how, and for what purpose we should be free to establish a sense of we-ness.

We need to create and study initiatives that provide opportunities for those who have diametrically opposed life views and life experiences – some that many may find highly offensive – to engage in civil dialogue and debate. We can turn to the Middle East to learn much about developing a productive and safe space for bringing people with different life views together. For decades, the Israelis and Palestinians have been waging a devastating and bloody conflict with little hope of finding a peaceful, viable solution. Amidst this chaos and distrust, however, the Parents Circle – Families Forum (PCFF) was founded in 1995.[65] It represents a joint education and reconciliation venture that includes over six hundred Israeli and Palestinian families. Each family has lost an immediate family member to the ongoing conflict.

PCFF is a unique and hopeful nonprofit organization that has experimented with various types of activities (e.g., dialogue meetings, youth camps, field trips, workshops, exhibitions, Memorial Day ceremonies, written narratives) designed to promote reconciliation and provide the foundation for an acceptable political agreement. One of PCFF's former activities was the Israeli-Palestinian Dialogue Meeting campaign. Although it was closed as of June 2022, the purpose of this innovative program was to bring Israelis and Palestinians together to share their bereavement stories and establish common ground based on personal loss. Separate Dialogue Meetings were organized for parents and youth in schools, community centers, and other sites. The ninety-minute meeting included both an Israeli and a Palestinian PCFF member who each shared their own story of bereavement and described why they chose an approach of reconciliation rather than revenge. The speakers also described the organization's other activities and then led a Q & A session with the audience. As of September 2020, over two hundred thousand youth and adults had participated in these meetings. An external evaluation of Dialogue Meetings showed that 68 percent of participants want to take action to promote peace and reconciliation, and 73 percent indicate that the program helped them develop a deeper understanding of the conflict.

Although the PCFF is not currently active, it demonstrated that it is possible to foster productive dialogue and some healing in situations where most would assume it was not. The unique form of we-ness that PCFF facilitated in settings that feature the concerns of thought communities and primary groups should inspire us to consider what is possible in all areas of our lives. Thus, how we navigate the pursuit of we-ness in the thought communities that matter to us is likely to influence how we manage our lives in the other four social domains relevant to this book. So, too, our experience in the various social domains will affect the choices we make in belonging to specific thought communities as well as the way we navigate that social space.

Leisure and Sports

The joy and freedom of spirit we experience when we engage in leisure and sports activities allows us to relax and share meaningful experiences with others. When we play with others, we often open ourselves up to learn a great deal about others and ourselves. This social domain provides pleasurable opportunities for us to work informally on the critical *MEAL* life skills discussed earlier (mindfulness, empathy, altruism, and leadership) that will enhance our ability to nurture healthy forms of we-ness.

Radha Agrawal, the CEO of Daybreaker who sharpened our appreciation for energy in chapter 5, has made a successful career out of combining her love of dance with community building. She and her team created a fun physical and social setting for people to "connect, self-express, sweat, and dance." As of 2020, this project includes roughly half a million community members in twenty-five cities who thrive on gathering to dance early in the morning. Agrawal also advises others on how they can be a catalyst for developing their personal and organizational communities.[66] She provides the building blocks for people to engage in self-discovery and to chart a plan to find people who will enhance their lives and enable them to feel as though they belong. She emphasizes the intentionality of creating communities, whether they involve leisure endeavors or other activities.

Drawing on the lessons she learned by launching and running Daybreaker, she's integrated her take-home messages for community building into what she calls the CRAWL method: at the outset, she advises people to define their Core values, identify the core Community they want to serve, and recognize the Constraints that will influence the community's development. In addition, she encourages catalysts to design Rituals that promote longevity, pay attention to Aesthetics to help people feel good about the community space they use, answer several questions related to Why a person wants to lead the community and Why it will survive, and be thoughtful about the Language used to frame members' experiences within the community. Although she initially targeted millennials when she designed Daybreaker, she has since expanded her vision to embrace an intergenerational philosophy. By providing an inclusive, relaxing, and accepting space for an intergenerational group of adults and kids to comingle and have fun, she is promoting a contemporary version of a third place.

Agrawal and her organizational team, as well as Daybreaker's participants, highlight the potential overlap between experiences in the five social domains highlighted in this book. The leaders and many of the participants share a kind of ideational we-ness because they see themselves as part of the holistic health movement. Many also reinforce their dyadic we-ness with friends and family as they do yoga and dance to enjoy their leisure time.

The core values that provide the foundation for the program are wellness, camaraderie, self-expression, mindfulness, and mischief. These values emphasize both the importance of self-reflection and the social connection people can gain by their involvement in the program. To enjoy the sessions, participants must be attracted to the high-energy experience of dancing in the morning with hundreds of other participants. To facilitate this outcome, Agrawal tries to give participants a physiological boost by stimulating their powerful brain chemicals. She coined the acronym DOSE to capture this notion – Dopamine, Oxytocin, Serotonin, and Endorphin. Agrawal has designed her program to increase the odds that members will not only feel better physiologically, but they ideally will also experience a sense of belonging to a community of like-minded and supportive people.

We do much of our leisure and play in group settings of various sizes, sometimes pursuing these activities with others who share a sense of dyadic or ideational we-ness with us. Today, an increasing amount of our leisure and play life is spent online, yet we still find plenty of ways to interact face to face with others in this social domain. Whether in person or online, our recreational activity can lead us to discover and practice the rudimentary elements of what it means to communicate, organize, cooperate, compete, and resolve conflicts while we celebrate our sense of group belonging. Moreover, as sociologist Gary Fine concludes, small groups, in various forms and sizes, are essential to building the bonds and energy that inspire people to get involved in their local communities as well as to join social movements fighting for broader social change.[67]

Opportunities for small group interactions in a recreational setting are influenced by the interplay between various cultural discourses (especially those that target parenting and public safety), infrastructure options with leisure and sports implications, and personal life philosophies. These overlapping forces affect our options to build a sense of we-ness while navigating recreational time and space. In recent decades, the push to ascribe "good parenting" to more intense levels of monitoring, coupled with growing fears about American children's public safety, have restricted children's play and exercise patterns. Today, parents are less willing to allow their children to roam the community with their friends, to ride bikes to school, and to explore other unsupervised activities with or without their peers and mentors – the childhood culture that I personally thrived in while playing in the woods far away from my parents' view. In the twenty-first century, parents are much more inclined to manage their children's nonschool schedule, which means that youth have fewer options to engage in unstructured play with friends. Although it is unclear what effect these patterns have had on youth's chances for forging intimate relationships that result in a sense of we-ness, today's youth probably have fewer face-to-face opportunities to create informal small group arrangements on their own. Contemporary youth, however, have more opportunities than kids in previous generations to have online exchanges with friends and strangers that can foster some form of we-ness.

As Taylor Dotson persuasively argues, computer technologies and conventional urban planning policies have fundamentally altered our lives and the built environments of our communities for decades.[68] These changes have led to less communitarianism and more networked individualism. However, just as certain changes inside and outside the home have lessened individuals' time spent socializing face to face, more progressive community developers and designers have been working to reconfigure physical spaces to generate more chance meetings, socializing, and communal investments. For example, Dotson advocates developing adventure playgrounds to promote more communitarianism, especially among the children who participate.

Launched in the 1940s in the UK by Lady Marjory Allen, these playgrounds are now operating in countries throughout Europe, but only a small number currently exist in the US. Writing in *The Atlantic* in 2014, Hanna Rosin describes the intent of adventure playgrounds as providing children novel opportunities to share unstructured and creative play time. They run counter to the overprotected kid syndrome that has "stripped childhood of independence, risk taking, and discovery – without making it safer."[69]

The documentary film *The Land* captures the spirit of a Welsh adventure junkyard playground that is supported by trained "playworkers."[70] The philosophy behind the adventure playground initiative is to enhance children's developmental opportunities by providing them with tools, materials, the natural space, and most importantly the freedom to create their own play experience that can promote self-confidence and independence. In addition, it provides children with unique opportunities to cooperate and learn from each other during play. Presumably, kids who regularly play together in an adventure playground can form meaningful bonds with one another as creative playmates who have a sense of group belonging in this unique play space. Kids learn to assess risk, explore, and be creative. These playgrounds can offer kids cooperative opportunities to grow their skills of mindfulness, empathy, altruism, and leadership in a fun setting.

These skills can also be developed by participating in organized sports. Popular culture is littered with stories depicting how athletes and coaches forge bonds in the world of sports. Hollywood plays to our sentimental instincts by producing sports-related movies celebrating the power of chasing shared dreams. These movies high-light themes associated with group belonging, we-ness, team build-ing, and overcoming challenges. While these movies are often only loosely based on real-life events (e.g., *Coach Carter* starring Samuel L. Jackson; *Remember the Titans* with Denzel Washington; *Rudy* with Sean Astin; and *Heart of Champions* with Alexander Ludwig), they illustrate the value of developing dyadic and ideational forms of we-ness in our everyday lives. They also accentuate how many of us feel about those close to us and the small groups that bring meaning to our lives.

We typically think of bonds in the sports arena as emerging organ-ically. Teammates, sometimes guided by a coach, are inspired by their collective identity and common purpose. In the process, they frequently co-opt the language of families to reinforce the shared identity that pushes them to pursue their goals together. Our cul-tural folklore and sports talk provide us with the image of "broth-ers" and "sisters" who are committed to each other as they strive for a common goal.

Many of us, especially those who have invested and shared their time and energy with others in recreational activities, can appreci-ate the social significance that leisure and sports have for people who are willing to extend and deepen their sense of we-ness. These activities offer many participants convenient options to experience greater multiplexity in their relationships. Sharing meaningful time with specific others in different social domains helps to enhance group solidarity. It can also lead to thicker communities. Family members who swim, bike, and run together not only bond over their shared interest in the multisport lifestyle, they also deepen their sense of we-ness as a supportive family committed to health and fitness. If they attend religious services together and participate in the family business, they are likely to establish even deeper interde-pendencies that define them and shape their multilayered feeling of group belonging. In addition, if they can find the time, the multiple connections these family members have might even compel them to be more engaged in civic activities at the local, regional, or national level. But we must recognize, too, that high levels of multiplexity do not always produce desirable outcomes; spending more time together in multiple settings with a contentious person can heighten interpersonal stress and conflict.

As the father of a son who participated for many years as a youth triathlete, I witnessed numerous families training and sometimes racing together. To their credit, some race directors promoted family-friendly events by highlighting options for kids and adults to participate on relay teams or to race against each other, or to race separately in different races scheduled over a weekend. Entire families or parent-child pairs sometimes coordinated training and recreation sessions that created opportunities for multiple families to pursue leisure and sporting activities together. These occasions lent themselves to individuals building their family and interfamily sense of we-ness. In some cases, this meant reinforcing a shared group identity as members of a triathlon team or multisport community.

In our hurried world, many families have seemingly little free time for shared meals or activities. Consequently, there's a need for fresh options to encourage families to recreate together. We should establish viable options to help people enhance their chances of developing social capital based on intimate bonding as well as the bridging variety that links families to other families. A logical starting place is to develop the infrastructure to encourage family members to reinforce their sense of we-ness around issues of health and fitness. In this regard, faith leaders can step up to educate their respective faith communities. They can cultivate a supportive community for members of their congregation to become more health and fitness conscious. When a faith leader promotes family health, that leader also promotes a lifestyle that allows congregation members to practice their respective faith in a healthy manner. Faith leaders are well positioned to create health and fitness challenges that encourage kids to learn about health and fitness through family-based, interactive programs like the one I've outlined elsewhere.[71]

Whether the recreational site involves sports or other forms of leisure, we should do more to create recreational opportunities that bring adults and youth together. I share Oldenburg's disappointment in the precipitous decline in the number of traditional third places that once facilitated intergenerational exchanges. With traditional third places on a dramatic decline, we need to develop alternative strategies like Daybreaker to encourage youth to spend productive time with unrelated adults, as well as family members, in community settings. The adult-youth triathlon training mentioned above is one type of intergenerational setting, but we need additional venues to build cross-generational ties. Modifying zoning ordinances so that retirement villages, schools, and day-care centers could be clustered together is one possibility. This type of community planning would make it possible to create more viable intergenerational volunteering arrangements. Older persons could walk or be quickly shuttled to schools to volunteer as teacher aides. Middle and high school students could provide helpful services and friendship at a retirement village before or after school. And students of varying ages might be able to mentor and help at nearby or on-site day-care facilities.

Community leaders should take the initiative to develop creative partnerships between civic organizations. Many schools already have service-learning requirements for their students, so these intergenerational arrangements can be incorporated into existing practices. Ultimately, such arrangements could promote different forms of intergenerational we-ness that would benefit all participants.

When we turn our attention to the we-ness present in professional sports, we see that athletes' experiences often bridge various social domains. Consequently, athletes can leverage their social capital to shape their sense of we-ness and group belonging. For example, teammates have increasingly capitalized on their shared bonds as fellow athletes to present a united voice against racial injustice in America. Compared to the reaction to Colin Kaepernick, who began to make his voice heard in 2016, and the prominent African American sports figures of the twentieth century (e.g., Muhammad Ali, Jim Brown, Bill Russell, Kareem Abdul-Jabbar) who spoke out about racism, a number of protests against racial injustice in the past ten years have featured fuller team- and league-based displays of solidarity centered on race issues. For example, the 2012 Miami Heat, an NBA basketball team that included LeBron James and Dwyane Wade, posed in hoodies after the shooting death of Trayvon Martin (who was wearing a hoodie, often associated with racist stereotypes of Black masculinity, at the time); members of the WNBA basketball teams Minnesota Lynx, New York Liberty, and Phoenix Mercury began wearing "Change Starts with Us" shirts in support of BLM in 2016; and numerous teams in different sports from high school to the pros used their public platforms to display their concerns about racial injustice in 2020.

Many of today's athletes are more open to blending their personal commitments to teammates with their convictions about social causes and civic engagement. The team chemistry and interpersonal bonds forged through athletics often enable teammates to become allies across racial lines and form both dyadic and ideational forms of we-ness.

Workplace

A growing chorus of expert voices is forecasting a significant transformation in how organizations and work are structured. As we learned in the previous chapter, Frederic Laloux has lent his creative voice to the cause while promoting what he labels the evolutionary-teal approach to management. His detailed research, based on a diverse set of case studies of innovative organizations from around the world, shows that his vision of a fresh organizational model is not only viable, but one well suited to foster healthy displays of we-ness and possibly team flow. He shows how diverse organizations have adopted a philosophy and set of practices that set them apart from more traditional organizations that operate using a hierarchical power structure. The top-down decision-making structure so pervasive today restricts the emergence of healthy options for experiencing a productive style of group belonging.

The teal approach embraces the types of mindfulness, empathy, and leadership skills outlined in earlier chapters. It calls for the work experience to be tailored so that it enriches our inner lives. The teal philosophy allows those of us under its guidance to be less committed to an organization per se. Instead, we direct our convictions toward a value-based purpose beyond a specific organizational goal. Thus, we have more fluid ties to specific organizations compared to those working in more traditional settings. Because competition is largely irrelevant to the teal organization, there are more opportunities to create bridging social capital between us and others as well as between different units and separate organizations. Teal organizations create unique options that expand our ability to align ourselves with "competitors" to pursue a shared purpose. Crisis management in these organizations also takes on a different feel because everyone is involved, so solutions are generated by "collective intelligence."

In today's world, the teal perspective is well suited for a workforce that includes high percentages of both mothers and fathers. Balancing home and work responsibilities is an increasingly critical source of stress for a growing segment of the workforce. Moving forward, business leaders will be challenged to display more empathy and restructure the work environment to help workers effectively manage their dual demands. Despite the hardships that COVID-19 dealt countless families, it forced many business leaders to rethink their management strategies. Many found resourceful ways to accommodate their workers' legitimate health and family needs to work remotely. These leaders, if guided by teal principles, can institute more permanent and progressive changes in a post-COVID-19 era. These policy shifts that are consistent with the teal philosophy should cultivate a work culture that encourages workers to express their full and authentic self in the work setting. If implemented, they can improve workers' long-term productivity and well-being. A revitalized work culture and infrastructure would most likely lead to workers having a network of relationships defined by more multiplexity.

Time will tell how much corporate culture in the United States shifts in the long run. Prior to the COVID-19 pandemic, American government and business leaders lagged their counterparts in other Western countries in making the necessary adjustments in their policies, corporate cultures, and work practices to assist workers in navigating their competing work and family demands.

Final Thoughts

Any serious attempt to understand and improve the human condition must account for our natural and powerful desire to experience a sense of we-ness and group belonging. Toward that end, I've framed this book to reveal why, how, and with what effect we pursue the deep dyadic, ideational, and spontaneous forms of we-ness that mean so much to us as social beings. A core premise of this work is that we must appreciate how our hunger to belong is shaped by cultural forces that either constrain or empower us to interpret our needs in specific ways through our mind, body, heart, and soul. The forces that shape who we are as individuals, in turn, compel us to embrace certain groups and ideas that foster a shared or collective identity. Unfortunately, some groups traffic in unethical agendas with the intent of restricting people's basic rights to life, liberty, and the pursuit of happiness. Thus, we cannot rightly claim that forming a sense of we-ness is always inherently good for us and others. But, as the stories presented earlier show, establishing a sense of belonging to a group can produce positive outcomes for all involved when a group's goals are ethically sound and life-affirming.

We live our everyday lives immersed in group dynamics. Our exchanges in group settings inform how we perceive and respond to our options to experience a state of group belonging. For most of us, navigating group life is a full-time activity amid our romantic and work relationships, families, friendships, teams, and other social arrangements. Our experiences in these areas give us the chance to express our identities and derive meaning from our actions. We long to be accepted and respected by those with whom we share something in common. Typically, this involves our mutual commitment to a group. Thus, we should reflect carefully on these matters if we hope to improve our ability to work collaboratively with others in groups, big and small, to cultivate forms of we-ness that promote our personal well-being and the common good. Achieving this objective is timely, yet quite challenging, because we live in divisive times, surrounded by the pervasive ethos of networked individualism. Moreover, our ties to the outside world are filtered through targeted and politicized messages – think CNN versus Fox – that limit our ability to have a common set of facts to orient our thinking. As a result, the thought communities we use to define our sense of we-ness are often restricted and isolated from one another.

My message underscores how the *MEAL* skillset of mindfulness, empathy, altruism, and leadership can be learned and applied in all five of the social domains I profiled: primary groups, thought communities, leisure and sports settings, community and civic groups, and paid work. Although our activities, identities, relationships, and perceptions in these domains are distinct in many respects, there is often significant overlap as well. Not surprisingly, then, the skills we learn in one domain are often transferable to others. Empathy lessons learned and practiced with our families are likely to assist us as we employ similar types of listening and interpersonal skills at work and in community groups.

The settings and dynamics of we-ness vary considerably across domains. However, many of the basic elements of why and how people chase a state of we-ness remain the same. Ideals about holistic health may motivate us to choose a specific romantic partner who shares our views, volunteer at our child's school, participate in a vegan online discussion group, and pursue a career in holistic medicine. We may also feel exhilarated by being in the flow as we interact with others and exchange ideas while participating in any of the five social domains. Although there is no magical formula to help people experience flow in a group context, the more mindful we are in structuring our institutions and group arrangements to encourage creativity, mutual respect, and empathy, the more likely people will experience life authentically and passionately. Whether it's hanging out in a third place, being part of a supportive team, immersing ourselves in a social movement venture, or basking in the love of a person who honors us for who we truly are, we have diverse options to experience a sense of belonging as well as the thrilling sensation of being in the flow or contributing to team chemistry.

If we are to forge an authentic and deep sense of we-ness as Americans, we must reframe and expand our understanding of the legacy of our racist caste system that has exploited millions and millions of people throughout the centuries. So, too, we are burdened by high rates of drug addiction, loneliness, domestic abuse, bullying, and other social ills that dramatically affect our quality of life. In short, we can be more effective in addressing a wide range of crises at home and abroad if we can implement progressive strategies to generate both bonding and bridging social capital across disparate groups. These strategies must foster productive forms of we-ness that integrate mindfulness, empathy, altruism, and leadership skills. Moreover, we should adapt modern communication technologies to enhance our ability to work collaboratively despite our differences. Creating more favorable social conditions and partnerships that improve our chances to manage the in-group and out-group tensions is critical. We must heed the warning that "coming together to find common cause, establish common ground, and develop a shared vision of the common good is vitally necessary, but mere 'kumbaya we-ness' will not ameliorate vast economic inequalities, curb deaths of despair, or end racism and sexism."[72] Decisive, collaborative, and multilevel action is required.

Historically, our society has built an infrastructure to teach the basics skills to function in an increasingly industrialized society. Our schools are expected to teach us how to read and write, do math, and manipulate computers. Unfortunately, we've done precious little in our school system to teach lessons about the *MEAL* life skills. We've left most of the instruction for such topics to our families, faith communities, recreational sports, and youth clubs. This needs to change. A proactive plan is needed to introduce a more diverse set of initiatives to enhance our interpersonal skills and emotional intelligence, with special attention devoted to youth and young adults. The national service initiative described earlier illustrates one possibility. In addition, we need a much more robust strategy to educate young people about how the government works and their essential responsibilities as citizens in a democratic society.[73]

Just as young progressives played a critical role in propelling the "upswing" in the early 1900s that led Americans to embrace a more communitarian spirit, young people must answer the call to confront our fractured society today. Informed by these historical insights about America's journey over the past 125 years, Putnam and Garrett add that solving today's challenges will "require just as much youthful courage, vigor, and imagination to overcome. And so, to a large extent, America's fate lies in the hands of the post-Boomer generations. Today's young people did not cause today's problems. But like their predecessors 125 years ago they must forgo the cynicism of drift and embrace the hope of mastery."[74] Putnam and Garrett underscore the need for contemporary reformers to follow in their predecessors' footsteps to work from the ground up not only "promoting political candidates, but also on building a grassroots, issue-based movement upon which they and future leaders will be able to draw in order to make lasting change."[75] This reform work must differ, however, from what took place in the first half of the twentieth century: "We must set our sights higher ... and stay fiercely committed to the difficult but ever-worthy project of fashioning an American 'we' that is sustainable because it is inclusive."[76] In other words, we must accelerate our stalled progress on securing racial, gender, and LGBTQ+ equality in its many forms so that every American is genuinely included in our expansive, shared understanding of the American "we." These matters should be framed in terms of being human rights not subject to the whims of advocates for states' rights or a closed-minded, powerful minority.

Journalist David Brooks, writing for the *New York Times*, sounded the alarm in 2016 that our institutions that once supported our "moral motivations" are being supplanted by "arrangements that arouse the financial lens." His admonition still rings true today. Writing about our life commitments, Brooks suggests that to be a good citizen or worker, "you often have to make an altruistic commitment to some group or ideal, which will see you through those times when your job of citizenship is hard and frustrating." He proposes that we redirect our attention to promoting our "moral lens" and "build institutions that harness people's natural longing to do good."[77] The nonprofits profiled earlier, Giving What We Can and Charity: water, are just two of many organizations that create opportunities for individuals to do good. Brooks's perspective reinforces Palmer's five basic habits of the heart noted earlier and is distinctly at odds with the transactional approach so dominant during the Trump presidency and in many political circles. As a loosely united network of people, we need to reject the Trumpian narrow-minded and selfish approach to navigating everyday life and public service. Instead, we need to nurture a more balanced perspective that espouses communitarian virtues while protecting the individual liberties that are so central to the American spirit.[78]

We are desperate for a more mature, wiser vision of our communal existence. In an inspirational speech he delivered over fifty years ago, Martin Luther King, Jr. challenged the nation to embrace a sentiment that coincides with Brooks's and Palmer's more recent commentaries:

> Through our scientific and technological genius, we have made of this world a neighborhood and yet we have not had the ethical commitment to make of it a brotherhood. But somehow, and in some way, we have got to do this. We must all learn to live together as brothers or we will all perish together as fools. We are tied together in the single garment of destiny, caught in an inescapable network of mutuality. And whatever affects one directly affects all indirectly. For some strange reason I can never be what I ought to be until you are what you ought to be. And you can never be what you ought to be until I am what I ought to be.[79]

Three years later, the legendary musician John Lennon released his iconic song "Imagine," cowritten with Yoko Ono. He captured MLK's aspirations in his refrain:

> You may say that I'm a dreamer
> But I'm not the only one
> I hope someday you'll join us
> And the world will live as one.[80]

A half century later, the gifted author Isabel Wilkerson passionately asserted how we would benefit from eradicating a destructive cultural force from the world: "In a world without caste, we would all be invested in the well-being of others in our species if only for our own survival, and recognize that we are in need of one another more than we have been led to believe."[81]

Whether they've done so in a speech, song, or the written word, the outspoken idealists of the world have over the years called upon their fellow citizens to elevate their shared humanity. They implore us to celebrate a type of we-ness that can cultivate the good life for everyone. The calls for action have spurred consequential social movements and social change. Yet Americans, as well as others around the world, continue to fall short in making changes to the social landscape that are sufficiently broad, deep, and permanent. The good news is that idealists are still among us, and the arc of history hints that we may someday realize our goal of establishing a genuinely inclusive global perspective on group belonging that incorporates all of humanity. The bad news is that we are awash in a polarized media environment that is toxic to civil discourse. Increasingly untethered to a common set of facts and perceptions, we face a system of information production and dissemination that breeds dishonesty and mistrust. Good faith efforts to understand and empathize with each other across political and cultural lines are declining rapidly. In short, our media system encourages a form of tribal we-ness while discouraging a broader, more inclusive style of we-ness rooted in shared values that celebrate truth and kindness.

As we look to the future with an eye on the big picture, dire consequences await us if we fail to forge a meaningful expression of we-ness based on our shared humanity. In the absence of a more globally inspired form of we-ness, we will be more susceptible to potential crises associated with climate change, misguided advances in AI, the spread of deadly viruses that are blind to borders, terrorism, nuclear war, food insecurity, as well as other twenty-first-century challenges that are rooted in global geopolitical circumstances and inequities in access to essential resources. Although this should be old news for anyone who is paying attention to recent current affairs, far too many seem unable or unwilling to look beyond their limited social orbit.

The idealist and prominent social thinker Jeremy Rifkin believes that we are moving toward what he calls a "biosphere consciousness" and a more empathic civilization that could propel our species into a new, promising stage of human evolution. The biosphere represents the earthly space that extends from the bottom of the ocean where primitive life forms exist all the way to our upper stratosphere – less than forty miles. The biosphere is the product of ongoing symbiotic relationships and interdependencies shared by living creatures and the connections between life forms and geochemical processes. Human existence and our quality of life are dependent on a well-functioning biosphere.

As Rifkin points out, beginning in the twentieth century, theorists in the physical and social sciences have increasingly adopted paradigms that focus on systems and network themes while emphasizing the interconnectivity between living forms and geochemical processes. These models have encouraged new ways of thinking about science and human relationships that have implications for how we see ourselves and our connection to humanity. These new perspectives urge us to express a biosphere consciousness that reflects our heightened level of awareness about how the biosphere works and our sense of responsibility to be conscientious stewards of Planet Earth. "If we can harness holistic thinking to a new global ethics that recognizes and acts to harmonize the many relationships that make up the life-sustaining forces of the planet," Rifkin optimistically speculates, "we will have crossed the divide into a near-climax world economy and biosphere consciousness."[82] This type of thinking is consistent with a holistic form of ideational we-ness that centers us as mindful, cooperative beings in a complex system that includes both living forms and geochemical forces.

We are moving incrementally on a path to realize this type of biosphere consciousness, in part, because most of today's kids are being taught that they and others can modify the footprint they leave on the physical environment. As a result, many are building a deeper appreciation for their interconnectivity to one another and to the planetary system. Youth and young adults are also increasingly being exposed to collaborative learning strategies and encouraged to develop experiential knowledge by participating in service-learning, field trips, and internships. Collaborative learning emphasizes "mindfulness, attunement to others, nonjudgmental interactions, acknowledgement of each person's unique contributions, and recognition of the importance of deep participation and a shared sense of meaning coming out of embedded relationships."[83]

As our species has become more self-reflective and aware of our elaborate evolutionary history as well as our potential to transform our world, we continue to juggle the dual urges to establish close ties with a small number of people and to experience a broader sense of union with humanity. Rifkin again helps us wrap our minds around the interplay between these parallel tendencies:

> Human beings are forever searching for "universal intimacy" – a sense of total belonging. What appears to be a strange confluence of opposites is really a deeply embedded human aspiration. It is our empathic nature that allows us to experience the seeming paradox of greater intimacy in more expansive domains…. The empathic predisposition that is built into our biology is not a fail-safe mechanism that allows us to perfect our humanity. Rather, it is an opportunity to increasingly bond the human race into a single extended family, but it needs to be continually exercised.[84]

Unfortunately, the type and level of collective empathy that would make this shared appreciation for humanity a reality is typically discarded for selfish and often politicized interests. Despite our general capacity to empathize with others if we choose, social forces and our immediate circumstances often discourage us from employing this vital skill, either with those who circulate in our inner circle or the masses with whom we have no direct contact. In 2020–2, this shortcoming was on full display when millions of people shunned their communal responsibilities by refusing to get vaccinated or to wear masks that could have protected their fellow citizens from COVID-19.

Ultimately, the future of humanity requires us to learn to manage our selfish tendencies and cooperate with others. The Buddhist monk Matthieu Ricard writes that we "must dare to embrace altruism. Dare to say that real altruism exists, that it can be cultivated by every one of us, and that the evolution of cultures can favor its expansion."[85] Our expression of altruism needs to be integrated into our daily lives as well as the institutions that organize our society and global community. In short, "Altruism is not a luxury, but a necessity."[86] It pushes us to experience ideational and deep dyadic we-ness in a productive way.

On the American front, idealists keep hope alive by imagining our ongoing efforts to establish a more perfect union, one that includes a shared sense of we-ness with persons from all walks of life. However, the turbulent reality on the ground witnessed in recent years demonstrates that plenty of formidable obstacles impede such dreams from being fully realized any time soon on a national or global scale. Let's hope that historians look back on the bizarre events during this period as an inflection point for the twenty-first century that compelled Americans to begin the arduous task of lessening their divisiveness as they've done in previous centuries. Perhaps they will describe how those of us living in this era ultimately forged more respect for each other and our precious institutions while adopting a more inclusive vision of the world.

Such a story about framing more inclusive forms of we-ness can only be written if we are astute and determined enough to adapt to, and transform, the destructive media landscape that breeds our tribalism. A free press has always been a vital part of the American experiment with democracy. However, in recent years, the media debate has grown more complex. With the dramatic changes to journalism and the press, and the emergence of social media that is anchored in clicks and views, "news" production represents an increasingly pivotal force beyond the traditional three branches of government (executive, legislative, and judicial) that shapes how we see and govern ourselves. In recent years, the ordinary citizen's enhanced ability to create and disseminate unfiltered information to the masses has fundamentally altered the public square. We also live in a post-truth era that promulgates misinformation and disinformation at an alarming rate. Conspiracy theories and fake news abound, creating confusion and distrust among the masses. Our information streams are segmented more than ever before by business incentives, pushing us further apart – perpetuating exclusive "we" identities at the expense of forging more inclusive types of group belonging. Nicole Cooke, an information sciences professor at the University of Illinois, warns that misinformation and disinformation are dangerous because they prevent "collective knowledge and understanding" and they also pose a threat "by prioritizing and promoting biased, misleading, or false agendas and opinions."[87]

Unfortunately, political and business operatives are employing tricks to spread and weaponize disinformation faster than the public is adopting the competencies necessary to process overwhelming amounts of controversial "news" critically. Reputable fact-checking sites like PolitiFact and Snopes exist to help those dedicated to sorting fact from fiction, but many are either unaware of these options or content to consume and disseminate rumors and hoaxes in a cavalier manner. In addition to normalizing fact-checking sites, we need more organizations like the Center for Humane Technology to inspire us to develop the infrastructure, knowledge, and norms that will make it easier to navigate the information age with a discerning eye. Our formal education system must also be more rigorous in how it prepares young people to be thoughtful consumers of news in the information age. Finally, we need creative and ethical leaders in political and business circles to promote forums (e.g., town halls and panel sessions) that bring together thought leaders and media pundits with different perspectives to engage in *civil* debate, that is, debate that succeeds in having participants answer questions directly and honestly while acknowledging the value of common sense. The public deserves a more complete and critical treatment of social issues that will provide them the means to make informed decisions when they pursue their politically oriented forms of we-ness. Instead of the pervasive business model that seeks to carve out a limited but loyal niche, we must incentivize efforts that broaden the information consumer base. This must be orchestrated in a fashion that includes individuals at the grassroots level as well as powerful influencers.

Following the Buddhist tradition, change of this magnitude must begin with a fundamental shift in how we see ourselves. Fortunately, we don't need everyone to adopt this mindset to generate major social change, but we do need a critical mass of enlightened persons, including a sufficiently large number who hold significant positions of power. As we've discussed, contemplatives have given us the tools to begin this process by demonstrating how adults and children can benefit by developing a meditation practice that encourages mindfulness. But beyond our efforts to center ourselves and become more self-reflective, we need to learn how to incorporate skills involving empathy, altruism, and leadership into our relationships with those we value most. These are the people in our immediate social orbits – the family, friends, neighbors, and coworkers who bring meaning to our lives. We need to create more authentic, wholesome ties with these individuals.

Accomplishing this goal demands that individuals not only take the initiative to get their minds right, but there must also be a collective response reflected in public discourse, policy, and programs to empower us to negotiate our personal relationships in a healthy and productive fashion. Together, we must redesign our built environments to make them more inviting to communal living. Likewise, we need to revamp systematically our institutional norms and practices to construct a social context more amenable to healthy social relations. In short, we must empower ourselves by making it more convenient to establish healthy forms of we-ness and group belonging.

A key element in this regard involves having the kind of "epistemological humility" that compels us to listen, so that we listen to learn. Having an open mind when we encounter those with whom we disagree is especially important. We should recognize that most of the people we see as belonging to our groups were once outside our entrusted circle of influence. If we listen to others' views with respect, the odds increase that we will eventually invite some of these acquaintances or strangers to share in our sense of we-ness. By doing so, we will expand the scope of our group we-ness and build valuable social capital. Wanting to feel connected to others is who we are; but establishing we-ness with a loving, mindful intention that honors our interdependence is who we must become.

Notes

Preface

1 Jon Meacham, *The Soul of America: The Battle for Our Better Angels* (New York: Random House, 2018), 16.
2 Arlie Russell Hochschild, *Strangers in Their Own Land: Anger and Mourning on the American Right* (New York: New Press, 2016).

Introduction

1 Charles Horton Cooley, *Social Organization: A Study of the Larger Mind* (New York: Charles Scribner's Sons, 1909).
2 Cooley, *Social Organization*, 23.
3 Mitch Albom, *Tuesdays with Morrie: An Old Man, a Young Man, and Life's Greatest Lesson* (New York: Broadway Books, 1997), 180.
4 Toby Ord, *The Precipice: Existential Risk and the Future of Humanity* (New York: Hachette, 2020).
5 Annette Baier, "The Rights of Past and Future Persons," in *Responsibilities to Future Generations: Environmental Ethics*, ed. Ernest Partridge (Buffalo, NY: Prometheus Books, 1981), 171–83, 177.
6 Ord, *The Precipice*, 61.
7 Marilyn B. Brewer and Wendi Gardner, "Who Is This 'We'? Levels of Collective Identity and Self Representations," *Journal of Personality and Social Psychology* 17 (1996): 83–93.
8 John T. Cacioppo and William Patrick, *Loneliness: Human Nature and the Need for Social Connection* (New York: Norton, 2008), 80.
9 Cacioppo and Patrick, *Loneliness*, 81.
10 George Simmel, "The Number of Members as Determining the Sociological Form of the Group," *American Journal of Sociology* 8 (1902): 1–46, 158–96; Gary Alan Fine, *Tiny Publics: A Theory of Group Action and Culture* (New York: Russell Sage Foundation, 2012).

11 Fine, *Tiny Publics*, 21.
12 Fine, *Tiny Publics*, 1.
13 Fine, *Tiny Publics*, 36.
14 Fine, *Tiny Publics*, 17.
15 Nicholas A. Christakis and James H. Fowler, *Connected: The Surprising Power of Our Social Networks and How They Shape Our Lives – How Your Friends' Friends' Friends Affect Everything You Feel, Think, and Do* (New York: Little, Brown, 2009), 9.
16 John Bowlby, *The Making and Breaking of Affectional Bonds* (London: Tavistock Publications, 1979); Donald W. Winnicott, *Human Nature* (London: Routledge, 1988); Cacioppo and Patrick, *Loneliness*.
17 Jacqueline Olds and Richard S. Schwartz, *The Lonely American: Drifting Apart in the Twenty-First Century* (Boston: Beacon, 2009), 44.
18 Mark W. Moffett, *The Human Swarm: How Our Societies Arise, Thrive, and Fall* (New York: Basic Books, 2019). Moffett provides a more extensive discussion of the evolutionary processes that place humans on the path to creating societies.
19 Mary O'Brien, *The Politics of Reproduction* (London: Routledge and Kegan Paul, 1981).
20 Moffett, *The Human Swarm*.
21 Moffett, *The Human Swarm*, 27.
22 Nicholas A. Christakis, *Blueprint: The Evolutionary Origins of a Good Society* (New York: Little, Brown Spark, 2019).
23 Christakis, *Blueprint*, 16.
24 Isabel Wilkerson, *Caste: The Origins of Our Discontents* (New York: Random House, 2020).
25 Wilkerson, *Caste*, 381–2.
26 Ashley Jardina, *White Identity Politics* (Cambridge: Cambridge University Press, 2017).
27 Arlie Russell Hochschild, *Strangers in Their Own Land: Anger and Mourning on the American Right* (New York: New Press, 2016), 225.
28 Daniel Acker, "Don't Let the Loud Bigots Distract You. America's Real Problem with Race Cuts Far Deeper," *Time*, September 17, 2018; Dana Milbank, "A Massive Repudiation of Trump's Racist Politics Is Building," *Washington Post*, July 3, 2020; "Rejecting Bigotry, Demanding Action: Communications to Direct Our Outrage toward Concrete, Lasting Change," The Opportunity Agenda, 2017, https://www.opportunityagenda.org/explore/resources-publications/rejecting-bigotry-demanding-action.
29 Jardina, *White Identity Politics*, 277.
30 Jardina, *White Identity Politics*, 275.
31 Robert Putnam with Shaylyn Romney Garrett, *The Upswing: How America Came Together a Century Ago and How We Can Do It Again* (New York: Simon & Schuster, 2020), 12–13.
32 Tom Brokaw, *The Greatest Generation* (New York: Random House, 1998).
33 See the YouTube video summarizing this fascinating interview: "Former Maid to Hitler Interview," *Israeli Broadcasting Corporation*, uploaded December 14, 2016, YouTube video, 14:57, https://www.youtube.com/watch?v=bqBiu45onyY.
34 Eviatar Zerubavel, *Social Mindscapes: An Invitation to Cognitive Sociology* (Cambridge, MA: Harvard University Press, 1997).
35 Cacioppo and Patrick, *Loneliness*.
36 Brad Stulberg and Steve Magness, *The Passion Paradox: A Guide to Going All In, Finding Success, and Discovering the Benefits of an Unbalanced Life* (New York: Rodale Books, 2019).
37 Sebastian Junger, *Tribe: On Homecoming and Belonging* (New York: Twelve, 2015), 125–6.
38 Esteban Ortiz-Ospina and Max Roser, "Trust," Our World in Data, 2016, https://ourworldindata.org/trust.

39 "Public Trust in Government: 1958–2021," Pew Research Center, May 17, 2021, https://www.pewresearch.org/politics/2021/05/17/public-trust-in-government-1958-2021/.

40 Lee Rainie and Andrew Perrin, "The State of Americans' Trust in Each Other amid the COVID-19 Pandemic," Pew Research Center, April 6, 2020, https://www.pewresearch.org/fact-tank/2020/04/06/the-state-of-americans-trust-in-each-other-amid-the-covid-19-pandemic/.

41 Lee Rainie, Scott Keeter, and Andrew Perrin, "Trust and Distrust in America," Pew Research Center, July 22, 2019, https://www.pewresearch.org/politics/2019/07/22/trust-and-distrust-in-america/.

42 Taylor Dotson, *Technically Together: Reconstructing Community in a Networked World* (Cambridge, MA: MIT Press, 2017).

43 Dotson, *Technically Together*, 59.

44 Dotson, *Technically Together*, 12.

45 Dotson, *Technically Together*, 29.

46 Dotson, *Technically Together*, 14.

47 David W. Haines, *Safe Haven? A History of Refugees in America* (Sterling, VA: Kumarian Press, 2010).

48 Ben Zimmer, "Where Does Trump's 'Invasion' Rhetoric Come From?" *The Atlantic*, August 2019, https://www.theatlantic.com/entertainment/archive/2019/08/trump-immigrant-invasion-language-origins/595579/.

49 Charlotte Alter, Suyin Haynes, and Justin Worland, "Time 2019 Person of the Year – Greta Thunberg," *Time Magazine*, December 23/30, 2019, https://time.com/person-of-the-year-2019-greta-thunberg/.

50 Alter, Haynes, and Worland, "Time 2019 Person of the Year," 13.

51 Youth4Climate, https://youth4climate.be/en/. This group is part of a larger movement to promote digital democracy that is supported by new companies like CitizenLab. Founded in 2015 by a small group of developers and citizen participation experts, CitizenLab provides individuals and groups with the tech toolbox to increase civic engagement in new ways; see "About Us," CitizenLab, https://www.citizenlab.co/about.

52 Elyssa Spitzer and Nora Ellmann, "State Abortion Legislation in 2021: A Review of Positive and Negative Actions," Center for American Progress, September 21, 2021, https://www.americanprogress.org/issues/women/reports/2021/09/21/503999/state-abortion-legislation-2021/; "Dobbs v. Jackson Women's Health Organization," Center for Reproductive Rights, updated May 22, 2022, https://reproductiverights.org/case/scotus-mississippi-abortion-ban/.

53 Michael Smerconish, "On Cable TV and Talk Radio, a Push toward Polarization," *Washington Post*, June 11, 2010.

54 Brian Stelter, *Hoax: Donald Trump, Fox News, and the Dangerous Distortion of Truth* (New York: One Signal Publishers, 2020), 18.

55 Hochschild, *Strangers in Their Own Land*, 126.

56 "22 Weeks into the Year, America Has Already Seen At Least 246 Mass Shootings," *NPR*, updated June 5, 2022, https://www.npr.org/2022/05/15/1099008586/mass-shootings-us-2022-tally-number.

57 Olds and Schwartz, *The Lonely American*.

58 Barbara Ehrenreich, *The Worst Years of Our Lives: Irreverent Notes from a Decade of Greed* (New York: Pantheon, 1990).

59 Cacioppo and Patrick, *Loneliness*; Vivek H. Murthy, *Together: The Healing Power of Human Connection in a Sometimes Lonely World* (New York: HarperCollins, 2020).

60 Rob Whitley, "Loneliness in Young Adults: A Growing Mental Health Issue," *Psychology Today*, January 29, 2020, https://www.psychologytoday.com/us/blog

/talking-about-men/202001/loneliness-in-young-adults-growing-mental-health
-issue; Katie Hafner, "Researchers Confront an Epidemic of Loneliness," *New York
Times*, September 5, 2016, https://www.nytimes.com/2016/09/06/health/lonliness
-aging-health-effects.html; "The Epidemic of Loneliness," Aspen Ideas Festival, 2017,
https://www.aspenideas.org/sessions/the-epidemic-of-loneliness.

61 Jean M. Twenge, Brian H. Spitzberg, and W. Keith Campbell, "Less In-Person Social
Interaction with Peers among U.S. Adolescents in the 21st Century and Links to
Loneliness," *Journal of Social and Personal Relationships* 36, no. 6 (2019): 1892–1913,
1894.

62 Cacioppo and Patrick, *Loneliness*, 13.

63 Sherry Turkle, *Reclaiming Conversation: The Power of Talk in a Digital Age* (New York:
Penguin, 2015), 10.

64 Cacioppo and Patrick, *Loneliness*, 7.

65 Murthy, *Together*.

66 "Income Plays a Role in Older Adults' Happiness, According to New AARP
Foundation Study," AARP, March 7, 2017, https://press.aarp.org/2017-03-07
-Income-Plays-a-Role-in-Older-Adults-Happiness-According-to-New-AARP
-Foundation-Study.

67 AARP Foundation, *The Pandemic Effect: A Social Isolation Report*, October 6, 2020,
https://connect2affect.org/wp-content/uploads/2020/10/The-Pandemic-Effect
-A-Social-Isolation-Report-AARP-Foundation.pdf.

68 Twenge, Spitzberg, and Campbell, "Less In-Person Social Interaction."

69 Whitley, "Loneliness in Young Adults."

70 "Loneliness and the Workplace," Cigna, 2020, https://www.cigna.com/static
/www-cigna-com/docs/about-us/newsroom/studies-and-reports/combatting
-loneliness/cigna-2020-loneliness-factsheet.pdf.

71 Stephanie Cacioppo, John P. Capitanio, and John T. Cacioppo, "Toward a Neurology of
Loneliness," *Psychological Bulletin* 140, no. 6 (2014): 1464–504; Julianne Holt-Lunstad,
Timothy B. Smith, Mark Baker, Tyler Harris, and David Stephenson, "Loneliness and
Social Isolation as Risk Factors for Mortality: A Meta-Analytic Review," *Perspectives
on Psychological Science* 10, no. 2 (2015): 227–37; Carla M. Perissinotto, Irena Stijacic
Cenzer, and Kenneth E. Covinsky, "Loneliness in Older Persons: A Predictor of
Functional Decline and Death," *Archives of Internal Medicine* 172, no. 14 (2012):
1078–83; J.M. Twenge, *iGen: Why Today's Super-Connected Kids Are Growing Up Less
Rebellious, More Tolerant, Less Happy – and Completely Unprepared for Adulthood* (New
York: Atria Books, 2017).

72 Robert Putnam, *Bowling Alone: The Collapse and Revival of American Community* (New York:
Simon & Schuster, 2000); see also Putnam with Garrett, *The Upswing*.

73 Putnam, *Bowling Alone*, 19.

74 Robert Putnam, "Bowling Alone: America's Declining Social Capital," *Journal of
Democracy* 6, no. 2 (1995): 65–78, 52.

75 Thomas H. Sander and Robert D. Putnam, "Still Bowling Alone? The Post-9/11 Split,"
Journal of Democracy 21, no. 1 (2010): 9–16, 11.

76 Sander and Putnam, "Still Bowling Alone?" 13.

77 "In U.S., Decline of Christianity Continues at Rapid Pace: An Update on America's
Changing Religious Landscape," Pew Research Center, October 17, 2019, https://
www.pewforum.org/2019/10/17/in-u-s-decline-of-christianity-continues-at-rapid
-pace/.

78 "Union Members Summary," US Bureau of Labor Statistics, January 20, 2022,
https://www.bls.gov/news.release/union2.nr0.htm. For a state-by-state report of
union membership, see "50 Years of Shrinking Union Membership in One Map," *NPR*,

February 23, 2015, https://www.npr.org/sections/money/2015/02/23/385843576/50
-years-of-shrinking-union-membership-in-one-map.

79 Brittany Murray, Thurston Domina, Linda Renzulli, and Rebecca Boylan, "Civil
Society Goes to School: Parent-Teacher Associations and the Equality of Educational
Opportunity," *RSF* 5, no. 3 (2019): 41–63, https://www.ncbi.nlm.nih.gov/pmc/articles
/PMC6545986/. Although there is an error in the narrative text that reports the percentage,
I confirmed with the authors that the graph's depiction of 11.4 percent is correct.

80 "Where Are America's Volunteers? A Look at America's Widespread Decline in
Volunteering in Cities and States," Do Good Institute, School of Public Policy,
University of Maryland, October 2018, https://dogood.umd.edu/sites/default
/files/2019-07/Where%20Are%20Americas%20Volunteers_Research%20Brief%20
_Nov%202018.pdf.

81 "Bringing Out the Best of America," AmeriCorps, https://www.nationalservice
.gov/newsroom/press-releases/2018/volunteering-us-hits-record-high-worth-167
-billion; "Volunteering in America," AmeriCorps, https://www.nationalservice
.gov/serve/via/research; "America's Volunteer Spirit Continues in the Face of the
Pandemic," United States Congress Joint Economic Committee, May 19, 2020, https://
www.jec.senate.gov/public/index.cfm/republicans/analysis?ID=61A912D3-8641
-4F5C-9A23-34E6AA3AF619.

82 Fine, *Tiny Publics*, 127.

83 Tim Ryan, *Healing America: How a Simple Practice Can Help Us Recapture the American
Spirit* (Carlsbad, CA: Hay House, 2018).

84 Jon Kabat-Zinn, *Meditation Is Not What You Think: Mindfulness and Why It Is So
Important* (New York: Hachette, 2018), XX.

85 Kabat-Zinn, *Meditation Is Not What You Think*, 130.

86 Jamil Zaki, "In a Divided World, We Need to Choose Empathy," *Greater Good
Magazine*, May 29, 2019, https://greatergood.berkeley.edu/article/item/in_a
_divided_world_we_need_to_choose_empathy.

87 Jamil Zaki and Kevin N. Ochsner, "The Neuroscience of Empathy: Progress, Pitfalls
and Promise," *Nature Neuroscience* 15 (2012): 675–80, 675.

88 Lior Abramson, Florina Uzefovsky, Virgilia Toccaceli, and Ariel Knafo-Noam, "The
Genetic and Environmental Origins of Emotional and Cognitive Empathy: Review
and Meta-Analyses of Twin Studies," *Neuroscience and Biobehavioral Reviews* 114
(2020): 113–33.

89 Zaki, "In a Divided World."

90 Sara H. Konrath, Edward H. O'Brien, and Courtney Hsing, "Changes in Dispositional
Empathy in American College Students Over Time: A Meta-Analysis," *Personality and
Social Psychology Review* 15, no. 2 (2011): 180–98.

91 Jean M. Twenge and Joshua D. Foster, "Mapping the Scale of the Narcissism Epidemic:
Increases in Narcissism 2002–2007 within Ethnic Groups," *Journal of Research in
Personality* 42, no. 6 (2008): 1619–22; Jean M. Twenge and Joshua D. Foster, "Birth
Cohort Increases in Narcissistic Personality Traits among American College Students,
1982–2009," *Social Psychological and Personality Science* 1, no. 1 (2010): 99–106.

92 Turkle, *Reclaiming Conversation*.

93 Jamil Zaki, *The War for Kindness: Building Empathy in a Fractured World* (New York:
Crown, 2019).

94 Helen Riess with Liz Neporent, *The Empathy Effect: 7 Neuroscience-Based Keys for
Transforming the Way We Live, Love, Work, and Connect across Differences* (Boulder, CO:
Sounds True, 2018).

95 Jeremy Rifkin, *The Empathic Civilization: The Race to Global Consciousness in a World in
Crisis* (Cambridge: Polity, 2009), 543.

96 Roman Krznaric, *Empathy: Why It Matters, and How to Get It* (New York: Perigee, 2014), xxiii.

97 Svetlana Feigin, Glynn Owens, and Felicity Goodyear-Smith, "Theories of Human Altruism: A Systematic Review," *Journal of Psychiatry and Brain Functions* 1, no. 5 (2014); John Doris, Stephen Stich, and Lachlan Walmsley, "Empirical Approaches to Altruism," *The Stanford Encyclopedia of Philosophy*, ed. Edward N. Zalta, Spring 2020 ed., https://plato.stanford.edu/archives/spr2020/entries/altruism-empirical/.

98 Brené Brown, *Dare to Lead: Brave Work. Tough Conversations. Whole Hearts* (London: Penguin, 2018), 4.

99 Brown, *Dare to Lead*, 12.

100 David Snow, "Collective Identity and Expressive Forms," CSD Working Papers (Irvine: UC Irvine Center for the Study of Democracy, 2001), 2212–19, https://escholarship.org/uc/item/2zn1t7bj.

101 Adam Waytz, *The Power of Human: How Our Shared Humanity Can Help Us Create a Better World* (New York: Norton, 2019), x.

1. Self-Meanings

1 *The Social Dilemma*, https://www.thesocialdilemma.com/.

2 Sherry Turkle, *Reclaiming Conversation: The Power of Talk in a Digital Age* (New York: Penguin, 2015), 9–10.

3 Kenneth Gergen, *The Saturated Self: Dilemmas of Identity in Contemporary Life* (New York: Basic Books, 1991).

4 Lyn H. Lofland, "The Social Shaping of Emotion: The Case of Grief," *Symbolic Interaction* 8, no. 2 (1985): 171–90.

5 The basic features of these competing views of reality are as follows. One major point of opposition directed at dualism involves trying to explain how a nonphysical entity associated with a mental state or consciousness can causally influence the physical body. We have been conditioned to think about causal effects as physical matter influencing another physical substance. Materialism comes under attack because it is unable to explain how various brain states are conscious. Scientists have precise instruments to detect brain functioning, but they cannot explain how brain functioning and consciousness are linked. Moreover, scientists can measure brain waves, but they are not yet able to determine what people are thinking: people must be asked.

6 Joseph Liu, "Scientists and Belief," Pew Research Center, November 5, 2009, https://www.pewforum.org/2009/11/05/scientists-and-belief/.

7 Jeremy Rifkin, *The Empathic Civilization: The Race to Global Consciousness in a World in Crisis* (Cambridge: Polity, 2009), 23.

8 Rifkin, *The Empathic Civilization*, 24.

9 H. Markus and P. Nurius, "Possible Selves," *American Psychologist* 41, no. 9 (1986): 954–69; R. Strauss and W.A. Goldberg, "Self and Possible Selves during the Transition to Fatherhood," *Journal of Family Psychology* 13, no. 2 (1999): 244–59.

10 "Menopause Care," Rush, https://www.rush.edu/health-wellness/support-groups/menopause-support-group.

11 "The Worldwide Cosmetic Surgery and Procedure Industry Is Expected to Reach $107.2 Billion by 2027 – ResearchAndMarkets.com," Businesswire, June 3, 2022, https://www.businesswire.com/news/home/20220603005380/en/The-Worldwide-Cosmetic-Surgery-and-Procedure-Industry-is-Expected-to-Reach-107.2-Billion-by-2027---ResearchAndMarkets.com.

12 *ISAPS International Survey on Aesthetic/Cosmetic Procedures Performed in 2019*, International Society of Aesthetic Plastic Surgery, 2019, https://www.isaps.org/wp-content/uploads/2020/12/Global-Survey-2019.pdf.

13 Dana Berkowitz, *Botox Nation: Changing the Face of America* (New York: New York University Press, 2017), 3.

14 Michel Foucault, *Discipline and Punish: The Birth of the Prison* (New York: Vintage Books, 1995).

15 Stephen C. Poulson, *Why Would Anyone Do That? Lifestyle Sport in the Twenty-First Century* (New Brunswick, NJ: Rutgers University Press, 2016).

16 Richard Kestenbaum, "The Biggest Trends in the Beauty Industry," *Forbes*, September 9, 2018, https://www.forbes.com/sites/richardkestenbaum/2018/09/09/beauty -industry-biggest-trends-skin-care-loreal-shiseido-lauder/.

17 Rafael Schwarz, "Why Social Media Marketing Will Only Become More Popular in the Beauty Industry in 2022," *Forbes*, February 15, 2022, https:// www.forbes.com/sites/forbescommunicationscouncil/2022/02/15/why-social -media-marketing-will-only-become-more-popular-in-the-beauty-industry -in-2022/?sh=784f45b12bb3.

18 "Dollar Sales of the Prestige Beauty Industry in the United States from 2010 to 2021 (in Billion U.S. Dollars)," Statista, February 2, 2022, https://www.statista.com /statistics/419668/dollar-sales-of-the-us-prestige-beauty-industry/.

19 Jacob Porteous, "The Top 21 Beauty Influencers Brands Need to Watch in 2021," Socialbakers, January 12, 2021, https://www.socialbakers.com/blog /top-beauty-influencers; Dina Gerdeman, "How Influencers Are Making Over Beauty Marketing," *Forbes*, December 13, 2019, https://www.forbes.com/sites /hbsworkingknowledge/2019/12/13/how-influencers-are-making-over-beauty -marketing/.

20 Christena E. Nippert-Eng, *Home and Work: Negotiating Boundaries through Everyday Life* (Chicago: University of Chicago Press, 1996).

21 Nippert-Eng, *Home and Work*.

22 Julie Beck, "In a Brainy Age, the Heart Retains Its Symbolic Power," *The Atlantic*, August 2016, https://www.theatlantic.com/health/archive/2016/08/the-enduring -metaphors-of-the-heart-this-mortal-coil-fay-bound-alberti/494375/.

23 Amy Eskind, "Nurse Who Went Viral Lifting Up Coworkers with 'Amazing Grace,' Starred in Inauguration's COVID-19 Memorial," *People*, January 21, 2021, https:// people.com/politics/covid-nurse-at-memorial/.

24 Barry Koltnow, "Director Says 'Paris' Isn't Just Dance Film," *Orlando Sentinel*, September 4, 1991, https://www.orlandosentinel.com/news/os-xpm-1991-09-04 -9109010113-story.html.

25 "*Kiki* (2016 Film)," Wikimedia Foundation, accessed December 11, 2021, https:// en.wikipedia.org/wiki/Kiki_(2016_film).

26 Jack O'Keeffe, "'Pose' Is Set in the '80s, but House Mothers Are Still Walking in Underground Balls Today," *Bustle*, June 3, 2018, https://www.bustle.com/p /ball-culture-in-2018-shows-that-pose-is-celebrating-a-movement-that-has-serious -staying-power-9245438.

27 "How a Hashtag Defined a Movement," EmergingUS, uploaded September 26, 2016, YouTube video, 7:48, https://www.youtube.com/watch?v=-8-KZ0RIN3w; Black Life Matters, http://www.blacklifematters.org/home.

28 Anderson Cooper, "Parents of a 2012 Aurora, Colorado, Shooting Victim Travel the Country to Help Others Impacted by Mass Shootings," *CBS News 60 Minutes*, August 4, 2019, https://www.cbsnews.com/news/parents-of-a-2012-aurora-colorado-shooting -victim-travel-country-mass-shootings-60-minutes-2019-08-04/.

29 Michael S. Kimmel, *Angry White Men: American Masculinity at the End of an Era* (New York: Nation Books, 2013).

30 Parker J. Palmer, *Healing the Heart of Democracy: The Courage to Create a Politics Worthy of the Human Spirit* (San Francisco: Jossey-Bass, 2014), 6.

31 Palmer, *Healing the Heart of Democracy*, 18.
32 Julien Musolino, *The Soul Fallacy: What Science Shows We Gain from Letting Go of Our Soul Beliefs* (Amherst, NY: Prometheus Books, 2015).
33 Jack Kornfield, "Identity and Selflessness in Buddhism: No Self or True Self? Examining Buddhist Notions of Identity and Selflessness," *Tricycle: The Buddhist Review*, https://tricycle.org/magazine/no-self-or-true-self/.
34 Steven Pinker, *How the Mind Works* (New York: Norton, 1997), 64.
35 Musolino, *The Soul Fallacy*, 16.
36 Musolino, *The Soul Fallacy*, 21–2.
37 Mark C. Baker and Stewart Goetz, eds., *The Soul Hypothesis: Investigations into the Existence of the Soul* (New York: Continuum, 2011).
38 William I. Thomas and Dorothy S. Thomas, *The Child in America: Behavior Problems and Programs* (New York: Knopf, 1928), 571–2.
39 John 14:23.
40 "About Us," Promise Keepers: Men of Integrity, https://promisekeepers.org/promise-keepers/about-us/.
41 "About Us," Promise Keepers.
42 Sara Eldén, "Gender Politics in Conservative Men's Movements: Beyond Complexity, Ambiguity and Pragmatism," *NORA – Nordic Journal of Feminist and Gender Research* 10, no. 1 (2002): 38–48.
43 Rabbi Naftali Brawer and Rabbi Jonathan Romain, "Does Our Dog Have a Soul?" *The Jewish Chronicle*, July 9, 2017, https://www.thejc.com/judaism/rabbi-i-have-a-problem/does-our-dog-have-a-soul-1.441160.
44 Yanki Tauber, "What Is a Soul (Neshamah)?" Chabad.org, https://www.chabad.org/library/article_cdo/aid/3194/jewish/What-is-a-Soul-Neshamah.htm.
45 "Body and Soul: Indispensable Partners for Doing Life's Sacred Work," My Jewish Learning, https://www.myjewishlearning.com/article/body-soul/.
46 "Olam Ha-Ba: The Afterlife," Judaism 101, http://www.jewfaq.org/olamhaba.htm.
47 Ibrahim B. Syed, "The Nature of Soul: Islamic and Scientific Views," Islamic Research Foundation International, Inc., https://www.irfi.org/articles/articles_51_100/nature_of_soul.htm.
48 Syed, "The Nature of Soul."
49 "Understanding the Three Types of Nafs," Zaynab Academy: Classical Islamic Learning for Women, http://www.zaynabacademy.org/understanding-the-three-types-of-nafs/.

2. Motives

1 Christopher, "Blood Is Thicker than Water (Conflicting Meanings Explained)," Symbolism and Metaphor, https://symbolismandmetaphor.com/blood-is-thicker-than-water-origins/.
2 Antonio Regalado, "More than 26 Million People Have Taken an At-Home Ancestry Test," *MIT Technology Review*, February 11, 2019, https://www.technologyreview.com/s/612880/more-than-26-million-people-have-taken-an-at-home-ancestry-test/.
3 Antonio Regalado, "Is the Consumer Genetics Fad Over?" *MIT Technology Review*, January 23, 2020, https://www.technologyreview.com/2020/01/23/276092/is-the-consumer-genetics-fad-over.
4 Research and Markets, "World Consumer DNA (Genetic) Testing Market Report 2021," GlobeNewswire, June 28, 2021, https://www.globenewswire.com/news-release/2021/06/28/2253793/28124/en/World-Consumer-DNA-Genetic-Testing-Market-Report-2021.html.

5 Libby Copeland, *The Lost Family: How DNA Testing Is Upending Who We Are* (New York: Abrams, 2020).

6 Jennifer Mason, "Tangible Affinities and the Real Life Fascination of Kinship," *Sociology* 42, no. 1 (2008): 29–45.

7 Jennifer Mason, *Affinities: Potent Connections in Personal Life* (Cambridge: Polity, 2018).

8 Deborah Dempsey, "Surrogacy, Gay Male Couples and the Significance of Biogenetic Paternity," *New Genetics and Society* 32, no. 1 (2013): 37–53.

9 "What You Need to Know about the History of Adoption," American Adoptions, https://www.americanadoptions.com/adoption/history-of-adoption.

10 Nicholas Zill, "The Changing Face of Adoption in the United States," Institute for Family Studies, August 8, 2017, https://ifstudies.org/blog/the-changing-face-of-adoption-in-the-united-states.

11 Allon Kalisher, Jennah Gosciak, and Jill Spielfogel, *The Multiethnic Placement Act 25 Years Later: Trends in Adoption and Transracial Adoption* (Washington, DC: Office of the Assistant Secretary for Planning and Evaluation, US Department of Health and Human Services, 2020). Available at https://aspe.hhs.gov/pdf-report/mepa-transracial-adoption.

12 "Dollhouse (Melanie Martinez Song)," Wikimedia Foundation, accessed June 9, 2022, https://en.wikipedia.org/wiki/Dollhouse_(Melanie_Martinez_song).

13 Aron Ralston, *Between a Rock and a Hard Place* (New York: Atria Books, 2004). See also Ralston's NBC interview with Tom Brokaw: "Aron Ralston, Part 1 of 6, Desperate Days in Bluejohn Canyon," uploaded February 14, 2011, YouTube video, 14:37, https://www.youtube.com/watch?v=ObPb01zGYRA&list=PLhkcUkmp_cDMD5kcFiQuLG6E3EBIv4qbj&index=1; "127 Hours," Wikimedia Foundation, accessed June 9, 2022, https://en.wikipedia.org/wiki/127_Hours.

14 Michael Inbar, "Hiker Who Cut Off Arm: My Future Son Saved Me," Today.com, December 8, 2009, https://www.today.com/news/hiker-who-cut-arm-my-future-son-saved-me-wbna34325633.

15 Fred Bronson, "Top 50 Love Songs of All Time," *Billboard*, February 4, 2021, https://www.billboard.com/articles/list/6792625/top-50-love-songs-of-all-time.

16 "The 33 Best Romantic Comedies of All Time," *Vanity Fair*, May 11, 2022, https://www.vanityfair.com/hollywood/2018/08/best-romantic-comedies-list.

17 Valerie Peterson, "What You Need to Know about Romance Fiction Genre," The Balance Careers, November 24, 2019, https://www.thebalancecareers.com/romance-novels-about-the-romance-fiction-genre-2799896.

18 "Fewer Consumers Celebrating Valentine's Day but Those Who Do Are Spending More," National Retail Federation, January 30, 2019, https://nrf.com/media-center/press-releases/fewer-consumers-celebrating-valentines-day-those-who-do-are-spending.

19 Martin Zwilling, "How Many More Online Dating Sites Do We Need?" *Forbes*, March 1, 2013, https://www.forbes.com/sites/martinzwilling/2013/03/01/how-many-more-online-dating-sites-do-we-need/.

20 Emily A. Vogels, "10 Facts about Americans and Online Dating," Pew Research Center, February 6, 2020, https://www.pewresearch.org/fact-tank/2020/02/06/10-facts-about-americans-and-online-dating/.

21 Millie Fender, "Best Online Dating Sites and Apps 2022," TopTenReviews, July 1, 2021, https://www.toptenreviews.com/best-online-dating-sites.

22 Cameron Costa, "How Singles Are Meeting Up on Dating Apps Like Tinder, Bumble, Hinge during Coronavirus Pandemic," *CNBC*, March 31, 2020, https://www.cnbc.com/2020/03/24/how-singles-are-meeting-up-on-dating-apps-during-the-coronavirus.html.

23 "Tinder Review," Dating Sites Reviews.com, updated April 1, 2022, https://www.datingsitesreviews.com/staticpages/index.php?page=tinder-reviews.

24 "Bumble Information, Statistics, Facts and History," Dating Sites Reviews.com updated April 6, 2022, https://www.datingsitesreviews.com/staticpages/index .php?page=Bumble-Statistics-Facts-History.

25 Urszula Pruchniewska, "'I Like That It's My Choice a Couple Different Times': Gender, Affordances, and User Experience on Bumble Dating," *International Journal of Communication* 14 (2020): 2422–39.

26 Hayley Matthews, https://www.datingadvice.com/about-us/hayleym, accessed December 11, 2021.

27 Andrew O'Hara, "Mobile App Development: The 8 Best Apps for Couples in 2021," Fueled, March 2, 2021, https://fueled.com/blog/8-best-apps-for-couples/.

28 Elise Moreau, "Couple: The Long Distance Relationship App," Lifewire: Tech for Humans, March 13, 2020, https://www.lifewire.com/pair-the-long-distance -relationship-app-3486478.

29 Mark McGonigle, WiseMind Apps, https://www.markmcgonigle.com/apps.htm.

30 Sherry Turkle, *Reclaiming Conversation: The Power of Talk in a Digital Age* (New York: Penguin, 2015).

31 E.E. Evans-Pritchard, "Zande Blood-Brotherhood," *Africa: Journal of the International Institute of African Languages and Cultures* 6, no. 4 (1933): 369–401.

32 Miller McPherson, Lynn Smith-Lovin, Matthew E. Brashears, "Social Isolation in America: Changes in Core Discussion Networks over Two Decades," *American Sociological Review* 71, no. 3 (2006): 353–75; see also Miller McPherson, Lynn Smith-Lovin, Matthew E. Brashears, "Errata: Social Isolation in America: Changes in Core Discussion Networks Over Two Decades," *American Sociological Review* 73 (2008): 1022.

33 Jacqueline Olds and Richard S. Schwartz, *The Lonely American: Drifting Apart in the Twenty-First Century* (Boston: Beacon, 2009).

34 Claude S. Fischer, "The 2004 GSS Finding of Shrunken Social Networks: An Artifact?" *American Sociological Review* 74, no. 4 (2009): 657–69.

35 Claude S. Fischer, *Still Connected: Family and Friends in America since 1970* (New York: Russell Sage Foundation, 2011).

36 Fischer, *Still Connected*, 94.

37 "U.S. Adults Have Few Friends – and They're Mostly Alike," Barna, October 23, 2018, https://www.barna.com/research/friends-loneliness/.

38 "This Woman Built a Soccer Team Using Bumble BFF," Bumble, https://bumble. com/en/the-buzz/soccerbff.

39 David Brooks, "The Cruelty of Call-Out Culture: How Not to Do Social Change," *New York Times*, January 14, 2019, https://www.nytimes.com/2019/01/14/opinion/call -out-social-justice.html.

40 Emily Witt, "How the Survivors of Parkland Began the Never Again Movement," *The New Yorker*, February 19, 2018, https://www.newyorker.com/news/news -desk/how-the-survivors-of-parkland-began-the-never-again-movement.

41 United Nations, *Counter-Terrorism: Introduction to International Terrorism* (Vienna: United Nations, 2018), 1, https://www.unodc.org/documents/e4j/18-04932_CT _Mod_01_ebook_FINALpdf.pdf.

42 "What Is Jihadism?" *BBC News*, December 11, 2014, https://www.bbc.com/news /world-middle-east-30411519.

43 Jessica Trisko Darden, *Tackling Terrorists' Exploitation of Youth*, American Enterprise Institute, May 2019, https://www.un.org/sexualviolenceinconflict/wp-content /uploads/2019/05/report/tackling-terrorists-exploitation-of-youth/Tackling -Terrorists-Exploitation-of-Youth.pdf.

44 "A Look at How ISIS Is Recruiting Young Americans through the Internet," *ABC News*, uploaded November 4, 2017, YouTube video, 11:04, https://www.youtube.com/watch?v=4FZC0WWzHQs.

45 Howard Altman and James R. Webb, "Informal Group of Troops, Vets, Working to Help Afghans Seeking Refuge in US," *Military Times*, August 16, 2021, https://www.militarytimes.com/flashpoints/afghanistan/2021/08/16/informal-group-of-troops-vets-working-to-help-afghans-seeking-refuge-in-us/.

46 Sebastian Junger, *Tribe: On Homecoming and Belonging* (New York: Twelve, 2015), 53.

47 Junger, *Tribe*, 54.

48 Marjorie A. Geisz-Everson, Dianne Dodd-McCue, and Marsha Bennett, "Shared Experiences of CRNAs Who Were on Duty in New Orleans during Hurricane Katrina," *Journal of the American Association of Nurse Anesthetists* 80, no. 3 (2012): 205–12; A.J. Willingham, "Civilians and Strangers Become Heroes for Harvey Victims," *CNN*, August 28, 2017, https://www.cnn.com/2017/08/28/us/harvey-good-samaritans-cajun-navy-trnd/index.html.

49 Rebecca Solnit, *A Paradise Built in Hell: The Extraordinary Communities That Arise in Disaster* (New York: Viking, 2009), 8.

50 Solnit, *A Paradise Built in Hell*, 3.

51 Elizabeth Lee, "Paradise Football Players Emerge from Fire Stronger and Undefeated," *Voice of America*, December 1, 2019, https://www.voanews.com/usa/paradise-football-players-emerge-fire-stronger-and-undefeated.

52 "Community of Paradise Come Together for High School Football," *KCRA News*, uploaded August 24, 2019, YouTube video, 1:48, https://www.youtube.com/watch?v=O24pu2iyXho; "Paradise Football Team Brings New Hope One Year After the Camp Fire," *NBC*, uploaded November 16, 2019, YouTube video, 2:32, https://www.youtube.com/watch?v=PsyYwUufJnc.

53 Phil Helsel and Alex Johnson, "Paradise Regained: A Year After the Camp Fire, a Resilient Town Rebuilds," *NBC*, November 8, 2019, https://www.nbcnews.com/news/us-news/paradise-regained-year-after-camp-fire-resilient-town-rebuilds-n1077991.

54 Olds and Schwartz, *The Lonely American*, 163.

55 William Marsiglio, *Men on a Mission: Valuing Youth Work in Our Communities* (Baltimore: Johns Hopkins University Press, 2008); see also Ed De St. Aubin, Dan P. McAdams, and Tae-Chang Kim, *The Generative Society: Caring for Future Generations* (Washington, DC: American Psychological Association, 2004); John R. Snarey, *How Fathers Care for the Next Generation: A Four-Decade Study* (Cambridge, MA: Harvard University Press, 1993); and Eric H. Erikson, *Life History and the Historical Moment* (New York: Norton, 1975).

56 Tony Briscoe, Dan Hinkel, and Genevieve Bookwalter, "Millions at Wrigley, Downtown for Cubs' World Series Parade, Rally," *Chicago Tribune*, November 4, 2016, https://www.chicagotribune.com/sports/cubs/ct-cubs-parade-world-series-1104-20161104-story.html.

57 "Meta," https://about.facebook.com/meta/.

58 Sheera Frenkel and Cecilia Kang, *An Ugly Truth: Inside Facebook's Battle for Domination* (New York: Harper, 2021).

3. Social Domains

1 "Social Workers: Job Outlook," *Occupational Outlook Handbook*, US Bureau of Labor Statistics, April 18, 2022, https://www.bls.gov/ooh/community-and-social-service/social-workers.htm#tab-6.

2 Jefferson A. Singer and Karen Skerrett, *Positive Couple Therapy: Using We-Stories to Enhance Resilience* (New York: Routledge, 2014).

3 See, for example, John M. Gottman, *The Science of Trust: Emotional Attunement for Couples* (New York: Norton, 2011); Daniel J. Siegel, *The Developing Mind: How Relationships and the Brain Interact to Shape Who We Are*, 2nd ed. (New York: Guilford Press, 2012).

4 Karen Skerrett, "'We-ness': The Key to a Positive Relationship," Kripalu Center for Yoga & Health, https://kripalu.org/resources/we-ness-key-positive-relationship.

5 Alexander Karan, Robert Rosenthal, and Megan L. Robbins, "Meta-Analytic Evidence That We-Talk Predicts Relationship and Personal Functioning in Romantic Couples," *Journal of Social and Personal Relationships* 36, no. 9 (2019): 2624–51.

6 Karen Skerrett, "The Power of a We-Story," Kripalu Center for Yoga & Health, https://kripalu.org/resources/power-we-story.

7 Singer and Skerrett, *Positive Couple Therapy*, 4.

8 "Trauma and Families," Better Health Channel, Victoria State Government Department of Health (Australia), https://www.betterhealth.vic.gov.au/health/healthyliving/trauma-and-families.

9 "A Conversation with Koko the Gorilla," *PBS Nature*, YouTube video, 56:06, recorded August 8, 1999, https://www.youtube.com/watch?v=joevfNYnbJI.

10 Katherine C. Grier, *Pets in America: A History* (Chapel Hill, NC: University of North Carolina Press, 2006).

11 Nickie Charles, "'Animals Just Love You as You Are': Experiencing Kinship across the Species Barrier," *Sociology* 48, no. 4 (2014): 715–30.

12 Clinton R. Sanders, "Actions Speak Louder than Words: Close Relationships between Humans and Nonhuman Animals," *Symbolic Interaction* 26, no. 3 (2003): 405–26.

13 Helen Peterson and Kristina Engwall, "'Why Would You Want a Baby When You Could Have a Dog?' Voluntarily Childless Women's 'Peternal' Feelings, Longing and Ambivalence," *Social Sciences* 8, no. 4 (2019): 126; Nicole Owens and Liz Grauerholz, "Interspecies Parenting: How Pet Parents Construct Their Roles," *Humanity & Society* 43, no. 2 (2019): 96–119.

14 Leslie Irvine and Laurent Cilia, "More-than-Human Families: Pets, People, and Practices in Multispecies Households," *Sociology Compass* 11, no. 2 (2017): e12455.

15 Leslie Irvine, *My Dog Always Eats First: Homeless People and Their Animals* (Boulder, CO: Lynne Rienner, 2013).

16 "Pawsitive Change," Marley's Mutts, 2021, https://www.marleysmutts.org/pawsitivechange/.

17 "Dog Psychology/Pack Leadership," K9BreakThru Behavior Rehabilitation & Training, https://k9breakthru.com/.

18 "Sophia 2020 – A Glimpse at What's to Come," Hanson Robotics Limited, uploaded January 14, 2020, YouTube video, 1:40, https://www.youtube.com/watch?v=XrSAQoetF0A; see also "Sophia the Robot Interviews Neuroscientist Dr. Heather Berlin on Consciousness," uploaded April 15, 2020, YouTube video, 9:00, https://www.youtube.com/watch?v=Gmr4i6ZcSdo.

19 "Cute Robots You Can Buy – Robots Are Your Ultimate Life Hack," Let's Do This, uploaded March 26, 2017, YouTube video, 13:47, https://www.youtube.com/watch?v=-OTd-S7rY98.

20 Sherry Turkle, *Alone Together: Why We Expect More from Technology and Less from Each Other*, 3rd ed. (New York: Basic Books, 2017).

21 Turkle, *Alone Together*, 9.

22 "Love by Female Companion Robots – Are They Real? Artificial Intelligence and Harmoni 2020," TFlex Tech, uploaded April 28, 2020, YouTube video, 3:46, https://www.youtube.com/watch?v=TSdLV6d06e4; "You Can Soon Buy a Sex

Robot Equipped with Artificial Intelligence for about $20,000," *ABC Nightline*, uploaded April 25, 2018, YouTube video, 7:27, https://www.youtube.com/watch?v =-cN8sJz50Ng.

23 Markus Appel, Caroline Marker, and Martina Mara, "Otakuism and the Appeal of Sex Robots," *Frontiers in Psychology* 10 (2019); David Levy, *Love and Sex with Robots: The Evolution of Human-Robot Relationships* (New York: Harper Perennial, 2008).

24 "You Can Soon Buy a Sex Robot," *ABC Nightline*.

25 Turkle, *Alone Together*, 125.

26 Turkle, *Alone Together*, 287.

27 Turkle, *Alone Together*, 125.

28 Roey Tzezana, "Singularity: Explain It to Me Like I'm 5-Years-Old," Futurism, March 3, 2017, https://futurism.com/singularity-explain-it-to-me-like-im-5-years-old.

29 "Ray Kurzweil: Get Ready for Hybrid Thinking," TED, uploaded June 2, 2014, YouTube video, 9:52, https://www.youtube.com/watch?v=PVXQUItNEDQ&list=P L57LVnlwhJiWtHOrP4_htVAyeuj3L8jZZ&index=13&t=0s.

30 Open Cog, https://opencog.org/; DeepMind, https://deepmind.com/; OpenAI, https://openai.com/.

31 Ben Goertzel, *The AGI Revolution: An Inside View of the Rise of Artificial General Intelligence* (Humanity+ Press, 2016).

32 Stephen Hawking, *Brief Answers to the Big Questions* (New York: Bantam, 2018), 188; see also Abigail Higgins, "Stephen Hawking's Final Warning for Humanity: AI Is Coming for Us," Vox, October 16, 2018, https://www.vox.com/future-perfect /2018/10/16/17978596/stephen-hawking-ai-climate-change-robots-future -universe-earth.

33 "An Open Letter: Research Priorities for Robust and Beneficial Artificial Intelligence," Future of Life Institute, https://futureoflife.org/2015/10/27/ai-open-letter/.

34 "Preparing for the Age of Intelligent Machines," Leverhulme Centre for the Future of Intelligence, http://lcfi.ac.uk/about/.

35 Lorraine Smith Pangle, *Aristotle and the Philosophy of Friendship* (Cambridge: Cambridge University Press, 2003); see also Bennett Helm, "Friendship," *The Stanford Encyclopedia of Philosophy*, ed. Edward N. Zalta, Fall 2021 ed., https://plato .stanford.edu/entries/friendship/.

36 Helm, "Friendship."

37 Naveen Joshi, "7 Types of Artificial Intelligence," *Forbes*, June 19, 2019, https://www .forbes.com/sites/cognitiveworld/2019/06/19/7-types-of-artificial-intelligence/?s h=11e95ea233ee.

38 Carl T. Rogers, "Why You Will Never Be Friends with an AI," *Medium*, February 28, 2020, https://medium.com/the-philosophers-stone/why-you-will-never-be-friends -with-an-ai-c1abb8d735de.

39 Turkle, *Alone Together*.

40 Parmy Olson, "This AI Has Sparked a Budding Friendship with 2.5 Million People," *Forbes*, March 8, 2018, https://www.forbes.com/sites/parmyolson/2018/03/08 /replika-chatbot-google-machine-learning/#2b5c124ffaba.

41 "The AI Companion Who Cares," Replika, https://replika.com/.

42 Oliver Balch, "AI and Me: Friendship Chatbots Are On the Rise, but Is There a Gendered Design Flaw?" *The Guardian*, May 7, 2020, https://www.theguardian .com/careers/2020/may/07/ai-and-me-friendship-chatbots-are-on-the-rise-but-is -there-a-gendered-design-flaw.

43 Olson, "This AI Has Sparked a Budding Friendship."

44 Nicholas A. Christakis, *Blueprint: The Evolutionary Origins of a Good Society* (New York: Little, Brown Spark, 2019).

45 Nicolas A. Christakis, "How AI Will Rewire Us," *The Atlantic*, April 2019, https://www
.theatlantic.com/magazine/archive/2019/04/robots-human-relationships/583204/.

46 "[VR Human Documentary] Mother Meets Her Deceased Daughter through VR
Technology," MBC Life, uploaded February 6, 2020, YouTube video, 9:38, https://
www.youtube.com/watch?v=uflTK8c4w0c&list=TLPQMDUwNTIwMjBikJEKXhiL
5A&index=3.

47 "Jeannette, Pennsylvania," Wikimedia Foundation, accessed December 11, 2021,
https://en.wikipedia.org/wiki/Jeannette,_Pennsylvania.

48 Taylor Dotson, *Technically Together: Reconstructing Community in a Networked World*
(Cambridge, MA: MIT Press, 2017).

49 Ray Oldenburg, *The Great Good Place: Cafés, Coffee Shops, Bookstores, Bars, Hair Salons,
and Other Hangouts at the Heart of a Community* (New York: Marlowe, 1999), 16.

50 Oldenburg, *The Great Good Place*, xix.

51 Oldenburg, *The Great Good Place*, xxi.

52 Oldenburg, *The Great Good Place*, xxiii.

53 Rebekah Levine Coley and Melissa Kull, "Cumulative, Timing-Specific, and
Interactive Models of Residential Mobility and Children's Cognitive and Psychosocial
Skills," *Child Development* 87, no. 4 (2016): 1204–20.

54 Jennifer, "The Crazy Reason Idaho Is Full of Underground Hermit Caves Will
Surprise You," Only in Your State, May 27, 2017, https://www.onlyinyourstate.com
/idaho/dugout-dick-id/; to see a video of Dugout Dick see "YERTpod19: Diggin'
Dugout Dick in Idaho," YERT – Your Environmental Road Trip, uploaded April 18,
2012, YouTube video, 14:34, https://www.youtube.com/watch?v=lYOfdpnoayY.

55 Jennifer, "The Crazy Reason Idaho Is Full of Underground Hermit Caves."

56 "List of Indian Reservations in the United States," Wikimedia Foundation, accessed
December 11, 2021, https://en.wikipedia.org/wiki/List_of_Indian_reservations
_in_the_United_States; "Indian Reservation," Wikimedia Foundation, accessed
December 11, 2021, https://en.wikipedia.org/wiki/Indian_reservation.

57 "Living Conditions," Native American Aid, http://www.nativepartnership.org/site
/PageServer?pagename=naa_livingconditions.

58 "Traditions & Culture," Running Strong for American Indian Youth, http://
indianyouth.org/american-indian-life/traditions-culture.

59 "Indian Affairs: About Us," US Department of the Interior: Indian Affairs, https://
www.bia.gov/about-us.

60 Sterling HolyWhiteMountain, "The Blackfeet Brain Drain," *The Atlantic*, November
2018, https://www.theatlantic.com/feed/author/sterling-holywhitemountain/.

61 Corey Walsh, "Blackfeet Writer, UM Grad Awarded Prestigious Stegner Writing
Fellowship at Stanford," *Missoulian*, November 5, 2019, https://missoulian.com
/news/local/blackfeet-writer-um-grad-awarded-prestigious-stegner-writing
-fellowship-at/article_e2ef113d-a692-5ddb-a4b7-c4c3f55d866e.html.

62 Walsh, "Blackfeet Writer."

63 "Fact for Features: American Indian and Alaska Native Heritage Month: November
2014," United States Census Bureau, November 12, 2014, https://www.census.gov
/newsroom/facts-for-features/2014/cb14-ff26.html.

64 "Mission & History," Running Strong for American Indian Youth, http://indianyouth
.org/about-us/mission-history.

65 Rebecca Laurence, "Come from Away: Why We Need the '9/11 Musical,'" *BBC*,
February 14, 2019, http://www.bbc.com/culture/story/20190212-come-from-away
-why-we-need-the-911-musical.

66 Laurence, "Come from Away."

67 "Tristan Harris Congress Testimony: Technological Deception in the Social Media Age,"
Center for Humane Technology, recorded January 8, 2020, YouTube video, 11:16, https://
www.youtube.com/watch?v=LUNErhONqCY.

68 May Friedman, "Daddyblogs Know Best: Histories of Fatherhood in the Cyber Age," in *Pops in Pop Culture: Fatherhood, Masculinity, and the New Man*, ed. Elizabeth Podnieks (New York: Palgrave Macmillan, 2016), 87–103; May Friedman, *Mommyblogs and the Changing Face of Motherhood* (Toronto: University of Toronto Press, 2013).

69 Casey Scheibling and William Marsiglio, "#HealthyDads: 'Fit Fathering' Discourse and Digital Health Promotion in Dad Blogs," *Journal of Marriage and Family* 83, no. 4 (2021): 1227–42.

70 Casey Scheibling, "'Real Heroes Care': How Dad Bloggers Are Reconstructing Fatherhood and Masculinities," *Men and Masculinities* 23, no. 1 (2020): 3–19.

71 "About Us," Dad 2.0, https://dad2.com/about/.

72 Rebecca Nicholson, "Star Gazing: Why Millennials Are Turning to Astrology," *The Guardian*, March 11, 2018, https://www.theguardian.com/global/2018/mar/11/star-gazing-why-millennials-are-turning-to-astrology.

73 Lily Wakefield, "World Famous Astrologer Eloquently Explains the Special Relationship between Queer People and Astrology," *PinkNews*, January 8, 2020, https://www.pinknews.co.uk/2020/01/08/astrology-chani-nicholas-queer-phenomenon-star-sign-sonya-passi-lgbt/.

74 Nicholson, "Star Gazing."

75 Bradley Aden, "50 Pioneers in Alternative Health & Medicine," Worldwide Wisdom Directory, https://worldwidewisdomdirectory.com/50-pioneers-in-holistic-and-alternative-health.html.

76 Meghan K. Edwards, and Paul D. Loprinzi, "Comparative Effects of Meditation and Exercise on Physical and Psychosocial Health Outcomes: A Review of Randomized Controlled Trials," *Postgraduate Medicine* 130, no. 2 (2018): 222–8; Subhadra Evans, Saskia Subramanian, and Beth Sternlieb, "Yoga as Treatment for Chronic Pain Conditions: A Literature Review," *International Journal on Disability and Human Development* 7, no. 1 (2008): 25–32; Søren Ventegodt and Joav Merrick, "Meta-Analysis of Positive Effects, Side Effects and Adverse Events of Holistic Mind-Body Medicine (Clinical Holistic Medicine): Experience from Denmark, Sweden, United Kingdom and Germany," *International Journal of Adolescent Medicine and Health* 21, no. 4 (2009): 441–56.

77 "Highlights from the 2016 Yoga in America Study," Yoga Alliance, January 13, 2016, https://www.yogaalliance.org/Learn/About_Yoga/2016_Yoga_in_America_Study/Highlights.

78 National Center for Health Statistics, "Use of Yoga, Meditation, and Chiropractors among U.S. Children Aged 4–17 Years," Centers for Disease Control and Prevention, November 2018, https://www.cdc.gov/nchs/products/databriefs/db324.htm.

79 Rachel Grate, "Yoga Statistics: Surprising Data on the Growth of Yoga," Eventbrite blog, March 7, 2019, https://www.eventbrite.com/blog/yoga-statistics-demographics-market-growth-trends-ds00/.

80 Lindsey I. Black, Patricia M. Barnes, Tainya C. Clarke, Barbara J. Stussman, and Richard L. Nahin, "Use of Yoga, Meditation, and Chiropractors among U.S. Children Aged 4–17 Years," *National Center for Health Statistics Data Brief 324* (November 2018): 1–8, https://pubmed.ncbi.nlm.nih.gov/30475687/.

81 Eva Bukina, "The Rise of Veganism with Social Media," The Panoptic, July 8, 2016, https://thepanoptic.co.uk/2016/07/08/rise-popularity-veganismvegetarianism-influence-social-media/.

82 Saulius Šimčikas, "Is the Percentage of Vegetarians and Vegans in the U.S. Increasing?" Animal Charity Evaluators, August 16, 2018, https://animalcharityevaluators.org/blog/is-the-percentage-of-vegetarians-and-vegans-in-the-u-s-increasing/.

83 "40% of Consumers Are Trying to Include More Vegan Foods into Every Meal," Livekindly, https://www.livekindly.co/40-percent-consumers-want-plant-based-foods/.

84 Joei Chan, "Vegan Social Media: How Food Trends and Social Movements Grow Online," Linkfluence, https://www.linkfluence.com/blog/vegan-social-media-how -food-trends-grow-online.

85 R.J. Reinhart, "Snapshot: Few Americans Vegetarian or Vegan," Gallup, August 1, 2018, https://news.gallup.com/poll/238328/snapshot-few-americans-vegetarian -vegan.aspx.

86 Ljubica Cvetkovska, "34 Vegan Statistics to Help You Be Kind to Every Kind," Petpedia, updated October 13, 2021, https://petpedia.co/vegan-statistics/; "Top Trends in Prepared Foods 2017: Exploring Trends in Meat, Fish and Seafood; Pasta, Noodles and Rice; Prepared Meals; Savory Deli Food; Soup; and Meat Substitutes," Report Buyer, June 2017, https://www.reportbuyer.com/product/4959853/top -trends-in-prepared-foods-2017-exploring-trends-in-meat-fish-and-seafood-pasta -noodles-and-rice-prepared-meals-savory-deli-food-soup-and-meat-substitutes .html.

87 Pippa Bailey, "An Exploration into Diets Around the World," Ipsos MORI, August 2018, https://www.ipsos.com/sites/default/files/ct/news/documents/2018-09 /an_exploration_into_diets_around_the_world.pdf.

88 Ana Djurovic, "General Vegan Statistics for 2022 – What Vegans Fight For," Deals on Health, August 4, 2021, https://dealsonhealth.net/vegan-statistics/.

89 "The Ultimate Guide to Vegan Marketing," Creative Compass, December 12, 2021, https://vegancreativecompass.com/blog/the-ultimate-guide-to-marketing-vegan -products.

90 Chelsea Chuck, Samantha A. Fernandes, and Lauri L. Hyers, "Awakening to the Politics of Food: Politicized Diet as Social Identity," *Appetite* 107 (December 2016): 425–36.

91 John B. Nezlek and Catherine A. Forestell, "Vegetarianism as a Social Identity," *Current Opinion in Food Science* 33 (June 2020): 45–51; Chuck, Fernandes, and Hyers, "Awakening to the Politics of Food"; Matthew B. Ruby, "Vegetarianism: A Blossoming Field of Study," *Appetite* 58, no. 1 (2012): 141–50.

92 "What Is Wellness," Global Wellness Institute, https://globalwellnessinstitute .org/what-is-wellness/.

93 Chloe E. Bird and Patricia P. Rieker, *Gender and Health: The Effects of Constrained Choices and Policies* (Cambridge: Cambridge University Press, 2008).

94 William Marsiglio, *Dads, Kids & Fitness: A Father's Guide to Family Health* (New Brunswick, NJ: Rutgers University Press, 2016); William Marsiglio, "Healthy Dads, Healthy Kids," *Contexts* 8, no. 4 (2009): 22–7.

95 "What Is Wellness," Global Wellness Institute.

96 Nezlek and Forestell, "Vegetarianism as a Social Identity," 48.

97 Julia A. Minson and Benoît Monin, "Do-gooder Derogation: Disparaging Morally Motivated Minorities to Defuse Anticipated Reproach," *Social Psychological and Personality Science* 3, no. 2 (2012): 200–7.

98 "About Adriene," Yoga with Adriene, https://yogawithadriene.com/adriene-mishler/.

99 "U.S. Public Becoming Less Religious," Pew Research Center, November 3, 2015, https://www.pewforum.org/2015/11/03/u-s-public-becoming-less-religious/.

100 Patricia M. Mische, "The Significance of Religions for Social Justice and a Culture of Peace," *Journal of Religion, Conflict, and Peace* 1, no. 1 (2007), http://www .religionconflictpeace.org/volume-1-issue-1-fall-2007/significance-religions-social -justice-and-culture-peace.

101 Hillel Gray, "They're Still Here: The Curious Evolution of Westboro Baptist Church," *Religion News Service*, July 17, 2018, https://religionnews.com/2018/07/17/theyre -still-here-the-curious-evolution-of-westboro-baptist-church/.

102 Megan Phelps-Roper, *Unfollow: A Memoir of Loving and Leaving the Westboro Baptist Church* (New York: Farrar, Straus, and Giroux, 2019), 134.
103 For access to the documentary, short films, and other information, see YERT: Your Environmental Road Trip, http://www.yert.com/.
104 Brian Stelter, *Hoax: Donald Trump, Fox News, and the Dangerous Distortion of Truth* (New York: One Signal, 2020).
105 Oldenburg, *The Great Good Place*, 11.
106 Kristie M. Engemann and Michael T. Owyang, "Working Hard or Hardly Working? The Evolution of Leisure in the United States," Federal Reserve Bank of St. Louis, January 1, 2007, https://www.stlouisfed.org/publications/regional-economist/january-2007/working-hard-or-hardly-working-the-evolution-of-leisure-in-the-united-states.
107 Turkle, *Alone Together*, 203.
108 Nick Yee, *The Proteus Paradox: How Online Games and Virtual Worlds Change Us – and How They Don't* (New Haven, CT: Yale University Press, 2014), 32.
109 Yee, *The Proteus Paradox*, 29.
110 Fanny Anne Ramirez, "From Good Associates to True Friends: An Exploration of Friendship Practices in Massively Multiplayer Online Games," in *Social Interactions in Virtual Wolds: An Interdisciplinary Perspective*, ed. Kiran Lakkaraju, Gita Sukthankar, and Rolf T. Wigand (Cambridge: Cambridge University Press, 2018), 62–79.
111 Simon Gottschalk, "The Presentation of Avatars in Second Life: Self and Interaction in Social Virtual Spaces," *Symbolic Interaction* 33, no. 4 (2010): 501–25.
112 Gottschalk, "The Presentation of Avatars in Second Life," 504.
113 Joline Buscemi, "Who's Still on 'Second Life' in 2020," MIC, February 16, 2020, https://www.mic.com/p/second-life-still-has-dedicated-users-in-2020-heres-what-keeps-them-sticking-around-18693758.
114 Yee, *The Proteus Paradox*.
115 Rabindra Ratan, David Beyea, Benjamin J. Li, and Luis Graciano, "Avatar Characteristics Induce Users' Behavioral Conformity with Small-to-Medium Effect Sizes: A Meta-Analysis of the Proteus Effect," *Media Psychology* 23, no. 5 (2020): 651–75.
116 Tom Boellstorff, *Coming of Age in Second Life: An Anthropologist Explores the Virtually Human* (Princeton, NJ: Princeton University Press, 2008).
117 Gottschalk, "The Presentation of Avatars in Second Life," 508.
118 Ramirez, "From Good Associates to True Friends"; Hong Joo Lee, Jaewon Choi, Jong Woo Kim, Sung Joo Park, and Peter Gloor, "Communication, Opponents, and Clan Performance in Online Games: A Social Network Approach," *Cyberpsychology, Behavior and Social Networking* 16, no. 12 (2013): 878–83.
119 Ramirez, "From Good Associates to True Friends," 75.
120 Brad McKenna, "Creating Convivial Affordances: A Study of Virtual World Social Movements," *Information Systems Journal* 30, no. 1 (2020): 185–214.
121 McKenna, "Creating Convivial Affordances," 194.
122 Associated Press, "U.S. Women's Soccer Team Boldly Embraces Off-the-field Activist Role," NBC, July 9, 2019, https://www.nbcnews.com/feature/nbc-out/u-s-women-s-soccer-team-boldly-embraces-field-activist-n1027726.
123 Steve Wyche, "Colin Kaepernick Explains Why He Sat during National Anthem," NFL.com, August 27, 2016, https://www.nfl.com/news/colin-kaepernick-explains-why-he-sat-during-national-anthem-0ap3000000691077.
124 Bryan Armen Graham, "Donald Trump Blasts NFL Anthem Protestors: 'Get that Son of a Bitch Off the Field,'" *The Guardian*, September 23, 2017, https://www.theguardian.com/sport/2017/sep/22/donald-trump-nfl-national-anthem-protests.

125 Roger Goodell, "Statement from NFL Commissioner Roger Goodell," NFL Communications, https://nflcommunications.com/Pages/Statement-From-NFL-Commissioner-Roger-Goodell.aspx.

126 "NFL Chief Admits He Was Wrong for Not Listening to Players Protesting Racism," *The Telegraph*, uploaded June 6, 2020, YouTube video, 1:23, https://www.youtube.com/watch?v=serZLRKtsNY.

127 Bill Bostock, "People Are Destroying Their Nike Shoes and Socks to Protest Nike's Colin Kaepernick Ad Campaign," *Business Insider*, September 4, 2018, https://www.businessinsider.com/nike-advert-with-colin-kaepernick-has-people-burning-products-2018-9.

128 *With Drawn Arms*, directed by Glenn Kaino and Afshin Shahidi, http://www.tommiesmith.com/.

129 Rupert Cornwell, "Great Olympic Friendships: John Carlos, Peter Norman and Tommie Smith – Divided by Their Colour, United by the Cause," *Independent*, August 5, 2016, https://www.independent.co.uk/sport/olympics/rio-2016-olympic-friendships-john-carlos-peter-norman-tommie-smith-mexico-city-1968-black-power-7166771.html.

130 Erin Blakemore, "How the Black Power Protest at the 1968 Olympics Killed Careers," History Channel, updated August 9, 2021, https://www.history.com/news/1968-mexico-city-olympics-black-power-protest-backlash.

131 Cornwell, "Great Olympic Friendships."

132 "Peter Norman, Australian for Human Rights 1968 Olympics," uploaded October 23, 2011, YouTube video, 8:14, https://www.youtube.com/watch?v=fu5K2cOeD4M.

133 Pierre Bourdieu, *Outline of a Theory of Practice* (Cambridge: Cambridge University Press, 1977).

134 William Marsiglio, *Kids Who Tri: Transforming Youth and Youth Sports Culture* (Bookbaby, 2019).

135 Valerie Wilson and Janelle Jones, "Working Harder or Finding It Harder to Work: Demographic Trends in Annual Work Hours Show an Increasingly Fractured Workforce," Economic Policy Institute, February 22, 2018, https://www.epi.org/publication/trends-in-work-hours-and-labor-market-disconnection/.

136 Bureau of Labor Statistics, "National Census of Fatal Occupational Injuries in 2020," US Department of Labor, December 16, 2021, https://www.bls.gov/news.release/pdf/cfoi.pdf.

137 Christopher Austin and Tahira M. Probst, "Masculine Gender Norms and Adverse Workplace Safety Outcomes: The Role of Sexual Orientation and Risky Safety Behavior," *Safety* 7, no. 3 (2021): 55; Mary Stergiou-Kita et al., "Danger Zone: Men, Masculinity and Occupational Health and Safety in High Risk Occupations," *Safety Science* 80 (2015): 213–20.

138 Matthew Desmond, *On the Fireline: Living and Dying with Wildland Firefighters* (Chicago: University of Chicago Press, 2007).

139 Bruce Watson, "Helen Keller's Moment," The Attic, https://www.theattic.space/home-page-blogs/2018/11/29/helen-kellers-moment.

140 Azita G. Hamedani, email message to author, December 19, 2021.

141 Dragomir Simovic, "The Ultimate List of Remote Work Statistics – 2022 Edition," SmallBizGenius, February 4, 2022, https://www.smallbizgenius.net/by-the-numbers/remote-work-statistics/#gref.

142 Lawrence Black, reply to "Do Long Haul Truckers Still Communicate with Each Other While Driving?" Quora, 2017, https://www.quora.com/Do-long-haul-truckers-still-communicate-with-each-other-while-driving.

143 "DoorDash Community," Reddit, accessed December 12, 2021, https://www.reddit.com/r/doordash/.

144 Eliza Levinson, "Meet the Gig Workers Collective: 11 Women Who Organize Nationwide Strikes but Have Never Met," *Next City*, May 21, 2020, https://nextcity.org/urbanist-news/meet-gig-workers-collective-11-women-organize-nationwide-strikes-never-met.

145 Lauren Kaori Gurley, "Gig Workers Are Forming the World's First Food Delivery App Unions," *Vice*, October 9, 2019, https://www.vice.com/en/article/59nk8d/gig-workers-are-forming-the-worlds-first-food-delivery-app-unions.

4. Judging Outcomes: Good, Bad, and Mixed

1 "Mitch Albom: Making Each Moment Matter," Chicago Ideas, uploaded April 16, 2013, YouTube video, 12:51, https://www.youtube.com/watch?v=Gr0COGuAA4U.

2 Mitch Albom, *Tuesdays with Morrie: An Old Man, a Young Man, and Life's Greatest Lesson* (New York: Broadway Books, 1997), 174.

3 Matthieu Ricard, *Altruism: The Power of Compassion to Change Yourself and the World* (New York: Little, Brown, 2013), 277.

4 Tom L. Beauchamp and James F. Childress, *Principles of Biomedical Ethics*, 6th ed. (New York: Oxford University Press, 2009); Stephen C. Taylor, "Health Care Ethics," Internet Encyclopedia of Philosophy, https://www.iep.utm.edu/h-c-ethi/#SH2d.

5 Bernard Lefkowitz, *Our Guys: The Glen Ridge Rape Case and the Secret Life of the Perfect Suburb* (Berkeley: University of California Press, 1997).

6 Lefkowitz, *Our Guys*, 21.

7 "Why Support St. Jude," St. Jude Children's Research Hospital, https://www.stjude.org/about-st-jude/why-support-st-jude.html.

8 "100 Best Companies to Work For," *Fortune*, https://fortune.com/best-companies/2019/search/?industry=Health%20Care.

9 Richard H. Hall, J. Eugene Haas, and Norman J. Johnson, "An Examination of the Blau-Scott and Etzioni Typologies," *Administrative Science Quarterly* 12, no. 1 (1967): 118–39.

10 "Stonewall Riots," *History Channel*, updated June 25, 2021, https://www.history.com/topics/gay-rights/the-stonewall-riots.

11 Bonnie J. Morris, "History of Lesbian, Gay, Bisexual, and Transgender Social Movements," American Psychological Association, 2009, https://www.apa.org/pi/lgbt/resources/history.

12 Harry Hay and Will Roscoe, *Radically Gay: Gay Liberation in the Words of Its Founder* (Boston: Beacon, 1996).

13 Jonathan Ned Katz, *Gay American History: Lesbians and Gay Men in the U.S.A.* (New York: Crowell, 1976).

14 "Stonewall 50 – WorldPride NYC 2019," Wikimedia Foundation, accessed December 13, 2021, https://en.wikipedia.org/wiki/Stonewall_50_–_WorldPride_NYC_2019.

15 Elizabeth A. McConnell with Ashley Simons-Rudolph, "People of Color Experience Discrimination within LGBT Spaces," Community Psychology: Social Justice through Collaborative Research and Action, https://www.communitypsychology.com/people-of-color-experience-discrimination-within-lgbt-spaces/; "A Conversation on White Supremacy and Racism in the Queer Community," San Francisco AIDS Foundation, June 12, 2020, https://www.sfaf.org/collections/status/a-conversation-on-white-supremacy-and-racism-in-the-queer-community/.

16 "Queer," Wikimedia Foundation, accessed December 13, 2021, https://en.wikipedia.org/wiki/Queer.

17 "Queer"; *Queers Read This*, June 1990, http://www.qrd.org/qrd/misc/text/queers.read.this.

18 Ryan J. Reilly, "Here's What Happens When You Complain to Cops about Cops," *HuffPost*, updated October 13, 2015, https://www.huffpost.com/entry/internal-affairs-police-misconduct_n_5613ea2fe4b022a4ce5f87ce.

19 Wilf Dunne, "The Effectiveness of Police 'Internal Affairs Departments' in Limiting Corruption in Police Services – A Literature Review," CurbingCorruption.com, October 2018, https://curbingcorruption.com/wp-content/uploads/2019/03/181004-Dunne-Literature-review-of-police-internal-affairs-departments.pdf.

20 Associated Press, "Abu Ghraib Whistleblower Testifies," *NBC*, August 5, 2004, https://www.nbcnews.com/id/wbna5613636#.XVrdwOhKh9M.

21 "The Stanford Prison Experiment: A Simulation Study on the Psychology of Imprisonment," The Stanford Prison Experiment, https://www.prisonexp.org/.

22 Peter Gray, "Why Zimbardo's Prison Experiment Isn't in My Textbook," *Psychology Today*, October 19, 2013, https://www.psychologytoday.com/us/blog/freedom-learn/201310/why-zimbardo-s-prison-experiment-isn-t-in-my-textbook.

23 Marshall Cohen, "FBI Director Says White Supremacy Is a 'Persistent, Pervasive Threat' to the US," *CNN*, April 4, 2019, https://www.cnn.com/2019/04/04/politics/fbi-director-wray-white-supremacy/index.html.

24 "Homeland Threat Assessment October 2020," US Department of Homeland Security, https://www.dhs.gov/sites/default/files/publications/2020_10_06_homeland-threat-assessment.pdf, 18.

25 Talia Lavin, *Culture Warlords: My Journey into the Dark Web of White Supremacy* (New York: Hachette, 2020).

26 Southern Poverty Law Center, *The Year in Hate and Extremism 2020*, 2021, https://www.splcenter.org/sites/default/files/yih_2020-21_final.pdf.

27 Matt Stieb, "Ex-White Nationalist Says Tucker Carlson Hits Far-Right Messaging 'Better Than They Have,'" *New York Magazine*, April 1, 2019, http://nymag.com/intelligencer/2019/04/ex-white-nationalist-says-they-get-tips-from-tucker-carlson.html.

28 R. Derek Black, "Why I Left White Nationalism," *New York Times*, November 26, 2016, https://www.nytimes.com/2016/11/26/opinion/sunday/why-i-left-white-nationalism.html.

29 Fareed Zakaria, "State of Hate: The Explosion of White Supremacy," *CNN*, June 30, 2019, https://cnnpressroom.blogs.cnn.com/2019/06/27/cnns-fareed-zakaria-on-the-explosion-in-white-supremacy-what-it-means-and-its-roots-sunday-june-30/.

30 Margaret Simms, "After 50 Years of Progress and Protest, America Is Still a Land of Unequal Opportunity," Urban Institute, September 19, 2018, https://www.urban.org/urban-wire/after-50-years-progress-and-protest-america-still-land-unequal-opportunity; Simms, "Say African American or Black, but First Acknowledge the Persistence of Structural Racism," Urban Institute, February 8, 2018, https://www.urban.org/urban-wire/say-african-american-or-black-first-acknowledge-persistence-structural-racism.

31 Emily A. Shrider, Melissa Kollar, Frances Chen, and Jessica Semega, "Income and Poverty in the United States: 2020," United States Census Bureau, September 14, 2021, https://www.census.gov/library/publications/2021/demo/p60-273.html.

32 Neil Bhutta, Andrew C. Chang, Lisa J. Dettling, and Joanne W. Hsu, "Disparities in Wealth by Race and Ethnicity in the 2019 Survey of Consumer Finances," *FEDS Notes*, Board of Governors of the Federal Reserve System, September 28, 2020, https://doi.org/10.17016/2380-7172.2797.

33 "Rate of Home Ownership in the United States in 2019, by Race," Statista, October 28, 2021, https://www.statista.com/statistics/639685/us-home-ownership-rate-by-race/.

34 "The 1619 Project," Wikimedia Foundation, accessed December 13, 2021, https://en.wikipedia.org/wiki/The_1619_Project.

35 Stephanie Russell-Kraft, "The Rise of Male Supremacist Groups: How Age-Old Misogyny Morphed into an Explicit Ideology of Hate," *The New Republic*, April 4, 2018, http://newrepublic.com/article/147744/rise-male-supremacist-groups.

36 "Daryush 'Roosh' Valizadeh," SPLC: Southern Poverty Law Center, https://www.splcenter.org/fighting-hate/extremist-files/individual/daryush-roosh-valizadeh.

37 Russell-Kraft, "The Rise of Male Supremacist Groups."

38 Jia Tolentino, "The Rage of the Incels," *The New Yorker*, May 15, 2018, https://www.newyorker.com/culture/cultural-comment/the-rage-of-the-incels; Ross Douthat, "The Redistribution of Sex," *New York Times*, May 2, 2018, https://www.nytimes.com/2018/05/02/opinion/incels-sex-robots-redistribution.html.

39 Lavin, *Culture Warlords*, 115.

40 Jeff Guinn, *The Road to Jonestown: Jim Jones and Peoples Temple* (New York: Simon & Schuster, 2017).

41 *Holy Hell*, directed by Will Allen, http://www.holyhellthedocumentary.com/.

42 Noah Berlatsky, "Holy Hell and the Truth about Cults: 'They're Not Going to Give It Up Easily,'" *The Guardian*, May 27, 2016.

43 For an example of a female cult leader, consider South Korean Shin Ok-ju who convinced four hundred people to move to Fiji (the center of the universe according to her) to avoid a famine she predicted in Korea. "Shin Ok-ju: S Korean Doomsday Cult Leader Jailed for Six Years," *BBC*, July 31, 2019, https://www.bbc.com/news/world-asia-49174634.

44 "Westboro Baptist Church," SPLC: Southern Poverty Law Center, https://www.splcenter.org/fighting-hate/extremist-files/group/westboro-baptist-church.

45 Megan Phelps-Roper, *Unfollow: A Memoir of Loving and Leaving the Westboro Baptist Church* (New York: Farrar, Straus, and Giroux, 2019).

46 Megan Phelps-Roper, "I Grew Up in the Westboro Baptist Church. Here's Why I Left," TED, uploaded March 6, 2017, YouTube video, 15:17, https://www.youtube.com/watch?v=bVV2Zk88beY.

47 Phelps-Roper, "I Grew Up in the Westboro Baptist Church."

48 Phelps-Roper, *Unfollow*, 275.

49 Ron Jones, "The Third Wave, 1967: An Account," 1972, https://libcom.org/files/The%20third%20wave.pdf.

50 Jones, "The Third Wave."

51 "Hate Groups Reach Record High," SPLC: Southern Poverty Law Center, February 19, 2019, https://www.splcenter.org/news/2019/02/19/hate-groups-reach-record-high.

52 Saba Imtiaz, "A New Generation Redefines What It Means to Be a Missionary," *The Atlantic*, March 2018, https://www.theatlantic.com/international/archive/2018/03/young-missionaries/551585/; Kaitlin Curtice, "Missions: Is It Love or Colonization?" *Religion News Service*, November 27, 2018, https://religionnews.com/2018/11/27/missions-is-it-love-or-colonization/.

53 "What Is a Gang? Definitions," National Institute of Justice, October 27, 2011, https://nij.ojp.gov/topics/articles/what-gang-definitions.

54 Elizabeth Mastropolo, "Child Soldiers in America: Criminal Manipulation of Minors," *Journal of Civil Rights and Economic Development* 27, no. 2 (Spring 2014): 322–46.

55 Giuseppe A. Finelli, "Slash, Shoot, Kill: Gang Recruitment of Children and the Penalties Gangs Face," *Family Court Review* 57, no. 2 (2019): 243–57.

56 "Karl Lokko," Independent Talent Group, https://www.independent-360.com/presenters/karl-lokko/; Karl Lokko, "Leading and Leaving the London Gang

World," TEDx Talks, uploaded July 9, 2015, YouTube video, 14:17, https://www
.youtube.com/watch?v=URAxnXjKXKY.

57 Craig J. Forsyth and Rhonda D. Evans, "Reconsidering the Pseudo-Family/Gang
Gender Distinction in Prison Research," *Journal of Police and Criminal Psychology* 18,
no. 1 (2003): 15–23.

58 Sarah K. Murnen and Marla H. Kohlman, "Athletic Participation, Fraternity
Membership, and Sexual Aggression among College Men: A Meta-Analytic Review,"
Sex Roles 57, no. 1 (2007): 145–57; Elizabeth Miller, Maria Catrina D. Jaime, and
Heather M. McCauley, "'Coaching Boys into Men': A Social Norms Change Approach
to Sexual Violence Prevention," in *Sexual Violence: Evidence Based Policy and Prevention*,
ed. Elizabeth L. Jeglic and Cynthia Calkins (Springer: Cham, Switzerland, 2016),
227–48; Kristy L. McCray, "Intercollegiate Athletes and Sexual Violence: A Review of
Literature and Recommendations for Future Study," *Trauma, Violence, & Abuse* 16, no.
4 (2015): 438–43.

59 "Ray and Janay Rice Speak Out on Recent NFL Assault Incidents," *CBS This
Morning*, December 18, 2018, https://www.cbsnews.com/video/ray-and-janay
-rice-speak-out-on-recent-nfl-assault-incidents/.

5. Navigating Transitions

1 Nell Lake, *The Caregivers: A Support Group's Stories of Slow Loss, Courage, and Love*
(New York: Scribner, 2014), 53.

2 Kathlene Tracy and Samantha P. Wallace, "Benefits of Peer Support Groups in the
Treatment of Addiction," *Substance Abuse and Rehabilitation* 7 (September 2016):
143–54.

3 Chyrell D. Bellamy, Michael Rowe, Patricia Benedict, and Larry Davidson, "Giving
Back and Getting Something Back: The Role of Mutual-Aid Groups for Individuals
in Recovery from Incarceration, Addiction, and Mental Illness," *Journal of Groups in
Addiction & Recovery* 7, nos. 2–4 (2012): 223–36, 232.

4 Jane Ussher, Laura Kirsten, Phyllis Butow, and Mirjana Sandoval, "What Do Cancer
Support Groups Provide Which Other Supportive Relationships Do Not? The
Experience of Peer Support Groups for People with Cancer," *Social Science & Medicine*
62, no. 10 (2006): 2565–76.

5 Ussher, Kirsten, Butow, and Sandoval, "What Do Cancer Support Groups Provide,"
2568.

6 Ussher, Kirsten, Butow, and Sandoval, "What Do Cancer Support Groups Provide,"
2569.

7 Sasha Mallya, Maureen Daniels, Cheryl Kanter, Alyson Stone, Amanda Cipolla,
Kim Edelstein, and Norma D'Agostino, "A Qualitative Analysis of the Benefits and
Barriers of Support Groups for Patients with Brain Tumors and Their Caregivers,"
Supportive Care in Cancer 28, no. 6 (2020): 2659–67, 2662.

8 "Survey: COVID-19 Affecting Access to Addiction Treatment and Key Services,"
Addiction Policy Forum, June 9, 2020, https://www.addictionpolicy.org/post
/survey-covid-19-affecting-access-to-addiction-treatment-and-key-services.

9 "A.A. Groups Using Digital Platforms to Find Sobriety during Coronavirus
(COVID-19) Outbreak," Alcoholics Anonymous, 2021, https://www.aa.org/sites
/default/files/literature/en_pr_20200323.pdf.

10 Mihaly Csikszentmihalyi, *Beyond Boredom and Anxiety: Experiencing Flow in Work and
Play* (San Francisco: Jossey-Bass, 1975); Csikszentmihalyi, *Finding Flow: The Psychology
of Engagement with Everyday Life* (New York: Basic Books, 1998).

11 Radha Agrawal, *Belong: Find Your People, Create Community & Live a More Connected
Life* (New York: Workman, 2018), 71.

12 Agrawal, *Belong*, 68.
13 Jef J.J. van den Hout, Orin C. Davis, and Mathieu C.D.P. Weggeman, "The Conceptualization of Team Flow," *The Journal of Psychology* 152, no. 6 (2018): 388–423, 413.
14 Van den Hout, Davis, and Weggeman, "The Conceptualization of Team Flow," 414.
15 Van den Hout, Davis, and Weggeman, "The Conceptualization of Team Flow," 413.
16 Joan Ryan, *Intangibles: Unlocking the Science and Soul of Team Chemistry* (New York: Little, Brown, 2020), 237.
17 William Marsiglio, *Stepdads: Stories of Love, Hope, and Repair* (Lanham, MD: Rowman & Littlefield, 2004), 43.
18 Susan Walzer, *Thinking about the Baby: Gender and Transitions into Parenthood* (Philadelphia: Temple University Press, 1998).
19 Walzer, *Thinking about the Baby*, 183.
20 Abbie E. Goldberg, *Gay Dads: Transitions to Adoptive Parenthood* (New York: New York University Press, 2012); Ellen Lewin, *Gay Fatherhood: Narratives of Family and Citizenship in America* (Chicago: University of Chicago Press, 2009); Ellen Lewin, *Lesbian Mothers: Accounts of Gender in American Culture* (Ithaca, NY: Cornell University Press, 1993); Petra Nordqvist, "'I've Redeemed Myself by Being a 1950s Housewife': Parent-Grandparent Relationships in the Context of Lesbian Childbirth," *Journal of Family Issues* 36, no. 4 (2015): 480–500.
21 Karen Benjamin Guzzo and Sarah R. Hayford, "Unintended Fertility and the Stability of Coresidential Relationships," *Social Science Research* 41, no. 5 (2012): 1138–51.
22 Barbara Katz Rothman, *Weaving a Family: Untangling Race and Adoption* (Boston: Beacon, 2005).
23 Rothman, *Weaving a Family*, 8.
24 Jeffrey Weeks, Brian Heaphy, and Catherine Donovan, *Same Sex Intimacies: Families of Choice and Other Life Experiments* (London: Routledge, 2001).
25 Weeks, Heaphy, and Donovan, *Same Sex Intimacies*.
26 William Manchester, *Goodbye, Darkness: A Memoir of the Pacific War* (New York: Little Brown, 1979), 391.
27 Desiree Verweij, "Comrades or Friends? On Friendship in the Armed Forces," *Journal of Military Ethics* 6, no. 4 (2007): 280–91.
28 Verweij, "Comrades or Friends," 289.
29 Verweij, "Comrades or Friends," 290.
30 Megan MacKenzie, *Beyond the Band of Brothers: The US Military and the Myth That Women Can't Fight* (Cambridge: Cambridge University Press, 2015), 3.
31 MacKenzie, *Beyond the Band of Brothers*, 1.
32 MacKenzie, *Beyond the Band of Brothers*, 3.
33 "Demographics of the U.S. Military," Council on Foreign Relations, updated July 13, 2020, https://www.cfr.org/article/demographics-us-military.
34 "Embattled: Retaliation against Sexual Assault Survivors in the US Military," Human Rights Watch, May 18, 2015, https://www.hrw.org/report/2015/05/18/embattled/retaliation-against-sexual-assault-survivors-us-military.
35 "Sexual Assault Accountability and Investigation Task Force," United States of America Department of Defense, April 30, 2019, https://media.defense.gov/2019/May/02/2002127159/-1/-1/1/SAAITF_REPORT.PDF.
36 "Vanessa Guillen's Body Found, Suspect Flees and Dies by Suicide: Part 2," *ABC News*, uploaded September 12, 2020, YouTube video, 8:16, https://www.youtube.com/watch?v=9EGH2kZQJVA.
37 Lawrence Colebrooke, *Special Operations Mental Toughness: The Invincible Mindset of Delta Force Operators, Navy SEALs, Army Rangers & Other Elite Warriors!* (self-pub., 2015), 9–10.

38 Chris Lambertsen, *Navy SEAL Mental Toughness: A Guide to Developing an Unbeatable Mind* (self-pub., CreateSpace, 2016), 17.

39 Colebrook, *Special Operations Mental Toughness*.

40 Lambertsen, *Navy SEAL Mental Toughness*, 24.

41 Gary O'Neal with David Fisher, *American Warrior: The True Story of a Legendary Ranger* (New York: Thomas Dunne, 2013).

42 Lambertsen, *Navy Seal Mental Toughness*, 26.

43 Mike Ives, "First Woman Completes Training for Elite U.S. Navy Program," *New York Times*, July 16, 2021, https://www.nytimes.com/2021/07/16/us/navy-woman-warfare-program.html.

44 Ron White, "What Are the Odds of Making It into the Navy Seals?" *Chron.*, June 27, 2018, https://work.chron.com/odds-making-navy-seals-26032.html.

45 Mary Jordan and Dan Lamothe, "How Did These Two Women Become the First to Complete Army Ranger School?" *The Washington Post*, August 19, 2015, https://www.washingtonpost.com/world/national-security/how-did-these-two-women-become-the-first-to-complete-army-rangers-school/2015/08/19/a745c962-46af-11e5-8ab4-c73967a143d3_story.html?noredirect=on; John Black, "Exclusive: Woman Makes History by Becoming the First to Graduate Modern Special Forces Training," SOFREP, June 17, 2020, https://sofrep.com/news/exclusive-woman-makes-history-by-becoming-the-first-to-graduate-special-forces-training/.

46 Nicole Alexander and Lyla Kohistany, "Dispelling the Myth of Women in Special Operations," Center for a New American Security, March 19, 2019, https://www.cnas.org/publications/commentary/dispelling-the-myth-of-women-in-special-operations.

47 Gayle Tzemach Lemmon, *Ashley's War: The Untold Story of a Team of Women Soldiers on the Special Ops Battlefield* (New York: Harper Collins, 2015).

48 Rosellen Roche, Jerome Trembley, Christina Trembley, Joel Manzi, Nicholas Thompson, and Anthony LaPorta, "The Unseen Patriot: Female Cultural Support Team Members and Combat Definition," *Journal of Veterans Studies* 7, no. 1 (2021): 271–9.

49 Lemmon, *Ashley's War*, 278–9.

50 Gayle Tzemach Lemmon, "The Army's All-Women Special Ops Teams Show Us How We'll Win Tomorrow's Wars," *The Washington Post*, May 19, 2015, https://www.washingtonpost.com/posteverything/wp/2015/05/19/the-armys-all-women-special-ops-teams-show-us-how-well-win-tomorrows-wars/.

51 Lemmon, *Ashley's War*, 266.

52 Jennifer Jantzi-Schlichter, "Integration of Women in SOF – The U.S. Perspective," Stratagem, September 11, 2019, https://www.stratagem.no/integration-of-women-in-us-sof/.

53 Ramon Hinojosa and Melanie Sberna Hinojosa, "Using Military Friendships to Optimize Postdeployment Reintegration for Male Operation Iraqi Freedom/Operation Enduring Freedom Veterans," *Journal of Rehabilitation Research and Development* 48, no. 10 (2011): 1145–58.

54 Hinojosa and Sberna Hinojosa, "Using Military Friendships," 1152.

55 John Ismay, "'I Am Fearless Again': New Veterans' Group Gives Women a Sense of Belonging," *New York Times Magazine*, updated October 4, 2019, https://www.nytimes.com/2019/10/02/magazine/women-veterans-network.html.

56 Jessica Lynn, https://www.jessicalynn.website/.

57 Cindy Gericke, "A Father Named Jessica," The Good Men Project, June 17, 2014, https://goodmenproject.com/featured-content/father-named-jessica-jvinc/; Chris Roney, "How a Transgender Parent in Grief Won Over the Ivy League," *HuffPost*, October 11, 2016, https://www.huffpost.com/entry/how-a-transgender-parent-in-grief-won-over-the-ivy_b_57fcfc53e4b0d786aa52bdd0.

58 Helen Rose Fuchs Ebaugh, *Becoming an Ex: The Process of Role Exit* (Chicago: University of Chicago Press, 1988).

59 Nell Lake, *The Caregivers: A Support Group's Stories of Slow Loss, Courage, and Love* (New York: Scribner, 2014).

60 Lake, *The Caregivers*, 162–3.

61 Jacqueline Olds and Richard S. Schwartz, *The Lonely American: Drifting Apart in the Twenty-First Century* (Boston: Beacon, 2009), 48.

6. We-ness, Empathy, and Altruism

1 Bruce J. Schulman, *The Seventies: The Great Shift in American Culture, Society, and Politics* (New York: Free Press, 2001).

2 Tom Junod, "My Friend Mister Rogers," *The Atlantic*, December 2019, https://www.theatlantic.com/magazine/archive/2019/12/what-would-mister-rogers-do/600772/?te=1&nl=morning-briefing&emc=edit_NN_p_20191118&section=whatElse.

3 Matthieu Ricard, *Happiness: A Guide to Developing Life's Most Important Skill* (New York: Little, Brown, 2007), 19.

4 Ricard, *Happiness*, 24.

5 Mortimer Jerome Adler, *We Hold These Truths: Understanding the Ideas and Ideals of the Constitution* (New York: Macmillan, 1987), 52.

6 Mortimer J. Adler, "Aristotle's Ethics: The Theory of Happiness – II," Self-Educated American, March 23, 2015, https://selfeducatedamerican.com/2015/03/23/aristotles-ethics-the-theory-of-happiness-ii/.

7 "About Greater Good: Our Mission," *Greater Good Magazine*, https://greatergood.berkeley.edu/about.

8 Roman Krznaric, *Empathy: Why It Matters, and How to Get It* (New York: Perigee, 2014), 95–6.

9 Neha P. Gothe, Imadh Khan, Jessica Hayes, Emily Erlenbach, and Jessica S. Damoiseaux, "Yoga Effects on Brain Health: A Systematic Review of the Current Literature," *Brain Plasticity* 5, no. 1 (2019): 105–22.

10 Center for Building a Culture of Empathy, http://cultureofempathy.com, and "Edwin Rutsch," Scoop.it!, https://www.scoop.it/u/edwin-rutsch; Empathy Library, https://empathylibrary.com/; "'It's Strangely Powerful' – Step Inside the Empathy Museum," Empathy Museum, uploaded September 8, 2016, YouTube video, 4:50, https://www.youtube.com/watch?v=60em6n_j8Io&t=53s; "Empathy and Relational Science Program," Massachusetts General Hospital, https://www.massgeneral.org/psychiatry/research/empathy-and-relational-science-program/; and "Why Empathy Training?" Empathetics: Neuroscience of Emotions, http://empathetics.com/.

11 "Barack Obama Promotes Empathy with Oprah Winfrey: 'My Mother Taught Me Empathy,'" recorded October 18, 2006, YouTube video, 3:36, https://www.youtube.com/watch?v=LgVAygC-ap0; and "Importance of Empathy: Barack Obama at Morehouse College Commencement," recorded May 19, 2013, YouTube video, 2:28, https://www.youtube.com/watch?v=Ft_M5tXRx28.

12 Helen Riess with Liz Neporent, *The Empathy Effect: 7 Neuroscience-Based Keys for Transforming the Way We Live, Love, Work, and Connect across Differences* (Boulder, CO: Sounds True, 2018), 157.

13 Arlie Russell Hochschild, *Strangers in Their Own Land: Anger and Mourning on the American Right* (New York: New Press, 2016), 5.

14 Jeremy Rifkin, *The Empathic Civilization: The Race to Global Consciousness in a World in Crisis* (Cambridge: Polity, 2009), 10.

15 Steven Pinker, *The Better Angels of Our Nature: The Decline of Violence in History and Its Causes* (London: Allen Lane, 2011).

16 Pinker, *The Better Angels of Our Nature*, 143.
17 Krznaric, *Empathy*, 180.
18 "About Mind & Life," Mind & Life Institute, https://www.mindandlife.org/mission/.
19 Daniel Goleman and Richard J. Davidson, *Altered Traits: Science Reveals How Meditation Changes Your Mind, Brain, and Body* (New York: Penguin, 2017); Richard J. Davidson and Sharon Begley, *The Emotional Life of Your Brain: How Its Unique Patterns Affect the Way You Think, Feel, and Live – and How You Can Change Them* (New York: Hudson Street Press, 2012).
20 Matthieu Ricard, *Altruism: The Power of Compassion to Change Yourself and the World* (New York: Little, Brown, 2013).
21 Richard J. Davidson and Brianna S. Schuyler, "Neuroscience of Happiness," in *World Happiness Report 2015*, ed. John F. Helliwell, Richard Layard, and Jeffrey Sachs (New York: Sustainable Development Solutions Network, 2015), 88–105.
22 Jeremy Adam Smith, Kira M. Newman, Jason Marsh, and Dacher Keltner, eds., *The Gratitude Project: How the Science of Thankfulness Can Rewire Our Brains for Resilience, Optimism, and the Greater Good* (Oakland: New Harbinger Publications, 2020).
23 Krznaric, *Empathy*.
24 Jamil Zaki, *The War for Kindness: Building Empathy in a Fractured World* (New York: Crown, 2019).
25 Lior Abramson, Florina Uzefovsky, Virgilia Toccaceli, and Ariel Knafo-Noam, "The Genetic and Environmental Origins of Emotional and Cognitive Empathy: Review and Meta-Analyses of Twin Studies," *Neuroscience and Biobehavioral Reviews* 114 (2020): 113–33.
26 Zaki, *The War for Kindness*.
27 Lisa Feldman Barrett, Ralph Adolphs, and Stacy Marsella, "Emotional Expressions Reconsidered: Challenges to Inferring Emotion from Human Facial Movements," *Psychological Science in the Public Interest* 20, no. 1 (2019): 1–68.
28 "Koko Provides Emotional Support to Kik Users, from Kik Users," Kik, https://www.kik.com/casestudy/koko/; Ben Popper, "The Empathy Layer," *The Verge*, March 2, 2017, https://www.theverge.com/2017/3/2/14764620/koko-social-network-mental-health-depression-app-kik.
29 Krznaric, *Empathy*.
30 Lynn Avery Hunt, *Inventing Human Rights: A History* (New York: Norton, 2007), 48.
31 Mary Prince, *The History of Mary Prince, A West Indian Slave: Related by Herself* (Chapel Hill: University of North Carolina Press, 2017), https://muse.jhu.edu/book/52335.
32 Riess with Neporent, *The Empathy Effect*.
33 *A Mile in My Shoes*, The Empathy Museum, https://www.empathymuseum.com/a-mile-in-my-shoes/.
34 "Shawna – A Mile in My Shoes," *A Mile in My Shoes*, Acast, audio file, 8:00, February 12, 2020, https://play.acast.com/s/amileinmyshoes/af50ab97-1f48-4e63-9d79-56bcd67af46e.
35 Erika Weisz and Jamil Zaki, "Empathy-Building Interventions: A Review of Existing Work and Suggestions for Future Directions," in *Oxford Handbook of Compassion Science*, ed. Emma M. Seppälä, Emiliana Simon-Thomas, Stephanie L. Brown, Monica C. Worline, C. Daryl Cameron, and James R. Doty (New York: Oxford University Press, 2017), 205–17.
36 Roots of Empathy, https://rootsofempathy.org/. See also pp. 532–51 in Ricard's *Altruism* for a description of other projects designed to promote empathy among children in educational settings.
37 Mary Gordon, *Roots of Empathy: Changing the World Child by Child* (New York: The Experiment, 2009), 10.

38 Gordon, *Roots of Empathy*, 13.
39 Gordon, *Roots of Empathy*, 7.
40 "Empathetics Introduction," uploaded May 11, 2016, YouTube video, 0:54, https://www.youtube.com/watch?v=zghLVcpb7qo&feature=youtu.be.
41 Riess with Neporent, *The Empathy Effect*, 41.
42 Helen Riess, email message to author, June 23, 2020.
43 Sherry Turkle, *Reclaiming Conversation: The Power of Talk in a Digital Age* (New York: Penguin, 2015).
44 Thích Nhất Hạnh, *Teachings on Love* (Berkeley, CA: Parallax, 1998), 69.
45 Nhất Hạnh, *Teachings on Love*, 98.
46 Rifkin, *The Empathic Civilization*, 571.
47 Rifkin, *The Empathic Civilization*, 573.
48 Rifkin, *The Empathic Civilization*, 573.
49 Christian Picciolini, *Breaking Hate: Confronting the New Culture of Extremism* (New York: Hachette, 2020), xxxiv.
50 Ricard, *Altruism*.
51 Kristen Renwick Monroe, *The Heart of Altruism: Perceptions of a Common Humanity* (Princeton, NJ: Princeton University Press, 1996).
52 Monroe, *The Heart of Altruism*, 4.
53 Monroe, *The Heart of Altruism*, 7.
54 Monroe, *The Heart of Altruism*, 7.
55 C. Daniel Batson, *Altruism in Humans* (New York: Oxford University Press, 2011).
56 Batson, *Altruism in Humans*; C. Daniel Batson, *A Scientific Search for Altruism: Do We Care Only about Ourselves?* (New York: Oxford University Press, 2019).
57 Ricard, *Altruism*, 25.
58 Ricard, *Altruism*, 55.
59 Alex Lickerman, "What Compassion Is, Redux," *Psychology Today*, March 3, 2013, https://www.psychologytoday.com/us/blog/happiness-in-world/201303/what-compassion-is-redux.
60 Scott Harrison with Lisa Sweetingham, *Thirst: A Story of Redemption, Compassion, and a Mission to Bring Clean Water to the World* (New York: Currency, 2018).
61 "About Us," Charity: water, https://www.charitywater.org/about.
62 "Careers," Charity: water, https://www.charitywater.org/about/jobs.
63 Peter Singer, *The Most Good You Can Do: How Effective Altruism Is Changing Ideas about Living Ethically* (New Haven, CT: Yale University Press, 2015); Paul Bloom, "Forum: Against Empathy," *Boston Review*, August 20, 2014, https://bostonreview.net/forum/paul-bloom-against-empathy.
64 "About GiveWell," GiveWell, https://www.givewell.org/about.
65 "Maximize Your Charitable Impact," Giving What We Can, video, 1:23, https://www.givingwhatwecan.org/; "Introduction to Effective Altruism," Effective Altruism, March 1, 2020, https://www.effectivealtruism.org/articles/introduction-to-effective-altruism.
66 Toby Ord, *The Precipice: Existential Risk and the Future of Humanity* (New York: Hachette, 2020); William MacAskill, *Doing Good Better: How Effective Altruism Can Help You Help Others, Do Work That Matters, and Make Smarter Choices about Giving Back* (New York: Penguin, 2016).
67 "About Us: What Do We Do, and How Can We Help?" 80,000 Hours, https://80000hours.org/about/.
68 Riess with Neporent, *The Empathy Effect*, 71.
69 Ricard, *Altruism*, 691.
70 Riess with Neporent, *The Empathy Effect*, 150.

7. Leadership

1 Connective Leadership Institute, https://connectiveleadership.com/.
2 "Achieving Styles," Connective Leadership Institute, https://connectiveleadership.com/achieving-styles/.
3 "Matrix Leadership Institute Consulting Services," Matrix Leadership Institute Consulting, https://matrixleadership.org/.
4 "The Empathic Leadership Institute (ELI)," Empathic Leadership Institute, accessed December 15, 2021, https://www.empathicleadershipinstitute.com/.
5 Robert Merton, "The Social Nature of Leadership," *The American Journal of Nursing* 69, no. 12 (1969): 2614–18, 2615.
6 William A. Gentry, Todd J. Weber, and Golnaz Sadri, *Empathy in the Workplace: A Tool for Effective Leadership* (Greensboro, NC: Center for Creative Leadership, 2007); Brené Brown, *Dare to Lead: Brave Work. Tough Conversations. Whole Hearts* (London: Penguin, 2018).
7 Brown, *Dare to Lead*, 96.
8 "Leadership Styles Based on Myers Briggs/Jungian Theory," Team Technology, https://www.teamtechnology.co.uk/leadership/styles/.
9 Barbara Kellerman, *Followership: How Followers Are Creating Change and Changing Leaders* (Boston: Harvard Business School Press, 2008).
10 Steve Holland and Ginger Gibson, "Confidant Trump Says Could 'Shoot Somebody' and Not Lose Voters," *Reuters*, January 23, 2016, https://www.reuters.com/article/us-usa-election/confident-trump-says-could-shoot-somebody-and-not-lose-voters-idUSMTZSAPEC1NFEQLYN.
11 Lee De-Wit, Sander Van Der Linden, and Cameron Brick, "What Are the Solutions to Political Polarization?" *Greater Good Magazine*, July 2, 2019, https://greatergood.berkeley.edu/article/item/what_are_the_solutions_to_political_polarization; Jeremy Adam Smith, "Can the Science of Lying Explain Trump's Support?" *Greater Good Magazine*, March 29, 2017, https://greatergood.berkeley.edu/article/item/can_the_science_of_lying_explain_trumps_support; Zaid Jilani and Jeremy Adam Smith, "What Is the True Cost of Polarization in America?" *Greater Good Magazine*, March 4, 2019, https://greatergood.berkeley.edu/article/item/what_is_the_true_cost_of_polarization_in_america.
12 Andrew Roberts, *Leadership in War: Essential Lessons from Those Who Made History* (New York: Viking, 2019), 221.
13 Roberts, *Leadership in War*, 211.
14 John Wooden and Steve Jamison, *Wooden on Leadership* (New York: McGraw Hill, 2005), 119.
15 Wooden and Jamison, *Wooden on Leadership*.
16 Wooden and Jamison, *Wooden on Leadership*, 27.
17 Michael Lee Stallard with Jason Pankau and Katharine P. Stallard, *Connection Culture: The Competitive Advantage of Shared Identity, Empathy, and Understanding at Work* (Alexandria, VA: ATD Press, 2015), 1.
18 Sherry Turkle, *Reclaiming Conversation: The Power of Talk in a Digital Age* (New York: Penguin, 2015).
19 Evan W. Carr, Andrew Reece, Gabriella Rosen Kellerman, and Alexi Robichaux, "The Value of Belonging at Work," *Harvard Business Review*, December 16, 2019, https://hbr.org/2019/12/the-value-of-belonging-at-work.
20 Brown, *Dare to Lead*. See p. 188 for the complete list.
21 Brown, *Dare to Lead*, 103–4.
22 William Gentry, *Be the Boss Everyone Wants to Work For: A Guide for New Leaders* (Oakland: Berrett-Koehler Publishers, 2016).

23 Glenn Llopis with Jim Eber, *Leadership in the Age of Personalization: Why Standardization Fails in the Age of "Me"* (GLLG Press, 2019), 105.
24 Llopis with Eber, *Leadership in the Age of Personalization*, 32.
25 Llopis with Eber, *Leadership in the Age of Personalization*, 44.
26 Brown, *Dare to Lead*, 10.
27 Cassandra O'Neill and Monica Brinkerhoff, *Five Elements of Collective Leadership for Early Childhood Professionals* (St. Paul, MN: Redleaf Press, 2017).
28 O'Neill and Brinkerhoff, *Five Elements of Collective Leadership*, 7.
29 O'Neill and Brinkerhoff, *Five Elements of Collective Leadership*, 8.
30 Margaret Wheatley with Debbie Frieze, "Leadership in the Age of Complexity: From Hero to Host," *Resurgence Magazine*, Winter 2011, https://margaretwheatley.com/wp-content/uploads/2014/12/Leadership-in-Age-of-Complexity.pdf.
31 Parker J. Palmer, "Thirteen Ways of Looking at Community (… with a Fourteenth Thrown In for Free)," Center for Courage & Renewal, August/September 1998, http://www.couragerenewal.org/parker/writings/13-ways-of-looking-at-community/.
32 Frederic Laloux, *Reinventing Organizations: A Guide to Creating Organizations Inspired by the Next Stage of Human Consciousness* (Brussels: Nelson Parker, 2014); see also the video series that expands on many of these ideas: "Videos," Insights for the Journey, https://thejourney.reinventingorganizations.com/videos.html.
33 Brown, *Dare to Lead*, 107.
34 Laloux, *Reinventing Organizations*, 6.
35 Kristin L. Cullen-Lester and Francis J. Yammarino, "Collective and Network Approaches to Leadership: Special Issue Introduction," *The Leadership Quarterly* 27, no. 2 (2016): 173–80, 173–4.
36 Donna Chrobot-Mason, Alexandra Gerbasi, and Kristin L. Cullen-Lester, "Predicting Leadership Relationships: The Importance of Collective Identity," *The Leadership Quarterly* 27, no. 2 (2016): 298–311.

8. Transforming Our Future

1 Evan Osnos, *Wildland: The Making of America's Fury* (New York: Farrar, Straus and Giroux, 2021), 144.
2 Jenny Odell, *How to Do Nothing: Resisting the Attention Economy* (Brooklyn: Melville House).
3 Ezra Klein, *Why We're Polarized* (New York: Avid Reader Press, 2020), xix.
4 Anya Kamenetz, "A Look at the Groups Supporting School Board Protestors Nationwide," *NPR*, October 26, 2021, https://www.npr.org/2021/10/26/1049078199/a-look-at-the-groups-supporting-school-board-protesters-nationwide.
5 Jennifer D. Jenkins, "I'm a Florida School Board Member. This Is How Protesters Come After Me," *Washington Post*, October 20, 2021, https://www.washingtonpost.com/outlook/2021/10/20/jennifer-jenkins-brevard-school-board-masks-threats/.
6 Jeffrey M. Jones, "Americans Hold Record Liberal Views on Most Moral Issues," Gallup, May 11, 2017, https://news.gallup.com/poll/210542/americans-hold-record-liberal-views-moral-issues.aspx.
7 Taylor Dotson, *Technically Together: Reconstructing Community in a Networked World* (Cambridge, MA: MIT Press, 2017), 133.
8 Ray Oldenburg, *The Great Good Place: Cafés, Coffee Shops, Bookstores, Bars, Hair Salons, and Other Hangouts at the Heart of a Community* (New York: Marlowe, 1999).
9 Parker J. Palmer, *Healing the Heart of Democracy: The Courage to Create a Politics Worthy of the Human Spirit* (San Francisco: Jossey-Bass, 2014).
10 "The Responsive Communitarian Platform," The Communitarian Network, GW Columbian College of Arts & Sciences, https://communitariannetwork.org/platform.

11 "About the Communitarian Network," The Communitarian Network, GW Columbian College of Arts & Sciences, https://communitariannetwork.org/about.

12 "The Responsive Communitarian Platform," The Communitarian Network, GW Columbian College of Arts & Sciences, https://communitariannetwork.org/platform.

13 Jon Kabat-Zinn, *Mindfulness for All: The Wisdom to Transform the World* (New York: Hachette, 2018), 119.

14 Tim Ryan, *Healing America: How a Simple Practice Can Help Us Recapture the American Spirit* (Carlsbad, CA: Hay House, 2018).

15 "Our Mission," MindUp for Life – The Goldie Hawn Foundation, https://mindup.org/.

16 See Twitter feed, https://twitter.com/MindUP; Karen L. Thierry, Heather L. Bryant, Sandra Speegle Nobles, and Karen S. Norris, "Two-Year Impact of a Mindfulness-Based Program on Preschoolers' Self-Regulation and Academic Performance," *Early Education and Development* 27, no. 6 (2016): 805–21; Kimberly A. Schonert-Reichl, Eva Oberle, Molly Stewart Lawlor, David Abbott, Kimberly Thomson, Tim F. Oberlander, and Adele Diamond, "Enhancing Cognitive and Social-Emotional Development through a Simple-to-Administer Mindfulness-Based School Program for Elementary School Children: A Randomized Controlled Trial," *Developmental Psychology* 51, no. 1 (2015): 52–66.

17 Michael S. Carolan, *A Decent Meal: Building Empathy in a Divided America* (Stanford: Redwood Press, 2021), 190.

18 Carolan, *A Decent Meal*, 181.

19 Carolan, *A Decent Meal*, 182.

20 Isabel Wilkerson, *Caste: The Origins of Our Discontents* (New York: Random House, 2020), 384.

21 John M. Bridgeland, *Heart of the Nation: Volunteering and America's Civic Spirit* (Lanham, MD: Rowman & Littlefield, 2013).

22 Stanley B. Greenberg, "'We' – Not 'Me': Public Opinion and the Return of Government," *The American Prospect*, December 17, 2001, 25–7.

23 Robert Putnam, "Bowling Together," in *United We Serve: National Service and the Future of Citizenship*, ed. E.J. Dionne, Jr., Kayla Meltzer Drogosz, and Robert E. Litan (Washington, DC: Brookings Institution, 2001), 13–19, 17.

24 Bridgeland, *Heart of the Nation*.

25 The Aspen Institute Franklin Project, *A 21st Century National Service System Plan of Action*, 21st Century National Service Summit, June 24–25, 2013, https://www.aspeninstitute.org/publications/21st-century-national-service-system-plan-action/.

26 Stanley A. McChrystal, "'You Don't Have to Wear a Military Uniform to Serve Your Country,'" *The Atlantic*, July 2016, https://www.theatlantic.com/politics/archive/2016/07/you-dont-have-to-wear-a-military-uniform-to-serve-your-country/491765/.

27 John M. Bridgeland and John J. DiIulio, Jr., *Will America Embrace National Service?* (Washington, DC: Brookings Institution, 2019).

28 "Why the Peace Corps? 8 Volunteers Reflect on Their Decision to Serve," Peace Corps, June 19, 2019, https://www.peacecorps.gov/stories/why-peace-corps-8-volunteers-reflect-their-decision-serve/.

29 Bridgeland and DiIulio, Jr., *Will America Embrace National Service?*

30 John McCain, "Patriotism Means Reaching beyond Our Self-Interest," in *United We Serve: National Service and the Future of Citizenship*, ed. E.J. Dionne, Jr., Kayla Meltzer Drogosz, and Robert E. Litan (Washington, DC: Brookings Institution, 2003), 60–7, 67.

31 E.J. Dionne, Jr., and Kayla Meltzer Drogosz, "United We Serve? The Promise of National Service," in *United We Serve: National Service and the Future of Citizenship*, ed. E.J. Dionne, Jr., Kayla Meltzer Drogosz, and Robert E. Litan (Washington, DC: Brookings Institution, 2002), 1–10, 8.

32 Matthieu Ricard, *Altruism: The Power of Compassion to Change Yourself and the World* (New York: Little, Brown, 2013), 84, 240.
33 Bridgeland and DiIulio, Jr., *Will America Embrace National Service?*, 3.
34 "About: Our Impact," AmeriCorps, https://americorps.gov/about/our-impact.
35 Alan Khazei, "An America That Asks: 'Where Will You Do Your Service Year?'" *HuffPost*, updated April 22, 2014, https://www.huffpost.com/entry/an-america-that-asks-wher_b_4812880.
36 "Top 25 Universities for Non-Profit and Community Service Ranked by Return," Best Value Schools, March 24, 2021, https://www.bestvalueschools.com/non-profit-and-community-service-ranked-by-return/.
37 Bridgeland and DiIulio, Jr., *Will America Embrace National Service?*
38 Bridgeland and DiIulio, Jr., *Will America Embrace National Service?*, 9.
39 "What Is *Leader in Me*?" Leader in Me, https://www.leaderinme.org/what-is-leader-in-me/.
40 William Marsiglio, "When Stepfathers Claim Stepchildren: A Conceptual Analysis," *Journal of Marriage and Family* 66, no. 1 (2004): 22–39.
41 William Marsiglio and Ramon Hinojosa, "Managing the Multifather Family: Stepfathers as Father Allies," *Journal of Marriage and Family* 69, no. 3 (2007): 845–62.
42 Robert D. Putnam, Lewis M. Feldstein, and Don Cohen, *Better Together: Restoring the American Community* (New York: Simon & Schuster, 2003), 279.
43 Putnam, Feldstein, and Cohen, *Better Together*; Palmer, *Healing the Heart of Democracy*.
44 Putnam, Feldstein, and Cohen, *Better Together*, 283.
45 Putnam, Feldstein, and Cohen, *Better Together*.
46 "Organizations in Action," Me too, https://metoomvmt.org/take-action/organizations-in-action/.
47 Steven Pinker, *The Better Angels of Our Nature: The Decline of Violence in History and Its Causes* (London: Allen Lane, 2011); Steven Pinker, *Enlightenment Now: The Case for Reason, Science, Humanism and Progress* (New York: Viking, 2018).
48 Megan Phelps-Roper, *Unfollow: A Memoir of Loving and Leaving the Westboro Baptist Church* (New York: Farrar, Straus, and Giroux, 2019), 276.
49 Phelps-Roper, *Unfollow*, 276.
50 Phelps-Roper, *Unfollow*, 277.
51 Donovan X. Ramsey, "The Truth about Black Twitter," *The Atlantic*, April 10, 2015, https://www.theatlantic.com/technology/archive/2015/04/the-truth-about-black-twitter/390120/.
52 Meredith D. Clark, "To Tweet Our Own Cause: A Mixed-Methods Study of the Online Phenomenon 'Black Twitter'" (PhD diss., University of North Carolina, 2014), 82.
53 Randall Collins, *Interaction Ritual Chains* (Princeton, NJ: Princeton University Press, 2004).
54 Clark, "To Tweet Our Own Cause."
55 Starbucks Coffee (@Starbucks), "Black Lives Matter," Twitter, June 12, 2020, 10:55 a.m., https://mobile.twitter.com/Starbucks/status/1271440942591913986?ref_src=%20twsrc%5Etfw.
56 Geetika Rudra, "George Zimmerman Juror B37 to Write Book," *ABC News*, July 15, 2013, https://abcnews.go.com/US/george-zimmerman-juror-b37-write-book/story?id=19669496; Heather Kelly, "Zimmerman Book Dies after Twitter Campaign," *CNN*, July 18, 2013, https://www.cnn.com/2013/07/17/tech/social-media/twitter-zimmerman-book/index.html.
57 Kenya Evelyn, "Ahmaud Arbery Killing Reignites Debate over Sharing Graphic Viral Videos," *The Guardian*, May 7, 2020, https://www.theguardian.com/us-news/2020/may/07/ahmaud-arbery-video-shooting-sharing-viral.

58 Deen Freelon, Lori Lopez, Meredith D. Clark, and Sarah J. Jackson, *How Black Twitter and Other Social Media Communities Interact with Mainstream News* (Miami: John S. and James L. Knight Foundation), https://knightfoundation.org/features/twittermedia/.

59 Alex Kaplan, "In 2020, QAnon Became All of Our Problem," Media Matters for America, December 31, 2020, https://www.mediamatters.org/qanon-conspiracy-theory/2020-qanon-became-all-our-problem.

60 Alex Kaplan, "Here Are the QAnon Supporters Running for Congress in 2022," Media Matters for America, updated June 8, 2022, https://www.mediamatters.org/qanon-conspiracy-theory/here-are-qanon-supporters-running-congress-2022.

61 Adrienne LaFrance, "The Prophecies of Q," *The Atlantic*, June 2020, https://www.theatlantic.com/magazine/archive/2020/06/qanon-nothing-can-stop-what-is-coming/610567/.

62 Mike Rothschild, *The Storm Is upon Us: How QAnon Became a Movement, Cult, and Conspiracy Theory of Everything* (Brooklyn: Melville House, 2021), 10.

63 Brian Barrett, "Security News This Week: Facebook Finally Cracks Down on QAnon," *Wired*, August 22, 2020, https://www.wired.com/story/facebook-qanon-secret-ipod-carnival-ransomware-security-news/; Jonathan Wilson, "Reddit Crackdown on 7,000 Hate Pages, as Facebook Boots Out QAnon 'Extremists,'" *E & T: Engineering and Technology*, August 21, 2020, https://eandt.theiet.org/content/articles/2020/08/reddit-crackdown-on-7-000-hateful-subreddit-pages-while-facebook-boots-out-qanon-extremists/; Casey Newton, "Facebook's Big QAnon Crackdown Might Have Come Too Late," *The Verge*, August 20, 2020, https://www.theverge.com/interface/2020/8/20/21375381/facebook-qanon-purge-content-policy-tide-pods; Tony Romm and Elizabeth Dwoskin, "Twitter Purged More than 70,000 Accounts Affiliated with QAnon following Capitol Riot," *Washington Post*, January 11, 2021, https://www.washingtonpost.com/technology/2021/01/11/trump-twitter-ban/.

64 LaFrance, "The Prophecies of Q."

65 "About PCFF," Parents Circle – Families Forum, https://www.theparentscircle.org/en/about_eng/.

66 Belong Center, https://belongcenter.com/.

67 Gary Alan Fine, *Tiny Publics: A Theory of Group Action and Culture* (New York: Russell Sage Foundation, 2012).

68 Dotson, *Technically Together*.

69 Hanna Rosin, "The Overprotected Kid," *The Atlantic*, April 2014, https://www.theatlantic.com/magazine/archive/2014/04/hey-parents-leave-those-kids-alone/358631/.

70 *The Land: An Adventure Play Documentary*, New Day Films, https://www.newday.com/film/land.

71 "Faith Leaders' Corner," Dads & Kids Health & Fitness Talk, https://www.dadsandkidshealth.com/faith-leaders-corner.html.

72 Robert Putnam with Shaylyn Romney Garrett, *The Upswing: How America Came Together a Century Ago and How We Can Do It Again* (New York: Simon & Schuster, 2020), 335.

73 Deborah Cupples, *It Is about You: How American Government Works and How to Help Fix It* (Delfinium, 2017).

74 Putnam with Garrett, *The Upswing*, 335.

75 Putnam with Garrett, *The Upswing*, 334.

76 Putnam with Garrett, *The Upswing*, 339.

77 David Brooks, "The Power of Altruism," *New York Times*, July 8, 2016, https://www.nytimes.com/2016/07/08/opinion/the-power-of-altruism.html.

78 Putnam with Garrett, *The Upswing*.
79 Martin Luther King, Jr., "Remaining Awake through a Great Revolution, National Cathedral," recorded March 31, 1968, in Washington, DC, YouTube audio file, 46:39, https://www.youtube.com/watch?v=SLsXZXJAURk.
80 "Imagine (John Lennon song)," Wikimedia Foundation, updated June 11, 2022, https://en.wikipedia.org/wiki/Imagine_(John_Lennon_song).
81 Wilkerson, *Caste*, 388.
82 Jeremy Rifkin, *The Empathic Civilization: The Race to Global Consciousness in a World in Crisis* (Cambridge: Polity, 2009), 600.
83 Rifkin, *The Empathic Civilization*, 607.
84 Rifkin, *The Empathic Civilization*, 613.
85 Ricard, *Altruism*, 691.
86 Ricard, *Altruism*, 691.
87 Nicole A. Cooke, "Posttruth, Truthiness, and Alternative Facts: Information Behavior and Critical Information Consumption for a New Age," *The Library Quarterly* 87, no. 3 (2017): 211–21, 214.

Index

Printed in the USA
CPSIA information can be obtained
at www.ICGtesting.com
CBHW030041081224
18527CB00006B/14/J

9 781487 544775